The History of
the Catholic Church
in Latin America

The History of
the Catholic Church
in Latin America

From Conquest to Revolution and Beyond

John Frederick Schwaller

NEW YORK UNIVERSITY PRESS
New York and London

NEW YORK UNIVERSITY PRESS
New York and London
www.nyupress.org

References to Internet websites (URLs) were accurate at the time of writing.
Neither the author nor New York University Press is responsible for URLs
that may have expired or changed since the manuscript was prepared.

Library of Congress Cataloging-in-Publication Data

Schwaller, John Frederick.
The history of the Catholic Church in Latin America :
from conquest to revolution and beyond / John Frederick Schwaller.
p. cm.
Includes bibliographical references (p.   ) and index.
ISBN 978–0–8147–4003–3 (cl : alk. paper) — ISBN 978–0–8147–8360–3 (e-book)
1. Catholic Church—Latin America—History. 2. Latin America—
Church history. I. Title.
BX1426.3.S39   2011
282'.8—dc22   2010034800

New York University Press books are printed on acid-free paper,
and their binding materials are chosen for strength and durability.
We strive to use environmentally responsible suppliers and materials
to the greatest extent possible in publishing our books.

Manufactured in the United States of America
10 9 8 7 6 5 4 3 2 1

Contents

Acknowledgments

This book has its origins in a course on the history of the Catholic Church in Latin America, which I had the pleasure and honor to teach first at the Regional Seminary of Saint Vincent de Paul in Boynton Beach, Florida. After that I taught the course in the Franciscan School of Theology of the Graduate Theological Union in Berkeley, California. Subsequently, I would teach significant sections of the course as part of classes on Latin American history at the University of Montana and the University of Minnesota–Morris. I would like to thank the administrations of those fine institutions for providing me with the opportunity to develop the ideas of this book as I taught in those schools. It is the students, however, who played an even more important role as they struggled, along beside me, to better understand the broad sweep of the history of the Church in Latin America.

I began my research in the history of the Church in my doctoral research, which focused on the secular, or diocesan, clergy in sixteenth-century Mexico. The essential text and basis for most modern research on the Church in the early colonial period is Robert Ricard's *The Spiritual Conquest of Mexico*. Ricard focused primarily on the mendicant orders and made only passing references to the secular clergy. My study of the secular clergy also led me to look at the financial underpinnings of the colonial church, especially the importance of the tithe and of the creation and management of endowments to support individual clerics. Early in my career, friendships with Asunción Lavrin and Arnold Bauer were forged by our mutual interests in the investments of the Church. The Reverend Stafford Poole, C.M., has been a constant friend, mentor, and consultant on ecclesiastical topics. None of this could have happened without his aid. My interests soon expanded to look at both the religious orders and the diocesan clergy during the period. In particular because of my training in Nahuatl, the Aztec language, I was soon interested in the dynamics of conversion. I collected information about Nahuatl language manuscripts in the United States and studied their role and function in the larger effort at evangelization.

The landmark book by James Lockhart, *The Nahuas After the Conquest*, provided my research with a solid theoretical basis on understanding the dynamics of culture change during the contact period. In looking at the Church in the later colonial period, William B. Taylor has recently written a monumental book, *The Magistrates of the Sacred*, which is essential reading if one is to understand the Church in the eighteenth century and into the beginning of the independence era. One cannot understand the intricacies of Church and state relations in the nineteenth and early twentieth century without a close reading of Lloyd Mecham's *Church and State in Latin America*. The Reverend Jeffery Klaiber, SJ, became a friend during my residency in Peru and has remained so thereafter. His insightful studies on the history of the Church in Peru have inspired me and assisted me greatly as I have attempted to look at the whole of Latin America. For the most recent period, I was very fortunate to have been on the faculty at the Saint Vincent de Paul Regional Seminary when the seminary hosted a large conference on liberation theology.

There are many individuals who have assisted me in this adventure, but I can mention only a few here. I especially want to express my deep thanks to Jennifer Hammer, my editor at New York University Press. This project has taken far longer than either of us anticipated at the outset. She has been a tremendous help to me in the several revisions through which the book has passed. I would also like to thank the anonymous readers both of the original prospectus and of the finished manuscript. Their comments have helped to make this a better work. I also want to thank my many colleagues at the University of Minnesota–Morris, and at SUNY Potsdam for having indulged me as an administrator to remain moderately active in research. I have tremendous admiration for my colleagues who are not only heavily involved with teaching and the formation of our students but who also pursue very active programs of creative activity. Needless to say, the contributions of all these wonderful people and works have assisted me in improving the book. Any errors are completely due to my own shortcomings.

Through all of this my family has provided me with great support. My parents, Henry and Juliette Schwaller, brought me up in a loving home and encouraged me to pursue a life of the mind. As a child I remember the seemingly countless churches in Mexico that we visited every year during our annual trip south of the border. Little did I know then that I would dedicate a large part of my life to studying those very churches and the people who worshipped in them. My sons, Robert and William, indulge their father as he tries to balance family life, a career as an academic administrator, and a role as a scholar. For this, I thank them. My wife, Anne, has been the best friend a person could ever hope to have. She has accompanied me through three continents as we have pursued elusive documentation. She is the best sounding board for ideas and a solid proofreader once those ideas get put in print. Her ministry has shown me how small groups and an atmosphere of love and support can transform lives. Words simply cannot begin to express my thanks to her.

Introduction

Presenting the history of the Roman Catholic Church in Latin America is a mammoth undertaking. Few would doubt that Catholicism is the single most important institution in the region if for no other reason than it is perhaps the only one that has remained central to most peoples' lives over a period of some five hundred years. Yet to try to tell the story of this institution on two continents involving millions of people and five centuries is an extremely difficult task. In order to begin to come to grips with it, one must look for the themes that run throughout the whole story while examining the individual pieces as they develop.

First of all Latin America is a region poorly understood and difficult to define. The region of the Americas consists of two continents, North and South America, divided at Panama. In general, Latin America refers to those countries on the American continents that speak a language based in Latin. Using this rubric, then, a case might be made for Quebec to be considered a Latin American region: it is in North America and most of the inhabitants speak French. Nevertheless, in practical use, the region known as Latin America tends to be those areas settled by the Spanish and Portuguese, and not the French, although a case might be made for French Guiana, located on the northeast coast of South America. Yet, its history is quite different from that of its neighbors, such as Venezuela and Brazil, and so French Guiana is usually excluded. Consequently the term "Latin American" usually refers to those regions where Spanish or Portuguese predominate

The other area of difficulty is the Caribbean. The largest islands (Hispaniola, Cuba, Jamaica, and Puerto Rico) were all first settled by the Spanish. Yet the smaller islands, known collectively as the Lesser Antilles, were not heavily exploited by the Spanish, and consequently in the eighteenth century other European powers claimed them, as the world's demand for sugar increased and these islands were perfect for sugar cultivation. The Caribbean region has a very different history from the mainland. Cuba and half of Hispaniola, now the Dominican Republic, do have some similarities with mainland Spanish-speaking countries, but the similarities within the Caribbean far outweigh the similarities of underlying Hispanic culture, and so many scholars consider the Caribbean its own region for historical purposes. This book follows that typology and does not include the islands of the Caribbean as part of its principle focus.

The next most important consideration is the periodization of Latin American history. In the most basic scheme Latin American history is divided into two periods: the colonial period, and the modern period. From 1492 until the early nineteenth century most of Latin America consisted of colonies of European powers, namely of Spain and Portugal. Between 1810 and 1824 most countries in Latin America achieved their independence from their colonial rulers and set out on their own path. Nevertheless, the more one focuses on the region and the changes that occurred over this large sweep of time, some additional nuances come to the fore. Most importantly the region had a long and vibrant history of human occupation well before the arrival of the Spanish and Portuguese. Many important civilizations rose and fell between the arrival of the first human on the continents, tens of thousands of years ago, until the late fifteenth century. Prior to the colonial period, then, one really must include a pre-Columbian era, that time before the arrival of the Europeans.

Looking at the now three periods of Latin American History, additional distinctions come into focus. The first century or so after the arrival of the Europeans was an epoch of some warfare but certainly of rapid expansion by the Europeans and cultural change on the part of the natives of the region. As one enters the seventeenth century things change significantly. No longer are there many expeditions of discovery and conquest, but life settles down into a daily routine. The region seems to begin to focus internally on exploiting the resources at hand and at developing a unique style. As a result many scholars draw a distinction between the period of conquest and settlement, in the sixteenth century, with the more developmental seventeenth century. Looking at local economies, too, the seventeenth century was one more of steady production, as opposed to the rapid increase in economic development in the earlier period. Some scholars even say that it was a century of depression, since the economies seem to have almost stagnated after the rapid growth of the early period.

In terms of the arts, however, the seventeenth century was one of tremendous energy and productivity. A new style emerged, called the Baroque. Architecturally, it was characterized by great exuberance, intricate and complex carvings on altars, church facades, and other sculpture. Paintings were filled with action and complexity. In literature wordplay and complex labyrinthine plots were the hallmark. Musically, harmonic and rhythmic complexity and contrast, along with the solidification of musical forms defined the era. As we look more closely, we find that these developments were very different from the first century of European occupation of the Americas.

Yet the eighteenth century was dramatically different from the previous two. A new ruling house came to govern Spain, the Bourbons. They brought with them a new style of government and new tastes in the arts. They implemented a whole series of reforms in the imperial system. In Portugal and her colonies the eighteenth century also saw change, not caused by a new ruling house but by international competition. Portugal also implemented sweeping reforms in her imperial system, and her principal colony, Brazil, became one of the wealthiest places on earth thanks to extremely rich mines, the spread of sugar agriculture, and the beginnings of coffee production. And so, again, looking more closely, the eighteenth century was dramatically different from the periods that had come before.

The eighteenth-century reforms implemented in Spanish and Portuguese colonies in the Americas carried with them the seeds of their own destruction. The reforms created a large cadre of wealthy individuals who felt betrayed by the mother country. At the same time, new ideas began to filter into Latin America from Europe about liberty and equality. Without a triggering event, however, these ideas seemed destined to merely become topics for debate rather than battle cries. Nevertheless, in 1808 the French, under Napoleon Bonaparte, invaded Spain and Portugal, and provided a moment for critical decision in the colonies. With the imperial governments in Europe essentially held hostage by the French, the colonists needed to make some decisions about what constituted legitimate authority. It took several decades for this debate to work out, but eventually every country of Latin America would opt for independence by about 1824. Consequently, although at first glance the colonial period seems to be amorphous and uniform, upon closer scrutiny one can perceive three rather different eras, roughly corresponding to the three centuries.

The modern, or national, period in Latin America corresponds to the period since independence. Just as with the colonial period, when one looks more closely unique sub-periods emerge. To begin with, the period of the struggles for independence actually stretched far beyond nominal autonomy, as warring factions within the newly independent countries had to work out their many differences. Within a decade or so, one faction gained the upper hand. For the next three or so decades, most Latin American nations saw low levels of political disruptions as the governing faction had to continually fight, either politically or on the battlefield, against opposition factions. Toward the later part of the nineteenth century the situation reversed. The faction in power lost control, the faction out of power gained it. Many reforms occurred, and political sparring continued. By the early twentieth century built-up tensions in some countries erupted in violence, civil war, and revolution, especially in Mexico. In other countries the changes of the early twentieth century occurred in the ballot box, but change did come.

At about the time of the worldwide Depression of 1930, Latin America saw a wave of military governments take power. These lasted until immediately after the Second World War, when civilian governments briefly took over, only to be overthrown by a second wave of military takeovers. In the last two decades of the twentieth century nearly every country returned to civilian rule, with most countries experiencing sharp debates between major parties as to the best course for the future.

Everything outlined above is a gross oversimplification of what actually occurred in Latin America, but it at least provides a roadmap for understanding the general contours of Latin American history, but the exceptions to this are just as important as the cases that prove it. While Mexico experienced a violent revolution in the early twentieth century, Chile had a more peaceful transition from the politics of the nineteenth century to the demands of the twentieth. On the other hand, most counties had military governments for many decades in the twentieth century, but Mexico and Costa Rica did not. Again, the exceptions are just as important as the rule.

In considering the Roman Catholic Church in Latin America, there are a few special circumstances to keep in mind. Latin America was the first place in the world where peoples from four continents lived and worked side by side. As a result of the imperial systems of both the Spanish and the Portuguese, peoples from Europe, Africa, and Asia all met in the Americas. This created an extremely complex social system. Because of a long history of contact with Africa and with Muslims, the Spanish and Portuguese had developed a social system which took into account a person's ethnic and cultural origins. Under the Spanish and the Portuguese individuals had to come from what the powers that be felt was a pure Christian heritage in order for them to gain important political or social positions. They also recognized the economic and social status of slaves, who were relegated to a different social status. Slaves in Spain and Portugal in the fifteenth century tended to come from Africa, via an overland trade that ended at the Straits of Gibraltar. The Portuguese and Spanish carried these ideas about social systems with them when they established their colonies in the New World.

When the Spanish and Portuguese arrived and settled in the New World, they recognized that the natives were culturally very different. They accorded them a modicum of authority within their own communities but subjected everyone to imperial rule. The conquerors and colonists also brought along their own slaves, and some free blacks arrived both as conquerors and settlers. Soon enough there were children born of relations, legal and extralegal, among all of these different ethnic and social groups. In the Hispanic world, the offspring of a European and a native was called a *mestizo*. The child of an African and a European was a mulatto. There was no clear consensus on the label for the offspring of an African and a native, but a common term was *zambo*. Finally, a distinction came to be drawn between those Europeans born in the mother country and those born in the colony. A child of European parents born in the colony was a *criollo* (Creole). Eventually these distinctions became established in laws that prohibited certain groups from entering certain occupations.

Needless to say, such a simple system of racial and ethnic identity could not remain simple. In each succeeding generation children would be born of different combinations. A child might have one parent who was a mulato and the other a mestiza. While some colonists attempted to establish a system to account for all of the different admixtures, the reality was that most folks considered themselves to be a member of one of the major groups, and generally were recognized by others as such. Consequently mixed-race persons who manifested an African phenotype, that is, they looked African, were normally considered mulatto, regardless of the exact percentage of African blood they might have inherited. Similarly a mixed-race person who looked like a native but who dressed in European style was considered a mestizo, while the same person—if he or she lived in an indigenous village and acted and dressed accordingly—would be considered a native.

The social and economic systems reinforced each other. Persons of wealth generally were either from the Iberian Peninsula or Creoles, born in the New World. Various occupations, such as ranch hand, mine foreman, teamster, and the like, were generally the province of mestizos and mulattos. Lower occupations were relegated to slaves and sometimes to natives who had to provide labor as part of their tax and tribute obligation. At the same time, many persons who worked in the most elite households as cooks, cleaners, and personal servants were slaves. The general social system was understood by the participants. As a result, with a single glance one person could categorize anyone with whom they came into contact by looking at their phenotype (racial identity), their clothes, and their occupation. While independence did away with slavery, and over the course of the nineteenth century many of the laws dictating ethnic categories for occupations were abolished, even today in much of Latin America people understand the social structure on a very deep level simply by looking at others.

The role of native peoples in the history of Latin America has become a topic of immense interest in the last fifty years, after having been previously largely ignored. Scholars have come to study more native groups in the historical context, often using documentation sometimes written in native languages. As a result an entirely new perspective on the history of the region is beginning to appear.

Even without the recent emphasis on the native perspective, for generations scholars have recognized that natives played a critical role in the history of the region. The native peoples were not passive observers, absorbing customs and cultures, but rather took an active role in dealing with the new reality that the presence of Europeans brought to their homes. This perspective is called "native agency": that is, natives were active agents in their own lives, not simply passive in the face of the European cultural onslaught. It is remarkable that the vast majority of the native population of the Americas who received missionaries in the early colonial period did, in fact, adopt Christianity. While some conversions were accomplished through violence, the fact that a huge percentage of the native population remains Catholic to this day is striking. In the process of adopting Christianity, the native groups saw opportunities that were advantageous to them. In much of Latin American there was a tradition of a conquered people adopting the religion of the conqueror, which also played into this trend. Yet the Church also provided the natives with structures and institutions through which they could express their own social and political visions.

Even though native peoples embraced Christianity, they did not entirely give up their old culture. Rather they understood Christianity through their old culture, just as the Europeans understood the native cultures through the lenses of Christianity and European culture. With time, however, many aspects of the old native culture either disappeared or were transformed into variants of a truly native Christian culture. This kind of blending of old and new was not unique to New World Christianity. Although Christianity began in the Middle East, by the fourth century it had been adopted by the Roman Empire as an imperial religion. By that time it had taken on a significant component of what might be called a Mediterranean or Roman culture.

While native peoples adopted, and adapted, Christian institutions, they also remained at least partially in charge of their own destinies. Native peoples always exercised some control over their local affairs, which ran the gamut from political institutions for internal self-governance to various aspects of religious celebrations. As long as there were significant numbers of outside observers, such as parish priests, these activities tended to conform to the general norms tolerated by the imperial or national power. Once villages became isolated from the larger community, they began to develop along more autochthonous lines. As a result, in some regions there was a resurgence of nontraditional forms of Christianity in areas where native groups either were not well converted initially or where they had gone for many years with little or no contact with the larger Church. Similarly they developed local political structures to respond to their own reality and culture, which might be at odds with imperial or national cultures. These variants also caused friction as groups became more fully integrated into the national culture.

Within the history of Latin America there is another theme that has important implications in the history of the Roman Catholic Church. From the time of the conquest until the present there has always been a tension between centralized control and diffuse local control. One of the first major political events in the New World occurred when Hernán Cortés, the conqueror of Mexico, opted to throw off control exercised over him by the governor of Cuba and establish himself as the leader of the conquest. Once the imperial systems were established in the New World, there was constant tension between decrees and regulations issued by the kings in Europe and the actual application of those decrees and regulations in the colonies.

The independence of Latin America can be seen as a small victory for local control, as against the imperial control of the European monarchs. Nevertheless, with independence this tension did not disappear, for now the strains existed between control of the new country by elites of the capital city versus local control of the provinces and outlying cities by their local elite. Just as in the early United States there was tension between the large populous states like Virginia and New York versus the smaller less populated states like Delaware, so in Latin America politics immediately after independence split along lines of central versus regional control. Eventually each country would develop a system to accommodate this tension, but in much of Latin America, there remains an inherent division between the major metropolises and the regions.

The issue of central versus local control also had an important role in the development of the Roman Church in Latin America. Because of the vast distance between the Americas and Europe, the first missionaries were largely independent from the scrutiny of superiors. There were no bishops locally for several decades, and even when they did appear, the territories were so vast and communications so rudimentary that most regions developed largely independently from one another. Consequently there was a slow movement toward the centralization of the Church. The kings of Spain and Portugal claimed authority over the Church, as will be seen, but certainly local bishops had more immediate claims. When independence came to Latin America, any claims that the monarchs might have had regarding control over the Church were moot, and the Papacy began to exercise far more control over the Church than it had previously. It was not until the twentieth century that all of the details of that control were finally resolved, and the Church fell completely under papal control.

At the same time that questions regarding ultimate authority over the Church were being worked out, individuals were living and dying as members of local congregations. From the first moment of contact, some missionaries spread the Gospel in a manner that emphasized the emulation of Christ: teaching through example. Others believed that the Gospel needed to be spread by preaching, by engaging the natives in discussion and teaching the rules of the faith. Just as natives claimed agency for their own political lives, they also embraced the Church for the benefits that it could provide them. There was then yet another tension over the degree to which the various institutions of the Church needed to be controlled by the Church or could be delegated to the faithful. Similarly, some organizations within the Catholic Church did not willingly submit to the authority of the local bishop. And so there were tensions in the Church over local and popular religious expression and the central authority of the bishop.

In the nineteenth century this tension continued as national governments sought to exercise control over the Church in their territories, only to be denied that authority by the pope. In the parishes there continued to be tensions between popular or native religions and the formal teaching of the Church regarding submission to authority. The Church in general suffered from a lack of clergy in the nineteenth century. Parishes seldom saw a priest and bishops remained isolated from the vast majority of the faithful. Popular associations sprang up to bridge the gap wherein local people created prayer groups or mutual aid societies, but not all were willing to be subjected to the supervision of the bishops. Finally, the bishops encouraged new associations to provide social support services, which they could more directly control, in order to undermine the influence of the popular associations. In the end, this endeavor too reflected the working out of tensions between local authority and centralized control.

With these considerations, the general outline for this book is a chronological one, beginning with the roots of Latin American Christianity in Spain and in the local native cultures. Chapter 1 outlines both the history of the Church on the Iberian Peninsula and the religious experiences of the natives of the New World. The Church as it arrived in the New World was in fact a local variant of the Catholic Church, namely one that developed out of the Iberian Peninsula. By the late fifteenth century in Europe, each region had given a slightly different flavor to the Catholic Church. In Ireland, for example, there was an ancient monastic tradition that had a deep influence on the Church there. On the Iberian Peninsula seven centuries of warfare and contact with the Muslims had created a very special type of Catholic Church. It is important to understand the Iberian background because it colored the way the Spanish and Portuguese missionaries would approach the evangelization of the New World. Experience on the Iberian Peninsula had encouraged the hierarchy and structure of the Church, and royal government itself, to adapt in favor of warfare and the taking of new territories. This too would have an important effect on the spread of Christianity in the New World. This first chapter also provides an overview of native religion in the New World, looking specifically at the religions of some of the ancient American cultures, such as the Aztec, Maya, and Inca, along with general observations about tribal religions. The native peoples of the Americas would interpret the Christian message through the cultural lens of their existing religious beliefs. The end result of this dialogue between the missionary and the native generally was some type of hybrid understanding.

Chapter 2 studies the practical issues related to the so-called discovery of the New World by the Iberian powers, and their negotiations with the Papacy to exercise control over the Church in the newly found territories. The Iberian kingdoms had centuries of experience confronting non-Christian nations, due to their location facing Africa, and resulting from numerous voyages from Europe down the African coast. The monarchs received certain incentives from the Papacy to confront Muslims on the Iberian Peninsula and to spread Christianity as they voyaged down the African coast. These rights and privileges were eventually extended to the New World as part of a complex legal system, which was developed in the sixteenth century for this very purpose.

The conquest of the New World forms the theme for chapter 3 wherein the military aspects and the religious conversion of the natives are considered. An older generation envisioned the early evangelization of the New World as a "spiritual conquest." Nevertheless, most recent scholarship finds it to be far more nuanced than that. While armed forces did accompany missionaries, or vice versa, most of the early conversions to Christianity did not occur at the tip of a sword or barrel of a gun. The process was far less violent and far more intimate. Early on, dozens of missionaries arrived to spread the Gospel as best they could. The chapter looks at the different groups of missionaries and their different techniques in order to get a better overview of the process.

The colonial period, as noted earlier, lasted for some three hundred years. The Church was one of a handful of important institutions in Latin America at that time, and chapter 4 looks at how the Church developed in Latin America during this long period. The Church hierarchy played an important social and economic role in the colonies, while missionaries and parish priests became the points of contact for most people. Thanks to the charity of the faithful and individual desires for salvation, the Church also became one of the wealthiest institutions in the colony, and served as the principle economic engine—other than trade and mining—for the colonial world.

Chapter 5 focuses on the reforms that the new ruling house of Spain, the Bourbons, brought about in the colonial system in general and the Church in particular. At roughly the same time, the Marquis of Pombal became the leading advisor to the king of Portugal and implemented a series of similar reforms for the Portuguese empire. Important in both of the sets of reforms was to bring the Catholic Church more fully under the control of the monarch. Linked to this effort, both the Portuguese and Spanish monarchs expelled the very powerful Society of Jesus, the Jesuits, from their overseas colonies, and eventually from all of their realms. The monarchs also set about taking control of the great wealth that the Church had amassed over the centuries. Consequently, this was an era of tremendous change for the Church in Latin America.

Political events in Europe precipitated the movements for independence in Latin America, and this process is the theme for chapter 6. It looks at the roads to independence and also the various discussions that occurred in the former colonies regarding the role of the Church in the newly independent countries. The central debate was the degree to which powers enjoyed by the king of Spain might be inherited by the governments of the former Spanish colonies. The debates were also a means whereby two major political movements worked out their differences in each country. The patterns established in Mexico, for example, did not hold true in Argentina.

Chapter 7 continues to focus on the political turmoil that surrounded independence as the two major political movements, liberalism and conservatism, confront one another in the new countries. In each country the positions staked out by each party, while being similar, had important local nuances. Involved in this political debate was the role of the Church. While liberals tended to support a model similar to the United States with a strict separation of Church and state, there were instances where, in order to gain more control over the Church, they embraced highly controlling and centralized authority over the Church. Conversely, while the conservatives wished to retain the centrality of the importance of the Church within the nation state, they did so through separating the Church from the state. Also at issue in these debates was the strong economic role of the Church, a legacy it had carried over from the colonial period. The case of Brazil, however, was unique. While independent, Brazil was still ruled by a monarch, and this chapter also discusses the varying role of the Church within imperial Brazil.

The late nineteenth century and early twentieth century saw a wide variety of popular religious expressions, some of which were violently opposed by the national government. In chapter 8 we see how political developments finally fostered the opening up of many political systems to additional parties beyond the traditional liberal and conservative. The issue of the role of the Church was an important one in the political platforms of these new parties. In Brazil the empire finally came to a end with the overthrow of the emperor and the implementation of a republic. The Church played an important role in both the issues leading up to the revolt and the political developments thereafter.

The Mexican Revolution and other political turmoils of the early twentieth century provide the point of departure for chapter 9. Throughout Latin America in the early twentieth century change was in the air. In Mexico it came through a revolution; in other countries it came via the ballot box. The Church increasingly looked upon social movements with concern that they might draw people away from the Church. As a result, many bishops followed papal suggestions and encouraged the development of Catholic Action groups, wherein groups of the faithful would come together to address important social issues of the time. The confluence of political change and the Church moving out of direct political action mark two important trends for this period.

Chapter 10 looks at the Church in Latin America in the middle decades of the twentieth century. This period was marked by military governments, deep social tensions, and turmoil. The Church began to develop its own social message while remaining at arms length from the political process. Some priests, however, embraced radical political movements and revolutionary struggle. The period also saw the beginnings of a way of doing theology, which became known as liberation theology. Importantly, the bishops of the region also began periodic meetings to address important social and economic issues that transcended national boundaries.

The ultimate chapter brings the history of the Church into the twenty-first century. On the political scene the military governments largely disappeared. The Church embraced liberation theology and then began to back away from it. Native groups rediscovered their indigenous spirituality, Africans continued spiritual movements based in their cultural heritage, and Evangelical and Pentecostal Protestant groups began to make inroads in traditional Catholic areas. In short, the Church in Latin America in the first decade of the twenty-first century no longer enjoys the monopoly that it once did but still continues on the forefront of many of the important debates in the region.

This book is meant to serve as an introduction to the major themes and issues of the Catholic Church in Latin America. The literature is large and growing constantly. Without question, the history of the Catholic Church in Latin America is a very important facet of the history of the region. No other single institution has had such an impact in so many places over such a long period of time, and it is core to much of what we know about that part of the world. In each country in each period, the Church confronted different issues and different specifics. The best that this book can do is to provide a general framework, a set of guideposts to lead the reader through this complex and fascinating history.

1

Religious Origins of
Catholicism in Latin America

Thousands of pilgrims gather in the mammoth sanctuary of Santiago Campostela, in the northwestern corner of Spain, to celebrate the life of Saint James the Greater, brother of the apostle Saint John. A huge censer (a large pierced metal ball in which incense is burned) called the botafumeiro, swings on a chain from the highest point in the transept, making long passages over the heads of the pilgrims. The faithful wear cockle shells on their hats and sleeves, the symbol of the saint. The pilgrimage route to Santiago is one of the most traveled medieval trails of Europe. The focus of this devotion, Saint James, is credited with being the first Christian missionary to the region, arriving within a decade of the death of Christ.

A richly dressed Aztec noble stands atop a tall pyramid. He has a feathered headdress, and shell rattles on his ankle. He dances while playing a flute. He is surrounded by priests dressed in black. Their robes and hair are matted with dried blood. The nobleman performs a brief ritual, pricking his ear lobe and placing a drop of blood on a piece of paper. The paper is then burned in a large censer along with copal, incense made from pine resin. The multitudes break into song, dancing in the courtyard of the temple.

Reconquest

The story of the Catholic Church in Latin America, begins with the Church as a religious and political entity as it developed in Spain and Portugal in the fifteenth and sixteenth centuries. There is no doubt that Christianity has deep roots in the Iberian world. The missionaries who would carry the banner of Christ to the Americas came from an environment in which Christianity had thrived, suffered, and recovered again and again over fifteen hundred years. Yet for nearly all of its history on the Iberian Peninsula, Christianity never

enjoyed exclusive status. Even in early Roman times, significant Jewish populations existed there. Within the religiously pluralistic society of the peninsula, Christianity gained a strong hold in Iberia. Its predominance as a state
religion was confirmed and augmented when the Roman Empire adopted the
faith officially in 312 CE. This position of dominance was threatened in the
eighth century when Muslims from North Africa overran the peninsula. In
711 CE, as part of the initial Muslim expansion following the death of Moham-
med, Muslim forces crossed the Straits of Gibraltar and occupied the Iberian Peninsula. Within less than a decade of the invasion, the Muslims had
defeated all of the existing states lying south of the two northern mountain
ranges, the Pyrenees and the Cantabrian mountains. The nearly eight-hun-
dred-year period in which the Christians of the north engaged in an on-again,
off-again war against the Muslims is called the *Reconquista* or Reconquest.

The Reconquest did not involve continual warfare throughout those eight
centuries, but rather several sporadic eras of conflict. Moreover, the initial
conquest by the Muslims hardly swept away all traces of Christianity. For the
first few centuries under Muslim rule, Christians and Jews remained free to
practice their religion. In reality, Christians constituted the majority in most
areas. While tensions could and did flare up, in general the Christians lived
peaceably under Muslim domination. Indeed, the taxes they paid due to
their status as "People of the Book" under Muslim rule were frequently less
than they had paid to their older Christian overlords.

From the tenth through the thirteenth centuries, the Reconquest faced a
changing landscape. On the Muslim side African influence increased. Several Muslim fundamentalist movements originating in sub-Saharan and
North Africa spilled over into the Iberian Peninsula. The most pronounced
of these were advanced by the Almoravids, who preached an extreme form
of Islam. Their name later became synonymous with the term "Muslim" in
Spain, and is the origin of the term "Moor." By the middle phases, the Reconquest also took on an important philosophical character as a holy war. As the
Muslims became more extreme in their embrace of Islam, so the Christians
also emphasized the crusade-like quality of the conflict. Finally the papacy
came to recognize the struggle against the Iberian Muslims as part and
parcel of a greater crusade against Muslims throughout the Mediterranean
world, extending spiritual benefits to those who participated in the warfare.

The Christians of the north developed several institutions and mechanisms to assist both in the actual warfare and in the incorporation of the
newly conquered areas. In both the warfare and the resettlement the Church
played an important role. In order to assist with military operations against

the Muslims, the Christian kings of the north of the Iberian Peninsula enlisted the aid of warriors from France and other areas of Northern Europe. As early as the 1060s the pope offered dispensations to warriors who fought the Muslims on the Iberian Peninsula. The Christian lords of the north would invite foreign nobles to join in the Reconquest, offering them temporal control over the lands they gained, providing they pledged fealty to the king for whom they fought. Important counties, such as Portugal, were carved out of the Muslim-held territories by these noblemen.

The Christian realms were a patchwork of contesting authorities. Local nobles enjoyed many privileges, including the right to collect local duties and taxes, control the local judiciary, and make appointments to Church offices. Some of these privileges came as a result of participation in the Reconquest, others had simply been accumulated from time immemorial. In the later Middle Ages the local nobles exercised a great deal of authority and frequently opposed the designs of the monarchs to wrest that authority from them.

Cities and towns acquired certain privileges from the monarch and other nobles that allowed them to exercise a degree of independence. These rights and privileges were known as *fueros* (*forais* in Portuguese). Some cities held the privilege of always being called to parliaments, known in Spanish and Portuguese as *Cortes*. Other privileges included the right to hold markets, to collect certain local taxes and duties, and especially to have an independent judiciary to hear cases involving local laws and customs. Additionally, during the Reconquest, the Christian monarchs often granted additional rights and privileges to towns that organized units to fight in the wars. In order to stabilize the frontier between Christian- and Muslim-controlled territories, the monarchs also often granted special privileges to residents of border towns both to encourage settlement and also in recognition of their more tenuous link to the monarch because of distance and turmoil. Nevertheless, by the late fifteenth century, the monarchs of Spain and Portugal viewed the *fueros/forais* as troublesome and as limitations on regal authority.

Ecclesiastical institutions also enjoyed a certain independence from the crown. They generally benefited from the *fuero eclesiástico*—*fora eclesiastico* in Portuguese—or clerical immunity. This *fuero* specifically granted members of the clergy immunity from royal courts. If a priest was accused of a civil crime, or of many petty criminal offenses, he had the privilege of having the suit heard in an ecclesiastical, rather than a royal or local, court. This privilege was extended to all clerics, priests and nuns, friars and monks, as well as to members of some of the military orders, and many members of ecclesiastical households, such as retainers of bishops and the like. It also extended to the lands owned or controlled by these individuals and institutions, such that the crown could neither exercise justice upon them physically nor collect taxes from them.

Alfonso X of Castile (1221–84), known as *El Sabio*, "the Wise," initiated an early attempt to curb the power of the nobles and cities. A very devout Christian, his *Cantigas de Santa María* (*Songs to the Virgin Mary*) represent a high point in early Castilian letters. His legal code, the *Siete Partidas* (the Seven Books or Parts) represents a significant attempt to regain power to the crown at the expense of the cities, towns, nobles, and the Church. Alfonso based his code on several basic principles. Central to these was the notion that the core function of the king was judge. All other functions emanated from that. Alfonso also posited that royal law superseded local law, and he envisioned a uniform royal law that could be applied throughout the realm in spite of local laws and jurisdictions. Alfonso's successors would extend this principle so that the decision of any local court could be appealed to the royal courts, effectively challenging the Church and local nobles.

In the twelfth century two Christian orders, the Knights Templar and the Hospitalers of Saint John, arrived in Spain. These pious gentlemen had organized themselves into military-religious orders to seek to regain the Holy Land and to assist in the crusade against the Muslims. They provided an important example for the rest of Europe. For centuries warriors had felt moral conflict about killing vis-à-vis the teachings of the Church. The establishment of military-religious orders granted the blessings of the Church to the knight for his calling. The mission of the warrior was linked to that of the monk in that both participated in a unified effort, waging war, and ministering at the same time.

On the Iberian Peninsula, these orders spawned several imitators. The most famous of these were the military-religious orders of Calatrava, Alcántara, and Santiago in Spain, and the Order of Christ and Order of Aviz in Portugal. Although the Order of Calatrava was the oldest, Santiago became the most important in Castile. The military-religious Order of Santiago was founded with a dual purpose. As with the other Iberian orders, participation in the Reconquest was an important vocation. Yet the other vocation of the Order of Santiago was to provide hospitality to travelers and hospitals to the sick. Eventually the order came to protect pilgrims who traveled through northern Spain en route to the shrine of Saint James at Santiago Campostela.

The military-religious orders manifested a perfect combination of ministries to assist in the Reconquest: a military branch to defeat the Muslims on the field of battle, and a religious branch to provide moral, physical, and spiritual assistance. In recognition of their service to the crown, they received grants of lands from which they would receive taxes and over which they exercised temporal authority. Large sections of the middle of the Iberian Peninsula fell under the control of the military religious orders when Alfonso VIII of Castile granted huge tracts to protect the approaches to Toledo from the south, west, and east. The orders then chose officers to whom they entrusted the oversight of the territory. The territories were called *encomiendas*[1] and the officers who administered them were called *comendadores* or *encomenderos*. These officers received a stipend for their efforts and served at the pleasure of the order. The ultimate rights over the administration of these *encomiendas* remained vested in the order. The orders were also called upon to populate the region, founding towns and villages to better hold and pacify the local area. The orders received certain judicial and fiscal privileges in these territories: the right to collect local taxes and duties and the right to control the judiciary.

The Church participated in the Reconquest in other ways. The famous missionary orders of the Middle Ages were created to address the demands of converting the heathens, bringing heretics back into the Catholic faith, and renewing the faith of the community at large. One of these, the Dominicans, was founded by a Spaniard, Domingo de Guzmán, who would later be canonized as Saint Dominic, *Santo Domingo*. He came to believe that the proper method of bringing people to the faith, be they heathen, heretic, or already Christian, was through preaching. He developed a Preaching Order of mendicant brothers whose mission was preaching the Gospel. The friars of the Dominican Order took an active role in the reestablishment of the Catholic faith in the newly conquered regions of the Iberian Peninsula.

Since the time of Constantine in the early fourth century, Christianity had developed in a world in which the limits of political authority and the limits of ecclesiastical authority merged. The world of Christendom was politically and religiously homogeneous. Those who differed in faith also followed a different political system. Consequently, while some non-Christians physically were living within the state, they could not be part of the political state because their religious faith differed. They were excluded from holding office or taking a role in public affairs. From the eleventh through the thirteenth centuries, the atmosphere of religious tolerance that had marked the earlier centuries disappeared. Ultimately, the Reconquest became a crusade against the Muslims in which the Jews were also targeted, as the Christians began to develop a new ideology of "One Faith, One Law, One King." This stance was far more marked in the Spanish kingdoms than in Portugal. Portugal achieved its modern borders by the middle of the thirteenth century. Although it continued to assist in the ongoing struggle against the Muslims, the kingdom was far more concerned about Castile and León than about a Muslim threat. Moreover, Portugal increasingly looked to England and France as allies, as it feared the growing power of Castile and Leon.

At the end of the fifteenth century, Queen Isabel of Castile and King Fernando of Aragón found themselves as the inheritors of a complicated system of authority, which had developed in the Christian Kingdoms of Spain. At this time what is now modern Spain consisted of two independent kingdoms, León and Aragón. Castile, in turn, contained yet other kingdoms and jurisdictions such as León, Asturias, and Navarre. In the late 1460s, Isabel's brother, Enrique, declared her to be his heir. At approximately the same time she accepted a marriage to Fernando, the heir of the Aragonese throne. Isabel ascended to the combined Castilian and Leonese throne through a civil war. The civil war pitted her supporters against those of her half-sister, who was backed by the Portuguese crown. The war split the Castilian nobility and was also a war between Aragon and Portugal, each backing a different sister.

Isabel survived the civil war. Yet because of the demands of the Reconquest, her predecessors had given much power away to the other estates: towns, the nobility, and the Church. Following the civil war there were other uprisings of the Spanish nobility against royal authority. Fernando and Isabel recognized the political and ideological value of conducting a war against a foreign enemy in order to galvanize sentiment at home. The Muslim kingdom of Granada provided them with a foreign enemy on soil, which the Spaniards claimed was their own, unjustly taken in the Muslim invasion of 711.

The monarchs were successful in conquering Granada and in increasing their own control over their domains. At just the same moment that they were engaged in the final assaults on Granada, Christopher Columbus offered them the opportunity to continue the efforts at conquest beyond the bounds of Europe. As we know, he eventually gained their support. For their part, Fernando and Isabel, for having led the Reconquest of Granada, were awarded the title of the "Catholic kings" by Pope Alexander VI.

While the reign of Isabel and Fernando marked the end of the Reconquest, it was also a period of reform within the Church, both in the ecclesiastical hierarchy and in the religious orders. The efforts to reform the Church had three main targets. One was the concern over orthodoxy and the threat posed by the presence of unconverted Muslims and Jews in Christian Spain.

The second was the ecclesiastical hierarchy of bishops and archbishops who had gained considerable power during the Reconquest and whose offices were frequently points of contention between the monarchs and the papacy. Third, the religious orders of Spain had needed reform for years.

The religious character of Spain at the time of the Granada war had become less tolerant of the Jews and Muslims. In the thirteenth and fourteenth centuries Northern European states had expelled their Jewish populations, many of whom took refuge in Spain and Portugal, among other longtime Jewish residents. Jews were openly welcomed by the Iberian monarchs in the Middle Ages because of the skills they brought with them, particularly in the areas of finance and administration. As the Reconquest entered its final stages, however, religious tolerance turned against the Jews, who often were among the wealthiest subjects of the realm. The final success of the Reconquest also brought the expulsion not just of the Muslims but also of the Jews from the Spain and Portugal. Jews who converted to Christianity were known as *conversos*; Muslims who converted to Christianity were known as *moriscos*. While the act of conversion protected these individuals from the immediate threat of expulsion, jealousies subsequently occurred since many *conversos* were both wealthy and powerful. Furthermore, the popular opinion was that some *conversos* had betrayed their conversion to Christianity and secretly continued to practice Judaism. The *moriscos* faced all of the same issues of discrimination that were faced by the *conversos*, with status issues added to the mix, because *moriscos* who remained in Spain tended to be of a lower economic status than the *conversos* who remained.

As part of the larger program to extend Christendom within the Christian kingdoms, in 1478 the monarchs requested that the pope grant them permission to establish the Holy Office of the Inquisition under royal control. The Inquisition was historically an institution attached to the office of the local bishop as the ordinary of the diocese.[2] When the pope agreed with the request, what had been an essentially ecclesiastical institution was taken over by the state. Strictly speaking the Inquisition did not have jurisdiction over nonbelievers, merely over those who had professed the Christian faith and been baptized. In Portugal the Inquisition was not formally established until 1536.

The presence of so many Christians who had recently converted from Islam and Judaism caused concerns about the orthodoxy of their faith; for decades the *conversos* and *moriscos* would be viewed as second-class Christians. During this same period, all of the elite institutions and ecclesiastical councils increasingly demanded that aspirants for office and preference demonstrate purity of lineage, *limpieza de sangre*: that is, to demonstrate that they were not descended from Muslims, Jews, or heretics within four generations.

Purity of blood statutes had the effect of creating a caste system in the Iberian Peninsula. Because such statutes came to rule in the Church, universities, most religious orders, the military-religious orders, and most government positions, *conversos* and *moriscos* were prohibited from a wide range of occupations and important offices. The crown could, and did, provide some relief from these statutes by waiving the purity of blood statutes in some specific instances. Nevertheless, the statutes developed clearly defined categories based upon lineage and ethnic origin.

The other area of concern regarding orthodoxy came from within the Christian community. In Spain and in the rest of Europe many thinkers began to question the power of the Catholic Church and some of its practices. Two major reforms emerged in Spain, centering on the relationship of the Church to the crown and on the internal organization of the religious orders. Many believed that the clergy in particular needed reform. As a result of long-term traditions and privileges granted during the Reconquest, the Church hierarchy of bishops, archbishops, and cathedral chapters remained well beyond the control of the monarchs. While bishops and archbishops exercised dominant control in their territories, they were subject to scrutiny only from the papacy. Traditionally these princes of the Church were elected by the clergy of the diocese, or archdiocese, and certainly by the members of the cathedral chapter, those high-ranking clerics assigned to ceremonial and administrative posts in the principle church of the diocese.[3] Yet the papacy held the ultimate right to approve the election, or appointment, and to confer on the candidate all of the ecclesiastical authority of the office. In the fifteenth century many of the main dioceses suffered from internal divisions, which made the selection of a bishop nearly impossible. In light of this, the crown would also put forward candidates, and the papacy would exercise its right to make the final approval. Yet the papacy used this situation to place its own favorites in the leading cathedrals of Spain.

When disputes occurred in the selection of new bishops, Isabel and Fernando pressed the papacy to recognize what the monarchs felt were their innate powers. Embodied in the *Siete Partidas*, the legal code of Alfonso X, was the principle that the monarch could mediate in elections for bishops and had the final authority to present the candidate to the papacy, called the right of patronage. After several decades of negotiations, and concessions on both sides, in 1486 Pope Innocent VIII granted the right of patronage to the Catholic kings in the territory of Granada, where the monarchs were conducting the last war of the Reconquest. Finally, in 1523, the Spanish crown received the general right of patronage throughout its realms. Nevertheless, although the crown could appoint bishops, archbishops, members of cathedral chapters, and even parish priests, it did not follow that all of these officials would necessarily support the crown in all endeavors.

Priests who serve in parishes and who are subject to the authority of the local bishop are called secular or diocesan priests. A problem of secular priests was that they tended to manifest lax morality and insufficient training. From the Middle Ages on, the local parish priest did not always represent the highest goals and aspirations of the clergy. They were often poorly trained and venal; lapses in priestly celibacy were widespread. In the late fifteenth and early sixteenth centuries there were renewed attempts to improve the quality of the clergy. The kings appointed bishops with the charge that they reform the clergy. The monarchs mandated that parishes be filled through competitive exams, to select the most highly qualified priests. In many regions local nobles clung to their rights of presentation to specific parishes. Bishops and others were loath to give up the right to appoint persons to these moderately lucrative positions.

The religious orders in Spain also went through a great period of reform in the late fifteenth and early sixteenth centuries. Religious orders differ from the secular, or diocesan, clergy in that their members take additional vows beyond the normal clerical vows, and they pledge to live according to a special rule, *regula* (Latin for rule). As a result, members of religious orders are called members of the regular clergy. In Spain, and throughout Europe, many of the monasteries and convents no longer followed their rules with the originally intended rigor. Morality became lax, and the spiritual aspects of religious life were lost to more mundane and secular concerns. Many members of the regular clergy sought to reinvigorate their orders and to seek a simpler form of spirituality. These goals had much in common with the royal policy that also favored reform of the monasteries and convents, if for no other reason than to bring them more closely under royal scrutiny. Religious orders frequently held large endowments, and their very structure made them somewhat immune from royal interference, since they had their own internal hierarchies and reported eventually directly to the pope. The Catholic kings supported efforts to reform the regular clergy. In some instances this support was merely tacit, refusing to intervene when differing factions might appeal to the crown to mediate. In other instances they took a more active role. Quite simply, the Church in Spain and Portugal at the time of the discovery of the New World was in a state of flux as it transitioned from the epoch of the Reconquest to the more modern era.

When the Spanish and Portuguese arrived in the New World, they brought with them the legacy of the Reconquest, and of the political and ecclesiastical history that preceded them on the Iberian Peninsula. The institutions that developed during those eight centuries would assist the Iberian powers as they sought to conquer and settle a New World. The attitudes and beliefs that they carried with them would color their interactions with the native peoples they found there. Christianity, and specifically Christianity as practiced on the Iberian Peninsula, would become the model toward which missionaries would guide the newly discovered natives as they attempted to Christianize them.

Old World/New World

While the story of the Catholic Church in Latin America begins in Europe, the contribution of the native peoples of the Americas is an equally important theme. The natives of the New World had developed their own forms of religious expression, completely divorced from any in the Old World. When missionaries arrived in the New World it was in fact the first time that Europeans had moved beyond the Old World of Eurasia and Africa, and beyond the Eurasian religious and philosophical tradition. The diversity of religious expression in the New World posed real challenges to the Spanish missionaries as they attempted to spread Christianity.

It is impossible to talk about a single religious orientation of all of the native peoples of Latin America because of the tremendous geographical and cultural area to be encompassed, from Patagonia to California and from Florida to Chile. The native peoples of the Americas had a wide variety of religious expressions. Natives of Central Mexico, Central America, and the Andean highlands lived in highly organized sedentary societies. They had a complex religious system with a panoply of deities and a complex liturgical calendar. Peoples living in such areas as Florida or the American Southwest, the Argentine pampas or Amazon forests, had a more nomadic life, with only tribal-level political organizations. Their religions were less state-structured. More peoples lived under the highly organized state systems of Mexico, Central America, and the Andes, and thus we will first consider the social structures and religious notions of the Aztec, Maya, and Inca,[4] the principal civilizations in these areas at the time of the conquest, before studying the more nomadic or less centrally organized groups.

Maya and Aztec

Anthropologists call the region in which the Aztecs and the Maya lived Mesoamerica, defined in general as that area south of what is now Northern Mexico down into Central America. The arid regions in the north of modern-day Mexico were home to quite different peoples in terms of their cultural organization. Similarly, from what is now Costa Rica on to the south, the cultures were different from those found in Mesoamerica. Both the Aztecs and the Maya are reflections of the larger Mesoamerican culture.

The two cultures shared some similarities and reflected some differences. An important difference is that they spoke two totally different, unrelated, languages. The Aztec language is known as Nahuatl; the Maya speak Maya, with many modern dialects. Both languages are still widely spoken in Mexico and Central America. Several of the Maya dialects were mutually intelligible, yet others were unique enough not to be understood. The two languages, Maya and Nahuatl, are members of two completely separate language families and are as totally distinct from one another as English and Chinese are.[5] Nahuatl is part of a language family known as Uto-Aztecan, while Maya is part of the language family known simply as Maya.

While the Maya and Aztec cultures used two different languages, they shared some important similarities. The two cultures shared some gods. One of the most important gods was the god of rain and water, called Tlaloc by the Aztecs, and Chac for the Maya. The iconography or the way each culture depicted him is quite similar. He was shown with big goggled eyes, a long, often elephant-like, nose, a snarling mouth, and large ornamental ear plugs. The Maya and the Aztecs also had similar number systems. While Europeans use a decimal system, based on ten, the ancient Mesoamericans used a vigesimal system, based on twenty. Nevertheless, the Maya and the Aztecs had slightly different ways of writing their numbers.

The Maya enjoyed an extremely complex calendrical system. Both the Maya and Aztecs had a basic system that used two distinct calendars at the same time: a solar calendar of 365 days and a ritual calendar of 260 days. These two calendars worked in conjunction with one another. The solar calendar was very similar to the European calendar. It consisted of eighteen months with twenty days each, with five extra days. It is unclear whether the Aztecs and Maya used interstitial days, leap days, and so the calendar eventually could have failed to keep up with the seasonal changes. The ritual calendar had thirteen numbers and twenty day names. Each name was paired with a number, but when the count reached thirteen, it was necessary to start over with one again. Upon reaching the end of the list of names it started over again with the first name again, until 260 days had passed, and the calendar returned to the starting point. The solar and ritual calendars ran concurrently. Each day had both a date in the solar calendar and a date in the ritual calendar. Each discreet combination of dates from the two calendars would repeat only every fifty-two years. As a consequence of this calendar, the ancient Mesoamerican civilizations had a century, which was in essence only fifty-two years. Both of these calendars were important for religious celebrations. In the ritual calendar, individual days were assigned values, good luck or bad luck: each day, and each hour in the day, was ruled by a different god who brought to that day a host of characteristics. Personal names were given to infants based upon their date of birth in that calendar. The solar calendar provided guidance for agriculture and certain large-scale religious festivals.

Although the Maya constituted one of the New World's most important pre-Columbian civilizations, by the time the Spanish arrived they had passed into an era of decline. The Classic Maya period (250 CE–900 CE) was characterized by a number of very powerful city-states, which engaged in trade and warfare among themselves. They shared a common religion, writing system, artistic expression, and in short were of a single cultural identity. Some of the more powerful states controlled trade routes from deep in Central America up into the Mexican highlands. In the tenth century, however, there was a great disturbance. The cities of the Classic Maya fell into disrepair, and the region was invaded by peoples from Central Mexico.

The Maya shared many of the same religious ideas as their predecessors of the Classic period. They conceived of the world as existing between thirteen heavens and nine underworlds, a view they held in common with other Mesoamerican peoples. The visible world was four-cornered, with the four Atlantean figures holding up the sky. In the middle, as the central point of existence, was a great *ceiba* tree holding up the pinnacle of the sky. The Maya pantheon was populated by scores of gods. There seems to have been a notion of a supreme god, Hunab Ku, but he was not as widely recognized as Itzamná, "Lizard House," and his consort, Ix Chel, "Lady Rainbow." The other gods seem to have been their offspring. Equally important were the Chacs, the gods of rain.

The Maya envisioned three layers to the world: the underworld, the surface of the world, and the vault of heaven. The underworld was known as Xibalba, where rulers and shaman went in their trances. Xibalba was dark, dank, a world of rotting matter, which fed the vital forces of the surface of the earth. The Maya paid particular reverence to caves since they were the liminal places where the underworld and the surface world met. Mountains had a similar role in that they were points where the surface world met the starry world of the sky. Within this world sacredness was concentrated at specific points, like the caves and mountains. Temples sought to imitate the natural points of power and duplicate them through human invention.

As with other Mesoamerican peoples, the Maya believed the world had gone through a series of creations. They believed that the current existence of the world was the fourth creation. In each of the earlier eras the world had been destroyed because of imperfections. As noted, the regulating and celebrating of the passage of time was an important feature of the Maya religion. It was believed that the world continually passed through cycles and that by precise record keeping one could predict the future. The Maya fixated on the passage of time and had a calendar, known as the Long Count, that measured every day since the creation of the world, more than five thousand years ago.

The Maya placed great importance in sacrifice, which not only propitiated the gods but also allowed one to enter into a personal relationship with the divine. Sacrifice was important to feed and nourish the gods. The Maya practiced human sacrifice, although not on the level of other natives peoples of Mesoamerica. Far more common among the Maya were various forms of personal blood sacrifice and the sacrifice of goods, such as birds, pottery, small animals, corn, cacao, paper, rubber, and incense. Personal blood sacrifice, along with the ingestion of alcohol or hallucinogens, was a second form of religious practice. These allowed the person offering the blood sacrifice, or ingesting the alcohol or hallucinogen, to commune more directly with the gods through visions and altered states. Thus, the leaders of the Maya states would commonly offer prodigious blood sacrifice to enter into a trance-like state. In these trances the noble lords would go through spiritual travels and converse with the deities for the benefit of their people. This role of mediator between this world and the world of the gods gave the leaders great political power.

Unique among New World civilizations, the Maya possessed an intricate writing system. Using stylized symbols with fixed sound values, this elegant form of writing allowed them to keep precise historical accounts and record other important data. Archeologists have begun recently to decipher the glyphs and recover much Maya history and religion.

While the Maya had established cities and a highly organized civilization as early as the fourth century CE, the Aztecs, or more properly the Mexica, do not appear in historic records until about 1250. The Mexica originally came from an area in Northwestern Mexico, where they were hunters and gathers.

Sometime around the year 1111, they began a migration southward through the central plateau of Mexico, and in about 1250 they entered into what we now call the Valley of Mexico. The Valley of Mexico had been inhabited for many thousands of years prior to the arrival of the Mexica. According to the Mexica legends, they were led on by their tribal god, Huitzilopochtli (Hummingbird-on-the-Left). After many years of migration, he indicated the place where they should found their new city: an eagle resting on a cactus. In 1325 the Mexica founded their city, Tenochtitlan (later known as Mexico City), on a small island in the middle of a lake in the Valley of Mexico. The Mexica rapidly dominated the older civilizations that occupied the Valley of Mexico and eventually went on to conquer a large part of central Mexico. Their civilization was still rapidly developing and their empire still expanding at the time of the arrival of the Spanish.

Just as the Maya believed that the world had been created four times, the Mexica believed that they were living in the fifth creation. Each of the previous creations ended with a cataclysm. The current epoch began when the gods gathered at the ancient city of Teotihuacan, just north of modern day Mexico City. There they performed rituals and sacrifice by bleeding themselves (auto-sacrifice), thus creating mankind and the current world. Once mankind had gained life, the gods commanded that humans should sacrifice similarly, in order to feed the gods who had created the world, and to maintain the essential balance of the universe. The sacrifice the gods demanded was human sacrifice: the sacrifice of hearts and of blood. The Aztecs believed that without sacrifice, chaos would invade the world: the orderly processes of the sun and the moon would be stopped, chaos would ensue, and the world would be destroyed.

The pantheon of gods was headed by Ometecuhtli, the Lord of Duality, and his consort Omecihuatl, the Lady of Duality. The Mexica especially revered Huitzilopochitl. Yet Tlaloc, the god of rain, shared the most prominent place on the major temple of the capital Tenochtitlan with him. Another important god was Quetzalcoatl, the Plumed Serpent or Plumed Twin. Quetzalcoatl was a culture god, the patron of the arts. Most of the Mexica religious beliefs were shared with the other people who lived in the Valley of Mexico, even though the Mexica were latecomers to the region.

The Mexica believed in an afterlife: a series of heavens. The factor that determined where a person went in the afterlife was not how he or she had lived their life in an ethical or moral sense; rather, the determining factor was exactly how they died. A warrior who died on the field of battle went to the highest heaven, to the heaven of Tonatiuh, the sun god, and accompanied him on his heavenly journey for four years, only to return to earth as a hummingbird. A woman who died in childbirth went to the same heaven, because such a woman was seen as a warrior fighting to bring forth the infant.

The Mexica also had an institution of confession. If they had committed some act against the moral strictures of society, they had the opportunity to confess that sin and to go on with their lives. This was something done only under extraordinary circumstances: normally, only once in a lifetime. The confession was made specifically to the Tezcatlipoca, Smoking-Mirror, one of the supreme Mexica gods, and Tlazolteotl, goddess of love. Confronted by so many strange and different practices, the Spaniards were surprised because of the similarity of this ritual to the Christian sacrament of penance or reconciliation.

The Aztecs have a reputation for being bloodthirsty, which is well grounded in terms of some of their ritual practices. In 1503, at the end of one of the great fifty-two-year cycles, thousands of people were sacrificed in one day in Mexico City in order to assure that the calendar continued into the next cycle. Certainly some of the punishments meted out by Aztec society were severe, but this was not wanton violence. The Aztecs had an extremely orderly society with a tremendous social pressure toward conformity. Nonconformity was dealt with quite strictly.

Inca

Thousands of miles to the south, the Inca empire developed independently from the Maya and the Aztecs. The Inca came to occupy an area that stretched from modern day Ecuador south into what is modern-day Chile, concentrated in the highlands of Peru and Bolivia. Like the Aztecs, the Incas were also latecomers. Inca civilization arose in the early fourteenth century. The Inca specifically were a group of Quechua-speaking people with origins from near Lake Titicaca in the Andean highlands on the border of modern Peru and Bolivia.

The Inca creation stories exist in many variants. The common themes of the legends begin with a supreme deity, Viracocha, who created the primordial Inca ancestor, Manco Capac. Manco emerged on the earth accompanied by his wife Mama Ocllo. Manco Capac defeated the existing powers of the earth, who then became stone outcroppings, important religious objects venerated by the Inca. Manco was followed by a line of heirs who constituted the royal dynasty. Many argue that at least the first seven of the rulers and their consorts, in the Incan ruling line, were mythical and not historical.

Viracocha was one of three central deities worshipped by the Inca. He was a creator being who brought forth the heavens and the earth and created men. Worship of Inti, the sun, was a central feature of Inca religion. Inca rulers claimed a genealogical tie to the sun, who then imbued their reign with divine power. Inti was the tribal god of the Inca people, whom he favored by granting them success in war and protection of their empire. The last of the three central deities was Inti-Illapa, the god of thunder. He controlled the weather and many of the forces of nature. Along with Viracocha and Inti, he was worshipped in the most sacred temple of Cuzco, the Coricancha. The Incas also venerated the goddess of Earth, Pachamama, and the goddess of the sea and lakes, Mamacocha.

The Inca believed that the emperor was a kinsman of Viracocha and consequently was considered divine. A complex ritual surrounded the person of the emperor precisely to avoid chance contact between the emperor and common people. The bodies of former rulers were mummified, kept in bundles in the Coricancha, and were routinely removed to participate in important ceremonies.

The Inca were also keen observers of the passage of time. They used a combination of an annual lunar calendar and a solar calendar. These two calendars do not coincide easily; since the lunar cycle is slightly less than thirty days, it does not divide evenly into 365. The Inca made ad hoc adjustments continually to both calendars to keep them from falling into error. Many sites in the Inca empire were aligned with special celestial events: equinoxes, solstices, rising and setting of specific stars and constellations. These celestial cycles supplemented the basic annual calendars to provide additional accuracy. The Inca had two major religious celebrations each year, the Capac Raymi and the Inti Raymi. The greater of these, the Inti Raymi, occurred with the June solstice, the equivalent of the midwinter solstice for the Southern Hemisphere, and celebrated the sun. The Capac Raymi corresponded to the December solstice, and was dedicated also to the sun and celebrated the passage of boys into manhood. These celebrations struck a chord with the Spaniards who celebrated Christmas near the December solstice and Saint John the Baptist near the June solstice.

The Inca landscape, both physical and spiritual, was dotted with sacred spots, generically called *huacas*. The points where major historic individuals emerged, such as where Manco Capac emerged from the earth, were *huacas*. Spots where the Inca believed a transcendent power was at work were *huacas*. The whole of nature was felt to be divine, and local landmarks held divine power and thus were *huacas*. Passersby would deposit a small stone or some other offering to honor these spots. The maintenance of the rituals associated with these divine places occupied a major part of the daily ceremonial life of many individuals.

The *huacas* were in turn linked to one another and to the capital Cuzco. Invisible lines, called *ceques*, radiated out from the Corichancha in Cuzco to link the hundreds of *huacas* in its immediate hinterland. Most towns had scores, if not hundreds, of *huacas* linked to their own town center through the *ceque* lines. Spaniards working in the sixteenth century documented nearly four hundred *huacas* associated just with Cuzco in the immediate hinterland of the city. The Spaniards, when they arrived, had great difficulty understanding this ritual and mythical environment.

The Inca civilization was able to control a wide range of ecological zones to provide a stable agricultural basis for their civilization. Most cities and towns had territories in the highlands, the temperate mid-zones, and the coastal valleys. The highlands produced a wide variety of foods, the most important of which was the potato. In the temperate zones corn production was possible. In the coastal lowlands many vegetables were grown, and the ocean provided a rich variety of fish and seafood. It was only by controlling all of these regions that native peoples could secure a fairly dependable source of food. If there were unseasonable freezes or other crop destruction in the highlands, a civilization depending solely on potatoes would suffer badly. Likewise, a civilization tied to the ecology of the mid-zones would suffer if for some reason the corn crop failed. If strange currents and abnormal weather along the coast devastated the lowlands, a coastal civilization would be challenged to survive. However, since the Inca civilization controlled all of the ecological zones, its survival potential increased greatly.

Once established in Cuzco, the Inca captured the highland valleys toward Lake Titicaca. After that they conquered down to the coast. With these actions they quickly controlled all of the necessary ecological zones. The empire then expanded northward and southward, following each of the ecological zones. The Inca empire was known as *Tawantinsuyu*, the four districts. Each district, roughly oriented toward the four cardinal directions like segments of a circle with the center in Cuzco, contained some of the three ecological zones, with the eastern district containing jungle lowlands rather than coastal lowlands. *Collasuyu* stretched south toward Lake Titicaca and beyond into Chile and Bolivia. *Cuntisuyu* passed to the south and west of Cuzco toward the coast. *Antisuyu* was all of the empire to the east and north of Cuzco. *Chinchasuyu* stretched to the north and west along the coast and middle zone into Ecuador.

The empire was ruled centrally from Cuzco by an emperor whose title was *Capac Apu Sapa Inca*. It was from this title that the name was taken and was applied to both the people and the empire. The people were known as the *Hatun Runa*. Linguistically they are known as Quechua speakers, since Quechua was the official language of the empire, but there were other linguistic and ethnic groups within the empire. One of the most important was the Aymara, who also came from the Lake Titicaca region.

The expansion of the Inca empire occurred during the last century prior to the arrival of the Spanish and was brought about through warfare. Once conquered, however, the defeated territories needed to be incorporated into the empire. Each of the four *suyus* or districts was ruled by a relative of the Sapa Inca, called a *capac apu*. In turn, the *suyus* were further subdivided into provinces, the governorship of which was also restricted to kinsmen of the Inca. Since the empire eventually came to consist of many different local ethnic groups, one means of maintaining control over the local regions was to spiritually conquer them. Once conquered, the local religious items, mummy bundles, and *huacas* of various types, were taken for storage in Cuzco, while religious objects associated with the Inca religion were installed in the newly conquered territory.

One of the striking features of the Inca empire was the high degree of centralization. Through an extensive system of roads, wayside inns, and couriers, information, men, and materiel circulated through the empire. To support the widely flung army and the institutions of government, all Incas were required to provide labor service on lands dedicated to the emperor and to the official religious cult. The produce of these plots, along with tribute and other income, was stored in imperial warehouses, *collcas*, for use by the army or in case of disaster. If a crop failure should occur in some part of the empire, food could be found locally stored or transported from nearby regions, to lessen the disaster. To keep track of these supplies, and to merely keep tabs on the empire, the Inca developed a system of record keeping using knotted strings, *quipu*. The patterns of strings, knots, and colors served as mnemonic devices for the record keepers and merely assisted the memory but were not true writing systems. Consequently, once the keeper of the *quipu* died, the information contained in the *quipu* also passed away unless he had trained a successor.

When they Spaniards arrived, they perceived some aspects of native beliefs seemed to be similar to Christianity. Among the Inca there was a custom of cloistering women for the service of the cult of the sun and to serve the Inca emperor as servants within his household. These women, known as *acllacuna*, or chosen women, bore a vague resemblance to nuns of late medieval Europe. The Inca also had a tradition of oracles, the most famous of which was the oracle of Pachacamac, near modern Lima, and these oracles reminded the Spaniards of the ancient Greek and Roman traditions.

While the sedentary, highly organized civilizations of the Maya, Aztec, Inca, and others accounted for the majority of the native peoples of the New World at the time of the arrival of the Spaniards, there were hundreds, if not thousands, of smaller groups manifesting various types of cultural development. Certainly one of the most common cultural group was that of the hunters and gatherers, which practiced primitive agriculture. These peoples could be found in all areas, and each had unique religious beliefs. Because each group might number only a few thousand persons, they represented some major problems for the Spanish missionaries.

Guaycuruans and other Tribal-level Groups

As an example of these tribal-level people in South America, the natives of the Gran Chaco in what is now Paraguay and Bolivia were collectively known as the Guaycuruan. The various tribes within this group were dedicated to hunting and gathering, and shared many cultural traits. While they shared similar languages, they did not have common political organizations. Their loyalty fell completely to their immediate group and not to a larger pan-tribal unit. The Guaycuruans believed in a spiritual creator, who created the world and provided for moral and spiritual guidance. This god was seen as a benefactor to people, especially giving prowess in hunting and war. The sky was inhabited by spirits who could act upon people's lives—mostly for ill. Similarly there were scores of malevolent terrestrial spirits with which people had to contend. Active intercession with the spirits could neutralize their effect or even use the spirits for good.

The Guaycuruans embraced hunting and militarism. They believed that they had to fight for their hunting lands against all challengers. Like the Maya, they divided the world into the heavenly regions, the surface of the earth, and the subterranean world. While in ages past these realms were linked, by a tree in many legends, the tree was destroyed. The various spirits and supernatural powers demanded that the Guaycuruans maintain a balance with their natural environment. Consequently, hunting was deeply imbued with spiritual values simply because there was a reciprocal relationship between animals and humans. Human souls, at death, became part of animal's bodies; the animals sacrificed themselves for the benefit of humankind. Yet upon death, the animal spirits could be very dangerous to humans. Because of this, hunters limited themselves to only what they needed. Alcohol played an important ceremonial role, especially to ward off illness and as part of funerary practices. The Guaycuruans had priests, or shamans, who were religious specialists. The shamans controlled, or mediated, the spirit world in which the people lived.

The Spaniards, upon their arrival and eventual conquest of the native groups, confronted two great obstacles. One the one hand, the religions and cultures that they encountered were very different from those with which they had some familiarity in the European context. While they might see minor rituals and beliefs, which the native peoples had in common with the Europeans, such as forms of confession or beliefs in a worldwide flood. Yet by and large the native religions were a mystery to the Spanish. On the other hand, they had great difficulty explaining Christianity and European cultural values to the native people of the Americas. The language barrier was only a partial impediment. The Europeans conceived of themselves, the natives, and of nature in a completely different manner from the Native Americans. While they might be able to translate the words, the concepts and the thought processes that lay behind them were totally different. The process of ongoing dialogue between the natives and the Europeans led Christianity in the Americas to develop in a unique way.

2

Spain and Portugal
in the New World

On the deck of the *Santa María* a crewman rang the bell to mark the hour. Christopher Columbus and his crew paused momentarily from their labors, and each said a prayer to the Virgin Mary to protect them in their voyage. While the small expedition consisted of scores of men, nowhere was there a clergyman. Nonetheless, Columbus and his crew believed that their voyage needed not just divine protection but was part of a larger divine project to spread the Word of God.

If the history of Christianity in the New World begins with the voyage of Columbus, Columbus's voyage begins several decades earlier, as the Portuguese initiated explorations in the Atlantic far beyond the confines of Europe. Portugal completed the Reconquest in their territories by the thirteenth century and remained largely free of conflict for several centuries. From the thirteenth century on, various Portuguese monarchs conceived of expanding the Reconquest by capturing Muslim strongholds on the African side of the Straits of Gibraltar, concluding in 1415 when they captured Ceuta in North Africa.

The Portuguese realized that the Muslims of North Africa were merely the farthest outpost of a vast political and economic network. Many of the goods, particularly gold, that the Portuguese and other European powers sought passed through Muslim traders. West Africa was a major producer of gold during the Middle Ages, which came from deposits in sub-Saharan Africa, and was traded northwards, across the Sahara, and eventually into Europe. Other goods, such as silks and spices, were produced in the Far East and passed through a series of merchant networks until they entered the Muslim world and then into Europe. The Portuguese reasoned that if they could reach the source of supply, they could eliminate the Muslim merchants and gain direct access to African gold and Asian trade goods. The Portuguese also continued the Reconquest in a more dramatic way, sending missionaries to gain converts to Christianity and thereby undermine Muslim rule. And, the Portuguese sought to find the Christian kingdom legend held to be located somewhere to the east, so that they might create an alliance that would in effect surround the Muslims.

The Portuguese maritime explorations began in 1419. During the next eighty years, the Portuguese would systematically sail the North Atlantic and the Atlantic coast of Africa. The Portuguese voyages of exploration fall into two basic periods. The first consisted of voyages in the North Atlantic. In the first twenty years of exploration, the Portuguese discovered and began to settle on many of the small islands of the North Atlantic, including Porto Santo (1418), Madeira (1419), the Azores (1427), and the Canaries (ca. 1431). The Portuguese sailors had determined that the winds and currents of the North Atlantic followed a generally clockwise flow, with the southern boundary being immediately north of the equator in what is now called the inter-tropical convergence zone.

The second phase of the Portuguese explorations overlapped slightly with the first, but consisted of voyages down the west coast of Africa. By 1434 the Portuguese had reached Cape Bojador, Cape Verde by 1444, and by 1460 the coast of Sierra Leone. The method pursued by these voyages was to sail as far down the coast as possible. Voyages to the region between Cape Bojador and Cape Verde required a return voyage that went west far out into the Atlantic, since the prevailing winds and currents went south and west. The Portuguese knowledge of the islands of Madeira and the Azores provided them with fuel and water stops for the return voyage. Once the expeditions had passed Cape Verde, the direction of the winds and currents shifted. In the inter-tropical convergence zone the winds and currents predominately go from east to west, but south of there the winds come up from the southeast. Sailing beyond this point required them to abandon the use of the square-rigged ship (*não* in Portuguese), which required wind from behind, and to adopt the caravel, which relied on triangular, or lateen, sails, allowing it to sail much closer to the wind. In order to return from the region south of Cape Verde, the expeditions sailed significantly westward and caught the northward winds and currents, stopping for supplies on one of the mid-Atlantic islands and then eastward to Portugal.

These voyages had important financial and political implications. They sought to discover the source of African gold and possibly divert its flow from Muslim traders of the Sahara. They also wanted to establish political ties with whatever powers controlled those regions. But their third impetus was to Christianize the peoples of the regions they discovered in order to create allies in a worldwide confrontation with the Muslims. In keeping with this third goal, the Portuguese asked for and received papal support for their efforts.

In a series of papal decrees, or bulls,[1] between 1452 and 1456, Nicholas V and Callistus II granted certain rights and privileges to the Portuguese crown. The pope allowed the Portuguese to attack and conquer any Muslims, pagans, or heathens who opposed the Christian word and to take both the goods and lands of these opponents, making slaves of them and granting the goods and lands to the Portuguese crown. Another bull granted a monopoly on navigation, fishing, and trade in all those regions, from Ceuta in northwest Africa all the way to the East Indies. The Portuguese monarchs were required to build churches and other ecclesiastical buildings as well as send priests to administer the sacraments. A third papal decree empowered the Order of Christ (a Portuguese military-religious order devoted to the spread of Christianity) and its leader, the grand prior, the spiritual jurisdiction of all the territories gained by Portugal under the authority of the earlier bulls. The grand prior could appoint priests to all benefices, administer ecclesiastical justice, and hold all of the powers of a local bishop. The order received this power specifically in territories outside of any established diocese, so no bishop or other ecclesiastical authority could claim jurisdiction. Taken as a whole, these bulls, and a few others, provided the basis for the Royal Patronage (known in Portuguese as the *Padroado Real* and in Spanish as the *Patronato Real*) In brief, the Royal Patronage consisted of the rights and privileges given by the papacy to the kings of Spain or Portugal over the Church in their overseas empires.

The critical moment in Portuguese explorations along the African coast occurred in 1488. Bartolomeu Dias departed from Lisbon in 1487 to sail down the African coast beyond the mouth of the Congo River. After having accomplished this goal, Dias continued his southward voyage. Around New Year's Day in 1488 he was blown off course while sailing along the coast of modern-day Namibia. When he finally weathered the storm, he began to sail north and east, hoping to regain the coast. To his surprise, and that of the crew, when land was sighted it was not to the east, but rather to the north and west. He had sailed around what he would call the Cape of Storms, later known as the Cape of Good Hope, the southern tip of Africa.

His voyage was hailed as the key to the opening up of the Indian Ocean for the Portuguese. Yet it took nine years after Dias's return for the voyage of Vasco da Gama to set sail definitively for India. By that time, the Portuguese also understood the general nature of the winds and currents of the South Atlantic. Rather than following the coast as previous expeditions had, when da Gama reached the inter-tropical convergence zone he sailed westward until he could pick up the prevailing winds that blow to the south. Da Gama probably had no idea that he was sailing close to the continent of South America. Just three years later, Pedro Alvares Cabral, commanding a second fleet to India, would make landfall in what would become Brazil, while retracing the route of da Gama.

Columbus and the Church's Mission

Just as the Catholic kings of Spain were engaged in the final assault on Granada, Christopher Columbus proposed sailing westward to reach Asia. The goals he presented to them were essentially the same goals that had driven the Portuguese expeditions: access to gold and spices, political alliances with friendly powers, and Christianization of natives. Columbus had sailed for the Portuguese and had made the same offer to the Portuguese king, João II. Columbus did not in fact propose to demonstrate that the world was round: all educated persons, and those with any reason to be informed on the issue, knew that the earth was round. What Columbus questioned was the size of the sphere. He posited that it was some six thousand miles smaller than generally believed. This was an important difference, since it made a voyage to Asia via the west within the limits of the technology then available. A longer voyage would have been frankly impossible. Columbus did find land at approximately the distance he anticipated. It was not, however, the eastern edge of Asia, but rather a new world altogether.

The missionary importance of the voyage of Columbus is great. One of his specific goals was to take Christianity to the Far East. While Columbus never reached the Far East, he did take Christianity with him. Interestingly enough, Columbus did not bring a priest along on his first voyage to the New World. Confident though he was, Columbus was uncertain of exactly how far he would have to sail. In sailing vessels of the period, there was a very demanding ratio between supplies and men. More men required more supplies. Yet the holding capacity of the ship was finite, as was the number of men needed to sail her. Columbus had no room for error; each and every man aboard was expected to do everything necessary to sail the ship, and bringing a priest aboard would have been a luxury. In light of this, he decided not to carry a priest.

This does not mean that there was no religious life aboard Columbus's three ships. In fact, the daily cycle of activities aboard ship was punctuated by prayers and religious songs. Columbus regularly led the men in prayer and was himself a deeply spiritual man. He sincerely believed that he had been chosen by God for a divine mission to carry Christianity to the ends of the earth. Later in his life he would sign his name as "Xpto ferens" (*Cristo ferens*), "he who carries Christ," referring to his role in spreading the Gospel. On his third voyage (1498), Columbus believed that he had discovered the gates of the Garden of Eden as he sailed by the mouth of the Orinoco. He was deeply influenced by the Franciscans, with whom he had lived after leaving Portugal, while negotiating with the Spanish monarchs. When he made his historic voyage he entrusted his legitimate son, Diego, to their care. In this period, many Franciscans firmly believed that the end of the world was near. The end was to come once the Gospel had been taken to the farthest reaches of the earth, and Columbus saw himself as a tool in that mission.

Although no priest accompanied Columbus's first voyage, on the second voyage several priests joined the expedition: four Franciscans and a Jeronymite—another religious order, led by Fr. Ramón Pané. The leader of the Franciscans was Fr. Buil. His origins are unclear, although he was probably a Catalan. Fr. Buil is credited with saying the first Mass in the Americas, on the Feast of the Epiphany, January 6, 1494, on the island of Hispaniola.[2]

Columbus envisioned his mission as a continuation of the Reconquest. In his negotiations with the Catholic monarchs he sought all the traditional honors: exclusive rights to govern the lands he had discovered, a monopoly right to all of the trade to and from the islands, and supervision of the courts and of the Church. Nevertheless, the Catholic monarchs, having recently won back powers and privileges from the nobles and cities in Spain, were unwilling to give up so much authority to someone new, and especially to somewhere several thousand miles away. They negotiated a contract with Columbus: *Las Capitulaciones de Santa Fe*, which granted various privileges to the explorer. He would enjoy the hereditary titles of the Admiral of the Ocean Sea, and Viceroy and Governor of the Indies. He could retain 10 percent of all taxes levied in the territories and enjoy the right to nominate all colonial officials. Notably absent from the agreement were any grants of judicial authority, the right to impose taxes, to restrict trade, or to control the Church.

In 1500 Fernando and Isabel abrogated the contract. The Catholic monarchs had serious questions about Columbus's ability to govern. At this point a series of lawsuits began over who had the right to name the governors of Hispaniola, the island in the Greater Antilles that Columbus recently discovered and settled. In 1516, in order to make peace on the island, three Jeronymite friars were sent out to govern the island as commissioners of the crown. Early on, the crown began to use clergy to pacify and stabilize the troubled area. The Jeronymites ruled only until 1519, when Columbus's son Diego became governor and retained power for some four years. Eventually all the Columbus claims to the governance of the New World were rejected and a series of civil governors ruled.

The arrival of the Spaniards on the island brought about conflict with the natives, against many of whom the Spanish launched expeditions of conquest, while also seeking to peacefully engage others. With increasing numbers of Europeans, the royal government needed to allocate the limited resources of the island, since the first settlers sought rewards from the crown for their participation in these adventures. In the New World there were two limited resources that needed to be allocated: land and labor. Both provided the economic basis of the colonies. Labor presented the thornier issue, because there was principally just one source of labor: the natives. While Spaniards were generally willing to work to supply their own needs, there was just too much to be done to make the colonies successful. Houses and other structures had to be built and crops planted. Additionally the colonists needed to search for commodities that could be sold profitably in Spain, such as gold, silver, and precious stones.

The first Spanish settlement occurred on the island of Hispaniola, the modern-day Haiti and the Dominican Republic. From their base of operations in the city of Santo Domingo, the Spanish launched expeditions to the nearby islands of Puerto Rico, Jamaica, and Cuba. By 1512 these large islands had been conquered and settled by the Spanish. From there expeditions to the mainland of the Americas began to expand Spanish influence. First among these was the settlement of the Isthmus of Panama. Shortly thereafter, expeditions from Cuba encountered the North American mainland in what is now Mexico. That phase of exploration and conquest ended in 1519 with the expedition of Hernán Cortés to Mexico.

In these expeditions and conquests, the royal government followed a policy begun in the Reconquest of recognizing the accomplishments of those who served in conquest, pacification, and settlement. To refer to the participants in the conquest of the New World as soldiers would be a misnomer. The term "soldier" implies that they received a salary, but these men and women did not receive any pay. Rather, they were members of a band or company, *hueste* or *compañía.*, and all were all limited investors. They provided their own food, their own armor, their own muskets, dogs, and horses. Whatever implements of war they happened to bring were theirs. As a result, one and all expected to receive booty in proportion to their investment.

In order to reward the members of the expedition, Columbus allocated plots of land to settlers. The land, in and of itself, had very little value unless someone could work it. In order to augment the labor pool beyond the Spanish population, specific communities of natives were granted, in trust, to Spanish settlers to provide them with labor. A specific settler received the right to the labor of a specific community. The settler could use that labor to build a house, to mine for gold, or to work the land. The grant of native communities as a labor force was called an *encomienda*. The institution of the *encomienda* existed previously in Spain, but in a far different form. In the New World the term implied that a population of natives was entrusted to the Spanish, meaning that the colonist did not actually own the natives. In some regions the distribution of natives among settlers was called the *repartimiento*.[3] In the early sixteenth century, *repartimiento* and *encomienda* were synonymous. The recipient of the *encomienda*, called an *encomendero*, could also collect taxes from the natives. Whatever tribute paid by the natives to their indigenous rulers was allocated to either the crown or to the *encomendero*.

The land grant was distinct from the grant of tribute. According to the principles of Spanish law as applied in the New World, if no one occupied a specific parcel of land, the crown was free to allocate it. This provision soon caused problems for the natives because Spanish perceptions of native occupation of land and the natives' actual occupation of land were quite separate and distinct things. Native agricultural practices demanded far more land than the natives ever occupied at any given time. Indians usually had three to four times more land lying fallow than they actually farmed. As far as the Spaniards were concerned, the fallow land was vacant land. The fallow land provided the Spaniards with more than enough land to settle, without exploiting lands currently occupied by the natives, yet had a disastrous impact on the natives' ability to support themselves.

While Columbus and other governors in the Indies felt free to make these grants, both of land and *encomiendas* in the name of the monarch, the grants constituted a major political and legal question to the thinkers of the age. At the heart of the issue were questions regarding the basis for Spain's dominion in the Indies.

Papal Bulls and the Royal Patronage

Spain's earliest claims to dominion over the New World were based in a papal bull of 1493. Upon the return of Columbus to Spain in 1493, the Spanish monarchs sent dispatches to Rome, informing the newly elected pope, Alexander

VI, of the event. The Spanish monarchs wished to secure some confirmation from the pope of the discovery and settlement of the recently discovered lands. In May 1493, Alexander issued his bull *Inter caetera divinae*, which recognized the Spanish accomplishment and divided the known world into two spheres of influence: the western half fell to Spain, the eastern half was Portuguese, in keeping with earlier privileges already granted to the Portuguese. The bull also provided for an imaginary line drawn through the North and South poles one hundred leagues west of the Azores and Cape Verde islands.[4] Alexander further defined the legal extent of the Spanish dominion in a follow-up bull titled *Dudum siquidem*, on September 26, 1493, which, in effect, created an exclusively Spanish sphere of influence in the New World.

A bilateral treaty between the Spanish and the Portuguese quickly followed the unilateral action of the pope. Ambassadors from the two kingdoms met in the Spanish town of Tordesillas where they molded the papal grant into a treaty. The Treaty of Tordesillas, dated June 7, 1494, accepted the provisions of the papal bull, but pushed the line of demarcation from 100 leagues west of the Cape Verde islands to 370 leagues. The papal bulls and the treaty would form yet another component in the Royal Patronage, the foundation of Spanish claims over the administration of the New World Church.

Many legal thinkers questioned the validity of the papal bulls to grant dominion to the Spanish. Not accepting papal justification, critics then turned to natural law. In the fifteenth and sixteenth centuries there was little notion of international law, as each European state had its own customary law, local laws, and statutes. Yet there was no law that could serve to amicably resolve disputes between nations. With overseas exploration and the expansion of Europe around the world, it became very important to develop a system of international law. This system of international law would govern two types of activities: relations between foreign nations and European states, and conflicts among European states themselves. The two types of the international law had different ends and different means.

A Dominican, Francisco de Vitoria, at the University of Salamanca, is generally credited with being the father of international law. He developed the *ius gentium*, the law of nations or the law of peoples. In developing this concept, Vitoria looked into the legal basis for Spain's claims to the New World. In studying canon law, he could find nothing that allowed a nation to expand and literally take over the territory of another people. Vitoria then turned to civil law and likewise found that in civil law there were no specific provisions for territorial expansion. He then turned to natural law: that is, what would be reasonable in relationships based upon the common ethical, moral, and legal precepts of the time. In so doing Vitoria developed an entirely new type of law. Yet even in natural law, the law of man in a natural state, Vitoria could find no cogent, logical arguments that could explain, or even have bearing on, European powers and establishing hegemony over others.

For Vitoria and his intellectual followers, there were two basic issues: *imperium* (sovereignty) and *dominium* (property rights). The supporters of the monarchy claimed that Spain enjoyed both sovereignty and property rights over the newly conquered regions. Vitoria and his followers, including another outspoken Dominican, Fr. Bartolomé de las Casas, argued that Spain's only claim might be that of sovereignty, and even that was doubtful. While the Spanish could govern the lands by virtue of conquest, they could not take the lands nor the wealth of the lands.

Another Dominican, Fr. Melchor Cano, posited that the cornerstone of Spain's claims was the *ius predicando*, the law of preaching: that a nation could establish hegemony over a non-Christian power for the purpose of spreading the Gospel, based upon principles of natural law. Heathens, pagans, and heretics could be subjected to foreign rule, specifically for Christianization.

Cano also provided that one power could dominate another power for the purpose of opening up that foreign power to commerce—what we now know as the law of free commerce. This law or right presupposed that the foreign country previously had been closed or unknown. Unfortunately, other European powers might seize on this idea, with reference to Spain's own holdings in the New World, and thus claim a right to free commerce there. Consequently, Spain did not use the law of free commerce to justify its claims to the New World.

Spain now had to rely on the *ius predicando* (law of preaching) as one of the legal bases upon which she held the New World, based on the primacy of the papal grants. By the early years of the sixteenth century, the Spanish justification for holding the New World became an integral part of the Royal Patronage. The crown had already promised to financially support missionary activity. In order to establish a firm legal claim on the New World using the *ius predicando*, the crown had to then send out missionaries.[5]

At the same time that Vitoria and others developed these rules of international law, there also emerged widely accepted rules about what constitutes a just, or legal, war. Force could be used only under very specific conditions, which defined the "just" war. Again, scholars extrapolated from canon, civil, and natural law. All of these sources agreed that if one were attacked, armed response was allowed. But under what circumstances could one nation attack another? The scholars studying just war concluded that if a foreign people openly rejected Christianity, war might be made to subdue them in order to spread the Gospel. Based on the concept of the *ius predicando*, conquest could not occur before efforts had been made to peaceably preach the Gospel. If the Gospel were rejected violently, war would be possible. Nevertheless, the purpose of war was to pacify the people, to Christianize them.

The Spanish crown drafted a rather curious document, known as the *Requerimento* (Requirement), to have Spanish expeditions comply with these restrictions. The Requirement consisted of a statement of Christian dogma and an explanation of Spanish royal authority. It called upon the natives to whom it was presented to embrace Christianity and be subjects of the Catholic kings of Spain. It was in effect a notification to the natives of the intents of the Spaniards and an attempt, in a very legalistic way, to peaceably bring the natives into submission.

Obviously there were difficulties with the system. The Requirement was seldom read to the natives in their own language. Even if the Spanish complied with all the details, seldom did the reaction of the natives represent an informed response. The existence and occasional use of the Requirement indicates that the Spaniards seriously thought about their legal claim to the New World, which claim was intimately related to the Christianizing mission. The Requirement called on the natives to first acknowledge the Christian Church, the pope, and the Spanish monarchs as superiors and lords, and second, to allow the Gospel to be preached. If another European power could demonstrate, or at least use propaganda to show, that the Spaniards were not dutifully Christianizing the natives, claims to the New World could be made against Spain. What concerned crown officials and intellectuals in Spain did not necessarily cause equal concern in the New World. Spaniards in the New World widely ignored, abused, and ridiculed the Requirement more than complied with it.

The New World was a powerful attraction to many Spaniards. Arriving in the islands of the Greater Antilles, Spanish immigrants posed a real problem to local officials, in that all sought a better life, usually at the expense of the natives. The treatment of the natives under the *encomienda* was deplorable, especially on the islands of Hispaniola, Puerto Rico, and Cuba. The conditions under which they lived were horrific: legally they were free, but they were made to work like slaves. Mistreatment under the *encomienda*, plus newly introduced European diseases, precipitated a very dramatic drop in the native population of the islands of the Caribbean. By approximately 1540, there were no more natives on either of the two big islands of Puerto Rico and Hispaniola, and within a few decades most would be gone from Cuba.

In the early sixteenth century, many observers attributed the drop in native population to mistreatment. They claimed that the Spaniards literally worked the natives to death. The list of abuses that the Spaniards supposedly handed out to the natives is nearly endless. Many of these claims were probably correct; the crucial question, however, is one of degree, volition, and cognition: the abuses occurred. One cannot determine how widespread the abuses were nor what all of their consequences were.

One important cause of the mortality of the natives was the introduction of Old World diseases. The New World was populated across a land bridge from Siberia by small bands of hunters. During the migration of Eurasians to the New World some forty thousand to ten thousand years ago, many European diseases simply did not arrive in the New World, especially those such as measles, small pox, and many kinds of influenza. The diseases of Europe that plagued cities and concentrated in populations in temperate and subtropical areas were not transmitted to the New World, as they did not survive among small groups of nomadic hunters and gatherers traveling through arctic and subarctic climate zones over thousands of years.

When the Europeans arrived in the sixteenth century, many of whom were suffering from these diseases, they infected the natives, who had no immunity. During any given outbreak of these diseases, more than half the native population would succumb, and in some instances, 80 or 90 percent of the native population of a given location might die. By comparison, among a European population one might expect a quarter of the population to die. When one also considers the disruption and the dislocation of conquest along with the later exploitation, one might expect the virulence of the diseases to be increased. The disease environment of the islands further deteriorated when certain African diseases arrived and became endemic.

The mortality of the natives did not pass unnoticed. Many voices on the islands were raised in their defense. The Dominicans on the island of Hispaniola became vocal critics of the *encomienda* and of Spanish mistreatment of the natives. The *encomienda* was identified as the single most important source of exploitation of the natives and that which caused the worst abuses of the natives.

A major controversy erupted in 1511 on the Fourth Sunday of Advent, the Sunday before Christmas, when the Dominican friar Antón de Montesinos delivered a scathing attack on the *encomienda* and the Spaniards who profited from it. The sermon was based on John 1:23 where the Pharisees asked John the Baptist who he was, and he replied "I am . . . the voice of one that cries in the desert: Prepare a way for the Lord. Make his paths straight."[6]

Montesinos lambasted the colonists for their ill-treatment of the natives. The sermon caused a major disturbance among the elite Spanish population of Santo Domingo. When the local citizens complained to the Dominican superior, Fr. Pedro de Córdoba, he indicated that he would do nothing to stop Montesinos from preaching in the future. The subsequent Sunday, Montesinos continued his polemic against Spanish exploitation of the natives, this time using as his text Job 36:2, "Be patient a little longer while I explain, for I have more to say on God's behalf" (NJB).[7]

As the criticism grew, in 1512 the Spanish king convened a high-level conference of scholars, religious, lawyers, and others to debate and discuss Spain's claim to the New World and the legality of the *encomienda*. This discussion resulted in the Laws of Burgos that gave a formal legal structure to the *encomienda*. They recognized the *encomienda* as a legal institution but sought to provide some regulation of the worst abuses. While natives could still be coerced into providing labor for the settlers, the *encomenderos* had to undertake the construction of churches, purchase ornaments and religious images, and see that the natives were Christianized. Under this provision the *encomendero* had to provide a priest to see that the natives were instructed in Christian doctrine and received the sacraments of the church. The *encomendero* was required to allow the natives some time off: religious holidays, Sundays, and other major feast days. That provision allowed the natives the opportunity to tend their own fields and to work for themselves. Moreover, the natives were still required to labor for and pay tribute to the *encomendero*. The *encomendero* for his part was required to provide horses and arms to defend the territory against attack. In short, the Laws of Burgos attempted to define the *encomienda* legally and restrain its excesses. The Laws of Burgos were accompanied by another document that sought to define the crown's relationship to the Church, called the Concordat of Burgos.

In 1512 Diego Velazquez led the conquest of Cuba. One of the participants in the conquest was Fr. Bartolomé de las Casas, who had first come to the Indies in 1502. For his service in the conquest of Cuba, he received a small *encomienda* on that island. In preparing a sermon to be delivered on Pentecost Sunday he had a midlife conversion. In considering the text appointed for that day, Ecclesiasticus (Sirach) 34:18–19, he came to the opinion that the Spanish exploitation of the New World was not lawful, based on divine law.[8] He returned to Spain where he joined the Dominican Order. Las Casas[9] became the most outspoken critic of Spanish policy toward the New World natives and spent the rest of his life seeking protection for the natives. His vision was that the Church needed to take an active role in the protection of the rights of the native peoples of the New World.

Las Casas wrote several books on the history of the New World and the Spanish excesses there. Both the English and French used Las Casas's writings for ammunition in the international court of public opinion. If the Spaniards could be shown to be violating the *ius predicando* and otherwise acting in violation of the conditions implied in the papal grants, in other words not earnestly Christianizing the natives, then Spanish claims to the New World could be found null and void. This vision of Spanish exploitation of the New World came to be known as the Black Legend.

Curiously enough, some of the men whose writings formed the basis for the Black Legend were the men who were trying the hardest to see that the natives were treated well, such as Las Casas. The White Legend, on the other hand, held that the Spanish did many good things in the New World. This position argues that they found the natives in varying degrees of barbarism and brought them the Gospel and all the benefits of European culture. The White Legend further holds that given the tone of the times, one cannot say that the Spaniards were any more cruel to the natives than any other European power, and were in most instances considerably more benign.

Although Las Casas has been credited for being the most outspoken defender of the rights of the natives of the Americas, he has been criticized in the modern era for having encouraged the use of African slaves as an alternative labor supply, suggesting that in order to alleviate the burden of labor on the natives, Spain should import African slaves into the New World. Las Casas felt that Africans were better suited to hard labor in the tropics and so could withstand conditions in the islands better than the natives. However, he later recognized that it was as unjust to enslave Africans as native Americans.

When Bartolomé de las Casas entered the fray, there developed in Spain a rather vocal and outspoken opposition to the *encomienda*, even the legally established *encomienda* of the Laws of Burgos. So much opposition was mounted that in future conquests in the New World, royal officials were specifically prohibited from granting *encomiendas*.[10] The supporters of the rights of the natives of the New World, such as Las Casas, succeeded in 1537 when the pope declared the American natives to be fully human, and thus fully capable of embracing Christianity, and of enjoying full human rights recognized by the Church.

Granting the natives full rights within the Church was no simple issue. Some Spaniards argued that the natives were not fully human but rather more like beasts, capable of imitation but not imagination and independent, thoughtful action. Fortunately, this school of thought was limited to very few people. In general, both the crown and the Church officials agreed on the humanity of the natives because it was essential to both their interests. Part of the political claim the Spanish crown had to the New World was based on Christianizing the natives. If the natives were beasts and not fully human, they could not be Christianized. Similarly for the missionaries, there was little doubt that natives were human. The priests and friars had learned their languages, conversed with them, learned of their thoughts, and successfully converted many to Christianity. In 1537 Pope Paul III issued the papal bull that brought an end to the discussion. Titled *Sublimus deus*, the document took the official position of the Church that the natives were indeed fully human and capable, even eager, to embrace Christianity.

Until this point the religious orders, the Franciscans, Dominicans, and to a lesser degree the Jeronymites, had dominated the development of the Church in the New World. Yet in the second decade of the sixteenth century the number of secular, or diocesan, priests was beginning to grow. The Spanish population also had increased. Two of the islands of the Greater Antilles were already settled, Hispaniola and Puerto Rico, and in 1512 Cuba was added to the list. Now it was time that dioceses be created to govern the Church.

As the population grew and the need for local bishops became clear, the Spanish monarch petitioned the pope to create the necessary dioceses. This marked the further development of the Royal Patronage. In a very general sense patronage consisted of the right to appoint a qualified person to an ecclesiastical office. It derived from the practice in the Middle Ages of persons endowing particular offices in the Church. In return for the endowment, the patron was given the right to appoint individuals to serve the office. In the case of the New World, the Spanish kings and the pope developed a complex system whereby the cost of Christianizing the natives was born by the king, and in recognition of this the pope granted certain administrative powers over the New World Church to the king.

The Royal Patronage was based upon grants made by the popes to the Spanish and Portuguese monarchs before the discovery and conquest of the New World. The popes had granted rather broad administrative powers over the missionary Church in Portuguese Africa to the prior of the military-religious Order of Christ, and eventually to the Portuguese monarch. Likewise, when the Catholic monarchs, Isabel and Fernando, successfully defeated the Muslim kingdom of Granada, the pope granted them rather extensive administrative powers over the Church in that territory, and eventually they sought the right of appointment to all high ecclesiastical offices in all of their realms.

In 1493, when Alexander VI divided the world into two spheres of influence, he also granted various political powers to the Spanish. Alexander VI and his successor, Julius II, gave the Spanish monarchs the basis for supervising missionary activities in the newly discovered lands and the means whereby to financially support that activity. Alexander VI issued three bulls, all titled *Eximie devotionis*, on May 4, 1493, March 21, 1499, and November 16, 1501. The first of these granted to the Spanish monarchs all the powers that the Portuguese enjoyed in their overseas possessions. The second of the three provided the monarchs with a means of providing financial support for the missionary activity by means of a royal tax. The third bull, dating from 1501, granted the Spanish monarchs the right to collect and use the ecclesiastical tax, the tithe, in the New World.[11] The revenues were to be used in the construction of churches, to support the priests, and to furnish the churches. It was assumed that when the Church grew large enough, the monarch would give the tithes back to the Church. Of these three bulls, the first and last would become key in the development of crown control over the Church. The first provided that the Spanish monarch would, in essence, control much of the administrative structure of the overseas Church through the power of appointment. The last bull granted the monarchs the control of the ecclesiastical purse strings, since the Church hierarchy down to the local parish priest relied on the tithe for the basis of their income.

While these grants constituted the first concrete privileges given by the popes to the Spanish crown, they were not the whole Royal Patronage. In 1504 Julius II, a famous humanist pope, granted the Spanish monarchs the right to nominate the first bishops in the New World to dioceses located on the islands of Hispaniola and Puerto Rico. Ferdnando chose not to act upon that privilege until the pope had granted him broader powers of patronage over the church. The fuller development of the patronage came in 1510, when Julius, in the bull *Universalis ecclesiae regimini*, granted to the Spanish kings the exclusive privilege of building and endowing churches, benefices, and other pious activities. Through these powers, the kings could appoint and nominate candidates to serve the newly created bishoprics, ecclesiastical dignities, and benefices forever.[12] Offices in the lower clergy were left to the local bishop, while appointments within the religious orders were subject to the internal approval processes of the orders. In the last of his bulls, Julius granted to the monarch the perpetual right to collect and enjoy the tithe on gold, silver, and other precious metals. With these grants the papal legislation creating the Patronato Real essentially was complete.[13] The monarchs still had to take an active role and positively use the powers that they had been granted in order for the Patronage to become a reality.

The key piece of legislation demonstrating the powers within the Patronage as envisioned by the Spanish monarchs was drafted in 1512, during the debates over the *encomienda* and over the legal status of the natives which occurred in Burgos. On May 8, an agreement was reached between the crown and the bishops of the new dioceses. The document, mentioned earlier, was called the Concordat of Burgos, but it was not a true concordat in that it did not directly involve the pope. In the agreement, the crown gave the tithes back to the Church, but the king retained one-ninth. This means that the crown accepted the principle of being responsible for the tithe, but empowered the local church to collect the tax. In return the crown received one-ninth of the total value of the tax. The agreement also stipulated that the crown could present candidates to any and all vacancies that would occur in the cathedrals, benefices, and other high ecclesiastical offices. Benefices would preferentially go to the children of Spanish settlers and Spanish inhabitants of the Indies. The crown then legislated on many very specific issues such as which feasts would be celebrated, and other administrative details. The agreement demonstrated the wide range of authority that the crown expected to enjoy in exercising administrative control over the Church in the New World.

Portuguese donatários

While the Spanish crown was engaged in developing the ecclesiastical system that would govern their territories in the New World, the Portuguese had been more focused on their possessions in the Far East. Yet in the early sixteenth century, the Portuguese began to take a more active interest in lands within their sphere of influence to the west. The Portuguese tradition, developed over the decades of exploration of the African coast, was to establish trading posts rather than colonies. Only a few Portuguese traders would be stationed at these locations. They would acquire goods from the interior to be traded to the Portuguese merchants. The merchants would leave supplies of European goods to be traded throughout the year, in between the arrival of the Portuguese vessels. The Portuguese in Brazil began in a very similar fashion, although for many years there was not even a permanent presence. The only product that interested Europeans was a tropical wood used for dying cloth called brazilwood, thus giving the name to the land.

After many years of intermittent trade, the Portuguese began to fear that other European powers might attempt to wrest Brazil away from them. The biggest threat was France, whose king, Francis I, is credited with having asked where in Adam's will was the whole of the earth divided between the Spanish and Portuguese, tacitly questioning the authority of the pope to divide the world into two spheres of influence. With growing concerns over other European powers attempting to claim Brazil, the Portuguese crown began to develop methods to better hold the territory.

In 1533, King João III initiated a limited settlement system for Brazil by dividing the territory into fifteen regions and granting control over each region to a captain, appointed by the crown. Each captain would have hereditary rights over the territory, including the right to appoint justices and collect local taxes. Because these territories were donated, the captains, usually favored courtiers, came to be known as *donatários*. The Portuguese had used this system to some success in settling the islands of the Atlantic. Although fifteen captaincies were created in Brazil, only two eventually became reality: São Vicente in the south, in the region of modern São Paulo, and Pernambuco, in the north. The *donatário* was also responsible for the development of churches in the territory and could collect some of the tithe to defray these costs. By mid-century it became clear that the *donatários* were not going to settle the whole of Brazil.

In 1548, João abrogated the grants to those individuals who never attempted to settle their territories, and he revised the two existing grants, to provide for a supreme local governor general with authority over all of Brazil, while still recognizing most of the hereditary rights granted to the *donatários*. The first governor general was Tomé de Sousa, a member of the Portuguese nobility who had already served in Africa and India. Recognizing that the seat of government could not be in either of the two already established territories, a capital was established in the deep-harbor port of Salvador da Bahia. The royal government for Brazil began with Sousa's appointment, and missionaries from the Jesuit Order, under the leadership of Manuel de Nobrega, came along with him.

The Portuguese crown claimed patronage over the Brazilian Church, based upon the papal bulls granting the crown authority in all lands they might conquer and settle. Unfortunately the bulls consistently referred to lands between Cape Verde in Africa and the easternmost reaches of India. The crown, however, extended these grants to possessions in America, based upon the Treaty of Tordesillas. Initially the Portuguese monarchs exercised a relaxed control over the Brazilian Church, because the very small Portuguese population in the colony meant there were very few ecclesiastical officials to control. On the other hand, the Portuguese crown maintained an amicable enough relationship with the Jesuits. Nevertheless, the Jesuits were characterized by a high degree of autonomy and independence from local authorities, which made them successful in the wilds of Brazil. In the long run, the Portuguese monarchs defended their patronage rights in Brazil.

In the end the *Patronato* (under the Spanish crown) and *Padroado* (under the Portuguese crown) represented highly complex agreements between the Papacy and the two Iberian powers. Historically the Portuguese predated the Spanish, and the latter was at least initially modeled on the former. Both relied on certain basic assumptions. The Iberian powers had gained control over lands outside of the European confines of the Church. The goal of the Church was to extend Christianity. The Papacy desired the extension of Christianity, especially at a time when the Catholic Church was confronting the rise of the Protestant Reformation. The Church was ill prepared financially to send missionaries to the far reaches of the globe. The Iberian monarchs were willing to do so, but under certain conditions. They desired papal recognition of their claims of authority over the newly conquered lands. Consequently, the Portuguese and Spanish saw that their support of the spread of Christianity could bring along with it additional recognition for their claims of authority over the newly conquered areas. They also appreciated any financial assistance in their efforts to extend the Gospel: the larger the Church grew, the more authority, power, and wealth the Papacy would eventually enjoy. Yet the popes gave away concessions to lands they did not control. Even though the Iberian monarchs gained significantly in their control over the Church, the Church gained too, although diminished by the concessions to the monarchs. It would not be until the seventeenth century that the Papacy began to recognize the full implications of these concessions.

The period of discovery in the late fifteenth and early sixteenth century is of tremendous importance in the development of the American Church. The legal history of the era manifests a dialogue between the pope and the monarchs of the Iberian Peninsula over the limits of the power and authority of each party. On the one hand, the pope was desirous of keeping as much control over the American Church as possible. On the other hand, that endeavor would cost a great deal of money. Neither the crown nor the pope was financially ready for the costs of evangelization. Thus the extension of the tithe to the New World and the crown's tacit acceptance of the role of Patron provided for a minimal return on investment. The Papacy had begun an era of devolving power to local secular authorities. In Spain in the sixteenth century the Spanish monarchs gained much authority over the administration of the Church. Throughout the period of exploration and discovery, the Portuguese crown had similarly gained significant considerations for its efforts from the Papacy. In this way both the Spanish *Patronato Real* and the Portuguese *Padroado Real* developed, which also meant that the Church in the Americas would be highly reflective of the secular state that supervised its activities.

3

Conquest—Spiritual and Otherwise

On Good Friday, 1519, Hernán Cortés and his expedition of some ten ships and five hundred men landed on the coast of Mexico. This marked the beginning of the conquest of Mexico. Cortés and his followers promptly set about founding a town on the site, and the expedition elected Cortés as governor. In commemoration of their landing on such an important Christian holy day, Cortés named the town *La Villa Rica de la Vera Cruz*, the Rich Village of the True Cross, commonly known as Veracruz. On Easter Sunday, a High Mass was celebrated by the expedition's chaplain, Fr. Bartolomé de Olmedo, which event helps to demonstrate the spread of the Gospel and the imposition of Christianity as an important aspect of the conquest of Mexico. While the conquerors unquestionably sought personal gain, they also believed that they were participating in a divinely inspired adventure to bring all of the world's population to the Gospel of Christ.

Cortés was a member of the lesser nobility back in Spain. He had a better than average education, perhaps even prepared for university study. Because of a lack of opportunities in his home region of Spain, in 1504 he set off to the New World in search of a better life. He eventually settled in Cuba in 1512 as part of the retinue surrounding the governor of that island, Diego Velázquez. Velázquez was interested in sponsoring voyages of exploration in the Gulf of Mexico and Caribbean, and had already sent out two such voyages prior to 1519 when he contracted with Cortés for another expedition. Once preparations were complete, Cortés abrogated the contract and sailed off without the express permission of Velázquez. In order to protect himself against lawsuits from Velázquez, Cortés ordered the foundation of Veracruz. Thus, as the governor of the settlement, Cortés gained legal standing to oppose Velázquez and upon which to base his further explorations and possibly conquest.

Cortés proceeded inland from Veracruz, moving slowly and encountering the millions of natives who lived in Central Mexico at the time. He defeated some native armies and negotiated with others. He acquired two interpreters: a Spaniard who had been shipwrecked on the Yucatan coast a few years earlier and who spoke Spanish and Maya, and a native woman given to him in the aftermath of a battle. She spoke both Maya and the Aztec language, Nahuatl. Using these two interpreters Cortés could communicate with most native groups in Mexico.

Cortés heard of a rich and powerful state in the highlands of Mexico, which we now know as the Aztec empire, and marched inland toward it. Along the way he was engaged in battle by another group, the Tlaxcallans. Upon their defeat by the Spanish, the Tlaxcallans became allies to fight against their mutual enemy, the Aztecs. Cortés marched into the Aztec capital, Tenochtitlan, having been greeted along the way by the Aztec emperor, Moteuctzoma, known in English as Montezuma. The city was located on several large islands located in the middle of a lake in what is now the Valley of Mexico, where Mexico City currently stands. Not knowing who these strange visitors were, Moteuctzoma invited them into his city and housed them in one of his palaces. The Spanish responded to the hospitality by taking the emperor prisoner and using him to eventually take control of his government. While the Spaniards were in Tenochtitlan, Diego Velázquez sent an expeditionary force to arrest Cortés and stop the conquest. Cortés sent a small army to confront them, and eventually the two armies united under Cortés. Meanwhile, in Tenochtitlan, the natives began to protest the imprisonment of their emperor, and matters grew even worse when the emperor died. The Spanish and their allies found themselves surrounded by hundreds of thousands of natives who had become increasingly antagonistic toward them. The Spanish were forced to flee the city, leaving behind the gold and silver they had collected.

After their flight from Tenochtitlan, Cortés regrouped his army and established a base on the shore of the lake, in a city called Texcoco. He ordered that his ships, which had been left at Veracruz, be dismantled and the parts be brought up to Texcoco, where he constructed twelve floating gun platforms. He used these to lay siege to Tenochtitlan. While the Spanish and their native allies laid siege to the city, many natives had begun to die from smallpox, which the Europeans had inadvertently brought with them. The siege and the pestilence worked together to defeat the natives, and the city fell on August 13, 1521, the feast of Saint Hippolytus, who would become the patron saint of the city, ending the opening stage of the conquest of Mexico. There were many more expeditions over the next twenty years, which would bring all of Central America and what is now Mexico under Spanish control. The region of North and Central America conquered by the Spanish was named New Spain.

The discovery and settlement of South America occurred after the conquest of Mexico. As early as 1526, Francisco Pizarro had begun exploration of the west coast of South America. He found evidence of a powerful native civilization located in the highlands, called the Inca. Armed with this information, he returned to Spain and secured royal permission for an expedition to conquer the native civilization. By 1528 he had organized his expedition and sailed to the coast of modern-day Peru. Sailing down the west coast of South America is extremely difficult since the winds and currents tend to run from south to north. Once the expedition landed, however, travel was easier. The Spanish received word that the Inca emperor, Atahualpa, was encamped in the city of Cajamarca, not too far from their location.

Pizarro divided his army into two companies. He led one company inland to Cajamarca, where they arranged a meeting with Atahualpa. The other company remained on the coast to create a defensive position should the Spaniards be forced to withdraw from the interior. At Cajamarca, Pizarro met with Atahualpa and, not surprisingly, took him prisoner, not unlike what Cortés had done in Mexico. Pizarro indicated that he would release the emperor if a ransom was paid. The ransom consisted of filling several rooms of the palace at Cajamarca with gold and silver. Once Pizarro had received the ransom he executed Atahualpa, distributed the booty to the men in the company in Cajamarca, and took over the governance of the empire.

The conquerors then proceeded to pacify the natives of the region and to establish Spanish towns and cities. They entered the Inca capital of Cuzco in November 1535; by March 1536 they had conquered it and proclaimed it a Spanish city. In January 1536 the city of Lima was founded to serve as the coastal capital of the Spanish province of Peru.

The company of Spaniards who had been left behind on the coast when Pizarro captured Atahualpa joined with one of Pizarro's captains, Sebastián de Benalcázar, in the conquest of the northern capital of the Inca empire, the city of Quito. Pedro de Alvarado, who had gained fame and fortune in the conquest of Mexico and Guatemala, joined the conquest of Quito, arriving with a contingent of colonists from Guatemala. Juan de Almagro, another of Pizarro's captains, and his followers also joined in the expedition to Quito. When Quito fell to the Spanish, Almagro and his men then went off to Chile, via Cuzco, with some of Alvarado's men, and other recent arrivals.

In the spring of 1537, Almagro and his followers returned from a disastrous expedition to Chile. By and large these men had been excluded from the division of booty at Cajamarca. Many of them had been in Peru as long, or nearly as long, as the men who had benefited from the distribution; they had been members of the company that had remained on the coast and not in the company present at Cajamarca. Almagro returned to Cuzco at the same time as a native uprising there against the Spanish. Almagro defeated the natives and recaptured Cuzco, claiming it for himself. Pizarro and his followers interpreted this act as outright treason and mounted an army to put down Almagro, and civil war broke out among the Spanish forces. Pizarro and his followers eventually defeated and killed Almagro, but the rebellion had sown the seeds of acrimony. In 1541 followers of Almagro assassinated Francisco Pizarro, and the battle was truly joined. Although the crown sent out royal officials to attempt to pacify all the parties, these efforts were to no avail. It was not until 1547 that the colony enjoyed a semblance of peace.[1]

The First Missionaries

Secular, or diocesan, priests and members of religious orders, called the regular clergy, accompanied Cortés and Pizarro.[2] In both instances the official chaplain of the expedition was a regular priest—in Mexico a Mercedarian and in Peru a Dominican—whereas secular priests participated in the expeditions on a less official level. The secular priests were members of the conquering armies whose function was to administer the sacraments to their colleagues. In this activity they represented the first real effort at the Christianization of the natives, both in Mexico and in Peru. Priests of any type were very few in number in any of the conquering bands. Perhaps as many as five priests served in Cortés's army, which at its largest numbered under 1,500 men. Only two priests were among the 168 men with Pizarro at Cajamarca. Clearly, these priests served in a frontier area, thousands of miles from the nearest bishop or religious superior. Consequently the missionary activity that occurred during the conquest and in the immediate post-conquest was not part of any centralized program. It was neither widespread nor uniform.

Two priests in particular played important roles during the conquest of Mexico. One, a Mercedarian, was Fr. Bartolomé de Olmedo; the other was a secular priest, Juan Díaz. Yet perhaps as many as four other priests also participated in the company.[3] Olmedo was Cortés's personal chaplain: he ministered to Cortés's spiritual needs, but by extension he was the informal chaplain of the company. Juan Díaz was just another member of the company. He could not fight since that would be in conflict with his priestly vows and in violation of canon law. Rather, he provided spiritual services to the company. He said Mass, heard confessions, and provided spiritual support to the men in and out of combat. In effect, Díaz became the chaplain for the men. There developed a dichotomy between Olmedo and Díaz: Olmedo served Cortés and in an extended sense the whole company, and Díaz, who was a member of the company, served his comrades in arms.

In general, Olmedo said Mass at all of the important moments when Cortés wanted to impress the natives. Moreover, Olmedo acted as a member of Cortés's inner circle of advisors. During the conquest Cortés sent him on at least one sensitive mission, to negotiate with Pánfilo de Narváez, the leader of the expedition sent by Diego Velázquez to arrest Cortés and his followers. The very important task of attempting to convert the Aztec emperor, Moteuctzoma, was also entrusted to Fr. Bartolomé de Olmedo. On several occasions Olmedo met privately with the native leader in order to teach him the principles of Christian doctrine, but his efforts had mixed results. During his long captivity, Moteuctzoma learned much about the Spaniards, but he never accepted the Christian faith.

The secular priest, Juan Díaz, also played an important role. He was responsible for the baptism and Christianization of the four leaders of the independent city-state of Tlaxcala, the first important native group to become allies of the Spanish. Earlier, Díaz had led an unsuccessful revolt against Cortés, stirring up opposition to the conqueror among those men who wished to return to Cuba. Had Díaz not been a priest, in all likelihood he would have been executed for treason. Consequently his role within the company was a complicated one, identifying clearly with the men of the company and in opposition to many aspects of Cortés's leadership.

Clerical participation in the conquest of Peru was similar. Pizarro's expedition included two priests. Pizarro's personal chaplain, Fr. Vicente de Valverde, was a Dominican. A secular priest, Juan de Sosa, served as the chaplain of the company. Valverde was present when the Inca leader was captured at Cajamarca. Nevertheless, as a member of a religious order having taken a vow of poverty, he could not receive a portion of Atahualpa's ransom. Sosa, however, who was not with the company at the decisive moment at Cajamarca, got a large portion of the gold, probably because he served as a priest for the company.[4] Unlike other company members for whom being present at Cajamarca was the deciding factor as to whether they received a portion of the ransom, the priests all received portions out of respect for their status in the Church and services to the expedition as a whole.

While there were several events in the conquest of Peru in which Valverde played a critical role, perhaps none was more important than the moment in Cajamarca when the Spaniards took Atahualpa prisoner. In the first minutes of the encounter, Fr. Vicente advanced, carrying a cross and breviary to where Atahualpa was seated. Valverde proceeded to talk to him, presumably about Christian doctrine. He offered a small prayer book to Atahualpa, who having no experience with the written word, dropped the book. After much confusion the prayer book ended up on the ground, and the Spaniards attacked the emperor, taking him captive. The controversy centered on whether Atahualpa merely dropped the book, or whether he hurled it to the ground. Regardless of these circumstances, it was Valverde who stood at the center of that fateful encounter.[5]

Juan de Sosa became famous for having received a share of the ransom. He was among the first men given permission to leave Peru after the distribution of the booty. He took his portion to Spain and used it to organize an expedition of conquest and discovery to Veragua, on the Venezuelan coast. The expedition failed, and eventually Sosa returned to Peru, became caught up in the civil wars that followed the conquest, and after ten years was exiled to Spain.[6]

The participants in the conquests saw them as spiritual endeavors. For the Spaniards, the imposition of Christianity was an essential part of the establishment of Spanish political hegemony. In spite of the ongoing debate about the proper method of conversion, in the two major expeditions there was no real thought given to peaceful conversion. The Spaniards did not recklessly attack every native group upon which they came but rather attempted diplomacy to win the natives over, reserving military confrontation for those instances where diplomacy failed. Nevertheless, the Spanish assumed that the subjugated people would accept Christianity. If the natives did not convert, that in itself constituted rebellion, which was sufficient cause for Spanish military retaliation.

The Spanish recognized and valued the priests of the native cults. In several instances after a native group had been defeated and its pagan temple destroyed, Cortés would install the priests of the old cult as the guardians of the symbols of the new religion, which were often located in the old sacred precincts. Shortly after having established his base camp in Veracruz, Cortés set out to visit the surrounding territory. In Cempoala, he destroyed all the sacred images in the native temple and ordered it cleaned and whitewashed. After the cleansing, the Spaniards installed an altar and an image of the Virgin Mary. Cortés then called the native priests, whose robes, hair, and skin were matted black with dried blood from the sacrifices. Cortés ordered them washed and clothed in white, and, after a short admonition, charged them to take care of the newly established Christian altar upon which a cross was mounted. On some occasions a Spaniard was left behind to protect and take care of the sacred precinct.[7] Yet other times Cortés would leave crosses or statues of the Virgin without a European to take care of them, resulting in criticism from members of the company. Several weeks after the events in Cempoala, when Cortés suggested leaving a cross in one native village, Fr. Olmedo chided him saying:

> It seems to me, sir, that in these villages it is not yet time to leave a cross in their possession, as they are without shame nor fear, and as vassals of Montezuma might burn it or do some other evil thing. What you have said to them is enough, until they have a better understanding of our Holy Faith.[8]

Cortés held an ambivalent opinion regarding the native religion. He actively fought and destroyed the pagan temples and inveighed against the pagan rituals at every turn, but he also recognized native spirituality, which had the potential to be turned to the worship of the Christian god. While he destroyed and cleansed the pagan temples, he left the old priests in charge of the new Christian symbols, clearly believing that the force of his actions and the strength of the symbols would be sufficient to effect a conversion. His chaplain clearly did not share that sentiment.

In Peru the nature of the Inca religion caused other difficulties for the Spaniards. The civil state was intimately tied to a complex series of religious devotions; moreover, the countryside was marked with locales of particular devotion from which emanated spiritual power. Spaniards did not know how to react to the Inca religion. On the one hand, when confronted with clearly marked centers of native devotion, Pizarro reacted in much the same fashion as Cortés. Pizarro sent his brother, Hernando, to the sacred temple complex of Pachacamac, south of modern-day Lima. The temple complex, which housed a very famous oracle, was one of the most important of pre-conquest Peru, dating even before Inca dominance. The Spaniards were impressed with the size and complexity of the temple compound. In order to enter the chamber of the oracle, one needed to pass through a thatched cubicle perched high atop an adobe pyramid. Normally, the priests of the zone guarded the shrine of the oracle and permitted no one to approach it without the necessary spiritual preparation. Hernando Pizarro and his men merely strode up the pyramid and smashed into the chamber. They found a close, dark, dank room, with a crudely carved human head on a post. Beyond that there was little of value to them except a few pieces of coral, turquoise, and other stones. They destroyed the image and the chamber, and went on their way. No effort at conversion was attempted; the search was for treasure.[9]

On the other hand, every region had several hundred minor and major religious sites, generically known as *huacas*. These might be as unobtrusive as a pile of stones along a road, or as imposing as a cliff or stone altar. Yet because they were intimate parts of the landscape and not clearly designated, the Spanish passed by unknowingly.

In all of the conquests, language played a very important role. As we saw in Mexico, Cortés benefitted from having two interpreters who could communicate, although awkwardly, with the natives. Pizarro had captured a native speaker of Quechua, the Inca language, years before he launched his conquest of Peru. This greatly facilitated both the conquest and communication about Christianity.

Pizarro and Cortés were primarily concerned with immediate strategic military and political concerns. Following that, they sought wealth, to defray the costs of the expedition and to provide for themselves and the members of their company after the conquest. In the face of these immediate and overriding concerns, the Christianization of the natives was less important. In the Aztec capital of Tenochtitlan, Cortés generally refrained from his idol-smashing behavior and was content to have a small chapel built in the apartments that Moteuctzuma allocated to the Spaniards. Only after the fall of Tenochtitlan did Cortés order a church built, specifically a chapel to Saint Hippolytus. Pizarro made no real effort to establish a church or chapel until Cuzco had been taken. Only then was one of the palaces allocated to Fr. Valverde as the site for the cathedral. It has remained there ever since: Valverde set up a chapel to Our Lady of the Conception.

Evangelization of Mexico

The term "spiritual conquest" has come to be applied to the evangelization of the New World in the wake of the military conquest. The term is inaccurate for the simple reason that the participants did not envision their efforts as a conquest but rather as the spreading of the Gospel: evangelization. The term "conquest" also suggests that the missionaries had a far more militant attitude and pursued a more confrontational method than the reality of the situation.

Following the fall of the Aztec capital in 1521, the process of evangelization entered into a different phase. Several missionaries traveled to Mexico as the war of conquest was winding down. These included several secular priests, a Mercedarian and several Franciscans. The most important of these was the Franciscan lay brother Fr. Peter of Ghent (Fr. Pedro de Gante).[10] As a lay brother, he followed all of the rules of the Franciscan Order without actually taking vows to become a member of the clergy. Even though he was a Franciscan, he was in reality a laic and not a cleric. Fr. Peter of Ghent is credited with establishing many of the essential missionary techniques used in the evangelization of Mexico.

In May 1524 the first major expedition of twelve Franciscans, led by Fr. Martín de Valencia, arrived at San Juan de Ulua, the port for Veracruz, joining Ghent and his colleagues. Cortés soon requested that more missionaries be sent to Mexico, and he specifically requested more Franciscans and some Dominicans.[11] He assumed that the religious orders would absorb their own costs, while secular priests normally were paid by the persons to whom they administered the sacraments. Thus the regular clergy would evangelize the natives thanks to the support of their orders, and the secular clergy would serve the Spanish.

The Franciscans and Dominicans were mendicant orders. That means that they supported their activities completely through alms and gifts, including support from their orders back in Spain. The secular clergy, on the other hand, relied upon the ecclesiastical tax, the tithe, for support. Secular priests also collected fees for the celebration of the sacraments of the Church. Cortés and the crown wished not to burden the natives with the tithe and the collection of fees for sacraments, but argued in favor of having the religious orders minister to them. Moreover, the religious orders had a strict internal system of governance and obedience. Consequently it was relatively easy, in terms of control, to move a group of religious missionaries into a new territory since they were largely self-governing. The secular clergy, on the other hand, required far more institutional support including the presence of a local bishop. It was difficult and costly to create a diocese, appoint a bishop, and develop the institutional structures necessary to govern the secular clergy.

In the early years following the conquest, there were no local bishops. While dioceses were created in the islands in 1504, they did not become fully functioning until after 1511, and in any case were only barely capable of supervising priests in their immediate area. The distance from bishops caused problems for the regular and secular clergy. Canon law reserves certain sacraments (Confirmation and Ordination) to bishops, along with the absolution of certain sins. Because of this, priests initially were not able to provide complete ecclesiastical services because of the absence of a bishop.

Cognizant of this and immediately following the conquest of Mexico, Pope Hadrian VI issued a papal letter in 1522 called *Omnimoda*, specifically for the Franciscans. *Omnimoda* gave full papal authority to the Franciscans who operated in the new frontier regions of the Americas, provided that they fulfilled certain requirements. The number of friars to be sent was to be limited by the crown. Each missionary group would elect its own superiors who served for three-year periods. The superiors would be subject to the commissary general of the order and to the pope. The pope granted the full authority of the minister general of the order to these superiors. This provision was important because of the great distances between the minister general of the order in Rome and the local superiors in the Americas. Speedy communication was simply impossible. When the friars and superiors in the Americas served in a region beyond the limits of any diocese, or in a place more than two-day's journey distant from a bishop, they would enjoy full papal authority: In the words of the letter "our own full power" (*omnimodam auctoritatem nostram*).[12] The pope imposed some limits. Although this authority included "every act that a bishop may perform," it did not include those which required a consecrated bishop: that is, the missionaries could not ordain priests.

The friars seldom used this privilege to the full extent of its powers. Principally it allowed the friars to preach, hear confessions, and grant dispensations without specific licenses from the bishop. Moreover, they could administer all the sacraments that did not require episcopal consecration. *Omnimoda* also allowed the religious superiors to have administrative control over any clergy, secular or regular, active in their particular region, provided it was outside of a diocese or a two-day distance from a bishop. Provisions such as these do not seem to have been widely applied. It seems highly unlikely that a secular priest would voluntarily submit to supervision by a religious, no matter how far away from a bishop he might find himself.

There were several basic questions the early missionaries had to confront. Most had to do with the administration of the sacraments. From the very first contact most missionaries were convinced that the Indians were indeed human beings. As we have seen, there was a small but vocal group of colonists and royal officials who felt that somehow the Indians were not fully human. These individuals held that the natives could be treated as animals, and should not or could not receive either the benefits of the sacraments of the Church or the protection of the law. While the clergy generally believed in the humanity of the natives, nevertheless, even among some of the clergy, when the initial efforts of conversion were met with either indifference or backsliding, they too began to look on the natives as less than fully human. While a papal bull confirmed the humanity of the natives in 1537, elements of the debate continued to be heard for centuries. The papal decision was tacitly confirmed by the Spanish crown in 1542, when the natives of the New World were declared to be vassals of the crown and thereby able to receive the benefits of the state and to participate in the obligations.[13] The benefits included access to the royal courts; the obligations included the payment of taxes and tribute.

While the Franciscans organized the first missions to arrive on the mainland of the Americas, in Mexico they were soon joined by the Dominicans in 1526 and the Augustinians in 1533. Although the Dominican contingent started out with twelve friars, within a year five had died due to illness. The Augustinian mission was to have consisted of eight religious, but one was detained in Spain, leaving only seven to travel to Mexico. These three orders constituted the full complement of religious orders in Mexico until later in the sixteenth century. The Jesuits arrived in 1570, the Carmelites in 1585, and in 1594 the Mercedarians.

Members of the secular clergy also participated in a more limited manner in the initial efforts of evangelization. Unfortunately the names and stories of many of these priests have been lost but a few names have come down to the present. In addition to Juan Díaz, another early missionary was Juan González. According to legend, he came out to Mexico in the final phases of the conquest to accompany a relative. González seems to have been ordained to the priesthood in Mexico by one of the early bishops, Fr. Julián Garcés. Although the king eventually appointed González to an important office in the cathedral òf Mexico, he renounced it in favor of missionary activity among the Aztecs and Otomí Indians of central Mexico. Juan de Mesa also was an early secular priest in Mexico. Born in Utrera in southern Spain, Mesa arrived in Mexico shortly after the conquest to live with a relative, an *encomendero* in the northeast of Mexico. Mesa soon dedicated his life to missionary work, spending thirty years in the Province of Pánuco, in the region surrounding modern-day Tampico.

All the religious orders followed the same general pattern of evangelization among the native peoples. The missionaries first had to learn how to communicate with the natives. This required that missionaries learn native languages, which they quickly did. Once they had a working knowledge of the language, they needed to consider how best to explain Christianity to the natives, and this issue would never be fully resolved. The process of conversion as been described as a case of double mistaken identity[14] The friars thought that they were explaining Christianity in terms the natives would understand. The natives interpreted Christianity in terms of their own religious background and consequently did not completely understand the friars. The natives communicated their doubts and ideas to the missionaries from the context of their own culture. The missionaries interpreted the questions and doubts within a European cultural context and thus did not understand the natives.

In order to communicate without the need for language, one missionary, Fr. Jacobo de Tastera, devised a system of depicting the important Christian prayers and creeds using pictures, not unlike a cartoon. These came to be known as Testerian catechisms. The friars also wrote grammars and dictionaries of the native languages to assist in the conversion. Catechisms and statements of Christian doctrine were also translated into native languages for use by missionaries, and many friars became quite adept at the native languages.

In Mexico the Franciscans established schools to train the sons of the native nobility in Christianity. Basing themselves in European history, the friars believed that by converting the native leaders their people would follow them in the faith. Some of the students became fluent not just in Spanish but in Latin and Greek as well. The role of these young men was to return to their villages and towns and serve as an example. None was ordained to the clergy in the sixteenth century.

The missionaries had different approaches to evangelization and the administration of the sacraments to the natives. The Franciscans believed that the natives would learn about Christianity by observing the way the friars acted. By emulating Christ they believed that they were teaching the natives about Christianity. The Franciscans believed that baptism was the very first step in becoming a Christian. Afterwards they would continue their Christian formation. The Dominicans, on the other hand, believed that the natives needed to be formally taught all of the basics of Christian doctrine, understand them, and make a profession of faith before they were willing to be baptized.

The sacrament of baptism initiates the Christian's life in the Church. Once the natives had received baptism they could receive the Eucharist. Commonly in colonial Latin America, however, natives were witnesses to the Eucharist and did not partake. As time passed, and the natives became more Hispanized in their customs and more thoroughly trained in Christianity, they began to also receive the Eucharist, but only the consecrated host, not the wine. The sacrament of penance was offered to the natives. Much of the religious training they received was to prepare them to live Christian lives and to reflect on their moral shortcomings in preparation for confession;

the sacrament of marriage was also available. Polygamous practices among many groups required the missionaries to address the Christian model of monogamy. Where polygamous husbands sought to have their marriages legitimized by the Church, the priests required that they formally marry only their first wife, and then cut off all contact with their other wives. The sacrament of confirmation was not widely practiced until much later in the colonial period, since many natives continued to receive baptism only as adults. The sacrament of unction caused much discussion. Many priests found it impossible to provide the sacrament of healing to their parishioners because there were a very few priests for thousands of natives. Last of all, ordination was not an option for native men until nearly a century after the conquest. The local bishops simply did not believe that the natives were well enough versed in Christianity to become priests.

The relatively small numbers of priests and the huge population of natives meant that there were thousands of parishioners for each priest. Priests routinely had to ride circuits of villages each week, traveling as much as a hundred miles. As the native populations began to decline in the late sixteenth century, the civil government instituted a program of reduction. Under this program, natives from small, isolated villages were reduced, or congregated (in simple terms, moved), into larger, more centrally located towns.

The physical distribution of the orders in Mexico was a function of geography and the time of arrival. The first group to come, the Franciscans, tended to dominate the central area around Mexico City. They also had missions in western Mexico, in the modern state of Michoacán, and around Guadalajara. Therefore, the greatest concentration of Franciscan parishes stretched east to west roughly from Veracruz to Guadalajara. The Dominicans, who arrived second, pushed toward the south. Their main concentration was in the Oaxaca region of southern Mexico and down into Central America. The Augustinians occupied the near northern and western areas of central Mexico since the Franciscans and the Dominicans had already taken the central and the southern areas. Specifically, the Augustinians established important missions immediately north of Mexico City toward the Pachuca mining district, and in some western areas in Michoacán, which had been first evangelized by the Franciscans.

By the end of the sixteenth century the Dominicans had developed three provinces: one centered on Mexico City, another centered in Oaxaca, in the south, and a third established in 1551 to encompass the southern region of Chiapas and Guatemala. Within the family of Franciscan orders, two different groups founded provinces in Mexico. In 1524 the Observant Franciscans founded the initial province, known as the Province of the Holy Gospel, which controlled Franciscan missions in all of New Spain. In 1559 the southern region became an independent province, and by 1565 it was further divided into two provinces: San José de Yucatán and Nombre de Jesús de Guatemala. The Discalced (literally, shoeless) Franciscans, a more ascetic branch of the Franciscan Order, became active in western Mexico, and in 1565 the Province of San Pedro y San Pablo de Michoacán separated from the Holy Gospel Province. In 1606 the far northwest became two independent provinces, one based in Guadalajara, the Province of Santiago de Jalisco, the other based in Zacatecas, the Province of San Francisco de Zacatecas. The Augustinians initially had only one province, which was centered in Mexico City, but in 1602 founded a second, San Nicolás de Tolentino, to govern the western and northern parts of the colony.

Evangelization of Peru

The religious orders also played an important role in the evangelization of Peru. The Franciscans, who had taken the lead in the conversion efforts in Mexico, were fewer in number and more limited in their impact in Peru. The Dominicans organized the first missionary expedition to Peru, sending six friars to accompany the Pizarro expedition, one of whom was Fr. Vicente de Valverde. Only two or three of these actually reached Peru. In 1534 Fr. Juan de Olias, one of those missionaries, established Dominican convents in Lima and Cuzco. The number of Dominicans remained small until 1538, when at least eight more friars arrived. In 1540 yet another expedition of twelve Dominicans traveled to Peru. By that time the Dominicans had established a province, San Juan Bautista del Perú, independent from the province in Spain, numbering about forty-two friars.

The Mercedarians also participated early in the evangelization of Peru. The Mercedarians based their effort on their earlier participation in the pacification of Nicaragua. In 1538 Fr. Juan de Vargas arrived in Cuzco as the leader of the order in Peru. The Augustinian presence was small and began quite late. It was not until 1548 that the first religious of the order, Fr. Antonio de la Santísima Trinidad, arrived in Peru, establishing a religious house in Lima. He would live there nearly three years before being joined by others of his order. Finally in 1550, an expedition of twelve Augustinians sailed from Spain to Lima, arriving in May 1551. Shortly thereafter, don Antonio de Mendoza arrived from Mexico, where he had just finished serving as viceroy, to take up the same post in Peru. In his company were two Augustinians who had previous experience in Mexico. One of these, Fr. Juan Estacio, was elected the superior of the new Augustinian Province of Peru.

The Franciscans were by no means absent from the initial evangelization of Peru; there were not, however, large well-organized missionary groups as had been the case in Mexico. The first Franciscan generally accepted as having arrived in Peru was Fr. Marcos de Niza, probably by early 1532, coming from Nicaragua and carrying an appointment from the General Chapter as commissary for the missions in Peru. The sources are unclear as to how many friars Niza brought with him, but estimates range from four to twelve. Fr. Pedro Rodeñas and two Flemings from modern-day Belgium, Fr. Jodoco Ricke and Fr. Pedro Gosseal, probably arrived in 1534, traveling first to Quito. Although the order received land upon which to found monasteries in Cuzco, Lima, and other cities, in most of these locations several years passed before they became a reality. For some eight years, from 1537 to 1545, Quito served as the headquarters for Franciscan activity in Peru.[15]

The secular clergy also participated in the early efforts at evangelization in Peru. Juan de Sosa, the cleric who accompanied Pizarro, had little impact on the ecclesiastical development of the Andean region. Others who came shortly after the events at Cajamarca served more actively as missionaries. Perhaps six secular priests traveled to Peru from Central America with the conqueror Pedro de Alvarado, arriving in February 1534. These priests then scattered, accompanying the bands of conquerors. One secular priest, Pedro Bravo, participated in the foundation of Arequipa; Juan Rodríguez was one of the first residents of Quito; Francisco Jiménez was an early citizen and curate of Cuzco. In 1534 alone some twelve secular priests were granted licenses to travel to Peru from Spain to engage in missionary activity.[16]

The efforts of the missionaries in early colonial Peru were greatly hampered by the civil wars that raged in the colony. The various missionaries were caught up in the conflicts and intrigues of the various factions. Moreover, the constant turmoil and ongoing internecine warfare did not create a proper atmosphere for evangelization.

In spite of the turmoil, colonists and missionaries continued to travel to Peru. In the period from 1544 to 1550, no less than 117 Franciscans arrived in Peru from Spain, with others coming from other regions of the Americas. There were sufficient Dominicans in the region that in 1539 they created the Province of San Juan Bautista. By the end of the century New Granada (modern day Colombia), Quito (Ecuador), and Chile would, in turn, become independent provinces. The Mercedarian order had very few missions in most of the Americas, but by 1540 had founded four houses in Peru, in San

Miguel Piura, Lima, Cuzco, and Huamanga, in addition to those in Nicaragua, Panama, and Quito. Difficulties with the Spanish crown eventually brought about the voluntary closure of two houses, Piura and Huamanga. After 1543 Charles V prohibited the order from building any more convents or sending missionaries to the Americas. An expedition of around twenty Mercedarians traveled to the Indies along with their superior Fr. Francisco de Cuevas in 1546. It was not until 1564 that the coastal Peruvian region became a Mercedarian province, along with others based in Cuzco and Guatemala. The Augustinians arrived in the late 1540s, and by that time many members of the existing religious communities had become identified with one or the other faction in the civil wars. As the Augustinians, having newly arrived, were not known to support any of the warring factions, they acted as mediators in these conflicts. Shortly after their arrival, the Province of San Agustín del Peru was created, followed by the Province of San Miguel de Quito in 1579, Nuestra Señora de Gracia in New Granada in 1603, and San Agustín de Chile in 1611.

The distribution of religious orders in Peru did not follow the same type of pattern as in Mexico. All the religious orders tended to establish convents and monasteries in Lima and Cuzco. Eventually they also founded houses in the other Spanish settlements of the colony. This meant that in any given city there might be houses of several of the orders. The number of religious who eventually went to Peru to serve was far smaller than in Mexico. These two factors meant that the religious orders in Peru tended to concentrate in the leading cities, provincial towns, and some rural areas, but there were many areas that they did not effectively cover. There were simply not enough priests and friars to take care of the entire territory. On the other hand, in Mexico, while not all the orders covered the whole region, in most areas there was a presence of at least one religious order. This geographic disparity had important repercussions for the implementation of Spanish law and the spread of Spanish culture and civilization. In Mexico, in general, the missionaries were fairly effective at spreading the Gospel in a relatively short period of time. In Peru, however, there were vast areas largely untouched decades after the conquest.

Evangelization in Brazil

Europeans remained on the coast of what is now Brazil for many decades. The first priests arrived in 1500 with the fleet of Pedro Alvarez Cabral. Early on, the Portuguese did not create any significant settlements. In 1549 the first governor general, Tomé de Sousa, came to Salvador da Bahía to organize the government. At the same time a group of six Jesuits, under the leadership of Manuel de Nóbrega, arrived to initiate the formal evangelization of the region. By 1550 a second group of four Jesuits landed, followed by more in the subsequent years. The Jesuits enjoyed a very close relationship with the representatives of the royal government. While they focused their efforts largely on the conversion of the natives, they also played an important role in the general life of the colony.

Although eventually many religious orders participated in the evangelization, the Jesuits took the lead and expanded steadily throughout the early colonial period. Starting in Bahía, the Jesuits began to spread Christianity along the Brazilian coast. The natives, who relied on some agriculture along with hunting and gathering, lived in small nucleated settlements widely dispersed in the interior. They frequently moved their villages to take advantage of new land and movements of wild animals and the fruiting cycles of plants. The Jesuits attempted to move the natives into larger villages and settlements to ease the process of conversion, thus beginning a practice that would continue throughout the colonial period. This also meant that the Jesuits had more control over the natives, who were also sought after by colonists as a source of labor. The crown and local governors had a mixed record in their decrees regarding Indian slavery, though. Some royal laws and local traditions allowed for the enslavement of the natives, while in general the crown discouraged it. The Jesuits fought to keep the natives free and under their immediate supervision.

While focusing their efforts largely on the coastal native population, the Jesuits also set out for the interior of what would become São Paulo. There the order not only founded a settlement but also a school to educate local native children, and to that purpose followed the pattern established in the Spanish colonies of learning local languages, the better to evangelize. The Jesuit Jose de Anchieta developed the first grammar of the local language, Tupí, and translated Christian teachings into that language. The Jesuits used a modified form of the language, vaguely intelligible to a broad number of tribes, which became the native lingua franca of the region. Although Nóbrega opposed African slavery, colonists increasingly imported Africans to work in sugar estates and other ventures. The Jesuits fought native slavery, and in the end the order was successful. Yet, as demand for labor increased, they relented with regard to African slavery. In fact, the Jesuits themselves would come to be some of the largest owners of African slaves in the colony.

The Jesuit Order was new at the time of its arrival in Brazil, having been founded only in 1540, and so carried with it much of the fervor imparted by its founder, Saint Ignatius Loyola. Moreover, the order was not a mendicant one. Individual Jesuits could have personal wealth, although they traditionally gave it to the order. But more importantly the order itself could acquire property and other forms of wealth, unlike the Franciscans. Although the order received subsidies from the Portuguese crown, the Jesuits established a series of rural estates, the profits from which helped to support their missionary activity.

The Jesuits controlled the Brazilian mission field exclusively until the 1580s when other religious orders—Franciscans, Benedictines, and Carmelites—began evangelization. Traditionally the expansion of Christianity in Brazil has been seen as falling into five periods, each focused on a different region. The evangelization began, as noted, along the coast, particularly in the northeast, where Portuguese settlement began. From there, the missionaries followed local rivers into the hinterland. The effort then turned to Maranhão and Pará, along the Amazon. This pattern continued, following the São Francisco River into the interior region of Minas Gerais and the west. The immediate interior of the southern region, particularly São Paulo and the south, were now Christianized.[17]

In both the Spanish and Portuguese regions of the New World, the early sixteenth century saw the conquest of the native peoples by bands of Europeans. In most instances members of the clergy participated in these expeditions of conquest, normally serving the spiritual needs of the members of the company but also conducting the first evangelization of the native peoples. After the military phase of the conquest had ended, the clerics, both secular and regular, increasingly engaged in evangelization along with administering the sacraments to their fellow Europeans. In general, members of the religious orders were more active in missionary activity, while secular priests tended to minister more to the European population. In Mexico seculars and regulars tended to disperse across the whole of the territory, so that eventually nearly every town and village of any size would have a priest. In Peru the clergy were generally more highly concentrated in the Spanish cities and towns, with fewer missionaries in rural areas. In Brazil, the European population was tiny and concentrated in only a handful of towns. The Jesuits spread out as far as their numbers would allow, bringing the Gospel to the natives. These efforts provided the foundation for the fuller evangelization and conversion of the later sixteenth century.

The first wave of evangelization sought to introduce the natives to Christianity. Different orders had different missionary techniques as they sought to teach Christian doctrine to the natives. The single greatest challenge was a linguistic one: the missionaries needed to learn the native languages before they could proclaim the Gospel. Even once the priests had become adept at native languages, the missionaries seldom understood the full nuance of the language. On the other hand, the natives also had difficulty understanding Christianity since it was so completely alien to anything in their own cultural experience. As a result, missionaries frequently misunderstood natives; natives frequently misunderstood missionaries.

4

The Colonial Church

In the city of Cuzco in the highlands of Peru, thousands of spectators filled the streets and plaza in the late 1670s. They were witnessing and participating in the feast of Corpus Christi, the celebration of the Holy Sacrament of the Eucharist, which occurs on the Thursday after Trinity Sunday, the first Sunday after Pentecost. Nowhere were the celebrations of this feast more stunning than in Cuzco. The central feature of the celebration was a procession of richly decorated carts upon which religious symbols were placed. The carts were then pulled through the streets of the city to the cathedral. This religious procession has its roots in Spain, where many cities also celebrate Corpus Christi in a similar manner. What made this celebration different was its size and scope. All ranks of society played an active role in the processions. None, however, took as enthusiastic a part as did the descendents of the Inca rulers. The high native nobility proudly displayed the traditional vestments and apparel of their status. The native nobles processed wearing the *uncu*, or embroidered tunic, which manifested their elite status. On their heads was the *mascaypacha*, or traditional crown or diadem, also an important social indicator. The celebration of the Christian sacrament became a means whereby the traditional native nobility could remind one and all of its former glory. Through the adoption of the religion and rites of the conquerors, these members of the conquered society reasserted their traditional authority in the colonial society.

The developing Catholic Church in Latin America reflected both the European traditions of the conquerors and the native traditions of the conquered. In many ways the colonial period figured as an ongoing cultural dialogue, which began with the conquest and early evangelization. The religious orders, the secular clergy, and all ecclesiastical institutions underwent change and modifications in light of the colonial reality.

The middle period of Latin American colonial history coincided with the seventeenth century. Culturally is it known as the Baroque period, one in which lavish manifestations of piety, such as the religious processions in Cuzco, were common. The great cathedrals of Latin America date from this period. Outside they were decorated with complicated and intricate carvings. Inside their altars were equally sumptuous, featuring much gold, heavily carved and highly detailed architectural pieces framing lifelike and minutely figured statues of saints. Large pipe organs, built in Spain and, later, in Germany, were shipped to the New World and installed by the master craftsmen from those countries with help from the local natives. The level of church music throughout Latin America in the seventeenth and eighteenth centuries was as opulent as the interior decorations and the organs; vocal and instrumental music by such well-known European composers as Josquin des Prés, Cabezón, Bermudo, and even Palestrina, resounded from the cathedral choir lofts. While the period of the conquest was marked by very simple, even plain, churches, interior decoration shifted from being merely added to the surface of the church façade or altarpiece to becoming an integral part of the overall architecture. Similarly the ceremonies and celebrations of the Church went from being simple affairs to lavish productions, with rich vestments, incense, organ music, choirs, and orchestras, celebrated by several priests. In rural areas, while the number of priests was limited and the level of decoration not quite so opulent, there was still fervor and exuberance to the celebrations.

At the same time, piety in worship became deeper and frequently more somber as devotional material tended to focus on penance and suffering. The figure of Christ on the cross became central not just to the liturgy but to devotions. Sorrow and lamentations were felt to make the faithful identify with the suffering of Christ, and consequently the period was almost schizophrenic with exuberance of joy and depths of penance all wrapped into the celebrations of the Church.

Layers upon Layers: Ecclesiastical Structure

The religious orders primarily conducted the initial evangelization of the New World. Their internal structure provided them with the logistical support and personnel management needed for activity far from their home base and ranging over many hundreds, if not thousands, of miles. Once the religious orders had converted significant populations of natives to Christianity, the normal hierarchical structures of the Church, including bishops and archbishops, fell into place. While there were numerous exceptions to this general pattern, it provides a general template for the early Christianization of Latin America.

The regular clergy, especially the Franciscans, Dominicans, and Carmelites, and to a lesser degree the Mercedarians and Augustinians, had evolved with specialized missions (charisms) involving evangelization. The Franciscans sought to spread Christianity by example, and from their very beginnings converted outsiders to the faith, initially Muslims as a by-product of the Crusades. The Dominicans advocated a Christian renewal and conversion through the power of preaching. The Carmelites emerged during the Crusades, seeking the redemption of Christian captives held by Muslims and other nonbelievers. As such, these orders evolved internal structures that allowed them to operate in war zones and in regions of poor communication.

After the initial phase of evangelization, the religious orders began to consolidate themselves into provinces. They established imposing convents and chapels in the towns and cities, and took up important roles in the Spanish colonial institutions. Yet even though missionary activity per se diminished by the end of the sixteenth century in the core areas of central Mexico and Peru, the entire colonial period was marked by a continual opening up of frontiers wherein the clergy played an important role in pacification and acculturation. In the late sixteenth and early seventeenth century, there was a significant change in the missionary technique of the religious orders. Immediately following the conquest, the missionaries traveled alone into unexplored regions to seek out and to Christianize the natives. While there might have been other Europeans in the region, the missionaries generally worked by themselves. The image of selfless missionaries entering into possibly hostile native territory seeking converts through example was a very powerful image for the missionary friars. Bartolome de las Casas propounded this method of evangelization as "the only way." Only once the natives had been introduced to Christianity and the conversion process had begun did other representatives of European authority enter the mission territory. But, throughout the seventeenth century, this pattern shifted so that increasingly missionaries and others accompanied military units as elements of European domination in previously unexplored regions.

An example of this shift can be seen in the activities of the Franciscan missionary Fr. Antonio Margil de Jesús. Margil was born in Valencia in 1657, joining the Franciscan Order at the age of fifteen. He studied philosophy and theology at various Franciscan houses and was ordained a priest in 1682. The subsequent year he joined a missionary adventure to New Spain organized by Fr. Antonio de Llinás. As a missionary in New Spain, Margil lived in the Missionary College of Querétaro. These colleges represented a hybrid form of missionary endeavor. While associated with the Franciscan Order, the authority for the colleges came from the Apostolic Congregation for the Propagation of the Faith (*Propaganda Fide*) in Rome. In New Spain Margil learned the practical aspects of missionary activity and was sent out on small expeditions to nearby towns and cities to preach. One of the goals of the missionary colleges was to reinvigorate the faith of those who were already Christian.

Having had some small success in these missions, Fr. Antonio set out to conduct a mission among the Talamancas of modern-day Costa Rica, some of the most fearsome natives in Central America. With only two traveling companions, one of whom was a fellow friar, he embarked on a thirteen-year mission in Central America, Guatemala, Chiapas, and Yucatan. In these missions, Margil emulated the style proposed by Las Casas and practiced by the early missionaries, namely to attract the natives to the faith by setting a Christ-like example. After his service in Central America, Margil helped to establish two other missionary colleges, one in Guatemala, Colegio de Cristo Crucificado, and another in Zacatecas, Nuestra Señora de Guadalupe. He continued his missionary efforts in Central America and also mounted an expedition to Nayarit among the Cora and Huichol people, located in the Mexican mainland facing the Gulf of California. Here, he attempted a peaceful conversion, as he had practiced in Central America, but was unsuccessful.

After the failure of the Nayarit expedition, the royal government cajoled the Franciscans of the missionary college to participate in a resettlement program in the province of Texas. The region had been settled, but once government support for the European settlers was withdrawn, the colonists left. Confronted with growing French influence along the coast of the Gulf of Mexico, the viceregal officials in Mexico saw resettlement of Spaniards and Hispanized natives and mixed peoples, and conversion of the natives, as a means of fortifying the frontier. Margil was sent as the leader of a major expedition. Unlike his other missions, Margil and the other missionaries were only one small component in a larger pacification and settlement program, accompanied by troops.[1] This pattern of a large expeditionary force accompanied by missionaries would become the norm rather than the exception as the eighteenth century wore on. This was due partially to changing attitudes about Christianization as well as a more practical approach by royal officials. Christianization was simply one tool for the incorporation of new territory into the empire. Colonization and the presence of armed forces were two other methods to stabilize frontier regions.

Although rigidly hierarchical and requiring vows of obedience from their members, the religious orders were highly democratic. The lowest unit within the religious orders was the friar. In most orders some friars never became priests, taking only the vows of the order and living in community with the other friars. Yet the majority did seek the priesthood. Along with the friars were lay brothers, individuals who lived according to the rule of the order,[2] dressed like the friars, and lived in community with them but never took the full vows of the order, and thus remained lay persons. Because most of these orders had vows of poverty, they subsisted on alms given by the devout: they had to beg for their support.

The friars lived in community, supporting one another. While in English these communities are commonly called monasteries, they are more accurately called convents or friaries. Monasteries house monks; monks and monasteries are associated with the Benedictine and affiliated orders, which were nearly absent in early Hispanic America and had only a small presence in Brazil. Thus the vast majority of religious in Latin America were friars, not monks. Each Franciscan community elected its superior, called an abbot, along with three other friars who would assist the superior in governing the convent. For the Dominicans, the convent was also the basic level of organization. Each house contained twelve friars and had as its head a prior. Within a province, all of the superiors, be they abbots or priors, would meet regularly to conduct the business of the province. Each of the friaries would also send a certain number of delegates to the provincial meeting. The delegates and superiors would elect the chief executive for the province. The Franciscans called this officer a provincial. The chapter also elected three friars, called definitors, who would assist the provincial in his duties. The Dominicans called their provincial superior a provincial prior and elected four counselors to assist him. The provincial meeting was a time when all friars could be reassigned from one convent to another, depending on the needs of the order. The vow of obedience required the individual friar to accept the orders of his superior, and required all friars to live according to the rule of the order.

Beyond the local province, there lay yet another layer of authority within the religious orders. On a regular basis, all of the provincials, and other elected representatives, would meet in a general chapter to conduct the business of the worldwide order. At this meeting they would elect a general officer for the order, who was the chief executive of the entire order. Similarly they elected a council of other friars to assist the general in the administration of the order. The general of the order was responsible to the general chapter and to the pope. Thus the organizational structure of the religious orders stretched from each individual local friar all the way to the pope in

Rome. The religious orders were rather democratic, at a time when elections were generally considered to be a form of anarchy. Yet the democracy was also tempered by strict rules of obedience.

The secular clergy, those priests who were not members of religious orders, received their power and authority from local bishops. Since initially the New World lacked bishops, the first secular priests acted under the direction of bishops on the Iberian Peninsula, frequently also under some authority from the kings. While religious orders could establish monasteries and other key elements of their organizational structure immediately upon arrival in the New World, the secular clergy had to depend on the crown and Iberian bishops until new dioceses could be created in the New World and bishops appointed to them.

A new diocese came into legal existence only when the crown had demonstrated a need for it and received confirmation from the pope, and this necessitated that the territory be defined legally. Because the Europeans had only vague notions of the geography of the New World in the first decades of the sixteenth century, the early dioceses were somewhat vaguely described. The first dioceses were created in 1504 on the islands of the Caribbean, based upon descriptions gleaned from Columbus's reports. They were called Yaguata (Santo Domingo), Magua (Concepción de la Vega), and Bayuna (Lares de Guahaba), all located on the island of Hispaniola. Much negotiation ensued between the papacy and the crown regarding these dioceses and the level of control that the Spanish crown wished to exercise over these new churches. It soon became clear that the island was small enough to require only two dioceses, namely that of Santo Domingo and Concepción, so the crown requested that the other one be transferred to San Juan (Puerto Rico). The early dioceses were suffragan to the Archdiocese of Seville; that is, their bishops conferred with the archbishop of Seville on certain matters, and that the dioceses were part of the ecclesiastical province of Seville.

In 1526 the Spanish crown created the first diocese for the mainland of North America called Carolina, after Charles V, king of Spain. The first bishop was Julian Garcés. This diocese was rather nebulous and not clearly defined. The papal documents creating the diocese referred specifically to the Island of Cozumel and the Yucatan, the only parts of the mainland known at the time. The jurisdiction was implied over whatever continent might be near.

The king ordered the creation of first true mainland diocese in 1527, with Fr. Juan de Zumárraga as the first bishop, requesting that the pope issue a bull to found or erect the diocese, commonly referred to as the bull of erection. Throughout Hispanic America in the colonial period, the bulls of erection of all the dioceses did not differ one from the other except in the name of the diocese and first bishop. They all were created according to a single model. The dioceses of South America date from after 1534, when Cartagena became the first diocese. Three years later Cuzco became the first diocese in South America outside of the Caribbean region.

In Brazil the creation of dioceses developed later than in Spanish America. The Jesuits played an important role in the early evangelization. The Portuguese crown claimed patronage rights over the church in Brazil, and some secular priests served the local Portuguese population, but it was not until the 1540s that the Portuguese presence in Brazil became concentrated enough to warrant a diocese. The first diocese was that of Bahía, dating from 1551. It was suffragan to the Archdiocese of Funchal on the island of Madeira in the Atlantic.

Although the bishop is the head of the secular clergy, many of the first bishops came from the religious orders. Both Zumárraga and Garcés, the first two bishops of the mainland, were Franciscans. It was not until 1534 that the original Caroline diocese became a physical reality, when it was transferred to Tlaxcala. Tlaxcala is located in central Mexico, sixty miles east of Mexico City and was the large native city that had allied itself to Cortés during the conquest. In Mexico the crown and pope created all of the other initial dioceses by 1548: the diocese of Guatemala in 1534; the diocese of Oaxaca in 1535; Michoacan in 1536; Chiapas in 1538; and finally, in 1548, Guadalajara.

In its simplest form, a diocese is an ecclesiastical territory governed by a bishop, also called a bishopric. The creation of a new diocese implied far more than simply drawing lines of jurisdiction on a map. The creation of a diocese carried with it the organization of an ecclesiastical structure to govern that territory. Obviously the chief executive officer of the territory was the bishop. He functioned within canon law as the ordinary: his powers resulted directly from his office, they were not delegated. He was responsible for supervising the secular clergy within his territory, the administration of the sacraments, the collection of the ecclesiastical tax (the tithe), and the execution of ecclesiastical justice (the enforcement of ecclesiastical [canon] law). One of the powers of the ordinary was also the maintenance of the purity of the faith in his territory. This responsibility carried with it the power of inquisition. Early on, New World bishops exercised this power by virtue of their authority as bishop. By 1570 the Spanish crown claimed the responsibility for the support of the Inquisition, and with papal approval it was removed from the jurisdiction of the ordinary.

The creation of a new diocese triggered two bureaucracies. One of these consisted of the offices surrounding the bishop, persons appointed by the bishop and deriving their power from him, and the most important of these offices was the vicar-general, who held the full range of episcopal powers and served in many ways like a "vice-bishop." In the Hispanic New World another office existed, that of provisor, a manager who also assisted the bishop in his administrative functions. Frequently the provisor and vicar-general were one and the same individual. Throughout the diocese, the bishop appointed local clerics to serve as ecclesiastical judges. Because they held their power vicariously from the bishop they were called *vicarios*. Although this is essentially the same as the English word "vicar," in the English Church a vicar is an individual who serves as a local parish priest in the place of another, and thus is a very different office.

The bull of erection also created a body known as the cathedral chapter, *cabildo eclesiástico*. While any given diocese will have many churches, one particular church will serve as the bishop's church and house the bishop's throne, his *cathedra*. Thus, this church is called the diocesan cathedral. Traditionally the priests who filled the special offices of the cathedral served as the advisors and assistants to the bishop in the administration of the diocese, as well as participating in the celebration of the sacraments in the cathedral. The cabildo eclesiástico consisted of twenty-seven members: five dignitaries (*dignidades*), ten canons (*canónigos*), six prebendaries (*racioneros*), and six half-prebendaries (*medio-racioneros*). The five dignitaries were the dean, the archdeacon, the precentor (*chantre*), the schoolmaster (*maestrescuela*), and the treasurer (*tesorero*). These individuals, by virtue of their appointment as dignitaries, also were entitled to use the honorary prefix "don" before their name. They were, in essence, granted nobility as the result of this appointment. There was an early implication that the dignitaries and canons were to be priests, the prebendaries were deacons, and the half-prebendaries were subdeacons. Nevertheless, by and large all the members of the chapter were actually priests.

Each of these offices carried with it certain rights and responsibilities. The dean was the chief executive officer of the cathedral and oversaw all of its activities and budget. The archdeacon customarily served as the vicar-general of the diocese and thus assisted the bishop. The precentor was responsible for all the liturgical aspects of the ceremonies within the cathedral, and this included supervising all the music and musicians. The schoolmaster controlled the educational activities, while the treasurer was the chief financial officer. As in the case of the archdeacon, many of these duties also extended to the entire diocese, depending on the pleasure of the bishop. The functions of the canons and prebendaries were far more restricted to the cathedral itself, unless the individual were appointed by the bishop to some diocesan role.[3]

One of the key duties of the cathedral chapter was the collection of the ecclesiastical tax, the tithe, a 10 percent levy on agricultural production. For example if a farmer produced one hundred bushels of wheat, he had to give ten to the Church. If a farmer had ten calves born in a year, he had to give one to the Church. The bull of erection stipulated the manner in which the tithe was to be divided among the various ecclesiastical offices. Of the whole sum collected, the bishop received one quarter to pay his own salary and to provide funds for the administration of the diocese. Another quarter went to the cathedral chapter and was distributed to the members of the chapter according to their rank. The second half was divided into nine parts. Two of these nine parts belonged to the king. The first papal bulls granted the power to collect the tithe to the crown, but in 1512 the king ceded the tithe back to the Church, keeping one-ninth of the whole for himself. Although the king's portion was one-ninth of the whole, because it was two-ninths of the half, it became known as the "two-ninths." Four-ninths of the second half provided funds to pay the parish clergy of the diocese. Initially this fund was far too small to pay all the clergy, so it was allocated to pay the salaries of just the priests of the cathedral parish. The remaining three-ninths of the second half were divided into two equal parts. One part went to support the physical structure of the cathedral and to purchase the vestments, chalices, and other supplies needed for the celebration of the sacraments in the church. The last portion was allocated to support a hospital for the diocese.

The cathedral chapter collected the tithe. Yet even under the best of circumstances it was a laborious and complex undertaking. Each and every farmer and rancher in the diocese had to be contacted and his production determined so that the tax could be paid. There were two options open to the cathedral chapter for the management of this process. On the one hand, the chapter could take control of the process directly, and send out members, or representatives, to all the farmers and ranchers and collect the tax directly. This also meant that the chapter could in essence control 10 percent of the annual agricultural and pastoral production of the territory. This allowed the cathedral chapter great influence over the price of goods on the market, depending on whether it chose to store the commodities or to sell them for cash on the open market. Some goods, such as oil and wax, could be used by the Church in its normal operations. If the chapter had storage facilities, it could, for instance, store grain and sell it when the price had increased. Therefore, the chapter could collect the tithe after the harvest when the price was relatively low due to the abundance, and then sell the product later in the year when shortages had begun to raise the price. This was an expensive and cumbersome system because the chapter had to pay people to take control of the collection of the tithe and pay for storage facilities, thus cutting into the total value collected.

The other option was to rent the collection of the tithe to others. Under this method the chapter would have a public auction for the right to collect a specific tithe, say, on wool. Persons interested in the commodity, or in speculating on the commodity, would bid for the right to collect that tithe. The chapter would grant the contract to the highest bidder. The person renting the tithe was gambling that the price paid at auction would be less than what was finally collected. Or, a merchant who owned a woolen mill might be interested in renting the tithe on wool since it could provide him with his raw materials at potentially less than the going rate. Obviously whoever won the contract was interested in collecting the goods as completely and as quickly as possible. It was to their benefit to be as thorough in collecting the tithe as humanly possible.[4]

The upper clergy, members of the cathedral chapter and members of the bishop's staff, received their incomes from the tithe. The local parish priest depended on the fees paid by the faithful for the exercise of the sacraments. Spaniards were expected to pay a nominal amount for certain sacraments, such as baptisms and marriages. In theory parish clergy also received a portion of the tithe, but this was the exception rather than the rule. Their main source of income was alms and offerings along with fees levied for the performance of various functions, such as weddings, burials, baptisms, and the like. The fees charged for ecclesiastical services became regularized by the early seventeenth century throughout most of Hispanic America. Each diocese would approve its particular schedule of fees, called an *arancel*. From the outset, however, the crown made it clear that the natives could not be charged fees, but only Spaniards and persons of mixed heritage.

The Spanish crown declared that the natives of the New World would pay tribute to the crown, replacing whatever taxes they had paid prior to the conquest. The tribute was a head tax, levied on each adult male and prorated to other members of society. From this money, the crown supported missionary activity and other services to the natives. In order to reward the conquerors and first settlers, the crown allocated the right to collect and enjoy tribute from specific Indian communities to private citizens. In return these citizens were required to pay for the Christianization of the natives in their grant, among other things. As we read earlier, those who received these grants of tribute were called *encomenderos*, from the Spanish word *encomendar*, to entrust.

In the sixteenth and early seventeenth centuries, priests who served parishes composed largely of natives received salaries from the *encomendero*. Since Spanish claims on the New World were based in part on the evangelization of the natives, and the natives paid tribute to the crown, the crown then declared that the cost of Christianizing the natives should be covered by the tribute. It was not proper that the natives would have to pay for the sacraments and pay their tribute as well. The crown itself was the largest *encomendero* and thus bore the greatest responsibility for this cost. It also standardized the salary of parish priests. The royal treasury developed an efficient, but complicated, system to pay priests who served towns under the crown. Those priests who served towns under a private *encomendero* had more difficulty collecting the salary as native populations declined and tribute remittances shrank. Increasingly parish priests in both Spanish and native parishes relied on the fees charged for services.

Unlike in Europe, the regular clergy served as local parish priests, especially in native regions and in those areas where the regulars had first established their missions. In these areas, the regular orders collected the stipend paid by the crown and *encomenderos* for the administration of the sacraments to the natives. Vows of poverty prohibited the individual friar from collecting. Beyond this, the regular clergy did not rely on the tithe for support but rather on gifts from the faithful, as well as fees charged for services.

The financial basis of the regular orders was extremely complex and varied from order to order. Nearly all of the religious orders were mendicant orders. Yet, most of the orders invested heavily in real estate, directly and indirectly. Gifts of real estate were very important for the orders in the early years in the New World: they provided urban locations for the creation of the churches, convents, and monasteries used by the orders; rural real estate could either provide the order with commodities, which could in turn be sold for income, or the properties themselves could be rented out to tenants and thus provide direct cash income to the order.

Pious Works and Confraternities

Central to the financial underpinning of both the secular and regular clergy was the institution of the "pious work." A pious work is any foundation created for the advancement of various works of piety and charity. The most common of these is the chantry (*capellanía*). A chantry provides for masses for the spiritual benefit of the founder and others, usually family members, designated in the foundation documents. It consists of a sum of money, the principle, which is then invested. The principle normally earns interest, originally 7 percent but reduced officially to 5 percent in the early seventeenth century. The interest provides the income for the priest who will say the masses as dictated by the founding patron. In order to generate the interest, Church officials only loaned out the principle in the form of a mortgage on real estate.

Individuals who wished to found a pious work, such as a chantry, had two additional options with regard to the principle capital investment. Rather than provide cash for the principle, they might opt to base the pious work on real estate. In this way the rents on the land, or the production of the land, could be used to fund the pious work. While in theory this seems a good practice and sound investment, in fact these foundations suffered the ravages of time. Frequently it was difficult to find tenants. For urban real estate, especially, there were costs of maintenance that had to be included in the calculations; for rural estates, crops might fail or otherwise not reach expected levels of return. Consequently, slowly but surely Church officials converted these endowments into cash and then invested the cash in mortgages.

The third way to create a pious work was to place a lien on a piece of property. In this method, the founding patron would present a piece of property and promise in the future to pay interest as if cash had been borrowed. This was a very popular form of endowing a chantry because it required very little capital outlay and only routine annual payments. Nevertheless, from the moment of endowment onward, it was a real mortgage and potentially had to be satisfied. Yet in colonial Hispanic America there was no effort to collect the principle of these mortgages. The debtor merely had to pay the annual interest. The Church officials did not expect the principle to be repaid, and in fact if it were repaid they would merely need to find another person to borrow the funds, since it was the interest that provided the income to the Church.

Pious works in general, and chantries in particular, became important financial tools for the Church and for colonists. Pious works could be founded in such a way as to maximize the benefit to the family of the founder in real as well as in spiritual terms. The founding patron of the pious work could stipulate that the money should be invested with family members, that future patrons be direct descendents, and that the priest who said the masses also had to be a direct family member. In these instances the Church intervened only to assure that the provisions of the endowment and canon law were satisfied. Yet some benefactors also established pious works under the patronage of the secular clergy and of the regular clergy. In these instances, in general, the Church assumed control of the principle and had the right to invest it as appropriate, as well as to name the beneficiary of the chantry, that is, the priest charged with saying the masses.[5]

Pious works and other ecclesiastical endowments served many good purposes in the Church. Many had only a tenuous relationship with any ecclesiastical institution. In order to retain a modicum of control over these investments, to make sure that they were managed according to canon law, and to guarantee that their proceeds were actually used for the purposes intended, an office was created under the bishop of each diocese. This office was known as the Chantry and Pious Works Court (*Juzgado de capellanias y obras pias*). While the court oversaw the operations of all such endowments, it actively managed endowments that for one reason or another fell to the bishop or which the patron had granted to the bishop. In some dioceses this could be a significant portion of all endowments and represented a huge capital investment.

The religious orders could rely on pious works and gifts of cash or property for their income. Yet there were other models for the economic support of religious orders. The Society of Jesus, the Jesuits, developed a unique system to provide income for their many endeavors. The basic unit of the order was the college, founded in the principal cities of the Americas. It was an educational institution, offering superior studies to both ecclesiastics and to the colonial elite, as well as the basis for the evangelical work of the order, sending missionaries out into the field. The college received income from the usual sources, including gifts of cash and property, and the foundation of pious works. Uniquely the Jesuits also used these gifts to create rural estates, which specialized in agricultural production for the commercial market. In Peru, for example, there were Jesuit estates producing wine and brandy for sale locally and for the export market. In colonial Ecuador they developed a system of estates and mills to both produce cotton and wool, and then turn these commodities into cloth. In Mexico their estates were cattle ranches producing meat, tallow, and other goods for the local market. In Brazil the Jesuits had sugar estates, growing the cane and then turning it into sugar and molasses for the international market. This model proved to be successful for the order and made them one of the wealthiest in the colonies.

The Church also provided opportunities to the residents of the New World for the creation of community activities and social networks. One of the most important institutions for these purposes was the pious association known as a *cofradia*, confraternity, or sodality. Cofradias were social organizations centered around the veneration of a particular saint, religious image, religious practice, or sacrament, with permission of the local bishop or archbishop, the primary activities of the confraternity being piety and charity. The most prevalent of the confraternities was the Confraternity of the Most Holy Sacrament (*Santísimo Sacramento*). This sodality had as its purpose the veneration of the consecrated host. Members of a confraternity gained indulgences and other spiritual benefits. Many of the confraternities functioned as burial societies. Upon joining a sodality, the new member would pay a membership fee and annual dues. In return, upon death the member would receive a funeral mass to be attended by the other members of the confraternity. These privileges also included memorial masses for the benefit of the soul of the departed member.

Membership in many confraternities was restricted to certain ethnic and social groups. For example, there were confraternities which only accepted members of pure European descent. Other social and ethnic groups organized their own cofradias, so that there were confraternities for freed slaves, mulattoes, and mestizos. By the eighteenth century, cofradias were founded by certain occupational groups, such as shoemakers and silversmiths. Even secular priests had their own confraternity, the Congregación de San Pedro.

Because confraternities existed as religiously based institutions, they had some limited ties to the Church. The celebration of some ceremonies, such as a corporate mass, required the participation of a priest. Other activities required no clerical representation. Frequently the sodality would hire a chaplain to provide for the spiritual needs of the group. The confraternities also amassed significant amounts of money. One of the basic activities of most confraternities was charity. While in many instances the confraternity merely received money from members and distributed it to needy persons or institutions, some of the money came to the sodality as part of pious works and targeted bequests. These types of donations had to be handled differently. As with all other pious works, funds had to be managed in order to protect the principle. The funds of the confraternity were invested in mortgages. The cofradía might also make short-term loans with some of its cash. It might own both urban and rural property. In short, in many communities the local cofradía was one of the wealthiest entities. This caused headaches for the ecclesiastical superiors because they had only limited control over the confraternities. In rural communities the local cofradía could be either fairly autonomous of the parish priest, or work closely with him, depending on the historical development of the sodality, since most existed under local tradition rather than canon law.

Confraternities played a major role in organizing local celebrations of major Church holidays, and special feasts associated with the patron saint of the confraternity, the patron saint of the local church, and other saints and feast days. Especially in native communities, the officers of the confraternity became an extension of the local municipal government, in that leading members of the community might serve as officers either in the town government or in the confraternity, frequently alternating between one and the other. By the twentieth century this pattern became known as the *cargo* system,[6] in which males alternated between the municipal government and the cofradía in leadership positions as they climbed the ranks of power. In this way the confraternity provided native peoples with more opportunities for leadership in their communities.

Just as native communities adopted cofradias as part of their religious experience and then adapted it to their social structure, so the very elements of the Christian faith were adopted into their culture. As Christianity expanded beyond the Holy Land and into Europe, local customs and practices were adopted and adapted to the religion. Celebrations of All Saints Day correspond to pagan traditions in Northern Europe, as does the use of a Christmas tree and other popular customs. Similarly, Christianity in native villages became an extension of the local culture. Pagan deities frequently reappeared in Christian guises, and celebrations from ancient traditions became associated with festivals in the Church calendar. Much of this resulted from the playing out of the double mistaken identity: that is, that the Spaniards and the native peoples each interpreted the actions of the other from within their own cultural experience. This gave rise to many different variants of religious practice throughout Latin America, all within the general parameters of Christianity.

The local bishop exercised a wide range of authority over the Church in his diocese including the power of inquisition. In the twelfth century, as a result of threats to the Catholic Church from heretical sects, the pope authorized the creation of a special tribunal of ecclesiastical judges charged specifically with the suppression of heresy and idolatry: the Holy Office of the Inquisition. In the New World, prior to the 1570s, local bishops initiated their own investigations into heresy as provided by canon law. One of the most famous of these early inquisitions focused on the local native ruler of the Mexican city of Texcoco, don Carlos Ometochtzin. Don Carlos was accused of apostasy and idolatry, in that he had reverted to worship of the old idols after having been baptized and made a Christian. His case was all the more poignant because the Franciscan friars had great hopes that the native rulers would set good examples of Christian living for their peoples. Don Carlos was eventually convicted of the charges, handed over to the royal authorities for execution, and burned at the stake. Nevertheless, the case caused a great stir in the society and in the ecclesiastical community. Many held that natives were newcomers to the faith—neophytes, and as such could not be expected to have the same level of understanding nor dedication to the new faith and that they rightly should be exempted from the Inquisition: the Spanish crown eventually exempted the natives. While the Holy Office of the Inquisition might be seen as an ecclesiastical institution, in reality it functioned more as a branch of royal government. Many of the inquisitors were not priests but rather were canon lawyers and others with training in canon law and procedure.[7]

The Holy Office focused mostly on the suppression of heresy and of violations of the sacraments. For example, many foreigners, especially French and English, more frequently came under the scrutiny of the Holy Office, under suspicion of heresy, than in the royal courts. Political thought was considered merely one manifestation of religious thought. As a result, the Inquisition functioned as a tool for the maintenance of the homogeneity of the body politic. Other cases heard by the Inquisition included bigamy (a violation of the sacrament of marriage), sexual solicitation by priests of women in confession (a violation of the sacrament of penance), and heresy. Many cases of oath taking, witchcraft, divination, and other minor forms of idolatry also made up a large proportion of cases early on. Later, the inquisitors focused less on the mundane issues of oaths and witches, and focused more on cases of true heretics and open violations of the sacraments.

Although the native peoples were exempted from the jurisdiction of the Holy Office, they still were subject to the local bishop's authority to root out idolatry. Throughout Hispanic America local bishops created tribunals to prosecute cases of native idolatry. In Peru this procedure became known as the extirpation, and it existed in Mexico and other regions as well. Under the extirpation, specially trained priests authorized by the bishop would conduct investigations in local Indian villages, seeking out idolaters. If they found cases of idolatry, the idolater would face spiritual punishments: public humiliation, public penance, and prayers. The articles associated with the idolatry (images, offerings, and other utensils) would be publicly destroyed. While much of the procedure seems similar to that of the Inquisition, the punishments were purely spiritual, other than the occasional flogging, and did not call on the local secular authorities to mete out capital or corporal punishments. These latter always existed as a possibility, but most Europeans considered the natives to be neophytes and thus inferior in their understanding of Christianity and less responsible for their errors. There is little evidence that the extirpations actually succeeded in eliminating idolatry, though. In most instances the idolatry merely shifted, becoming less obvious and less identifiable, blending into a host of folk beliefs and secular rituals already embraced by the Europeans, as would also happen with African religious traditions in many areas. Moreover, the priests charged with extirpating idolatry concluded, as had the inquisitors, that there were more important things to focus on than small-scale folk practices, as long as the core beliefs of the faithful were orthodox.

With the development of the New World colonies, the crown sought to strengthen its control over the Church using the privileges of the Royal Patronage. As part of a general period of reform, the Spanish crown began a program to codify laws and standardize the methods of administration in the colonies. This endeavor reached its climax with regard to the Church in 1574 with the promulgation of the Ordinances of the Patronage (*Ordenanza del Patronazgo*). This collection of royal decrees embodied some earlier orders and included several new ones. The decrees created a system whereby candidates for clerical offices would engage in competitions destined to select the best trained person for the office. The competitive exams, called *oposiciones*, sought to improve the quality of priests serving in the parishes. The crown favored this system to such a degree that in the early decades of the seventeenth century it ordered that four canonries on each cathedral chapter be filled through competitive exam. These were seats reserved for one person holding a doctorate who could teach canon law at the local university, another trained scholar who could teach general studies, a specialist in penitential theology to supervise confessions within the cathedral, and another who would supervise the liturgy of the Word, the reading of the biblical lessons and the sermons. They carried the titles of doctoral canon, magisterial canon, canon penitentiary, and canon lector. The *oposición* system governed the appointment of priests into most parishes in which the crown had guaranteed an income. This included most rural Indian parishes and many urban parishes that received funds from the tithe. Nevertheless, the religious orders continued to function in many of the rural parishes, and the crown did not control appointments within the orders.

The ordinances also called for "secularization," the removal of the regular clergy from rural parishes and their replacement with secular clerics. Although begun in the sixteenth century, it would take nearly two centuries to complete. In the Spanish colonies, while the bishops and secular clergy fell directly under crown control, the regular orders did not. The regulars effectively operated outside of direct royal scrutiny and, in many ways, beyond the scrutiny of the local bishop. The regular clergy had a structure that linked them directly to the pope in Rome, while the secular clergy in the Americas tended to be more directly controlled by the monarchs, thanks to the Royal Patronage. Moreover, thanks to papal grants from the time of evangelization, the Franciscans in particular, and other religious orders in general, claimed quasi-papal powers when operating out of the immediate area of control of the bishop, defined as a two-day ride. While it is unclear the degree to which the orders actually used that authority, they all vigorously claimed it. As a result, the regulars were perceived by many royal officials as operating outside of the control of the state, and thus constituted a serious threat to royal authority. Consequently, the crown sought to remove the regulars from the parishes and replace them with seculars in order to gain more effective control over the Church as a whole. This also had the effect of moving the regulars from rural parishes into their convents and houses, which tended to be in urban areas. This had been and continued to be the pattern in Europe, where most parochial duties fell to the secular clergy and regulars were confined to convents or monasteries, or engaged in very specific activities.

At the same time that the Spanish crown sought to increase control over the regular orders, the Catholic Church began a period of reform manifested by the Council of Trent (1545–63). The Council of Trent was called by Pope Paul III in order to address important theological questions which had arisen in the Church over the course of two hundred years and to reform the Church of abuses. Among other issues, Trent sought to address criticisms raised by the Protestant Reformation concerning the sacraments, indulgences, and the structure and authority of the Church. One of the important themes of the council was the centrality of the pastoral duties of priests and bishops. As part of these reforms the Council reaffirmed the rights of bishops to supervise the administration of the sacraments within their dioceses. The logical result of the reforms of Trent was that bishops would seek to gain greater supervisory control over the activities of the regular clergy in their dioceses. Specifically,

Trent called for bishops to license clergy who administered the sacraments in their dioceses, as well as to give licenses to preachers and others.

The episcopacy of don Juan de Palafox y Mendoza in the early seventeenth century exemplifies many of the difficulties inherent in the attempt to bring the religious orders under the control of the local bishop. Palafox arrived in New Spain in 1640, already appointed and consecrated as bishop of Puebla de los Angeles. In addition to his ecclesiastical duties, he came as a special investigator to look into irregularities in the viceregal government. Shortly after his arrival he was also appointed interim viceroy (due to the flagrant misconduct of his predecessor) and archbishop of Mexico, a dignity he renounced in favor of retaining his post in Puebla. After having received a new viceroy to replace the one who had been removed due to malfeasance, Palafox settled down to govern his diocese. Early on he had come into conflict with the mendicant orders over their claims of exemption from episcopal supervision. The tension came to a head when he removed the mendicants from thirty-six parishes and replaced them with secular priests. The confrontation, though heated, was resolved. Palafox then took on the Jesuits. The Jesuits refused to secure episcopal licenses for their priests to administer the sacraments. Palafox demanded that the order pay the tithe on the production of all of its agricultural estates, a very significant demand since the order was based financially on the production of its estates. The bishop and the order came to loggerheads. While Palafox continued to take action against the Jesuits, they found an ally in the new viceroy, who ordered Palafox's arrest. Eventually the crown supported Palafox, but shortly thereafter the monarch recalled him to Spain and appointed him bishop of Burgo de Osma. The Jesuits did submit to the license requirements but only after Palafox had left for Spain.[8]

Nuns and Convents

While much has been written on the role of male clergy in the ecclesiastical history of the Americas, only recently have historians directed their attention to female religious. Shortly after the Europeans settled the New World the colonists began to build cloisters for women. As early as 1551 the city fathers of Cuzco, for example, purchased property in their city to dedicate to a nunnery. This occurred barely a decade after the nominal conquest of the Inca and while the colony was itself still wrecked by civil war. This first establishment had as its goal the protection of *mestizas*, female children of Spanish conquerors and their native wives and lovers.[9] The object was to protect the virginity of the girls from the rough-and-tumble world of post-conquest Peru. While the worldview that spurred these efforts was highly patriarchal, with women viewed as receptacles of the honor of their families in need of protection, it also manifested the high regard that these men had for the children of their legal and casual relations. These were the daughters they recognized and whom they wished to raise in the Spanish tradition, not just forgotten offspring from illicit or forced relationships.

Throughout Latin America the conquerors and early settlers set about founding similar institutions. These establishments for women were but one of several types of formal, Church-sanctioned repositories for women. There were at least three other types. The classic nunnery was inhabited by women from good families who had decided to join a religious order and live apart from the world in contemplation and prayer. Other establishments housed women who were married, sometimes with their entire family, while the male of the house was away on business or in government service. In the case of the house for mestiza daughters, seen in Cuzco, the expectation was that girls might eventually marry and leave the nunnery. Similarly, the women who were married would presumably leave the institution when the head of the household returned. Last, some cloisters had as their purpose the reform of women who were considered by society at large to be sinful. These religious houses provided a safe place for prostitutes and public sinners to be taken out of the public eye and given a chance to reform their lives. The courts frequently placed such women in the cloister, and in other instances the women entered voluntarily. What all of these institutions had in common is that they provided a place for women to be separated from society in general. They tended to reinforce a patriarchal society in which women were viewed more as property than as independent actors.

The communities of female religious followed rules of life, like the rules of the male religious orders. Most of the male religious orders had female analogs. Women who wished to follow the rule of Saint Francis could join the Order of Saint Clare, Francis's companion, who founded an order of nuns along the lines of the Franciscan order for men. These orders for women are frequently referred to as the second order, with the male order being the first order, and religious orders for the laity being the third order.

In spite of the tenuous position occupied by women in the colonial society, the cloister provided some positive benefits as well. As evidenced by the writings of the famous Mexican nun of the seventeenth century, Sor Juana Inés de la Cruz, the cloister accorded her a place where she could pursue the life of the mind, in study and in writing. It was the cloister that gave her the freedom to pen such lines as: "Foolish men who accuse women without a reason, not seeing that you are the cause of the very thing that you blame" ["Hombres necios que acusáis / a la mujer sin razón, / sin ver que soís la occasion / de lo mismo que culpáis."].

While a few nuns of the colonial period gained fame and reputation for their learned writings, most remained invisible to the larger world. Many, however, did write of their experiences, both within the life of the cloister as well as of their own spiritual development. One of the spiritual disciplines frequently pursued was that of writing personal journals, in which the nun would trace her development in faith, telling of those parts of her life related to her calling in the religious order. Scholars are now discovering these journals and beginning to study them for the many insights they provide into the minds of these women. Although these journals are based in reality, they tend to be highly mystical and quite idiosyncratic to each author. Moreover, they are in essence part of a dialogue. The confessor explores areas of faith and sin with the female penitent, who in turn writes of it in her journal, to be read and edited in turn by the confessor.

The writings of these nuns fall into three basic categories. The first is the autobiography, usually requested by the confessor. It provides the reader with a glimpse of the lives of women in this period, as well as snippets of everyday life. It can offer some reflections on their moral and religious ideas. The second type is a spiritual journal or diary that traces the spiritual development of the woman, again at the behest of or guided by the confessor. Third, there are letters written by nuns to outsiders, confessors, that trace events in their interior life of spiritual growth. The letters written by Sor Juana to various individuals outside of her convent are examples of this type.[10]

Many cloisters, although dedicated to women who had formally withdrawn from society as opposed to those who temporarily entered for various reasons, closely emulated the social structures and range of entertainments found outside their walls. In Arequipa, Peru, for example, the convent of Santa Catalina (founded some forty years after the city) housed around 450 nuns, plus their servants and slaves, and occupied the equivalent of several city blocks. Rather than live in single cells along corridors, the nuns of Santa Catalina built their own cells, small houses in reality, creating a city within the city, with streets, plazas, and patios. In many ways within the walls the nuns re-created the society outside the walls. The convent was associated with the Dominican Order of men and followed the Dominican rule.

Several of the exemplary saints of colonial Latin America were women, in whose lives their contemporaries saw models worthy of emulation. Perhaps no more famous example exists than Saint Rose of Lima, born Isabel Flores in Lima, Peru, in 1586. The legend runs that her face was so angelic, her cheeks so like roses, that the family servants gave her the nickname of Rosa, and it became universal. Rosa was a remarkable child, emulating Saint Catherine of Siena. While still a child Rosa took a vow of perpetual chastity. As an adolescent she began to react strongly against her own physical beauty, cutting her hair and employing other tricks to look ill or otherwise unappealing. For years she wore the habit of a Poor Clare, and even considered entering the convent. One day en route to the cloister of the Discalced Carmelites, she passed the Chapel of Nuestra Señora del Rosario. There she became convinced that her calling was as a third-order Dominican nun, that is, that she would live her life according to the Dominican rule but not in the cloister. Instead, she made her home a cloister for the rest of her life and adopted the Dominican habit. Her spiritual devotions focused on the denial of sensual pleasure, humility, and prayer. Even within her lifetime she was recognized as saintly. She died in 1617, was beatified in 1668, and canonized a saint barely three years later.[11]

The cloisters for women played an important role—along with the religious orders for men and the secular clergy—within families, especially with regard to inheritance patterns. In both early modern Spain and Portugal and in their colonies in the New World, inheritance laws dictated that the estate of the parents be divided equally among the children. The parents could enhance the portion of one child so that the child could receive nearly a half of the estate, depending on the number of children. This inheritance system had the effect of dividing up large estates into smaller ones. As opposed to concentrating wealth, the system tended to disperse it from generation to generation. Placing children in religious orders and into the secular clergy provided families with a method of mitigating the effect of the inheritance laws. They could in essence limit the amount of the estate that was dispersed during the parents' lives, allowing for more wealth to be concentrated in one or a few of their offspring who went on to marry.

Another vehicle for protecting family assets was the entailed estate. These estates consisted of one or more properties, which were legally bound as a unit. There were legal prohibitions against selling or mortgaging the whole, or parts, of the estate. This method was very costly in that it required royal permission for setting up and the payment of heavy fees. Once an entailed estate was founded, it could never be sold or broken up.

The nunneries also played an important role in the economy of colonial Latin America. Just as with the male orders and the cofradias, the nunneries held property, chantries, and most other forms of ecclesiastical property. Just as with many institutions today, convents and monasteries had a constant need for funds. The care and feeding of a dozen nuns or friars represented a significant cash outlay, even for mendicant orders who had renounced a life of luxury and comfort. Upon entering a mendicant order, men were expected to give up their worldly possessions to the order. This transaction also meant a renunciation of their inheritance from their parents. These funds then passed to the order. Similarly, when women entered a religious order, the order collected what would have been their dowry should they have married. Most nunneries stipulated the minimum amount that they required. Upon entering the cloister, the woman would make a will, usually making two additional allocations. One of these was an outright bequest to the nunnery for a portion of her parents' estate. The woman could also create a reserve, really an endowment, the growth of which would allow her to have a private income for her personal needs beyond the communal living of the house. The constitutions of differing convents and monasteries had important variations, but in general the wealth gained upon the entrance of a new member was to be invested for that member's long-term sustenance. Only the interest generated by this principle could be used for day-to-day support, not the principle itself. This placed many convents and monasteries in a very precarious position of having substantial holdings of property, for example, but little income. Similarly they might hold numerous mortgages based on invested funds, but not really have enough cash to take care of daily needs. These considerations did not usually come to bear on those cloisters where married women entered for limited periods of time. Some orders and nunneries allowed their inmates to retain their own personal wealth, but those nuns were, in turn, responsible for their own maintenance beyond the minimum provided by the order. This was the case of the convent of Santa Catalina of Arequipa where individual nuns built their own accommodations.

While in Spanish America cloisters for women date from the first few years of settlement, in Brazil it was not until the late seventeenth century that the first official convent for women appeared, the Convent of Santa Clara do Destêrro in Salvador da Bahia. The colonial officials feared that the establishment of cloisters for women might impede population growth. It remained the only convent for women for at least fifty years. The hefty monetary requirements placed on entering novices meant that only the daughters of Bahia's elite could join. As a result the convent enjoyed a very solid endowment, based upon the dowries and donations provided by those upper-class novices.

While strictly speaking not a part of the Church, the universities of the colonial Americas had strong clerical participation. The major universities of the Hispanic world have their origins on the Iberian Peninsula in examples such as the University of Salamanca and the model Renaissance university in Alcalá de Henares, called the Complutense. The first three major universities in the Hispanic New World were founded in the 1550s. Over the years, each has demonstrated its claim for primacy, but the University of Santo Tomás de Aquino in Santo Domingo boasts that it actually has its roots in a 1538 papal bull. Universities in colonial Latin America were institutions established to govern independent colleges, where the teaching occurred. These colleges tended to be organized by religious orders, especially the Jesuits and the Dominicans, although a secular cleric in Mexico founded the Colegio de Omnium Sanctorum. The university merely provided for a collective governance of the colleges and held the ultimate authority to issue degrees, based on the power granted by the king and the pope.

The University of San Marcos in Lima had its origins in 1548 when the Dominican provincial chapter meeting in that city approved a college of general studies. The University of Mexico came into being upon the arrival of the royal decrees of 1551 authorizing its inauguration. The Church had a great need for universities in the New World, as an indirect result of some of Trent's reforms. Instituting stricter standards for ordination increasingly required young men to have university training, if not a degree itself. Those young men who had university degrees found better opportunities within the ecclesiastical hierarchy, be it in important urban parishes or on the numerous cathedral chapters.

The crown and clergy rapidly incorporated the newly settled territories of the Americas into the ecclesiastical structures. Because of the presence of various religious orders, and of the diocese, the map soon became a patchwork of overlapping jurisdictions. The middle years of the colonies also saw the establishment of many important ecclesiastical institutions. These included both offices of the Church, such as an expansion of the offices under the bishops, the creation of tribunals to extirpate idolatry, and offices for the collection of the tithe and the management of investments. The period also saw the creation of quasi-ecclesiastical institutions in the form of the Inquisition and the universities. Although both the Inquisition and the universities were deeply rooted in the Church, by the sixteenth century they had taken on independent existences. While men in religious orders had participated from the very beginning in the evangelization and settlement of the New World, it was only *after* the foundation of towns and cities that female religious orders made their appearance in the New World. In the Hispanic colonies convents for women appeared in the mid 1500s, while in Brazil the first nunnery did not gain approval until the late 1600s, some 170 years later. All of these institutions provided a deep and rich foundation upon which the Church would develop in the eighteenth century.

The Catholic Church in the seventeenth century developed a uniquely American flavor. As customs and rituals from Europe were established in the New World, the local people, both natives and those of European or African origin, adapted them into their own cultural experiences. Native communities embraced the cofradía as a structure for social organization and corporate action. Native peoples also adapted Christian beliefs and rituals into their own customs, making for a rich and diverse religious experience across the continents. At the same time the Europeans developed a more complex and ostentatious form of religious expression, filled with public ceremonies, processions, dramatic rituals, rich vestments, and opulently decorated churches. All of these features became part of the very essence of the Catholic tradition in Latin America, a rich and colorful tapestry of varied religious experiences, as groups adopted those elements of the Christian faith that touched them and served their social and cultural needs.

————————————————————————————— 5 ——

Reform and Enlightenment

_____

The southern region of Brazil has some of the richest mines of pre-cious stones on earth, in addition to immense deposits of gold and silver. Portuguese explorers discovered these deposits in the seventeenth century, causing a huge rush into the area, soon called *Minas Gerais,* the general mines. Mines in the New World were the ultimate source of all capital for the economy. As a result the Church had an interest in both the spiritual life of the miners and in the investment of money generated by the mines. In many ways the miners were dependent on the crown for the protections that royal law gave to their claims. Although this was a fairly primitive frontier region, the crown sought to govern and regulate it, obviously to improve its own financial situation thanks to the tariffs and taxes on mineral production. To provide for the spiritual lives of the miners, the crown established churches in the region administered by the secular clergy; they prohibited the regu-lar clergy from entering the mining districts because, as we have seen, the secular clergy were more easily controlled. An interesting dichotomy arose whereby the secular clergy served in the mining camps and cities that grew up around them, while the outlying native villages throughout the interior were served by members of the regular clergy.

In the eighteenth century, local observers frequently contrasted the secular clergy and members of religious orders in Minas Gerais. The secu-lar clergy serving in the mining districts and cities supported themselves through fees established for their services. For example, the clergy collected one-sixteenth of an ounce of gold each time a person received the Eucharist. The price for a sung mass was one full ounce. The price for a marriage was three-sixteenths of an ounce of gold, while a baptism cost one-fourth of an ounce. In the entire district of Minas Gerais there were only thirty priests in 1712, so each received a significant income. The appointment of priests was a closely guarded privilege of the bishop of Rio de Janeiro. And not surpris-ingly, colonists routinely complained about the quality of the secular priests in the district. In addition to their perceived extravagant income, priests were accused of sexual and moral improprieties. Life in a mining district clearly tested the vows of many priests.[1]

In the native villages of the interior, far from the mines, the regular clergy, led by the Jesuits and Franciscans, had established missions. Life in the missions could not contrast more strongly to life in the mines. Each of the orders established its own rules governing the missions. In general the orders worked with the royal government to keep other Europeans out. Each village had two priests, no doubt to provide support to one another. They were strictly controlled in their dealings with the natives; they had to pay for anything other than nominal gifts given to them by the natives; they could not meet with native women in private or allow native women into their quarters; they had to build and service a hospital or infirmary in the village. In addition, they gathered the village for prayers and teaching each morning. They dismissed the adults to their labors, while they continued to teach the children. After the midday meal and a period of rest, the lessons continued. In the evening the whole village again gathered for vespers. This cycle and model was inspired by the work of the Franciscans in Mexico immediately after the conquest in 1524. These villages, especially the ones organized by the Jesuits in interior Brazil and Paraguay, were viewed as nearly utopian communities. Even if they did not all reach this high level, their religious leadership did provide a stark contrast with the life of the secular clergy in the mining districts.

The eighteenth century in Latin America saw the coming together of two important trends in the history of the Church. First, the various institutions established earlier continued to develop and flourish, becoming essential parts of the social and cultural lives of the colonies. Second, political changes in Europe and new intellectual movements began to create an atmosphere of opposition to some aspects of the Church's activities. The Catholic Church was easily more important than any other single institution, perhaps even including the royal government. As we have seen, the Church was far from being a single, monolithic institution but was actually composed of many subsidiary parts, some of which acted in opposition to one another. In the eighteenth century the Church in Latin America grappled with the effects of modernization while attempting to increase its control over its many varied components.

The Church became a dominant economic force in the eighteenth century. Through the use of mortgages and liens the Church had some connection with much of the property of the colonies, both urban and rural real estate. Although most of the liens and properties appeared on the books of the *Juzgado de capellanias* (Chantry Court), they were parts of the endowments of scores of different institutions. Any given convent, friary, cofradía, or parish might have scores or hundreds of endowments supporting it. All of these endowments fell under the scrutiny of the Chantry Court, but not all were managed by that court. Consequently, while the total amount of money invested in property in the colonies was impressive—some have estimated at least one-quarter of all the property available—it was dispersed among many institutions within the Church.

Some of the funds invested in mortgages and liens represented long-term spiritual obligations. These funds, once invested, could never be alienated from the Church. The condition under which the Church held them was called mortmain (literally "dead hand"). Initially this legal principle applied to all property and other goods owned by the Church or any ecclesiastical corporation. Since the Church continued to exist beyond the life of any one individual, there could be no distribution of the property to any heirs: it was seen as being held by a dead hand, always and continually in the possession of a single corporation. Arising out of this primary sense, the term "mortmain" also came to refer to those holdings of the Church that could not be alienated, due to the restrictions placed upon them at the time the Church first received them.

Following from this second meaning, as mortmain developed in the Iberian world, only some of the property and funds obtained by the Church and its institutions fell under its provision. A prime example of funds falling under mortmain was the dowry paid by nuns upon their entrance into the cloister. Under Spanish law the dowry remained the possession of the bride in the marriage. It had to remain intact, and the husband had to account for it at the time of his death. The husband could manage the funds of the dowry, but only with his wife's explicit permission. The woman could designate an heir for her dowry. With a nun, the Church took the role of the husband insofar as the management of the dowry was concerned. Once the nun died, her dowry remained under the control and administration of the Church, which represented her spiritual husband.

Loans, Rents, and Interest

There were three basic sources for income to the various institutions within the Church, be they male or female religious orders, chantries, cofradías, or some other ecclesiastical corporation. These were the tithe, rents, and interest income from mortgages and liens. There were also three other smaller sources of income available to the Church and individual clerics. These were parochial dues (the fees charged for various services), alms, and first fruits.[2] The first fruits were the first animals born to a herd, the first bushels of wheat harvested, the first sugar milled in a given season. These were traditional offerings and never amounted to a significant source of revenue but were largely symbolic. For the bishop and cathedral chapter, the tithe and fees, along with interest and rents, provided the bulk of their income. By the late seventeenth century, very few parish priests received salaries from *encomenderos*; most relied on the collection of fees, along with modest stipends from chantries. Religious orders, both male and female, accepted gifts and some fees but overwhelmingly relied on rents and interest as did chantries and cofradias and most other ancillary institutions. The Jesuits supported their operations through commercial ventures and agricultural estates, which were geared toward the market economy. It is the growth in reliance on rents and interest that characterized the eighteenth century.

In 1820 it was estimated that the total revenue to the Church in Peru, for example, was approximately 2.3 million pesos, from all sources. At that same time, there were approximately three thousand secular and regular priests, with a larger portion coming from the ranks of the secular clergy.[3] These revenue figures fall in the same order of magnitude as those reported for Mexico from about twenty years earlier. The bishops and cathedral chapters did not rely as heavily on rural real estate as they did on urban real estate, mortgages, and the tithe. In Buenos Aires the average tithe collection to the archdiocese at the end of the eighteenth century was 35,000 pesos. This is much smaller than the figure for the Archdiocese of Mexico (500,000 pesos), but the population in Buenos Aires was much smaller.[4] It still, however, represents a significant sum of money. The Archdiocese of Lima was far more equal to that in Mexico in terms of population and importance in the imperial system. The tithe collected in Lima at the end of the eighteenth century hovered around 180,000 pesos. Although comparable in many ways, the Archdiocese of Mexico was the hub of an important agricultural district, which generated a huge income from the tithes. The desert locale of Lima simply could not support the same density of population. In sum, it is important to recognize that the Church and all of its subsidiary institutions represented an important economic engine. Yet different regions had different conditions while different units of the Church relied on different sources of income.

The financial role of religious orders is central to understanding the economy of eighteenth-century Latin America. There was a remarkable similarity among practices in Mexico, Brazil, Chile, Argentina, Mexico, and Colombia. In all locations the Church, and the various institutions within it, played an important role. In the case of Mexico in the late eighteenth century, a few figures are illustrative. The tithe for the Archdiocese of Mexico in the 1790s averaged about 500,000 pesos annually, representing a total agricultural and pastoral production of 5 million pesos annually.[5] With regard to rents, the income from buildings owned by Church related institutions in this same period averaged approximately 1 million pesos.[6] Somewhat later, just prior to 1820, the total value of the invested capital reported through the Chantry Court was 3.5 million pesos, generating nearly 180,000 pesos annually. The total received from these three sources is approximately 1.75 million pesos annually. At the same time there were approximately three thousand secular priests and four thousand religious, male and female.[7] There can be little doubt that in the late eighteenth and early nineteenth century the Church represented the largest single social and economic entity in the colony, and this pattern was repeated throughout Latin America.

What is crucial to understanding the position of the Church is that although it might have liens and mortgages on the books worth tens of millions of pesos, the borrowers, or debtors, were under no obligation to repay the principle, only the interest. The principle of the loans and encumbrances was not freely available to the Church. The Church did not have as much ready wealth as may have been portrayed on its books. It has been estimated that by the late eighteenth century most properties, urban or rural, in Mexico, Chile, Venezuela, Brazil, or throughout Latin America, carried an encumbrance, either from a loan or from a mortgage.

All of this activity involving loans and encumbrances might strike the modern reader as curious, especially dealing as it does with the Church and many subsidiary institutions that ostensibly were based on a mendicant lifestyle. The irony was not lost on contemporary churchmen and women. Some religious orders, notably the Franciscans, hardly participated in the loans. The other problem was that, strictly speaking, lending money at interest was considered sinful up until relatively recent times. In the sixteenth through the eighteenth centuries the Church reconciled its practices by focusing on the income generated. It declared that these were not loans, but in fact annuities: the Church would give a large sum of capital to a private citizen in return for an annual payment. Similarly it allowed individuals to pay annuities in lieu of lump-sum payments, such as the payment of a nun's dowry or to found a chantry. Thus these transactions were to be seen as the generation of annuities, not the lending of money at interest.

Yet by the eighteenth century the Church began to lose its squeamishness about interest. It began to openly recognize that it lent money at interest. Two types of loans appeared. One was similar to the liens of earlier period in that in return for the loan, the recipient placed a lien on his property; the loan was for a relatively short term, a few years perhaps, and was subsequently repaid. Estate owners and other entrepreneurs used these funds to renovate or modernize their activities. The Church even began to loan money without the requisite lien on property, simple unsecured loans with interest to be repaid in a few years. These took the name of *depósitos*, which unfortunately also refers to other financial transactions in which nuns allocate part of their wealth "on deposit" with the nunnery to provide for personal expenses.[8]

While the impact of Church loans and encumbrances on the economy of Latin America is difficult to determine, these instruments were of tremendous importance to the ecclesiastical institutions that depended upon them. For example, in a twenty-year period in the late eighteenth and early nineteenth century, the convent of La Encarnación in Mexico City received some 185,000 pesos in loan repayments. This figure probably represents at least a few instances of money paid back, loaned, and paid back again. In the early nineteenth century the convent of Santa Clara de Jesús in Querétaro, Mexico, had nearly 150,000 invested in loans and encumbrances.[9] One cofradía, that of Our Lady of Aranzazú of Mexico City, emitted nearly 120,000 pesos in loans in just eight years at the turn of the eighteenth century. These figures, however, only demonstrate the movement of capital, money collected by the ecclesiastical institution and then loaned out again. They do not represent the income generated by the investments.

Ecclesiastical institutions, convents, nunneries, cofradias, and hospitals all survived thanks to the rents and income on loans. As we read in chapter 4, the oldest nunnery in colonial Cuzco was founded for mestiza daughters of the conquerors shortly after the conquest. In 1793 it had an annual income of about 25,000 pesos, down from a high of some 31,000. These impressive figures, however, mask the fact that the nunnery also carried some impressive bad debts. One leading aristocrat of the city had accumulated nearly 53,700 pesos in debts to two Cuzco convents. This debt continued to grow such that in the mid 1780s it had reached 83,000 pesos.[10] Obviously, then, large numbers of loans on the books did not necessarily translate into a comfortable financial situation.

Many institutions frequently suffered from significant problems of cash flow: income was not available when they needed it. Many institutions tended to spend more than they actually had: expenditures outpaced revenue. The convent of Santa Clara in Mexico in the mid-eighteenth century, for example, routinely spent nearly 5,000 pesos more per year than it took in. Its income hovered around 14,500 pesos while its expenses ran at nearly 20,000. In situations like these, the convents took out loans from private citizens or from other ecclesiastical corporations in order to remain solvent. In 1774 the convent of La Concepción in Oaxaca reported that it owed 7,500 pesos to its steward and had debts totaling 22,100 pesos to nine other creditors. While the convent's total net worth was listed at 225,000 pesos, it was able to collect interest and rents on only 65,000 pesos of that. The rest of its endowment consisted of run-down properties or uncollectible liens.[11] In Brazil the oldest nunnery found that while collecting rents on its property was fairly simple, collecting interest on the loans was far more difficult. Contemporary observers and later historians have noted that nunneries more frequently ran into economic trouble than other institutions, for a variety of reasons. One reason was a lack of administrative experience on the part of the nuns who became the accountants and managers of their institutions. Another reason was a bias toward certain institutions. Some convents had more prestige than others and had an easier time both receiving donations and in collecting outstanding debts, possibly because of ties to powerful individuals in the local community. And finally, there was gender bias that made collecting their debts more difficult.

Convents and other ecclesiastical institutions also provided only part of the capital available in any given area to those in need of credit or cash. In colonial Latin America there was a relative absence of coinage, and so many transactions involved credit. While it is impossible to track all of the minor transactions that might involve credit, only the large ones that involved security for a loan or when a notary needed to witness appear in the record books. The best snapshot of all transactions comes from Guadalajara in the eighteenth century. For approximately a century, the records indicate that ecclesiastical institutions made just under half of all loans. The Church and its institutions accounted for 70 percent of all loans early in the eighteenth century, but only 25 percent in the first decade of the nineteenth century. In the last two decades of the eighteenth century ecclesiastical corporations loaned out over 3 million pesos, an average of 150,000 pesos annually. Of those loans, 85 percent were evenly split between the cathedral, the convents, and the Chantry Court. Other pious agencies—hospitals, cofradias, orphanages, and the like— accounted for approximately 17 percent of all Church-associated loans. The largest issuer of loans among the convents was Santa María de Gracia, which loaned out nearly 30,000 pesos annually in the twenty-year period, a truly astounding level of investment. The next closest was Santa Mónica, which loaned only some 5,000 pesos annually.[12]

The next form of income to the Church came from rents on property. Through various mechanisms, religious orders and other institutions within the Church acquired both urban and rural property. Some of this property was donated with the initial foundation of the institution. In other cases patrons gave property to support their favored institutions. In some instances the property came as a result of foreclosure on properties that had been pledged against liens. Ownership of land by ecclesiastical institutions caused much confusion in the late colonial period. The crown initially prohibited land grants from being issued if the land were to be given to the Church within two to three years of the grant. Town councils pleaded that land in their jurisdictions not be given to ecclesiastical institutions. Some of that fear had to do with the collection of various taxes based on real estate; other concerns had to do with the notion that land owned by the Church somehow fell out of production. Nothing could be farther from the truth.

In general, convents associated with the Franciscan Order held less property than others. The order frowned on the acquisition of property, but even when it did hold property the legal fiction was that a trustee (syndic) held the property for the benefit of the order. Several ecclesiastical institutions found landownership generally to be more trouble than it was worth. The cathedral chapter of Mexico in the sixteenth century resolved to sell all of its real estate, mostly houses and other urban properties, in favor of investing the money in loans. The convent of Santa Catalina in Cuzco also tended to sell real property in favor of investing capital in loans. These bodies made this decision because of the cost of maintaining real property. First of all, a tenant had to be found to pay the rent. Once found and installed, the property had to be maintained. With the passage of time the properties became run down, and for many institutions property and its maintenance simply represented too much investment for too small of a return. Curiously, as we saw in Brazil, some institutions found that collecting rents on property was easier than interest on loans. Moreover, property could be leased for a very long term, up to 450 years, with no obligation to the owner, and with the tenant taking on all the responsibility for upkeep and maintenance as well as for improvement of the property.

In spite of decisions made in the sixteenth century, the cathedral chapter of Mexico reevaluated its stance on property ownership, and by 1800 it, and various institutions subsumed within the cathedral, owned 107 pieces of property in the city with a total value of approximately 1 million pesos. Just a few years later, in 1812, the two leading nunneries in Mexico City had annual incomes from rental properties at just under 60,000 pesos for one and just under 70,000 pesos for the other. Thus combined with even paltry revenues from loans and mortgages, these establishments enjoyed a prodigious wealth. They represent the most elite institutions in one of the two most important cities in Latin America, and thus display the pinnacle of wealth from property, not the norm.

A look at the other capital of the Spanish American empire, Lima, gives a similar picture of landownership. In the early eighteenth century, one nunnery owned or managed more than one hundred properties in that city. The nunnery, La Encarnación, owned or had interests in thirteen stores, two barbershops, a general store, a warehouse, a cloth mill, several suburban vegetable gardens and orchards, and at least one rural estate. It is not clear if the nunnery owned them or if they represented properties upon which the institution had placed liens as part of their investment portfolio.[13]

Haciendas

In the highlands of Peru, Cuzco was home to a variety of ecclesiastical institutions with both rural and urban real estate holdings. In the last decades of the seventeenth and beginning of the eighteenth centuries, the Jesuits held a position of preeminence. The Society of Jesus used the production of rural estates to help finance its widespread activities. Following the Jesuits, the Augustinians held a total of twenty-three rural properties and two urban ones. None of these, however, generated an overwhelming income. Based upon various sources, it is likely that these properties only provided a mere 650 pesos a year in income. Fortunately, the order also had several loans earning an income of just under 4,000 pesos per year. Compared to the resources of the large convents and nunneries in the major colonial cities, this income was paltry, and it again demonstrated the need for a diversified portfolio of investments for financial security.[14]

A very special subcategory of property ownership consists of those ecclesiastical corporations that not only owned but managed their own rural estates. Under this model the religious order or other institution attempted to generate a profit from the property, planting and harvesting crops, and then selling them on the local market. The stars of this particular system were the Jesuits. Although they depended to a certain degree on rents from property and income from investments, the bulk of their wealth was generated by their rural estates.

The members of the Society of Jesus resembled other religious in that they took vows of poverty, celibacy, and obedience. Jesuits, however, after a certain number of years in the order, also made a fourth vow of loyalty to the pope. The mission of the Jesuits was flexible and priests could be assigned to any task as needed. A college, the central unit of the order, might own property, receive gifts, make loans, and participate in all the activities common to religious orders. The order provided food, clothing, and shelter, thus freeing the individual Jesuit from concerns for his personal well-being. Some members of the order specialized in raising the money necessary for their missions. By and large, the bulk of these funds in the American Jesuit colleges came from rural estates, known as *haciendas*.

Several of the college hacienda complexes in Mexico, Peru, Ecuador, and Argentina have been studied in depth. At the beginning, and often for several decades, some haciendas did not produce enough income to keep the colleges from operating in the red. Not until the late seventeenth and early eighteenth centuries did the ranches and estates actually produce enough to pay off all debts and provide support for the colleges. In the early years of operation much money was spent on developing the infrastructure of the estate, be it the acquisition of equipment, livestock, slaves, or other necessary items. Early profits were routinely invested back into the operation, so that remittances to the college were small. Furthermore, the Jesuits frequently borrowed large sums of money based on their holdings, and the interest on these loans needed to be paid. Only with time, the decrease in expenses, the increase in production, and the receipts of gifts did the estates begin to be profitable.

One example of the workings of a Jesuit college hacienda complex is the Jesuit College of Quito. This college owned estates that produced agricultural and pastoral goods: cattle, sheep, and the like. The college also owned a woolen mill where the wool from its sheep could be woven into cloth, making the entire operation a well-integrated one. In about 1700 the college owned some ten estates. The production on them probably constituted the single largest commercial agricultural enterprise in the region of Quito: as a whole these estates owned 8,000 head of cattle, just under 90,000 sheep, about 1,200 mules, 1,100 oxen, and several hundred pigs. The expenses of the estates—113,000 pesos—was slightly larger than the income, 103,000 pesos.[15] More than anything else, the estates provided adequate cash flow to keep all other operations running.

The Jesuits were not the only religious order to use rural estates to support their missionary activity. The Benedictines in Brazil supported much of their activity through the production of sugar estates. In 1764 the Benedictines reported a total income of some 25,000 *milreis*; of that 9,735 came from the production of their sugar mills, essentially 40 percent of total income. Unlike the Jesuit estates, the first few decades of the Benedictine operation did see significant income; although the middle decades suffered, income increased again in the late eighteenth century. While sugar and molasses made up 65 percent of the income, the Benedictines also sold tobacco, alcohol, hides, and milk produced on their estates.[16]

The Benedictines and the Jesuits, as well as most other religious orders, owned slaves. While some evidence points toward better treatment of slaves on clerical estates, nonetheless the orders reflected the attitude of their times. On the Jesuit sugar haciendas of coastal Peru the slave population grew from an average of about 100 per estate in the later seventeenth century to 256 in the mid-eighteenth century, a significant increase. Since the birthrate approximated the mortality, slaves were continually being imported to increase the numbers. The Jesuits had slaves on all types of estates, not just sugar plantations. Even the mixed agricultural estates in the Quito region accounted for 1,364 slaves in 1767. On the estate of Santa Lucía in Mexico, an extensive ranching and agricultural property, the Jesuits held a little more than 100 slaves in the later seventeenth century; forty years later that number had increased to nearly 300. Most were domestic slaves working in the housing facilities with domestic duties, such as cooking and cleaning, as well as working in the textile mills associated with the estate. The remainder worked in agriculturally related activities as herders, field slaves, and such.

The Jesuits became one of the leading single landowners in much of colonial Latin America. Their properties included urban and rural real estate. The model they created spread among other religious orders and on a small scale was emulated by many private landowners. Many residents of the Americas concluded correctly that much of the local economy was dominated directly or indirectly by the Church and its various institutions, because of the large number of rural estates, urban real estate, and the large number of mortgages and liens all held by the Church and its institutions.

The Bourbon Reforms

The eighteenth century witnessed major political changes. The Spanish ruling house changed in 1700 with the death of Charles II, the last of the Spanish Hapsburgs. Charles died without an heir, but he had earlier designated a member of the ruling house of France, Phillip, Duke of Anjou, a member of the house of the Bourbon, as his heir. The war that resulted from this odd accession, aptly named the War of the Spanish Succession, became a true "world war" since the English, Dutch, Portuguese, and various German states opposed the choice and fought the French and Spanish. And the Spanish proved successful. The rule of the Bourbons in Spain sought to improve colonial governance, tighten up regulations and tax collection, and generally improve both revenues and defense. In general the Bourbon Reforms as applied to the New World manifested an underlying assumption that in whatever the context, the colony existed to benefit the mother country.

The Church was the object of much of the reform brought about during the eighteenth century. The Royal Patronage had already granted extensive powers to the Spanish monarch over the Church in the New World. Of greatest importance was the power to appoint bishops, archbishops, and members of cathedral chapters. This power effectively converted the ecclesiastical hierarchy into a professional corps of royal servants. As a result of the Ordenanza del Patronazgo, the crown also claimed the right to appoint thousands of local parish priests. While this gave the monarch broad control over the secular clergy, the crown exercised no similar control over the religious orders. The orders operated quite separately from royal control, and only the implementation of the canons and decrees of the Council of Trent in the late sixteenth century began to bring them under the supervision of local bishops, and thereby indirectly under the purview of the monarch.

An important power posited by the monarchs was the *pase regio*, which allowed the monarch to intercept communications between Rome and the New World. No bull, brief, or other papal communication could proceed to the New World without royal permission. Moreover, with this privilege the pope granted to the Spanish monarch the right to hear appeals from ecclesiastical courts in the New World, ostensibly to save time and effort on the part of the appellants. These two considerations effectively required all communications between Rome and the Spanish American Church to go through the Spanish monarch. Although the pope recognized the authority of the monarch to hear appeals, he did not recognize the *pase regio*, but since the bishops were appointed by the king there was little that the pope could actually do.

The royal authorities had very few legitimate means of controlling the religious orders. Yet thanks to the Royal Patronage, no church, monastery, chapel, convent, or other ecclesiastical building could be constructed without permission from the monarch. The crown had already discouraged local governors from handing out land grants to the Church for fear of losing control over more land.

The Bourbon monarchs sought to gain added control over the Church in three important areas. First, they sought to tighten the control over the secular clergy. Second, they sought to gain some administrative authority over the regular clergy, at least to resemble the power they already had over the seculars. And third, the crown sought to benefit from the extensive holdings and capital amassed by the Church as a whole. The endeavor eventually would have dramatic effects on the Church in Hispanic America.

From the early years of the Bourbon monarchy, the crown began to limit the activities of the regulars. The crown first began to exercise privileges in the Patronato that had been generally accepted in the past, such as the right to license new churches and monasteries. In the early 1700s, the crown decreed a moratorium on new convents and monasteries. Following that, it declared a moratorium on the orders accepting new members. If the orders could neither accept new members beyond the numbers needed to replace those members who died nor construct new facilities, the orders could not grow beyond their current size. Since the early colonial period the crown had also reserved the right to allow or prohibit members of religious orders from traveling to the New World, a power exercised by the Bourbon monarchs.

One area in which the crown did not have to overreach its authority under the principle of Patronage was in the appointment of parish priests. As early as 1574 the crown had outlined the process whereby curates would be selected and that all parishes would be administered only by secular priests. It was not until the 1740s that the Bourbon monarchs made secularization a high priority. From this point on, the regular clergy focused their efforts on towns and cities where they already had a presence, as well as continuing their missionary activity on the frontiers. As early as the sixteenth century the crown had prohibited friars from performing marriages or baptisms in their convents, requiring these ceremonies to take place in the parish itself. The canons and decrees of Trent also required members of religious orders to secure licenses from the local bishop in order to administer the sacraments.

Although the secularization program in many ways remained incomplete, especially in very rural or frontier dioceses, such as Oaxaca or Arequipa, in the central regions such as Mexico and Lima it was remarkably effective. The other restrictions placed on the religious orders also had an impact. The oldest and largest province of friars was the Holy Gospel Province of Franciscans in Mexico. In the early eighteenth century it had 840 friars, including 700 professed members and 140 lay brothers. The province also counted 35 parishes and 88 convents. By 1765 the clerical population had declined to 727 religious (630 friars and 97 lay brothers). In 1786 there were 513 friars in 24 monasteries, serving 48 parishes and missions. By the end of the century the order had only two parishes, sixteen large convents, and two houses of recollection.[17]

During the early eighteenth century the crown also instituted a series of formal legal investigations, called visitations, of the religious orders, acting on the claims that many religious lived outside of their vows of celibacy, poverty, and obedience. Each order appointed four visitors, one each for the Philippines, and the viceroyalties of New Spain, New Granada (modern-day Ecuador, Colombia and Venezuela), and Peru. The religious orders in many ways were more willing to submit to closer scrutiny by the crown than to the domination of the local bishop. This was demonstrated through the use by friars of the *recurso de fuerza* increasingly in the eighteenth century. Under this provision of Spanish law, any subject of the crown had a right to due process. If the person believed that he had been denied due process, he could appeal to the *audiencia,* the local royal high court. What was unique about the *recurso de fuerza* on the part of religious is that they enjoyed a particular right to have their cases heard not in the royal courts but in ecclesiastical courts, a right called the *fuero eclesiástico.* By invoking the *recurso de fuerza,* the religious subjected the ecclesiastical court to scrutiny by the royal courts. If the royal court discovered that a violation of due process had indeed occurred in the ecclesiastical proceedings, the remedy included either beginning the process over again in the original court, at a point prior to the violation of due process, and continuing, or transferring the entire proceeding into the royal courts.

While in general the right of the *fuero* allowed those suits in which a cleric was the defendant to be heard in the ecclesiastical courts, there were some exceptions. In cases of treason or lèse-majesté, the cleric had to appear before a royal court. Everything having to do with the appointment of priests to offices under the Royal Patronage also fell to the royal courts, as did cases involving the interpretation of the bulls through which the dioceses were created and cases dealing with the collection of tithes. Since the crown had been granted the right to collect the tithe—a right it donated back to the Church—it withheld jurisdiction over disputes. As part of the Bourbon desire to increase control over the Church, the monarchs increasingly sought to limit the scope of the *fuero,* until in 1812 the Spanish government abolished it altogether.

At the same time that the crown sought to limit the power of the religious orders through their access to the courts, the crown had a concern that the religious orders held too much economic power. Royal theorists held that the orders exercised undue influence over the faithful at the time of making a will. Royal decrees consequently wanted to make the drawing up of a will a civil act, requiring only the presence of a notary and, in fact, forbidding the presence of a friar. In addition, ever since the early seventeenth century there had also been a simmering dispute between the Jesuits and the local bishops over the payment of the tithe on products from ecclesiastical estates, as in the case of Bishop Palafox of Puebla (see chap. 4). This problem was never fully resolved, although in various dioceses at various times a compromise was reached in which the religious order would make a token payment on the productions of the estates. As part of the Bourbon reform program, the monarchs began to place concrete limits on the wealth of the religious orders in particular and the Church in general. By limiting the number of new members and restricting the construction of new convents and monasteries, the monarch exercised a significant control over the growth of the orders.

The Pombaline Reforms

The tension between the religious orders and the monarch is nowhere more clearly manifested than in the conflict that erupted between the Society of Jesus (Jesuits) and the Iberian monarchs. The Jesuit order achieved significant successes in both Portuguese and Spanish America. The order's system of supporting its missionary activities through the production of commercial agricultural estates created a very powerful economic system that operated in every territory of the Americas. The Jesuits had an almost complete monopoly over higher education in the colonies. While other orders, particularly the Dominicans, also had university colleges, the bulk of higher education was in Jesuit hands. As a result , the order enjoyed a close relationship with the highly educated elite of the colonies. The Jesuit order simply ignored the importance of national boundaries. Although all orders tended to operate outside of royal control because of their direct communication to and from Rome, the Jesuits were more emphatic in claiming their exemption. To complicate matters, the Jesuits also tended to ignore national origins in assigning clergy to missions. For example, in the Americas one could find Bohemian, Florentine, or even German Jesuits. This openly violated royal laws restricting travel to the Americas to subjects of the Spanish and Portuguese crowns, respectively. And finally, the Jesuit order was more closely identified with the papacy than other orders, as each priest took a personal oath of fealty to the pope. For all of these reasons, then, the monarchs of Spain and Portugal could imagine that the order constituted a fifth-column within their American holdings.

The central figure of Portuguese reform was Sebastião José de Carvalho e Mello, the Marquis of Pombal. Pombal came from the lower nobility and began his service in the Portuguese diplomatic corps. After studying at the University of Coimbra, he became an ambassador to England and Austria. With the coronation of King José I in 1750, Pombal took on the role of de facto prime minister, but in reality something more like a dictator. Like his counterparts in Spain, Pombal sought to increase royal control over the Portuguese colonies throughout the world. He reorganized royal government in Brazil, added new jurisdictions and officers to govern them, and created a new judiciary in Rio de Janiero, nearer to the population centers of the south. Importantly, he suspended the last of the private captaincies that dated back to the very first decades of Portuguese colonization in Brazil. He actively encouraged emigration into Brazil from the Azores and other regions of the Portuguese empire. The reforms that Pombal imposed on Portugal and the empire are known as the Pombaline reforms.

In a manner similar to that pursued in Spain, he sought to totally subject the Catholic Church in the Portuguese realms to the authority of the crown. Although there had been no tradition of controlling appointments to bishoprics, Pombal insisted on royal intervention. Moreover, he established the crown's right to remove any prelate from a diocese. Pombal also asserted that no religious order could open a new institution without royal permission, and demanded that all parish priests and other local ecclesiastical officials recognize royal supremacy in the interpretation of canon law. Local royal judges were prohibited from consulting canon law and were required to make their decisions based on royal law and local custom. While the Inquisition had never played an active role in Brazil, it did have a major presence in Portugal. Pombal brought it under direct royal supervision as well, using it as an extension of the crown's political authority. He expelled the papal nuncio (equivalent of an ambassador) in 1760, and for the next ten years refused to communicate with the Holy See. Eventually Pope Clement XIV conceded to most of the demands that Pombal had made regarding royal control over the Church.

Pombal attacked the Church along a broad front. As with the Bourbon Reforms in the Spanish realms, under Pombal the chantries were a target of concern. In legislation that sought to reform inheritance laws, Pombal began a process of eliminating chantries by making it nearly impossible to establish new ones. The foundation of new chantries required payment of large sums in taxes to the crown. Pombal sought to limit the authority of the religious orders in Brazil's interior; he favored the secularization of parishes and the appointment of secular clerics. He brought the activities of the religious confraternities under the purview of the royal government. In turn, an empowered secular clergy also sought greater control over chantries and confraternities in their parishes.

The Jesuits vs. the Monarchs

Pombal developed a personal mania regarding the Jesuits. When he gained power, he used the state archives to document what he saw as the pervasive influence of the order over affairs of state. He wrote a three-volume indictment regarding the abuses of the Jesuits in the Portuguese realms, and he insisted that all officials receive a copy and read it. Pombal's own antipathy to the order stimulated other detractors of the Jesuits to become bolder in their accusations against the order. Pombal then moved to expel the order from Portugal and all Portuguese colonies.

Linked to a growing opposition to the Jesuits, the kings of Spain and Portugal both sought to improve the finances of their American colonies as well as improve their political integration. These goals called for more efficiency and tighter central control, according to the thinking of the era. These too played into the hands of the opponents of the Society of Jesus. They argued that the order wanted to undermine the authority of the monarchs, that it had organized uprisings, and that it had come to represent a threat to all monarchs. In response to these and other arguments, first Portugal then Spain expelled the Jesuits from their American colonies.

The expulsion of the Jesuits was dramatic and as close to instantaneous as any royal decree ever implemented. First in Brazil in 1759, then in the Spanish colonies in 1767, the monarchs ordered Jesuit houses and estates confiscated; the individual members of the order were offered the opportunity to renounce their vows and continue in the Americas as secular priests or to go into exile. Nearly all chose exile. The confiscated estates passed to the crowns and were then offered at auction to whomever could afford to buy them. The income on investments fell to the crown. In the case of New Spain, the crown then allocated the funds largely to the Franciscans and Dominicans, who took over the Jesuit missions in the far north and in the Californias. The speed and secrecy with which the order was expelled shocked and surprised everyone. Moreover, it served as a warning to other religious orders that if the Jesuits, the richest and most powerful order, could be suppressed in a single day, then the others had little ability to withstand a direct royal assault on their privileges.

The expulsion of the Jesuits had tremendous repercussions on colonial society. A significant number of the Jesuits were Creoles: locally born members of the order. The expulsion separated them from their families in the Americas. Moreover, as noted, the Jesuits had exercised a near monopoly in higher education. The expulsion created havoc in the education sector as other religious orders sought to fill the void. A whole generation of young men lost an opportunity for higher education as the universities reorganized in the absence of the Jesuits. The impact on the economy was also significant. The Jesuit estates represented some of the largest and most economically viable estates. When the crown offered these estates for sale, there were very few persons of sufficient wealth able to purchase them. Placing all the estates on the market at roughly the same time had the effect of driving down their value. This in turn caused a decrease in land values across the board. Since so many of the private estates carried mortgages and liens, the general decline in value then placed these investments at risk. In addition, land rents declined as more lands became available, causing further disturbances in the local economies.

The Bourbon monarchs of Spain continued to seek greater efficiencies and higher revenues from the American colonies. The expulsion of the Jesuits did provide the crown with an infusion of cash. Nevertheless, financial crises in Spain forced the monarchs to find additional sources of cash and credit. As early as 1797, the crown began to take over the mortgages and other investments managed by the Chantry Court in the peninsular dioceses. The crown then sold the properties and mortgages for cash, securing the original investment with bonds from the royal treasury, called *vales reales*. Although the exchange of the properties and mortgages for bonds was intended as a stopgap measure to generate cash until royal revenues improved, by 1804 and the beginnings of war with Britain the monarch had to not only make the alienation of the mortgages and properties permanent, but he had to pledge the income from the process to outside lenders who were providing ready cash. At this point the crown turned to the New World and recognized that millions of pesos of value were pledged to local chantry courts; thus the process of confiscation of ecclesiastical investments was then extended to the New World.[18]

The alienation of Church wealth in Hispanic America had a tremendous impact on the economies of the colonies. Because the crown demanded the repayment of the mortgages and liens, the process was also known as the amortization. While scholars debate the impact of the program, several aspects stand out. The intrusion of the crown into the pious funds of the New World exhibited a level of central control the colonists had not experienced before. The amortization cast a pall over the economy merely by disrupting people's confidence in the lending institutions of the time. It also called into question the actual value of real estate, and it interfered greatly with the income for priests and others who depended on the payment of interest for their livelihood. In the New World the crown took over the principle of the loans and pledged royal bonds for the payment of interest. One major problem was collecting on the bonds. Within the first five years of the program 2.5 million pesos passed from the Church in the Archdiocese of Mexico into the royal coffers. Yet because the crown was in such a difficult financial situation, many people could not collect the interest on the bonds.

As the Bourbon monarchs continued their efforts to gain further control over the Church, they soon began to look at the power of appointment they already exercised over positions in the secular clergy. This power was so effectively used that the bishops of the eighteenth century tended to be well aligned with royal policies and designs. This is manifested in the canons and decrees of the Fourth Provincial Council of Mexico. The Council of Trent mandated that councils be held in the provinces of the Church on a regular basis, but in Mexico this rule clearly did not have much sway. The Third Provincial Council was held in 1585, two decades after Trent, while the Fourth Council did not occur until 1771. This one consisted of all the bishops from the dioceses within the province of Mexico, what is now Mexico and Central America. In advance of convening the councils, the crown issued a set of guidelines for the assembled bishops to consider. In the case of Mexico, the bishops completely and nearly literally adopted them. So eager were the bishops to support the King that they endorsed various measures the crown had not even proposed, such as excommunication for anyone who opposed the monarch or who failed to show respect for royal decrees.

The eighteenth century in the Americas saw dramatic changes in the Catholic Church in both Hispanic and Portuguese territories. The Church at the beginning of the century was the one institution that received nearly universal respect. It was core to nearly everything that occurred in the colony. It regulated the life cycle of all inhabitants, marking birth, marriage, and death. It was an important social institution because of the various sodalities and confraternities, which organized celebrations and charity. It served as the principle source of credit, both for individuals and for businesses, by accepting endowments and then lending the funds in the form of liens and mortgages. It was one of the leading landowners. The Jesuits represented an experiment in developing commercial agriculture, which would enhance regional commercial activity. Nearly every elite family had at least one child in the secular clergy or religious orders. The sons of the elite were educated at Jesuit and Dominican colleges. And finally, the crown itself viewed the Church as an extension of royal authority. Every village and town throughout the empire had a church and a visiting priest. In short, the Church and the institutions it represented were the very fabric of colonial life.

In rural villages with significant native populations, the Bourbon Reforms had less of an immediate impact. Nevertheless, there was great turmoil. The secularization, the removal of religious orders from rural parishes and replacing them with secular, or diocesan, clergy deeply affected villages where it occurred. The alienation of Church wealth, the expulsion of the Jesuits, and the amortization of Church-held mortgages caused serious disruptions in the rural areas because so many depended on various estates for their livelihood. In many villages these two actions of the Bourbons created a great deal of hostility since it affect two of the most crucial aspects of their daily life: their spiritual life, and their livelihood. Villages also had come to take some control of their own spiritual lives as confraternities continued to play an important role in the social and political fabric of the rural areas. The Bourbon Reforms threatened some of the financial underpinnings of the confraternities, which inserted yet more uncertainty into native communities. Moreover, the Church itself also sought to bring confraternities more directly under its control, all of which angered and frustrated native villagers. In many regions, parish priests began to make increasing demands on their native parishioners to pay for services. The crown now stepped away from its direct support of parish priests, leaving the Church to rely more heavily on the tithe and on payments made by parishioners for services, which interjected tension into village life. In short, natives continued to play an active role in the development of the Church, especially in rural areas.

By the end of the eighteenth century the Church was under attack on a broad front by the crown. Its properties were threatened, its investments were confiscated. The most powerful order of all, the Jesuits, had been abolished, and its members forced to emigrate. The other religious orders could no longer accept new members, nor they could not accept new endowments or build new facilities. The secular clergy became, in essence, just another royal bureaucracy. Individual clerics lost the right to have their legal suits heard in ecclesiastical courts. Even something as intimate as ministering to the sick and dying was under close scrutiny by royal officials. The prestige that the Church had enjoyed for centuries was under attack. Some clerics responded by seeking to ameliorate the conditions and cooperate with royal officials; some simply did not take a position, while others saw the mandates of the crown as actions to be opposed, possibly with violence.

The first decades of the nineteenth century would witness a series of events in Spain that had deep repercussions in the New World. In the wake of the French Revolution, Napoleon Bonaparte would seek to extend his rule over most of Europe, targeting the Iberian Peninsula as one of his first goals. In the wake of the Napoleonic invasion of the Iberian Peninsula, the Spanish and Portuguese territories of the New World would be forced to come to grips with resolving the question of what constitutes legitimate authority in the absence of the monarch.

6

The Church and Clergy in the Time of Independence

Early in the morning of September 16, 1810, Father Miguel Hidalgo y Costilla climbed the stairs of his parish church of Dolores in the region of Querétaro, some three hundred miles northwest of Mexico City. Nearly every morning he rang the bells in the tower in order to call the faithful to prayers. But his concern that morning was political, not spiritual. Hidalgo was a member of a local reading group, made up of other Creoles who were interested in all the political and philosophical movements in Europe. This group had become increasingly opposed to the Spanish government of the colony and had begun to stockpile arms in order to lead a rebellion. Although sworn to secrecy, one of the members of the group had inadvertently spoken of their plans to a local postal official, who in turn had reported the conspiracy to the royal officials in Mexico City. Arrest warrants had been issued for the ring leaders, including Hidalgo, Ignacio de Allende, a captain in a local military regiment, and Juan de Aldama, also a military officer. Aldama had ridden through the night from the city of Querétaro to Dolores to warn Hidalgo. The priest had then resolved that in the face of his imminent arrest, he should launch the rebellion sooner rather than later.

Father Hidalgo rang the church bells and waited for his flock to gather. As they did, he began to preach his political sermon against Spanish dominion in the colony. While no one copied his words that morning, many people subsequently reconstructed his speech. His parishioners, consisting mostly of natives and mestizos, had suffered for years under the burdens of the colonial system. Relegated as they were to second-class status, they were burdened by taxes and tribute and excluded from power. Father Hidalgo ended his speech with a battle cry: "Long live our Lady the Virgin of Guadalupe! Death to bad government! Death to the *gachupines*! (a deprecatory term for peninsular Spaniards)" Hidalgo's speech about liberty and freedom from oppression resonated with his parishioners, and within a few hours he had a band of devoted followers ready to overturn the colonial regime.

This event marked the beginning of the rebellion that would ultimately bring about the fall of royal government in Mexico. What is interesting is that the father of Mexican independence was a priest. Many of the other leaders of the independence movement in Mexico, and throughout Latin American, were also priests. These men were attracted to the rebellion for several reasons: They believed that the Church had suffered mightily as a result of the reforms implemented by the Bourbons; they had seen their own social and political power and prestige wane as a result; they were generally better educated than the broad cross-section of society, and certainly more aware of the intellectual currents buffeting Europe.; and they were aware of the Enlightenment, had read many of the best-known authors and, while they were far from being revolutionaries themselves, could support a less authoritarian political system, especially a government located so far away.

In the late eighteenth century, the Spanish and Portuguese crowns engaged in a series of actions designed to gain greater control over many aspects of the Catholic Church. This effort was consistent with other governmental changes generally considered under the heading of the Bourbon Reforms for Spain and the Pombaline Reforms for Portugal (see chap. 5). In the political, economic, and social realms the crowns moved to establish a greater degree of control over affairs of the Indies. These reforms resulted from the application of a political theory that held that the overseas colonies needed to serve to the needs of the mother country. The unanticipated effect of the reforms was to create dissatisfaction among certain members of the elite in the New World. Particularly negatively affected were those individuals who had gained power in the seventeenth century thanks to crown policies in both Spain and Portugal, which fostered a degree of self-sufficiency in the colonies. This encouragement of self-sufficiency responded to the reality that communications were difficult at best and that loyal and competent local elites could better represent the larger interests of the crown.

At the same time that the European crowns were increasing direct control over the affairs of the Indies in the eighteenth century, the ideologies of the Enlightenment were beginning to find their way into the Americas. Although the Catholic Church prohibited the publication and dissemination of the works of many of the Enlightenment authors, these ideas, nevertheless, made their way into the New World, and were taught and discussed in the universities and colleges of the Americas. The result was that in the Americas leading intellectuals and elites understood the implications of the various reforms both in the context of European political ideologies as well as in terms of the practical implications on their lives. While the imperial governments sought to control the extreme versions of many of these ideologies, there was still a broad range of ideas that were tolerated, although certainly not encouraged.

Enlightenment thought also had an effect on the devotional life of many people. The new way of thinking tended to favor a more personal, inward devotion and less of the more public, collective devotion manifested in the Baroque era, with its religious processions, ornate altars, and large complicated public rituals. Many practices were viewed with a new scientific awareness. Among these, burial practices received much scrutiny. In particular the custom of burying the dead within the confines of the church, or even in a churchyard, was seen as unhygienic, especially in an urban context. Reformers called for the creation of dedicated cemeteries outside the confines of the city. This would prevent the spread of disease associated with dead bodies, while creating a space dedicated to burials.

By the early eighteenth century Enlightenment thought had triggered two powerful political debates. One focused on the local implications of the imperial reforms. Groups who had either benefited or been injured by the reforms confronted the principles and implications of the reforms. The other political debate engaged persons who supported the ideas of the Enlightenment, as opposed to the supporters of the traditional ways of thinking. The latter were highly influenced by the traditional teachings of the Catholic Church.

These various debates eventually came to illuminate the response to an important event, which shattered the relationship between the Iberian kingdoms and their colonies. In 1808 Napoleon Bonaparte invaded the Iberian Peninsula. The two Iberian crowns responded differently to the invasion and threat to their authority. The Spanish monarch and crown prince were placed under house arrest by the French and eventually forced to abdicate in favor of Napoleon's brother, Joseph, who was, in turn, proclaimed king of Spain. In the case of the Portuguese, the ruling family opted to flee their country, traveling to Brazil where they ruled their empire in a type of self-imposed exile.

Brazil

The Portuguese experience in Brazil was unique in Western history up to that point. A war in the homeland had forced the ruling family to flee into exile to a colony. While Brazil was a rich and populous territory, even its finest cities could not compare to Lisbon. The royal family and courtiers arrived in Salvador da Bahia and were shocked by what they found—a relatively poor provincial capital. Eventually the court moved to Rio de Janeiro and governed the empire from there, although Rio too was far less opulent than Lisbon. For the Brazilian colonists this was an extraordinary series of events. Rather than being governed by a monarch many thousands of miles away, now the colony not just hosted the monarch, they had to pay for the support and upkeep of the court. Even prior to the arrival of the court, many Brazilians had chaffed at the levels of taxation. In 1789 there was a revolt in Minas Gerais, the very important and rich mining district. While couched in terms of liberty against oppression, the revolt was actually in response to more efficient tax collection. At the same time, there was great popular support for the monarchy, especially because of local pride at hosting the court during the period of instability. For many, the arrival of the court offered employment. The number of persons associated with the court expanded rapidly once it was established in Rio, increasing local employment opportunities. Clerics accounted for a goodly part of this increase.

The presence of the Portuguese court in Brazil was thanks to the British, who for centuries had maintained cordial relations with Portugal. During the exile in Brazil, the Portuguese crown allowed for greater free trade with Brazilian ports, especially with British-flag shipping. While in Brazil, the Portuguese monarch maintained a highly centralized system of government, much to the chagrin of many regional oligarchs who had assumed a fairly wide range of local powers. This created a certain degree of tension in the colony. For the Church, too, the presence of the monarch was a mixed blessing. Although royal largess did provide funding for church construction and other pious activities, the bishops and other high churchmen were also under much closer scrutiny than ever before, by a monarch who continued in the Pombaline tradition of greater royal control over the Church.

With the expulsion of the French from Portugal in 1814, the Portuguese crown faced a decision as to when to return, if ever, to Lisbon. In preparation, the king declared Brazil to be a full kingdom, on a par politically with Portugal itself. By 1820 the political situation in the mother country had become critical. Following on the heels of a similar uprising in Spain, opponents of the crown had taken over the Portuguese government and proclaimed a republic. King João IV needed to return to Portugal to put down the uprising and assert royal control. At the same time, he feared the loss of the largest colony should he return to Portugal. As a result, he gave permission to his eldest son, Dom Pedro, to declare Brazilian independence, if need be, in order to keep it as closely tied as possible to the mother country, although he swore to uphold the monarchy and the integration of the Portuguese state. Young Pedro, then, remained in Brazil. João's fears proved to be well founded. The political situation in Brazil became increasingly tense. Cries for complete independence increased, as neighboring Spanish colonies broke from their mother country. In 1822, the young prince declared his intention to remain in Brazil and govern it as an independent kingdom, thus bringing about Brazilian independence.[1]

Hispanic America

The colonial response to the Napoleonic invasion of the Iberian Peninsula was by no means uniform. Clearly in the case of Brazil, the colonists gained a monarch in their midst rather than one living an ocean voyage away. In the Hispanic colonies the local authorities had to resolve the basic question: What constituted legitimate authority in the absence of the monarch? Both local officials and the imperial authorities had to decide if they would recognize the French claims to the Spanish crown or reject them. If they rejected the French claims, then two other options arose: (1) they could somehow rule their regions in the name of and for the benefit of the imprisoned Spanish monarch, or (2) they could take the first steps toward loosening or cutting their ties to the metropolis.

Each of the Spanish territories responded slightly differently to the situation, but in general there were two responses. By and large, no region embraced the French government, which was seen as lacking any legal authority and merely a puppet regime of Napoleon. Beyond that, the areas with the greatest history of imperial authority and the highest density of government officials tended to remain loyal to the imprisoned Spanish monarch and crown prince, Charles IV and Ferdinand VII, respectively. Consequently, in both Mexico and Peru the viceregal governments continued to exercise their authority in the name of the monarch. Soon a government protecting the interests of Charles and Ferdinand was established in Cádiz, on the Iberian Peninsula, to continue to direct the Spanish empire and those regions of the peninsula that remained loyal to the Spanish king.

In some regions of the Americas, especially those more distant from the imperial capitals, with a briefer history of imperial authority and more accustomed to local control, there were preliminary efforts to loosen ties with the metropolis. In particular in the regions surrounding Buenos Aires, Santiago de Chile, and Caracas some local governments and some colonists began to embrace a more independent attitude with regard to the imperial authority. One such response was to declare a conditional independence while respecting the authority of the monarch. In essence, these governments and individuals manifested the idea that in the absence of legitimate royal authority, power reverted to the local level, particularly local municipal councils, and other constituent assemblies. These then, ignored higher levels of the bureaucracy and governed locally but in the name of and under the nominal authority of the crown. The local councils began to communicate among themselves and to initiate contacts with foreign powers as they sought to develop their own authority. In these instances, the political and economic desires of the local elites found Enlightenment ideas to provide them with a political ideology to justify loosening their ties to the monarch.

In the core imperial areas, such as Mexico and Peru, while some intellectuals and elites embraced the Enlightenment, the imperial authorities did not and thus pursued a program of maintaining the status quo. Nevertheless, there were pockets of resistance to this course of action. As we have seen, in Mexico, Father Miguel Hidalgo launched a revolt against the imperial authorities. While the rebellion espoused many Enlightenment principles, the movement at the same time proclaimed the authority of the imprisoned Spanish monarch. It quickly became a mass uprising, attracting a large following among the native peoples and persons of mixed racial heritage. The rabble army grew so quickly that it caused great fear among the ruling elite. When the army failed to launch a final attack on Mexico City, imperial forces gained the upper hand and crushed the revolt. While the leaders were captured and executed, many followers remained and would launch an on-again-off-again insurgency for the next decade. Key among the demands made by Hidalgo was a restoration of the power and authority to the Church and clergy, which he believed to have been diminished by the Bourbon monarchs of Spain

In the region surrounding Buenos Aires, the movement for independence was fairly linear, from the early town council proclaiming independence but loyalty to the monarch, to a clearer rejection of ties to the mother country, to out-and-out independence, all within about a ten-year period. The path in Chile was not so simple. There was an early break, like that in Argentina, but royal authority was reestablished and the leaders of the early independence movement were forced to flee over the Andes to Argentina. Only later did they join with the Argentine independence supporters and return to gain Chilean independence militarily. A similar series of events occurred in Venezuela, where an early attempt at independence was quashed, only to have the leaders return to establish independence militarily.

While one might consider these developments to reflect the simple ebb and flow of forces on the scene in each colony, this is only part of the picture. The colonists in Hispanic America responded as much to developments on the Iberian Peninsula as they did to events in their local area. Following the arrest by the French and forced abdication of Charles IV, the Spanish court retreated to Cádiz and set up a government to rival that of Joseph Bonaparte. By 1812 the government had convened a constitutional congress to govern Spain and the empire in the absence of the monarch. This assembly drafted a constitution that reflected many of the Enlightenment ideals of the time and called for a constitutional monarchy and a general liberalization of the empire, allowing a modicum of local control, along with a parliamentary system of government for the whole empire. It did not, however, roll back the various restrictions that the Bourbon monarchs had placed on the Church.

This constitution was embraced by many of the allies of Spain in the war against Napoleon, particularly by England. The efforts of the Spanish resistance fighters—known by the name of "guerilla fighters"—along with their English allies, forced the French out and brought about the restoration of the Bourbon monarchy in the person of Ferdinand VII. One of the conditions imposed on Ferdinand by the British was the acceptance of the Constitution of Cádiz. Once the British troops had left the peninsula and Ferdinand began to rule on his own, he repudiated the constitution. This brought about an inevitable backlash from the supporters of the constitution. In 1820 Ferdinand was deposed by a republican uprising that sought to create a government that manifested Enlightenment ideals, not unlike that of the United States. Opponents to the royal government were known as republicans or liberals; the supporters of the regime were called royalists or conservatives.

Each of these changes in the political fortunes in Spain had repercussions in the New World. When the liberals in Spain gained ascendancy, more conservative elements in the colonies began to question the value of maintaining close ties to the mother country. When more conservative elements in Spain gained the upper hand, liberal elements in the New World reacted by calling for greater freedoms and less centralized control. In general the conservative elements, particularly the landed elites, the representatives of the upper clergy, royal government officials, and merchants tied into the royally sanctioned trade, were unwilling to cut ties to Spain. On the other hand, more liberal groups, the lower clergy, merchants who had lost economic power with the Bourbon Reforms, and many regional elites and landowners favored either loose ties with Spain or independence. After 1820, all of these groups began to find consensus in independence from Spain. The liberals had always favored loose or no ties to Spain and saw opportunities for themselves in a more free and open society and economy. The conservative groups favored a continuation of the status quo from before the Napoleonic invasion of Spain, under which situation they enjoyed primacy in the social and economic systems. With the rise of the liberals in Spain and their desire to open both society and the economy, the colonial elites who had favored close ties to Spain saw that the regime there was no longer sympathetic to their goals, and so eventually found common cause with the colonial liberals. While the two groups differed radically on the ultimate type of society and economy they envisioned, in the interim they could agree on independence.

The particular path to independence varied dramatically from country to country and from region to region. In Mexico, we saw how Father Miguel Hidalgo instituted a popular revolt. The revolt consisted of many native peoples, mestizos, and other persons of color but with a leadership that generally came from among the ranks of the Spanish and Creoles. The threat of social upheaval manifested by the large wave of popular support mounted by Hidalgo carried the seeds of its own destruction. The Creole elites of Mexico feared a popular uprising like one that had occurred in Haiti when thousands of slaves rose up and slaughtered their owners. As a result the Creole elites, both in the provinces and in central Mexico, opposed the Hidalgo movement and successfully sought to destroy it. After Hidalgo was captured and executed, the mantle of leadership of the movement passed to another priest, Father José María Morelos. Morelos furthered the movement and sought to institutionalize it. He convoked the first constitutional convention in Mexico in 1814, crafting a document that granted autonomy to the Church and political equality to the different races and social groups.

Upon the arrest and execution of Morelos, the movement fragmented. Guerrilla movements developed along the two major trade routes from the coasts to Mexico City, one astride the Veracruz road, the other toward Acapulco. Finally in 1821, an army of royal troops led by Agustín de Iturbide, a Spanish officer, sallied forth to put an end to the revolts once and for all. It engaged the guerrilla army led by rebel leader Vicente Guerrero along the road to Acapulco. After several months of skirmishes, the two leaders met and, in a surprising turn-around, jointly declared Mexican independence under the Plan of Three Guarantees. These included the guarantee of independence, the guarantee of union (recognizing equality of peninsular Spaniards and Creoles), and the guarantee of religion (that the Catholic Church would remain central to the nation). This action brought about independence. There were hopes among some that a democratic republic would ensue, but Iturbide eventually became emperor of a newly independent kingdom of Mexico. While this turn of events was supported by the more conservative members of the independence coalition, the more liberal members vehemently opposed it. Iturbide could not effectively govern, and was eventually forced to abdicate and flee Mexico, ushering in a period of liberal ascendancy.[2]

The Church played a key role in the political maneuvering. The lower clergy, represented by men such as Morelos and Hidalgo, favored independence and a more republican form of government. The upper clergy, members of the cathedral chapters and bishops, supported a more conservative approach of a constitutional monarchy.

Argentina and Venezuela

In Argentina and Venezuela, the process toward independence differed greatly from the pattern in Mexico. In Argentina, colonists demonstrated little support for the crown. In the years immediately prior to the Napoleonic invasion of Spain, British forces had attempted to take over Buenos Aires. In the absence of a large garrison of Spanish troops, local militias had to do most of the fighting. Sentiments toward the royal government were also diminished when the viceregal court withdrew from the city during the attempted invasion, thus leaving the colonists to fend for themselves, which created a certain sense of autonomy among the colonists. Furthermore, for two centuries the colony had been largely overlooked by the crown. Although located on the east coast of South America, for scores of years it had been governed from Lima, Peru, on the west coast. The Spanish imperial economic system dictated that goods to and from the colony be shipped through Callao, Lima's port. The cost of shipping goods overland, across the Andes, and then to Argentina was immense. The colony, necessarily, came to depend on "back door" approaches, trading with passing ships regardless of flag. In the late eighteenth century, the region was made a new viceroyalty and became the center of its own sphere of influence. Direct trade with Spain was also permitted, but this merely served to alienate many of the older merchants who had become prosperous under the clandestine trading system. As a result of all of this, sentiments in the colony regarding a continued relationship with Spain were quite mixed.

When news arrived of the French invasion of Spain, the Creoles of Buenos Aires began a process that would lead inexorably toward independence. First they created a local government to uphold the rights and interests of the deposed Ferdinand VII. The clergy of the territory embraced this effort, allowing them to move toward independence while ostensibly remaining loyal to the crown. Eventually that government became more autonomous, until by 1813 it was independent for all intents and purposes, although a formal declaration did not occur until 1816. The Church was not comfortable with this declaration. Foremost in the minds of the bishops was the question of who would exercise ultimate control over the Church. They wondered if the old Royal Patronage would dissolve or be embraced by the new government. One of the immediate repercussions of Argentine independence was a disintegration of the territorial integrity of the old viceroyalty. Upper Peru, which would become Bolivia, first revolted, then rejoined, then eventually fell back into Spanish royal control. The eastern shore of the Rio de la Plata, modern Uruguay, also rebelled in an attempt at autonomy but was forcibly brought back, only to gain independence in 1828. Paraguay also sought autonomy and after several battles gained it but then became an isolated, insular nation, led by one of the region's first dictators, Dr. José Rodríguez de Francia. The revolts of Paraguay, Uruguay, and Bolivia manifested the deep regional differences that existed and also foreshadowed the tensions in Argentina that would develop between centralists and federalists. Independence in Argentina came relatively easily, and certainly earlier than in most of the other countries of South America. All of these political changes had an extremely deleterious effect on the Church, since individual dioceses could be divided between two different countries, as the various provinces declared independence. And finally, as ecclesiastical offices became vacant, such as seats on the cathedral chapter, it was not entirely clear who had the authority to fill them.

The movement for independence in Venezuela ostensibly had much in common with Argentina. It too was an isolated colony, far from a center of viceregal power. It had been administered from Santo Domingo and then later from Bogotá. It had a long experience with contraband trade, but lay near the major Spanish trade routes. For a brief time commerce to the region was controlled by a joint stock company based in the Spanish Basque country: the Caracas Company (*Compañía Real Guipuzcoana de Caracas*). As in Argentina, upon arrival of the news of the French invasion of Spain, the local Creole elite seized control of the government, proclaiming their support for the Spanish monarch. Many loyalists, sensing the political tide, fled to Cuba and Puerto Rico. When independence was actually won in 1811, fighting broke out. An earthquake did tremendous damage to the regions controlled by the rebels, but left the loyalists largely unscathed. Loyalist clergy preached that the earthquake was a sign of divine anger at the rebels and support for the crown. When reinforcements arrived from the Spanish controlled islands, the rebels were defeated.

Many of the rebels fled to the Venezuelan hinterland, others to sympathetic ports in the Caribbean. Leadership of the rebels began to coalesce around a former royal officer turned rebel, Simón Bolívar. From his exile in Jamaica, Bolívar wrote to the dispersed rebel leaders analyzing the political situation and calling for unified efforts to expel the Spanish. He moved his operations to the Venezuelan coast and eventually made headway in the rich agricultural region of the Orinoco called the *llanos*. Rather than attack the main Spanish army near Caracas, he led his troops on an arduous overland crossing of the Andes into what is now Colombia and first took Bogota. Buoyed by this success, he then turned and drove toward Caracas. Allies still in the *llanos* drove northward and together they took the city. This assault occurred in 1820 against the backdrop of political unrest in Spain, which further undermined the royal presence in the New World. Bolívar then returned to Colombia and began his campaign southwards. The Venezuelan clergy tended to divide as did the clergy in most other regions: the local parish priests and members of religious orders were far more likely to support independence than were the members of the upper clergy.[3]

Chile and Perú

In Chile, an early attempt at Independence, led by Bernardo O'Higgins, son of a former colonial governor, had failed. By the eighteenth century, there were many bureaucrats of English and Irish origin in the Spanish imperial service. In Britain, Catholics were prohibited from attending colleges and universities. Starting the in the sixteenth century, many Spanish universities established colleges for the English and Irish. Many of the graduates went into royal service, such as Bernardo's father, Ambrosio O'Higgins. With the success of independence in Argentina, an army of Argentines and Chileans marched over the Andes in 1817, led by the military leader of Argentina, José de San Martín, and took Chile for the cause of independence. In 1820, San Martín, assisted by a British admiral, Lord Cochrane, led a successful assault on Lima and Callao, taking the viceregal capital of Lima in 1821. San Martín and Bolívar met in Guayaquil in 1822 to evaluate the course of the independence movement in South America. San Martín withdrew his bid for leadership and eventually sailed off to exile in Europe. This came as a great surprise to all involved, since San Martin was in a position to claim sole leadership of the independence movement in South America. It seems that he withdrew so that there would be no possible rivalry for the leadership, thus ceding the command to Bolívar. Bolívar then led the combined forces in the final campaigns of independence in Upper Peru that ended in 1824. The Church in Peru, Bolivia, and Chile took a very critical view of the independence movements. While a few members of the lower clergy were passionate supporters, by and large both secular and regular clergy opposed any change to the political relationship with Spain. This opposition would be critical as these two countries attempted to create constitutions and develop republican values.

Brazil

In Brazil, independence came through the rebellion of the crown prince Dom Pedro, who had been left behind in the colony following his family's return to Portugal. Yet Dom Pedro was to rule for only nine years and provided Brazil with a transition from colony to a truly independent monarchy. While fervent in his support for Brazilian independence, Dom Pedro would eventually return to Portugal to press his own claims to that throne. While he convened the first constitutional convention, he remained an absolutist monarch. And while he helped to establish the first representative government in Brazil, he also dissolved it and ruled by decree. With regard to the Church, however, his rule was more stable.

The political transition in Brazil allowed for stability for the Church. The Church in Brazil under Pedro differed little from previous periods. As the heir of the monarch, Pedro exercised the Royal Patronage over the Brazilian Church. Dom Pedro continued to appoint Portuguese rather than native Brazilians to high offices in the Church and royal government. The great liability of the new regime was its poverty. Dom João had taken most of the funds in the royal coffers when he returned to Portugal, so Dom Pedro found a largely bankrupt treasury. This in turn limited his ability to fund the Church, and increased his willingness to see the Church as a source of income. The Church itself, as with society at large, consisted of those who sought a more representational government and those who preferred an absolutist monarch. In addition, the country was divided between those who preferred some sort of regional autonomy and those who saw centralism as the best political structure. The far northern regions, along the Amazon and Atlantic coast, continually pressed for more regional autonomy, partially because communication was extremely difficult with Rio. Similarly, residents in the far south, neighboring Spanish-dominated lands, also preferred some sort of regional self-determination. In general those who supported regional aspirations tended to be supporters of a republican form of government, while those who were centralists tended to favor the monarchy.

Pedro's ecclesiastical policies, while not differing greatly from his father and other Portuguese monarchs, increasingly ran counter to the trend in the Vatican, which sought to create a more centralized Church where the pope retained the authority to appoint bishops and other high clerics. Although Pedro's government received the recognition of the Vatican in 1823, it was soon clear that the issue of patronage would become a stumbling block to continued good relations between the new Brazilian government and the Vatican.

Popular Religion at Independence

The questions raised in Brazil concerning the relationship of the state to the Church would at one time or another be confronted in each of the former Spanish colonies. Yet while political issues played a crucial role in the transition from colonial to national status in the Americas, religious practice was also undergoing a dramatic change. For most of Latin America, public displays of religious sentiment were commonplace. The festivals of the Church provided the society with a cycle of celebrations throughout the year. These were marked by different specific celebrations, which usually involved many of the faithful. Parades and processions served not only to celebrate a particular feast but also to provide a physical embodiment of the social and religious hierarchy. Many people belonged to religious sodalities and confraternities that further served as a small group within which to build a personal spirituality and to provide them with an identity in the larger society.

Confraternities and sodalities also provided a framework around which society at large was organized as part of a corporate social structure. In this corporate social structure a person's identity was defined in terms of what that person did and which social groups he or she belonged, rather than through race and ethnicity, on the one hand, or through social status and rank on the other. Yet the corporate structure did not supplant or replace the status and racial systems but rather complemented them. Religious sodalities tended to be created along racial and status lines, and also reflected professional and occupational categories. For example, the Congregation of Saint Peter was a sodality exclusively for secular priests. Since the priesthood in general was limited to males of European origin, no natives or mixed groups could join. Similarly, a sodality for silversmiths would also manifest a largely European membership. A sodality for muleteers, however, would have a very different composition, including low-status persons of European origin, as well as people of mixed racial background, a few free blacks, and wealthier natives. Additionally, in the eighteenth century many sodalities began to take on the character of a guild. As craftsmen began to join together in religious devotions, they also used the sodality to reinforce their professional ties. Increasingly, sodality members worked together not just for the celebration of the patronal feast or for other spiritual aims, but also to support their particular craft or trade.

As in the case of sodalities, religious practices responded to local pressures. Local politics also were crucial to the particulars of the manner in which independence was achieved in any particular area. In New Spain (which corresponds to Central America and Mexico, including the southwestern part of the United States), the break from Spain occurred more like a coup d'état with the leader of the royal army striking an agreement with the leader of the insurgents in which both agreed to independence from Spain and the beginnings of a constitutional state. In South America, the final break occurred as a result of a war that had insurgents from Venezuela and Argentina slowly gaining support from their neighbors as the rebel army moved from the geographical extremes of the continent to converge on Peru and Bolivia. While there were battles, in the end, the royalists in South America lost the broad support of the Creole elites. Without this support, even armies could not keep the colonies tied to the mother country.

Conservatives vs. Liberals

Independence in the Spanish American colonies came through an alliance of a wide variety of political movements that were in reality very different from each other. Some supported extreme social changes such as the abolition of slavery, the equality of native peoples with Spaniards and those of European descent, and opponents to the centrality of the Church. Some were in reality archconservative, seeking to reestablish a social and political system not unlike that of the seventeenth century, before the implementation of the Bourbon Reforms. In each country and region of Hispanic America, these different factions represented larger or smaller segments of the political spectrum. But what was common throughout the region was that each country had to come to grips with opposing political constituencies in order to create a functioning government. While many other issues confronted the early leaders, one issue took center stage in nearly every country—the role of the Catholic Church in the nation-state.[4]

Central to this role was the relationship between the Church and the newly independent government. In general, two guiding political philosophies emerged. One held that the Church and state should be strictly separated: the Church should control ecclesiastical affairs and the state would not meddle; neither would the Church meddle in affairs of state. Adherents to this philosophy looked at the example of the separation of church and state in the United States as a model. The other political philosophy held that the nation-state was the legitimate heir of the Spanish crown. The crown had exercised control over the Church through the Royal Patronage, and the new nation, as heir, would continue to exercise a national patronage over the Church. The papacy complicated this model, by insisting that the new states needed to negotiate a legal relationship with it in order to enjoy such patronage. Several nations did enter into such negotiations, reaching agreements, known as concordats, which outlined the rights and privileges of the nation *vis à vis* the papacy. These negotiations were long and complex, and most of the agreements did not become reality until the last quarter of the nineteenth century. In the meantime, the governments would routinely forward recommendations for episcopal appointments to the pope. In some instances civil governments also attempted to remove bishops from office, but in general the most they could accomplish was to remove the bishop physically from his territory, placing him in exile, either internal or external. The papacy reserved the right to remove bishops from the service of their office.

Looking at the issue another way, there were two major political philosophies that dominated Latin American politics through most of the nineteenth century, and each had a strong opinion regarding the role of the Church in society. The conservatives held that the Church should retain its role in all aspects of society: it should continue to be the institution in charge of supervising the key moments in a person's life, birth, marriage, death; continue to collect its tax, the tithe, to support its good works; continue to manage public education; continue to hold property, including both urban and rural properties for rent or exploitation, to further the good ends of the Church; and finally, continue to exercise a banking function in loaning out capital. In short, the conservatives wished to restore the Church to the position of authority it enjoyed in the seventeenth century.

The other major political philosophy of Latin America in the nineteenth century was liberalism. The philosophies of the Enlightenment heavily imbued liberal thinking. Liberals looked to constitutional democracies as their models, particularly the principles of the French Revolution and the practical application of these in the Constitution of the United States. Liberals did not believe that the Church should play a central role in the political and economic life of the nation. They sought to create a civil registry of births, marriages, and deaths to wrest control over these life passages from the Church; they also sought to abolish the tithe. If individual believers wished to donate a percentage of their income to the Church, well and good, but the state should not act as a collection agency. Liberals sought to strip the Church of its extensive land holdings. They believed that the effect of having large portions of land held by the Church acted as a restraint on economic development and felt that the land needed to enter into the public marketplace and not be protected from taxation or other state control. Similarly, the liberals believed that by controlling a large portion of the capital available for loans the Church restricted the economic development of the nation, and so they sought to continue the amortization policies of the Bourbons whereby long-standing mortgages and liens were called in and exchanged for bonds on the national treasury.

While logic might dictate that the conservatives would strongly support the idea that the nation-state was the heir to the Royal Patronage, and the liberals would demand the abolition of anything similar to a national patronage, in reality the two did not always support those contentions. Many conservatives, cognizant of the changing political tides, felt that the best way to protect the Church was to create a wall between Church and state. Conservatives might not always dominate, and in the event that the liberals took control, the conservatives wished to protect the Church from their intrusion and meddling. While the liberals generally supported the complete separation of Church and state, in order to achieve some of the more radical elements of their program they needed to have direct control over the Church itself. Using a national patronage to appoint sympathetic bishops and other clerics was a shrewd political move. Consequently, in some instances conservatives sought the separation of Church and state, while some liberals sought the continuation of the national patronage.

The Church was not, however, a single, monolithic institution in the midst of all this. There were deep divisions between the regular clergy and the secular clergy, between the upper clergy and the lower clergy. During the wars of independence it was not at all unusual to find different clergymen in all of the various factions. In general, though, the upper clergy and the regular clergy tended to support either continued ties to Spain or a conservative national government. These groups, in spite of the vicissitudes suffered during the Bourbon Reforms, depended to a large degree on the political system imposed by the Spanish crown. The crown had supported the Church for a very long time, and the members of religious orders and upper clergy assumed that it would continue to do so. The Spanish state also provided political stability in the midst of changing times, and this was seen as an advantage. Nevertheless, a few leading bishops and archbishops felt that the Spanish government had become too undependable.

The Napoleonic invasion and the ensuing political disruptions demonstrated clearly that the Church could no longer depend on the Spanish state for support. Many ecclesiastical authorities concluded that the Church would have better success regaining its power and authority in an independent, conservative nation rather than under any number of well-meaning Spanish regimes. The lower clergy, in particular, saw benefits in the Bourbon Reforms and were more heavily influenced by the thoughts of the Enlightenment. Less power for the Church did not necessarily translate into less privilege for the lower clergy. Since the clergy were some of the few representatives of the Spanish state in rural Latin America, less central control translated into more local control. Under an independent government, the local clergy had just as much political strength as any other political faction and might be able to secure a comfortable modus vivendi. Many were truly committed to social change, as espoused in the French Revolution. They wholeheartedly embraced the ideals of *liberté, egalité, fraternité*.

The first national governments spawned by the independence movements were, in general, dominated more by liberals than conservatives. This dynamic occurred in all likelihood because liberals had been in opposition to Spanish rule for a longer time, were better organized, and had a clearer agenda that they wished to accomplish. As a result, the first constitutions written in Latin America tended to manifest liberal philosophies. They called for the separation of Church and state, and the abolition of titles of nobility, slavery, the tithe, and other institutions closely associated with the old regime. The liberal constitutions called for public education, the creation of a system of civil registry, representative governments, and the lifting of restraints on trade, such as monopolies enjoyed by merchants' guilds. In most of the Hispanic American republics, the early liberal constitutions also called for a federal system of government. The elites of the peripheries had suffered more from the Bourbon Reforms than had those of the central regions, and the local elites outside of the capital regions sought to redress this situation by granting themselves a modicum of autonomy under a federal system. These regional elites felt placed at a disadvantage by the capital regions and were far more likely to embrace liberal philosophies as a means of gaining power and wealth. The elites of the capital regions, on the other hand, had always benefited from tight central control. They had been the last to abandon the Spanish crown and wanted to maintain their power and authority in the new state.

The exception to this general rule was Argentina. There the regional elites, while embracing federalism, were politically conservative, staunchly supporting the Church as a centrally important institution; the urban (exclusively the city of Buenos Aires) elites were liberal and supported a centralized government, not unlike what was found in Europe in the same period. Urban elites tended to be more engaged in international intellectual movements, more influenced by outside thinking, and hale from large metropolitan regions where there was a greater exchange of ideas and greater access to higher education. Urban elites were, in general, liberals but supported a centralized form of government.

Argentina also manifested a unique trajectory after independence because of regional differences. The old viceroyalty of the Rio de la Plata had broken into constituent parts: Bolivia, Paraguay, Uruguay, and Argentina. One of the goals of the political leadership following independence was to forge the pieces back into a single political entity. This effort was led by the Argentine politician and philosopher Bernardino Rivadavia from the province of Buenos Aires. Deeply imbued with notions from the English Enlightenment, especially the works of the British political thinker, Jeremy Bentham, Rivadavia instituted a wide range of liberal policies, which eventually became embodied in the first major constitution in 1825. Rivadavia emerged as the first president of the United Provinces of the Rio de la Plata. His program sought to balance the development of the region as a whole with the prosperity of Buenos Aires. The two major factions in the region were the wealthy merchants of the city of Buenos Aires, and the large landowners and ranchers of the hinterland. Their needs were for the most part antithetical to one another, which made for a difficult balancing act. On the one hand Rivadavia provided long-term leases to landowners over public lands, especially those pushing southwards into the grasslands. He also provided for a system whereby local estate owners controlled the movement of ranch workers and laborers, the famous *gauchos*. Yet he also promoted wide-scale economic reforms, sought to lessen barriers for trade among the provinces of the state, encouraged British investment and industrialization and even offered to federalize the city and port of Buenos Aires. As it was, the port revenues and duties collected in the city remained in the city, making it by far the wealthiest political entity in the nation.

In the area of Church relations, Rivadavia pursued a traditional liberal agenda. He abolished the ecclesiastical *fuero*, the right whereby clerics could have legal cases heard in ecclesiastical courts rather than national courts. He also suppressed some monasteries and other religious houses, confiscating their properties for the state. He refused to have the state enforce the collection of the tithe. While the Church could still ask the faithful to pay their fair tax, the state would no longer serve as the collection agent. Last, he promoted public primary and higher education. In his efforts to encourage British investments, Rivadavia also guaranteed freedom of religion so that Protestants who might settle or live in the country would be allowed to practice their brand of religion. Due to these efforts, the Catholic hierarchy opposed the Rivadavia government. Because of increasing opposition from the rural landowners who were confronted with new national taxes and a reduction of some of their traditional revenues, and who also opposed the new government, Rivadavia lost political control of the region. In 1827 he resigned and fled into exile. The Argentine government eventually fell into the hands of a powerful rural land owner, Juan Manuel de Rosas.

Rosas, using his political acumen in forging ties with other regional strongmen, gained the governorship of the province of Buenos Aires in 1829. Working with leaders of other provinces, Rosas seized the presidency of a federation of provinces in 1831. The federation provided for a single voice in external affairs but largely left the provinces free to determine their own internal policies. Importantly, Rosas controlled the all-important customs houses of Buenos Aires and thus all external trade; much internal trade also passed through his control. While Rosas was a strong federalist, he was also extremely conservative. He overturned most of Rivadavia's reform agenda, restoring control over education to the Church, and encouraging the return of the Jesuits to run the educational system. Rosas eventually expelled the order yet again when he found that he could not control its actions. He maintained close ties with the ecclesiastical hierarchy and even had his portrait, and that of his wife, placed beside the main altar of all churches. Rosas is most famous for his bloody suppression of his political opponents, collectively referred to as *unitarios* (Unitarians), who preferred a centralized state to a federation. He even had a secret police force called the *Mazorca* that terrorized and executed many opponents to the Rosas regime.[5]

Both Rivadavia and Rosas, however, sought to have the state inherit the Royal Patronage. For vastly different ideological reasons, both men felt that the nation was the legal heir of the monarch in terms of appointing high-ranking clerics. For Rivadavia, the position was based in the rights of the new state as a successor to the old. By having control over the appointment of bishops and others, the state could then see that more sympathetic prelates gained episcopal eminences. Rosas approached the issue from a different angle. He was already a strong supporter of the Church hierarchy. The continuation of the patronage merely assured that the Church would remain strong and central to the life of the federation. It also gave him a degree of control over the Church that he also exercised over other aspects of the nation.[6]

Another one of the constituent parts of the old viceroyalty of the Rio de la Plata was Bolivia. There independence came late, through success on the battlefield. The Venezuelan general Antonio José de Sucre commanded the army of independence, taking command at the behest of Simón Bolívar. Sucre also became the first president on Bolivia in 1825. Unfortunately, the early republic faced dire economic problems. While it had some of the largest mineral resources on the continent, many of the technicians who supervised the mines fled the region during the war of independence. The infrastructure of government dissolved and foreign trade diminished to nearly nothing. In order to begin to govern, Sucre needed funds. Like many of the leaders of independence movements, he was a political liberal and, if not actively anticlerical, was no strong supporter of the Church. He instituted some of the most sweeping legislation aimed at curtailing the economic power of the Church. One of his first acts was to seize control of the collection of the tithe. While many liberals advocated the abolition of the tithe, Sucre took it over because of the steady revenue that it could provide to the state. In fact, in the colonial period, the state participated in both the tithe collection and distribution in many regions, and just under 20 percent of the total collection went to the crown. Sucre also followed up on the amortization program, whereby the crown had taken control of the assets upon which chantries and other ecclesiastical endowments were based and so most of the capital invested by the Church passed to the state.

Sucre also confiscated much of the property of the Church. He ordered the closing of convents and monasteries with fewer than twelve inhabitants and consolidated the religious into larger houses. He took over the rural farms and estates owned by the orders, along with their urban real estate. While these actions provided the government with a massive infusion of cash, mortgages, and real estate, it did mean that the state became responsible for paying hundreds of clerics their salaries, which had been based on revenues generated by the investments and properties. The state also had the problem of trying to find potential buyers for all of the real estate. Given the fragile economic situation of the country, this was a difficult task. Finally, Sucre assumed complete power of patronage, even taking control of the silver ornamentation of the churches themselves. As contrasted with other regions in Latin America, all of these actions occurred without massive protests. The end result was that in Bolivia, more than in any other nation, the Church was completely under the domination of the state for many decades. Thus, the Church and high Church officials did not play a major role in nineteenth-century Bolivian politics.

In neighboring Chile the local hero of independence, Bernardo O'Higgins, ruled the country with the title of "supreme dictator" following the expulsion of the Spanish. O'Higgins, although born in Chile, had spent much of his life in Europe. While independence had served to unite liberals and conservatives, O'Higgins represented the liberal faction. He actively pursued an agenda common to many liberals in Latin America. He abolished titles of nobility, grants of entail,[7] and other policies favored by wealthy interior landowners, and he also angered the Church hierarchy by his actions. He expelled a bishop of Santiago who had openly supported the return of the Spanish; he tried to restrict religious processions and the public veneration of religious images. He also proclaimed freedom of religion, allowed for the construction of Protestant churches and the creation of Protestant cemeteries, and invited Protestant teachers to come and establish schools, all part of an effort to wrest control of education from the hands of the Church. Although O'Higgins promulgated a constitution in 1818, he increasing had difficulty in enforcing his program, largely due to the poverty of the government. Although early on he had abolished certain government monopolies, such as the tobacco monopoly, he was forced to later reinstitute them as a source of government revenue. By 1822 O'Higgins began to lose the support even of the liberals, due to his dictatorial stance on several issues, and in 1823 he resigned his office and went into exile in Lima.

The seven years following O'Higgins's departure were highly unsettled in Chile. The liberal faction, headed by a military hero of the independence movement, Ramón Freire, sought to continue most of O'Higgins's agenda. The conservative opposition wished to restore many of the institutions targeted by the liberals and generally provide for a more stable environment for the estate owners and merchants. These liberals tended to be federalists, representing both an intellectual elite from Santiago but also traditional elites from the far north and south of the country. The conservatives were centralists and largely represented the wealthy landowners and merchants of the central valley and the city of Santiago. The time of turmoil, which saw numerous different presidents and several constitutions, ended in 1830 with the military success of the conservatives.

Joaquin Prieto now headed the conservative government, and Diego Portales, one of his cabinet ministers, was the intellectual leader of the movement. Although Portales never actually served as president, he is widely regarded as the strongman of the era. The conservatives gained an absolute majority in Chile's congress in 1833 and moved to rewrite the constitution, creating a centralist document in opposition to the federal constitution supported by Freire, which was styled on the U.S. Constitution. Importantly, the Constitution of 1833 placed the Catholic Church at the heart of the state. It declared Chile to be a Catholic nation, required all elected officials to be Catholic, gave the Church absolute control over marriage and other civil ceremonies, and mandated that the state exercise the power of patronage over the Church. While liberal constitutions tended to open up suffrage to adult males, conservatives restricted the right to vote. In the case of Chile electors had to be twenty-five years of age, literate, and own property. To be elected to public office one had to own even more property than just the amount required to vote. The political system that emerged saw a strong president, who could appoint all government officials, who held an absolute veto over Congress, and who could freely declare a state of siege anywhere in the country and suspend constitutional rights. As a result of these extraordinary powers, the political system in Chile became a reflection of the president. For the next several decades Chile saw a relatively peaceful procession of presidents, each serving two five-year terms. The major issue of the patronage took many more years to be resolved.[8]

At the other end of Hispanic America, independence in Mexico effectively substituted one monarch for another. Although Agustín de Iturbide proclaimed Mexican independence and became its first president, he soon became more autocratic and established himself as Agustín I, emperor of Mexico, but there was very little political support for his monarchy and he was quickly overthrown. The liberals and conservatives represented the major political factions. Liberals tended to be federalists and represented the merchants and landowners from Mexico's wealthy outlying provinces. The conservatives tended to be merchants, miners, and landowners from the central region of Mexico, a region on either side of an imaginary line from Guadalajara in the west through Mexico City and on to Veracruz in the east. This dichotomy also reflected a division in external politics, since the liberals identified more with the United States, the conservatives with England.

With the expulsion of Iturbide, these two factions were able to unite enough to write a fairly moderate constitution in 1824. The document created a federal government but had an extremely conservative process of indirect election: the president and vice president were elected by the state legislatures, each of which had one vote. The federal government had a bicameral legislature of a senate and house of deputies, also indirectly elected through a different process. Regarding issues of the Church, the document created public education, thus loosening the ecclesiastical monopoly, but it declared the Catholic faith as the official state religion. More specifically it also guaranteed the ecclesiastical *fuero*. This period of moderation did not last very long, and by 1825 the last conservative was forced out of the government, headed by liberal war hero Guadalupe Victoria. The liberals then pursued their own policies more fervently.

The thirty years between 1824 and 1854 were ones of political turmoil for Mexico. The nation saw a seemingly endless parade of presidents. In general, these administrations alternated between the liberals and conservatives, and neither faction had sufficient political power to fully achieve its political objectives. With each passing administration the factions became more antagonistic and intransigent. The most constant feature of the political scene, especially from 1834 until 1854, was Antonio López de Santa Anna, a rancher and military hero, who represented one faction of the conservative movement. Further complicating the political scene in this period, the French, Spanish, and British all attempted various military actions against Mexico, mostly seeking payment of losses incurred in the war for independence and other subsequent events. The administrations faced not only opposition from within Mexico, but frequently from outside as well. The economy, shattered from the wars of independence, hardly had a chance to recover, especially in light of both political turmoil and foreign threats.

In this period the Liberal Party defined itself as desiring a political system not unlike that of the United States. It supported a federal system wherein the states had authority in all areas not specifically allocated to the nation. Liberals believed in a laissez-faire economic policy, which called for as little government control of economic activity as possible, although they did concede that some regulation was needed. This then dictated their opposition to government monopolies, such as on tobacco and other goods. They opposed internal tariff barriers between the states, but supported national tariffs on imported and exported goods. The idea of laissez-faire also applied to the social system. It combined with the liberal's pursuit of the political model like that of the United States and thus dictated a separation of Church and state. The liberals also opposed the state collecting the tithe; they required an abolition of the ecclesiastical *fuero*; they supported public education, both at the primary and secondary levels; and they were concerned by the vast land-holdings of the Church and religious orders, seeing them as an impediment to economic development. Under their ideal system, the liberals also sought civil registry: that births, marriages, and deaths be recognized by the state without need to access the ceremonies of the Church. Among other social policies, the liberals opposed slavery, which had been nominally abolished at independence. They also opposed the use of noble titles and opposed the existence of entailed estates, since they were manifestations of a system of social hierarchy and posed the same economic threat as the Church land-holdings by impeding the free flow of market forces.

The conservatives in Mexico favored a centralized state, indirect elections, and stringent requirements on voter eligibility. In general the conservatives sought to maintain the social and economic order that governed the country before the Bourbon Reforms. This implied that effective control should be in the hands of a few powerful families. The movement was heavily dominated by merchants, miners, ranchers, and high Church officials from the core region. Their political agenda included support for the Church, making it the official state religion; the government would collect the tithes, the ecclesiastical fuero would remain in force, and the Church would continue to be the official agency in charge of recording births, deaths, and marriages. In the economic realm the conservatives supported the continuation of government monopolies and high tariffs. They also supported the generalized sales tax that was inherited from the colonial period, along with internal tariffs and duties for goods moving inside of the country. The result of these policies was that the conservative governments normally had sufficient revenues with which to govern. The conservatives generally opposed the political authority of the states. Instead they looked to a centralized governmental system, not unlike France, where control over the states was exercised through governors appointed by the central government. The states, converted into departments, had little control over their own territory or policies. There were some conservatives who also supported the creation of a monarchy, or even becoming a quasi independent part of Spain again, but these were a very small minority.

The constant turmoil caused by ongoing conflict between the liberals and conservatives weakened the nation. In addition, revolts in outlying provinces also taxed the resources of the nation. In this period the northernmost province of Texas declared its independence and eventually was subsumed into the United States. Mexico sent an army into Texas, led by General Antonio López de Santa Anna, to reclaim the territory, without success. López de Santa Anna, in addition to being an important military leader, served as president of Mexico on several occasions in the nineteenth century.

In the early nineteenth century, there were also revolts in the Yucatan, led by federalists who vehemently opposed the central government's centralist tendencies. This was fueled by extreme social dislocations between the native peoples and the mestizos and Creoles, which led to the conflict being known as the Caste War. Eventually the loss of Texas, the protracted war in the Yucatan, and the invasion of Mexico by U.S. forces and the ensuing treaty that granted vast parts of the Mexican northwest to the United States caused a popular upheaval against the conservatives in general and López de Santa Anna, as the embodiment of conservative ideology and failure, in particular, leading to the eventual success of the liberals in election in the early 1850s. The Treaty of Guadalupe Hidalgo (1848) that ceded nearly half of the national territory to the United States in return for a cash payment and the cancellation of other claims was seen by many Mexicans as an indictment of the conservative agenda. Not only had the conservatives not established a stable economic and social system, but they had destroyed national integrity.[9]

Native peoples played an important role in the period of independence. The armies of independence in Mexico and South America consisted of a leadership, which tended to be of European ancestry, but mestizos, mulatos, and natives represented the majority. Some of their involvement came as a result of opposition to taxation and domination especially by local royal representatives. The turmoil caused in rural areas by the Bourbon Reforms and the loss of social structures also played into their willingness to take up arms. In some areas, such as the highlands of Peru and in the Yucatan, full-scale wars erupted pitting native peoples against the European and mixed groups.

Leaders of the newly independent states paid lip service to national unity and to freedom for all. In many countries tribute was abolished. The British made the abolition of slavery a condition for recognizing the new states. Yet after the first flush of independence, native peoples frequently found themselves in a worse situation than under the royal government. They were marginalized and excluded from the political system that granted the right to vote only to literate property owners, generally of European descent. In the face of the new regimes, the Church continued to offer support and social stability. Therefore, native peoples continued to be staunch supporters of the Church in many regions.

The period of independence and its immediate aftermath in Latin America thus saw dramatic changes in the relationship of the Church with the other institutions of society. The Church and ecclesiastical officials had become active in politics. While the bishops and other members of the upper clergy tended to support conservative policies that sought to keep the Church as a central institution in the new nations, many local parish priests, friars, and other religious supported the reforming policies of the liberals. Yet, the overriding political question that remained unresolved into the middle of the nineteenth century was that of patronage. At just the same time that the nations of Latin America sought to inherit the privileges of the Spanish kings relevant to the Church in their territories, the papacy had embarked on a program of gaining increased control over the Church worldwide. These two trends would form the backdrop against which the history of the Church in Latin America would be played out in the mid-nineteenth century. While conservatives believed that the patronage was important to maintain the strength and importance of the Church, events dictated that the patronage in the hands of liberals could easily undermine the very things that the conservatives hoped to accomplish. The end result was that in most countries both conservatives and liberals abandoned hopes of gaining the patronage.

$$7$$

Working Out the Differences

Amid flickering candlelight, when a person entered an Argentine church in the 1840, a very surprising sight would emerge. On one side of the main altar was the portrait of the president, Juan Manuel de Rosas; on the other side was a portrait of his dead wife, doña Encarnación. Although Rosas called himself a federalist, and he represented many of the interests of the interior ranch owners, he ruled despotically and became a de facto centralist. His official title was Restorer of the Laws, a direct criticism of his predecessors, whom he viewed as having led the country to anarchy. Rosas forged an alliance with the Church, while demanding the Church's compliance with his will. Thus temples of Christian worship came to participate in worship of the Restorer.

Esteban Echeverría, a young writer and an outspoken critic of Rosas, wrote an allegorical tale titled "The Slaughterhouse," in which he compared life in Argentina under Rosas to life in an abatoir. More directly, Echeverría described the slaughterhouse very much like one of the churches of the era. Just as one could find the portraits of Rosas and his wife at the high altar, so they were found on either side of the desk of the manager of the slaughterhouse. The allusion was drawn even tighter because the story takes place during Lent, when work at slaughterhouses should have been at its slowest. The symbolism, filled with references to Catholic thought and practice, was a scathing criticism not just of Rosas but of the Church as well. This allegory ignited the passions of the liberals and centralists who opposed Rosas on political grounds, yet it even led many conservatives who had supported Rosas to oppose him for his failure to hold the Church in the proper respect.[1]

At the other end of Latin America, Mexico was ruled on and off during this period by another strongman, Antonio López de Santa Anna. Like Rosas, López de Santa Anna, known to English speakers simply as Santa Anna, began his career as a ranch owner and military man, and ruled mostly as a dictator. Already well known from his military service in the War of Independence, López de Santa Anna became a national hero in 1837 when the French attacked Veracruz seeking to address claims of the French government and French nationals. Because one of the claims pressed by the French government was for losses sustained to a French pastry shop in Mexico City, this war became known as the Pastry War. In the defense of the port of Veracruz, a battle the Mexicans lost, Santa Anna's leg was badly wounded and had to be amputated. The general had it buried at his ranch, Manga de Clavo. A few years later, in 1842, when López de Santa Anna became president, he had his leg disinterred and brought to Mexico City. The archbishop and other high-ranking clergy greeted the limb and accompanied it on the way to its interment. With full military and ecclesiastical honors it was buried in the cemetery of Santa Paula, where citizens could go to venerate the limb. Beyond this event, López de Santa Anna also cultivated very close ties to the ecclesiastical hierarchy, which, in turn, offered him its full support. In 1844, the dictator again fell from power. The rabble of Mexico City, so upset by his mishandling of the nation, dug up the leg and dragged it through the streets of the city in public ridicule. These anecdotes demonstrate the sometimes too close relationship that Latin American dictators of the nineteenth century had with the Church. Bishops and prelates often catered to the whims of the leader in return for a favored place in the halls of government.[2]

In addition to politics internal to the Latin American nations, the United States came to play an important role in the region. As early as 1823 James Monroe's famous message to Congress (known thereafter as the Monroe Doctrine) stated that if one of the European powers made war against one of the newly independent American nations, that action would be considered as an act of aggression against the United States itself. At this point in its history, the United States was not capable of making good on its declaration. European powers, notably Spain, France, and Britain routinely invaded various Latin American countries, mostly seeking redress for other acts and financial claims against the new countries. Nevertheless, beginning in the 1840s the United States began to become more active in the affairs of Latin American states, whether or not it was a reaction to European aggression. This interventionist policy came to an early head in 1846 when a war was launched against Mexico. This war was not based on the tenets of the Monroe Doctrine but on needed westward expansion. The territory beyond the Louisiana Purchase was controlled by Mexico, and the United States attacked Mexico, hoping to defeat that country and thereby gain what would become the western part of the United States. The war was a success, for the United States. Ironically, some fifteen years later Mexico would be invaded by European powers—France, Spain, and Britain—yet the United States did not come to her aid. While the United States did invoke the Monroe Doctrine and oppose the invasion, it could effectively do nothing, being caught up in its own Civil War. Yet throughout the nineteenth and twentieth centuries the United States would intervene in the internal affairs of many Latin American nations, whenever it thought that such intervention was in its best interests, regardless of whether the Monroe Doctrine was involved. Mexico and the Central American nations were the most frequent targets of intervention.

While the independence of Latin America nations came about as a result of an alliance among various internal factions, all of which could agree on severing ties with the mother country, the ensuing decades saw turmoil as these various factions then disputed the leadership of the nations and the specific policies to be implemented. As we have seen, the two major factions consisted of liberals and conservatives. The liberals pursued policies to establish governments along the lines of the United States; conservatives sought to maintain a more closed social and political system, tended to favor the continued centrality of the Catholic Church, and pursued the interests of large landowners, merchants, and miners. While the issue of the continuation of the patronage had captured the imagination of many politicians early in the nineteenth century, most recognized that the Vatican would be unwilling to cede this power to republican forms of government, and thus they focused their attention elsewhere. The issue that would emerge in many countries was the role of the Church in the local economy and, related to that, the degree to which the Church should hold land and other assets. These issues would soon take center stage.

Mexico

Nowhere more than Mexico did these issues become so important. In the first few decades of the nineteenth century, Mexico saw a series of short-lived governments, alternating between liberals and conservatives. Antonio López de Santa Anna became the standard-bearer for the conservatives, but he also led the country into two tragic and debilitating wars, first over Texas independence and later to fight against the invasion of the United States. While López de Santa Anna was merely reacting to hostile actions of the Texas revolutionaries and protecting his nation from an invasion, the conduct of the war and the humiliating defeat caused his popular support to erode. By around 1850 the liberals enjoyed significant success at the polls and began to implement their reform policies. Santa Anna made one final comeback in 1853 supported by high Church officials, generals, and large landowners. He governed for less than two years, and by 1855 he was thrown out of office for the last time.[3]

The final defeat of Santa Anna allowed the liberals to more aggressively seek to implement their programs. Santa Anna had alienated even his strongest supporters, and his government had cast a pall over the conservative movement. The liberals proceeded to establish a provisional government and to govern by decree, until such time as a new constitution could be written embodying a federal organization of government and including reforms long sought by the liberals. In the two years of the provisional government, several important laws came into effect and eventually formed part of the Constitution of 1857. Three laws in particular stand out regarding the relations between Church and state in Mexico.

The first of these was known as the *Ley Juárez*, named after the minister of justice of the provisional government Benito Juárez, an Indian from the southern state of Oaxaca. This law abolished the ecclesiastical *fuero*, along with the similar military *fuero*, and subjected all citizens to federal law. Thereafter, the Church courts and courts-martial could serve only as internal courts to the Church and military respectively, dealing with issues that were purely canonical or military. Many conservatives railed that this law would destroy the integrity not only of the Church but of the military, and thus make both clerics and military personnel the target of outlandish civil law suits.

Rather than bow to conservative opposition, the liberal provisional government pressed ahead and promulgated the second law, known as the *Ley Lerdo*. This law, named after the treasury minister Miguel Lerdo de Tejada, was a direct attack on Church wealth. The *Ley Lerdo* prohibited any social corporation from holding land other than that necessary for its central purposes. This law was aimed at the Church, which continued to be the nation's largest landowner. The law sought to divest the Church of the property it owned and to allow for the creation of a middle class of small farmers and landlords. The Church could continue to possess only the churches themselves and the monasteries and convents where religious lived. All other properties, rural and urban, were to be sold to the tenants, with the current rent representing 6 percent of the value of the property. Any property that was not being rented was to be sold at public auction to the highest bidder. The way that the law was written, however, meant that it applied to many other institutions than just the Church. Private clubs and other social organizations came under the jurisdiction of the law. Most poignantly, so did many native villages, which had never adopted European landholding traditions and which continued to hold all of the village land communally. Over the ensuing years many wealthy speculators began buying up property as soon as it could be identified. Rather than creating a middle class of small landholders, the law actually had the effect of concentrating even more land in the hands of the very wealthy and those few speculators who were able to take advantage of the system. This had the further effect of devastating the economic underpinning of many native villages, forcing them off of their land and into unfair labor relations with the large landowners.

The third law was more limited in its scope but also more pointedly aimed at the Church. This law, the *Ley Iglesias*, named after yet another liberal minister José María Iglesias, restricted how much priests could charge for the exercise of their office. From the seventeenth century on, parish priests had begun to charge parishioners fees for specific functions, such as baptisms, marriages, and funerals. These fees became embodied in fee schedules, known as *aranceles*. In the colonial period they had been approved by the local bishop and were subject to the ecclesiastical court system. In the period following independence, the liberals felt that the Church took advantage of the poorest members of society and charged fees that were simply too high. On the surface, then this was supposed to benefit the natives and the peasants. But when the Church protested and withheld the sacraments of the Church, it was these same neediest members of society who remained without the benefits of the Church. Needless to say, the Church saw this legislation as being an unlawful intrusion into purely ecclesiastical matters by the state.[4]

These laws soon became part of the Constitution of 1857, which was crafted by many of the leading liberal intellectuals of the time. The document reinstituted the federal system of government, first established in the Constitution of 1824, loosely based on the U.S. Constitution. Like its model, it had a section of rights guaranteed to citizens, including freedom of the press, of speech, of assembly, and of education. It both abolished slavery and prohibited people from receiving labor tribute without fair compensation to the worker, attacking one of the important labor mechanisms of the colonial period. While the constitution did empower the states to act in all areas not specifically allocated to the national government, at the federal level it only had a single unicameral legislature. Moreover, there was no vice president. In case of the death of the president, the chief justice of the Mexican supreme court would succeed. Because of strong differences of opinion even within the liberal factions, no statement on religion per se became part of the constitution: it neither recognized the Church nor prohibited it; neither provided for freedom of religion nor mandated the Catholic faith. The constitution was silent on this point. In spite of this, the tone of the document was clearly anticlerical. Now, at the prodding of Mexican ecclesiastical officials, the pope rejected the constitution and condemned all the legislators who participated in the constitutional convention.

No sooner was the new constitution promulgated than the conservatives reacted against it. Under the battle cry of "Religion and Privileges," the conservatives launched a civil war to overthrow the liberals and expunge the constitution. Many bishops excommunicated the legislators who had participated in the convention, and the battle lines were drawn between the Church and conservatives on one hand and the liberals on the other. It was also a war between the central region and the states. The elites of the central region continued to see value in the conservative agenda, while those living in the outlying states sought the greater advantage provided by a federal system. Juárez was forced into a type of internal exile—on the road from provincial capital to provincial capital—while armies loyal to the liberals battled the armies of the conservatives. The conservatives had the advantage of better finances, since they could control tax collections in the major ports and some of the revenues coming into Mexico City. The liberals had to rely on whatever other taxes they could collect and distribute. Finally Juárez, out of financial desperation, nationalized all Church property without any compensation, suppressed all monasteries and convents, established a complete separation of Church and state, and proclaimed freedom of religion. This act went far beyond the earlier *Ley Lerdo*: while the earlier law would have compensated the Church for lost property, this act simply confiscated it all, to be sold with the proceeds going to support the state. Eventually, the liberals carried the day, and by 1860 the conservatives had been defeated on the battlefield. In the wake of the War of the Reform (or Three Years' War), as it was known, Juárez, seeing the need for national unity, proclaimed a general amnesty in favor of the conservatives and invited them into a national unity government.

What Juárez did not know is that some leading conservatives were in talks with European powers regarding the possibility of foreign intervention to overthrow the liberal government and establish one friendlier to conservative policies. England, France, and Spain had a long list of particulars against the Mexican state in general and the liberals in particular, and were hospitable to the conservatives' entreaties. In 1862 the three powers initiated an occupation of the Mexican ports in the Gulf of Mexico in order to collect funds due them over the years by previous governments. Once Spain and England had satisfied their debts, they withdrew. The French remained and marched on to Mexico City. Although the French army met with some defeats along the way, most famously in Puebla on May 5, 1862, they succeeded in overthrowing the Juárez government and established a new monarchy in its place.

Napoleon III of France used Mexico as an opportunity to create an overseas empire. In addition to his adventure in Mexico, the French and other European powers were also beginning to carve out areas of interest in Africa and South Asia. The French ruler complied with the wishes of the Mexican monarchist conservatives and in 1864 installed a monarch on the Mexican throne: Maximilian of Hapsburg, a distant relative of the Hapsburg monarchs of Spain. Juárez was once again forced into an internal exile, much of it spent in the far north along the border with the United States.

The conservatives carried the field, with French support. Unfortunately for them, Maximilian turned out to be a political realist and a pragmatist. The conservatives had anticipated that he would throw out all of the reforms instituted by the liberals in the Constitution of 1857, and restore the Church and large landowners to their role of centrality in the new empire. Maximilian found much to favor in the liberal agenda. He approached the *Ley Lerdo* and the expropriation of Church property as an accomplished act and was unwilling to dispossess the new landowners of their recently acquired property, because he did not have the money to indemnify them. While he maintained ostensibly cordial relations with the Church, he wished to exercise a degree of control over ecclesiastical appointments that the papacy and local Church officials were unwilling to allow. Moreover, realizing the need for national unity in order to govern the country effectively, Maximilian reached out to some of the liberal leadership, who saw in him a possibility of extricating Mexico from factionalism. The end result was that Maximilian lost the support of the Mexican conservatives who had plotted to install him.

At the same time that Maximilian was losing support from the Mexican conservatives, the United States was ending its own Civil War, and the government was increasingly worried about the presence of French troops on the North American continent. The United States began to actively support the cause of Juárez as the legal Mexican government and to undermine the French in diplomatic circles. The liberal insurgency opposing the French intervention and Maximilian's rule had never ceased to fight, but was relegated to fighting in isolated pockets around the country. With some meager assistance from the United States, the insurgency increased. At this point, Napoleon III eventually concluded that his Mexican adventure was no longer viable and in 1865 began to withdraw his troops. For a while Maximilian was able to hold on to power with Mexican troops loyal to his cause, but eventually he was captured. He and a handful of his generals were tried for treason and found guilty. Many groups requested that Juárez pardon Maximilian and grant an amnesty to conservatives who took up arms. Remembering that he had given an amnesty following the War of the Reform, which only led to the conservatives plotting with the French to invade, Juárez steadfastly refused any amnesty or pardon. Maximilian and his generals were executed in Querétaro in 1867.

The effect of the War of the Reform and the French invasion was the triumph of the liberals. While there would continue to be squabbles, often violent, in the last three decades of the nineteenth century in Mexico, all the leading politicians could point to their strong liberal credentials. The Church had to accept the new situation, and although bishops and other high Church officials continued to press for a return of Church property, no concrete action was ever taken. The Constitution of 1857 finally became the law of the land. Yet the reality of the situation was that the nation was still overwhelmingly Catholic. For all intents and purposes every politician and person in power was a Catholic. While the Church lost much of its land, and had been repudiated as a political movement, it still controlled the morality and faith of the nation. And so the closing decades saw less confrontation between the Church and state in Mexico and something of a rapprochement.

Nowhere in Latin America was the confrontation between Church and state as violent as in Mexico. The nineteenth century in South America, while filled with conflict between liberals and conservatives, saw the slow rise of power of liberals across the continent, and the Vatican routinely refused to establish formal concordats with any of the Latin American republics. Still, the governments continued to make nominations for bishop and archbishop, and to use their diplomatic relations with the Vatican to seek confirmation of those nominations. This awkward procedure allowed the papacy to support those clerics who had the approval of the local government *and* sufficient connections and renown to be known to the pope. It avoided giving the absolute power to appoint bishops into the hands of republican governments. Lacking a concordat, the papacy could freely communicate with bishops and other Church leaders without the intervention of the civil government. The complement to any agreement with a civil government was the grant of *exequatur,* whereby the civil government was granted power to promulgate papal decrees within its territory. This action would give the papal decree legal standing in a civil court. The papacy, as noted, was generally unwilling to grant either a concordat or the *exequatur* to the governments in Latin America. On the other hand, the papacy frequently explored the right to exercise prior approval of laws passed by national congresses. In general, however, it did not seek that power but relied on both diplomatic and canonical sanctions should a nation pass laws it found unsuitable.

Argentina and Chile

In Argentina, the dictator Rosas was overthrown in 1852 and the next year a new constitution was written, closely patterned on that of the United States. While it called for the Catholic Church to be the official religion of the state, it also provided for freedom of religion for followers of other faiths, mostly Protestants. Argentina had developed very close ties with Great Britain, and as a result Buenos Aires saw a significant increase in the number of merchants from Great Britain, many of whom were Protestant. In the end the constitution merely required that the president and vice president be Catholics. Argentina had not negotiated a concordat with the Vatican, but nevertheless continued to make recommendations regarding the appointment of bishops. The Vatican did include Argentina, Brazil, and Chile as stops when it sent an apostolic delegate to South America in 1865. One of the beneficial fruits of this trip for the Argentines was the creation of a new archdiocese of Buenos Aires with the other dioceses of Argentina suffragan to it. Yet in so doing the pope also stipulated that Argentina had to concede to the Vatican the power to create new dioceses, to determine the boundaries of those diocese, and to appoint the bishops and other high-ranking clerics, and that the government would allow the ecclesiastical officials to reside in their territory and collect the fees, dues, and other revenues peacefully.

In Chile the conservative state developed by Portales had begun to erode by the 1870s. While the leadership still came from among the conservatives, they implemented many liberal policies, such as public education, and various laissez-faire economic programs. In 1850 the liberals mounted a particularly vigorous campaign to gain the presidency, only to lose to the official government candidate, Manuel Montt. The liberals then attempted a revolt, only to be repressed vigorously by the government, with great loss of life. After offering an amnesty to the liberals, Montt proceeded to implement some of the key initiatives of their program, such as the abolition of entailed estates and the abolition of the tithe. He also refused to allow the Jesuits to return to the country after their reorganization in the Roman Church. He supported public education and took over the Church-run school system.

He placed parish priests under the jurisdiction of the government and developed a civil marriage procedure for non-Catholics. These actions infuriated various conservative Church and secular leaders, who broke with the government party to form their own conservative party. Montt, nevertheless, had sufficient support among the remaining conservatives and moderate liberals to continue to govern.

By 1871 the liberal transition of Chile was complete when the first liberal president was elected. The country had become very prosperous due to efficient exploitation of its mines and forests. German and British investors had come to the country and allied themselves with Chileans to create a new economic strength for the country. While the Catholic Church remained the official religion of the nation, measures allowing for tolerance of other faiths became law, recognizing the growing influence of Protestants, perhaps because the newly prosperous immigrants tended to marry into the families of the Chilean elite. Yet for the next two decades this "religious question," that is the degree to which the state should tolerate and accommodate non-Catholics, remained one of the central political themes in Chile.

Peru and Bolivia

In nearby Peru, the political reality differed greatly. Along with Bolivia, Peru had embraced the cause of independence in the later phases of the wars. The elites of the core region, living along a line stretching from Cuzco in the highlands to Lima and Callao, favored Spanish rule, because it was directly beneficial to them, and also they had participated to a higher degree in the institutions of the colony. The northern and southern elites favored independence sooner. Nearly all groups perceived the Church as a stabilizing influence. It tended to reinforce socioeconomic and racial categories; it supported royal government and opposed change. Unfortunately, as a result of this stabilizing approach many reformers, and the liberals in particular, felt that the Church abdicated its moral authority by reinforcing the status quo, given that the liberals perceived the status quo as being contrary to reason and faith.

As in many other countries, the early governments of Peru claimed the right of patronage. The papacy remained intransigent and refused to appoint any bishops to the region for as long as two decades. Furthermore, as with liberals in other areas, the government sought to reform religious orders by closing down small monasteries and convents. It also confiscated their property and forced men in religious orders to enter the secular clergy. This debilitated the Church in two important ways. On the one hand it deprived the Church of manpower. Without bishops, new priests could not be ordained. The government discouraged men from entering the clergy at all. On the other hand, the Church lost much of its financial underpinnings in the loss of property and investments confiscated by the government. Unlike in other countries, the liberals in Peru did not launch an all-out attack on the Church. They did not seek to eliminate it but rather to bring it more under the control of the state by uniformly endorsing the Catholic Church as the official state religion and the pope as the symbol of unity in the Church.

For the Church in Peru, the first decades of independence were chaotic. By the 1840s, the bishops, now appointed by the Vatican, set out to restore the Church to the position of power and authority it had occupied before independence. In Peru, liberalism was in reality the political philosophy of a small number of the elite. The vast majority of the population, natives and peoples of mixed heritage, such as Afro-Peruvians, were devout and tended to reject many of the liberal innovations. As a result, especially in rural areas, the Church continued to operate as it always had: as a source of stability for the people, the one single institution that could provide guidance and continuity in changing times. At the highest levels of government and the Church, a working relationship developed. The papacy, while rejecting government claims of patronage, did consult with the state before appointing bishops. This informal agreement continued for nearly three decades.

The last half of the nineteenth century in Peru saw a renewed conflict between the Church and state. In 1860 a new constitution was ratified. Many in the Church saw it as a direct assault. On the other hand, many older liberals rejected it as being too soft on the Church. In fact it was more balanced than people at the time probably recognized. While the constitution guaranteed the Catholic Church as the official state religion, the liberals became more clearly anticlerical and engaged in a series of assaults on the privileges of the Church. They tried to ratify an even more radical constitution in 1867, with no success. Nevertheless, they did promulgate a series of laws aimed at the Church, including authorizing civil cemeteries, freedom of worship for non-Catholics, and other acts. Curiously, Peru achieved a de facto concordat with the papacy at this same time. In 1874 Pope Pius IX issued a bull granting certain rights to the Peruvian state over the Church, including nominations to bishoprics. It reflected the practice that had evolved since mid-century. The Peruvian government, in turn, accepted the bull and issued an order of *exequatur*, promulgating the papal decree so that the document would have legal force in the country.[5]

Colombia and Venezuela

The neighboring countries of Colombia and Venezuela have markedly different histories with regard to the Church in the nineteenth century. Colombia was the seat of one of the more powerful *audiencias*, located in Bogotá. It eventually even became home to a viceroy. Thus the region was similar to Mexico and Peru, where the full weight of Spanish colonial administration was present and there were many functionaries serving the bureaucracy. By contrast, Venezuela had a checkered administrative history, being part of a territory governed from Santo Domingo for a time, then later from Bogotá. During the period of the Bourbon Reforms, the crown attempted to change the territory into a proprietary colony under the control of a joint stock company. This attempt failed, and Venezuela continued to be a frontier region of the empire. It never had the same density of government offices and services as did Colombia. The Church too had significantly fewer priests and other functionaries, making it a less visible presence.

In Colombia factions supportive of the centrality of the Church to national life gained ascendancy in the series of national governments after independence. In Venezuela the Church was far weaker and groups that were anticlerical or at least ambivalent to a continued role for the Church tended to gain power with greater frequency. In Colombia, then, the national government forged fairly close ties with the Vatican, promoted the role of the Church in national life, and built in protections for the Catholic faith in the life of the country. In Venezuela a series of anticlerical measures sought to strip the Church of its power and wealth similar to cases seen in Mexico. In both countries, as in many others, many of the peninsular clerics returned to Spain in the wake of independence, leaving the clergy significantly diminished in many places.

Colombia, after an initial experiment with liberalism, ratified early constitutions that either remained silent on issues dealing with the Church, or which upheld the central role of the Church in Colombian life. The Constitutions of 1832 and 1843 simply noted that the Catholic Church was the state religion and that there would be no religious tolerance. Nevertheless, liberal factions in the republic continually sought to reduce the power and influence of the Church in the nation, even triggering a civil war in 1839. Although supportive of the Church, civil officials in this period reduced the extent of the *fuero eclesiástico*, limited various types of clerical fees and other emoluments, sought to reduce the size of the religious orders, and assumed the patronage, over the protests of the clergy and ecclesiastical officials. The conservative government also exercised the *exequatur*, reserving to itself the approval of papal communications within its borders. The conservatives were supportive of the Church, and although they gained a large degree of control over the Church, it was for the purpose of keeping it strong. Colombia was the first Latin American republic to receive official recognition from the papacy.

To further complicate matters, conservative regimes after 1843 invited the Society of Jesus to return to Colombia. In many rural and mission areas there were insufficient priests to serve the whole population. The conservative regime reasoned that the Jesuits could both train more priests and improve the spirituality of the Colombian Church. Yet even though the Jesuits did return, they were unable to assist in the missions, only serving a college in Bogota. The legislature refused to allocate the funds necessary to support the Jesuits and, with the electoral success of the liberals, in 1850 the order was once more expelled.

The success of the Colombian liberals in 1850 led to other acts aimed against the interests of the Church. The liberals instituted divorce, abolished the *fuero*, curtailed the collection of the tithe, guaranteed freedom of religion, and formally separated Church and state. These changes were then embodied in the Constitution of 1853.

The liberal ascendancy in Colombia lasted more than thirty years. The government exiled both prelates and priests who opposed the anticlerical legislation. The separation of Church and state in Colombia also meant that the government would no longer exercise the patronage. Furthermore, it declared that the legal property of the Church be vested in the parishioners of a parish and the residents of a diocese. The government also cut its diplomatic ties to the papacy. While some regimes were more tolerant of the Church than others, the government of General Tomás Cipriano de Mosquera, which began in 1864, set the standard for anticlericalism. Although recognizing the separation of Church and state, he prohibited priests from serving in an ecclesiastical function without express government permission. He authorized the abolition of ecclesiastical mortgages and ordered that the property of the church pass to the state. All monasteries and convents were suppressed, and each male and female religious was provided with a living stipend. Only the buildings actually used for religious services would remain under the control of the Church. Although Mosquera was ousted in 1867, the liberals continued his ecclesiastical policies for another decade.[6]

In 1880 the liberals elected Rafael Núñez as president of Colombia. He had strong liberal credentials, and had been a socialistic radical in his early years, but he also felt that liberal excesses had harmed the country. By his second term he had become a conservative. He held a constitutional convention and proceeded to overturn much of the liberal agenda of the previous thirty years, and established a strong role for the Catholic Church. The constitution restored the Church to its central role in Colombia, but with some limitations. It became a self-regulating entity, free from government interference. At the same time, there was freedom of religion. And finally, the constitution authorized the state to seek a concordat with the papacy to further clarify the relationship between Church and state. Within two years such an agreement was signed.

The concordat between the Vatican and the Colombian government was unique among Latin American nations, since few followed the lead. The groundbreaking agreement remained in effect until 1973 when a revised document was signed.[7] The Concordat provided that:

- the Catholic Church was the official religion of the nation;
- the Church would have autonomy from civil jurisdiction;
- the ecclesiastical courts would be the sole venue for ecclesiastical cases;
- the Church could acquire property, yet only churches, seminaries, and residences of curates and bishops would be exempt from taxation;
- religious orders could be organized and exist subject to canon law;
- higher education would be subject to ecclesiastical regulation;
- only the Vatican could appoint bishops, but would give precedence to suggestions from the civil government;
- the Vatican would allow the civil government to consult once such an appointment had been made;
- marriages were subject to canon not civil law;
- the government would repay the Church for property confiscated under other regimes, with interest;
- and the government would provide financial support to the Church.

This document in essence swept away many of the liberal reforms of the previous decades and restored the Catholic Church to a prominent position within Colombia. It provided the state with a minimum of control over the Church, but most importantly it provided a vehicle whereby Church and state relations would be monitored and evaluated.

The concordat was followed by a series of additional agreements that served to clarify and expand on issues in the original document. In these subsequent agreements the state agreed to extend the *fuero ecclesiástico* on a limited basis to priests and religious. Cemeteries would fall under the ecclesiastical jurisdiction and supervision, with some exceptions. It allowed for the creation of public cemeteries for non-Catholics at public expense. And, the Church would provide copies of baptism, marriage, and burial records to the state on a regular basis for civil registry. Colombia achieved a modicum of stability in its relations with the Church through the concordat, and the Church continued to play an important political and social role in the country well into the twentieth century.

Venezuela followed a very different course from Colombia, although the two countries were neighbors. Prior to 1830, Venezuela, along with Ecuador and Colombia, formed part of the Republic of Gran Colombia. After that date it pursued its own independent course. In stark contrast to Colombia, and many other countries, Venezuela posited state control over the Church almost unwaveringly throughout its national history. Beginning with the promulgation of its first national constitution in 1830, the Venezuelan state clearly mandated that the state would control the activity of the Church, fully taking over all powers formerly vested in the Spanish monarch. In both liberal and conservative administrations the principle of state control over the Church remained a constant. The differences appeared in the specific policies adopted by each. liberals pursued policies expropriating Church lands and wealth, creating civil registry, and proclaiming freedom of religion. The conservatives countered by allowing foreign priests to enter the country to fill out the ranks of clergy depleted by war and conflict. The conservatives also provided some government financial support for the Church and appointed prelates friendly to their cause.

One of the leading figures of Venezuela's history in the mid-nineteenth century was General José Antonio Páez. Páez was a hero of the War of Independence, a liberal, and a rancher. He had served several times as president and de facto power broker, and with the years he became slightly more conservative. By about 1860 he supported a new arrangement with the Church and sought a negotiated concordat with the Vatican. The Venezuelan ambassador successfully negotiated such a treaty and signed it in 1862. Páez ratified it upon its arrival in Venezuela. Unfortunately, a large number of factions opposed Páez for many reasons and shortly thereafter he was ousted from the presidency. Opposition to the concordat was also widespread, and Páez' successor rejected the original agreement yet was unable to negotiate a new one. Venezuela thus remained faithful to its original policy of state patronage over the Church.

The government of Antonio Guzmán Blanco in 1873 imposed stringent restrictions on the Church, basing itself on the right of patronage. Upon coming to office, Guzmán Blanco had a feud with the archbishop of Caracas over the celebration of a *Te Deum* ordered by the president to celebrate his victory. The archbishop refused, offering to celebrate a thanksgiving Mass instead, and called on the president to first offer a general amnesty to those who had fought against him. Guzmán Blanco responded by sending the prelate into exile. He then saw to it that the congress declared the see vacant and he appointed a successor. Two years later the pope intervened, encouraging the exiled archbishop to resign and then confirming the person nominated by the president as the new archbishop. Guzmán Blanco proceeded to enact wide-ranging restrictions on the Church including absolute civil registry of births, marriages, and deaths; confiscation of all cemeteries; abolition of all convents, monasteries, and religious colleges; suppression of seminaries; and the confiscation of all ecclesiastical property. Guzmán Blanco even persuaded the congress to pass a civil matrimony act allowing, among other things, for priests to marry without jeopardy to their ecclesiastical posts. Public outcry forced the suppression of this latter clause. The remainder of Guzmán Blanco's rule saw a slightly improved climate for the Church, but it remained a cowed institution for many years.[8]

Brazil

Brazil offers a very different perspective on the development of the Catholic Church. Because Brazilian independence consisted of a successful monarchical *coup de état*, Brazil remained a monarchy well into the late nineteenth century, and consequently the issue of the devolution of the Royal Patronage to a nation-state was delayed. The only mild innovation to occur at independence, as provided for in the Imperial Constitution of 1824, was for freedom of religion. While the Catholic faith continued to be the official state religion, others were permitted to practice their faith in private. Yet non-Catholics were not permitted to vote in parliamentary elections. Otherwise the patronage continued under Emperor dom Pedro I. He presented bishops and archbishops, and all candidates for ecclesiastical benefices, for confirmation and canonical institution by the pope. The emperor could also withhold the *exequatur*, the approval for the publication of papal communications in his realm. The crown continued to collect the tithe and see that the priests were paid. Since the imperial government was in difficult economic straits, the clergy suffered as well. The pretensions of the emperor were ratified by the papacy in 1827, but the emperor, in turn, refused the *exequatur* for the papal grant, declaring that the Brazilian constitution was superior and did not need ratification by the pope.

Dom Pedro I ruled only until 1831 when he abdicated his Brazilian throne to seek the throne of Portugal, leaving his five-year-old son, dom Pedro II, as emperor. The country was ruled by regency until 1840 when the boy was declared of age. The decade of the regency was a complicated one in Brazilian history. Federalists sought to wrest some powers from the imperial government and return them to the provinces and municipalities. One of the leading politicians during this period was Father Diogo Antonio Feijó, who later became regent. Feijó, however, had a complex political orientation, which was not entirely sympathetic to the papacy if not openly antagonistic. While nominally a liberal, his views were strongly regalist. He supported the patronage as a method of keeping the Brazilian monarch strong even though not all clerics at the time supported this position. Some believed that the Church needed to be autonomous, but privileged. At the same time, a significant number of priests and prelates espoused liberal causes. Feijó himself even advocated an end to the requirement of clerical celibacy. In another example, as early as 1810, the bishop of Rio de Janiero negotiated an agreement with the British to allow a Protestant chapel to be built, provided it was in a private home and that no bells be used to call to worship. There were even calls to separate from Rome and create a national Church, as had occurred in England.

During the regency, the appointment of a bishop for Rio de Janeiro created a furor with the papacy. The Brazilian government nominated a distinguished cleric, and member of parliament, Father Dr. Antonio Maria de Moura, to the see. Moura suffered from ecclesiastical impediments: first of all, he was illegitimate. He had received dispensation for this upon entering the clergy, but needed papal dispensation in order to be consecrated bishop. He also suffered from an additional embarrassment, having endorsed legislation that had been opposed by the papal chargé d'affaires in Brazil. Specifically, he had supported three measures: one loosening restrictions on matrimony, another providing for ecclesiastical advisory boards within dioceses to assist the local prelate, and the third for the creation of an ecclesiastical fund in each diocese, administered by the state, that would collect ecclesiastical fees, tithes, and offerings, administer them, and pay out salaries to ecclesiastical officials. The papal representative in Brazil found these proposals absolutely reprehensible and advocated blocking the appointment. The Vatican followed this recommendation. The regency took this as an affront to its power and the monarch it represented. Diplomats were withdrawn and later exchanged, and then negotiations ensued, but the papacy never did appoint Moura to the diocese. The cleric eventually renounced the nomination and allowed the government to appoint another, with less political baggage. In the confrontation with the papacy, however, the notion of drafting a concordat was explored in order to avoid further conflicts between the imperial government and the Vatican. No concordat was forthcoming, and the monarchy continued to exercise the patronage and the papacy tolerated it, without any clear articulation of powers and privileges.

The regency government dealt with the important political issues of regional versus centralized control. During the regency many of the states claimed various degrees of self-rule, and had their requests confirmed by the imperial parliament. Nevertheless, revolts in the provinces, and the prospect of the disintegration of the nation, caused centralist politicians to push for greater centralization, which occurred on the eve of the end of the regency when dom Pedro II was declared of age. The emperor then ratified these acts and established a relatively stable system that lasted for nearly fifty years.

The ascension of dom Pedro II to the throne brought about a modicum of stability to the nation through a constitutionally vested "moderating power." Dom Pedro wielded far more authority than many monarchs. He had free rein in inviting political parties to form a government and an equally free hand in dissolving them as well. He selected senators from among nominees presented by the provinces; he continued to control both the ecclesiastical patronage and political patronage, directly appointing hundreds of office-holders. The political system was, however, restricted to a small proportion of the population. Only white landowners with an income above a certain level could participate in the political system. The millions of slaves, mulattos, and others were completely divorced from any claim to power.

The political development of Brazil created two factions within the clergy. One faction identified closely with the land and its people, held more liberal political views, and supported the monarchy. The other faction believed that the Church was lax and had fallen away from the true discipline demanded by the papacy, and that the monarch was intrusive into areas of ecclesiastical government to which he had no legal claim. Dom Pedro was philosophically caught between a deep appreciation and love for the Catholic Church but also a true interest in modern issues. In many ways he was a very traditional Catholic with a bit of free-thinker added to the equation. Some believed him to be tolerant of Protestant views, while others claimed that his administration was overpopulated by clergy. As monarch one thing was true: he would protect what he believed to be his privileges with regard to the church and the Royal Patronage.

In the middle of his reign, dom Pedro began to manifest liberal tendencies that concerned some members of the ecclesiastical hierarchy. One of these was his campaign against religious orders in the 1850s. He prohibited the creation of any new seminaries by religious orders and indicated that he would place limitations on those that already existed. In this matter, however, he received the quiet support of the bishops and other prelates who long had recognized the need to reform the orders. In short, his actions provoked no deep conflict between the Church and the state, although several factors played into this subdued response. Pedro was adamant about his authority to fill all ecclesiastical benefices, from the lowest parish to all the dioceses. Consequently, the secular clergy depended heavily on imperial largesse. As well, the secular and the regular clergy continually had a strong antipathy for one another. Thus, restrictions placed on the religious orders would not necessarily prompt a strong opposition from the bishops.

In the 1870s, dom Pedro confronted an issue that would have far greater impact of both his reign and on Church–state relations. In 1864 and 1872 the pope condemned various modern ideas and practices in the encyclical *Quanta Cura* and later in the *Syllabus of Errors*. Among other things, the pope condemned the Masonic Orders and declared excommunication on any Catholic who would join them. Since the early nineteenth century Freemasonry had become quite popular throughout Latin America, especially in Brazil, where Masonry was very stylish among the elite. Many clergy, government officers, and leading notables of Brazilian society were all Masons, and many of the religious confraternities served as Masonic Lodges. When the Vatican prohibited membership in these lodges, the Brazilians, by and large, ignored the pope. At the same time, because the Brazilian emperor continued to exercise the *exequatur*, these papal communications needed to have imperial confirmation before they could circulate in Brazil—and Pedro had not allowed their publication.

In 1872 the bishop of Rio de Janeiro removed a priest who had delivered a sermon in a Masonic Lodge. The bishop ordered him to either renounce Freemasonry or face ecclesiastical suspension. The prime minister, who happened to also be the Grand Master of the Masons in Brazil, convened a general session, calling on all Masons to battle the Church. The bishop of Rio promptly rescinded his order, but the Masons found another target in the person of the newly appointed bishop of Olinda. A newspaper account announced an anniversary celebration of the founding of the local Masonic Lodge to be commemorated with a Mass. The bishop responded by prohibiting any priest from celebrating the Mass. Moreover, he called upon all the confraternities and other Church-sponsored groups to expel any member who was a Mason. Those sodalities that failed to do so would be placed under interdict. The Masons of the diocese now appealed to the emperor. The government requested that the papal representative in Brazil order the bishop to relax his stance. The papal representative in turn only advised the bishop to soften his position. He refused and appealed to the pope for assistance. Of the twelve bishops in Brazil, only one came to the aid of the bishop of Olinda.

The government of dom Pedro mounted a spirited defense of the patronage. The Brazilian ambassador to the Vatican urged the pope to counsel the bishops to cooperate with the local civil authority and to withdraw their threats of interdict and excommunication. The initial reaction of the pope was to support the bishops against the civil government. Upon further reflection, and after consultation with the Brazilian ambassador, the pope lifted the interdict that had been placed on the brotherhoods, with the tacit understanding that the imperial government would take no action against the two bishops. The government, however, opted to accept the pope's position but to also prosecute the bishops. The imperial government ordered the offending bishops to acknowledge the authority of the government in the case, and when they did not, they were arrested. In their trials they were charged with impeding the will of the emperor and of his moderating power. Found guilty, the bishops were condemned to four years hard labor, but the government quickly commuted the sentence to imprisonment only. Nevertheless, the public outcry over having prelates of the Church sentenced to hard labor was extreme. In the public mind the bishops became popular martyrs, and eventually the emperor granted them amnesty. While the imperial government had in effect won the battle over the control of the Church, it eventually lost the war. The "religious question" would become one of the elements in the overthrow of the imperial government by a republic.[9]

Central America

Central America in the first few decades following independence had a very chaotic history. On the one hand, the forces of inertia dictated that the region remain under the authority of Mexico, as they had been in the colonial period. At the same time regional pride and the ideology of independence called for the provinces to seek their own course. The other complicating factor was that each territory wished to become a diocese, and no mechanism existed to petition the papacy to create a new diocese since the provinces of Central America existed only as a distant region of Mexico. When Mexican troops eventually withdrew in 1823, the provinces moved to become a formal federation, under liberal political leadership.

The constitution of the federation and of the member states all declared the Catholic faith to be the official religion. Yet the thorny issue of patronage was not addressed in any of these foundational documents. Unfortunately, both Costa Rica and El Salvador had for years aspired to be their own dioceses, rather than merely parishes in the archbishopric of Guatemala. In both territories the local assembly proclaimed the creation of an independent diocese and appointed prelates as bishops. The archbishop of Guatemala protested this action and threatened to impose ecclesiastical sanctions. El Salvador persisted. In the end the pope formally reprimanded the legislators and ordered them to cease and desist, and to subject themselves to the archbishop of Guatemala. The controversy manifested a political split in the region, since liberals had favored the unilateral creation of the new diocese, while conservatives had deferred to the pope and archbishop. In Costa Rica, although the process began the same, the priest chosen by the assembly to become the new bishop declined the honor, and the politicians decided to leave well enough alone. This controversy brought to light the political division that existed over ecclesiastical policy and the patronage within the federation.

For approximately a decade, the liberals were in control of the federation under the leadership of Francisco Morazán. The archbishop of Guatemala became an immediate target of the liberals. He had been appointed by the Spanish government in the waning years of colonial authority; he had branded the supporters of the independence movements as heretics. To control him politically, the government imposed a form of censure; no pronouncement of the archbishop could be published without the approval of the government. Finally Morazán charged the prelate with treason, declaring that the archbishop was plotting the overthrow of the government. He was arrested and, along with several hundred friars, was banished from the territory. The government then proceeded against the religious orders and abolished them, confiscating their land. Eventually the pope conceded that the archbishop could not return to Guatemala and declared the see to be vacant, allowing the members of the cathedral chapter to appoint an administrator until a new archbishop could be appointed.

Throughout the Central American federation, local provincial assemblies and their chief executives moved to limit the power of the Church. The federal government proclaimed freedom of religion and made marriage a civil contract. It also claimed the right of patronage for the entire federation. In the provinces similar actions were taken locally. The number of holidays was reduced, cemeteries secularized, convents closed, nuns turned out, and the properties confiscated.

The backlash against the liberals came in the form of a popular uprising led by the conservative General Rafael Carrera. Carrera led a movement heavily composed of native peoples, although he himself was a mestizo. They received strong backing from the conservative elite. In 1839 Carrera deposed the government of Morazán and dissolved the federation of Central America. From that point on each province began to exist as an independent state, with Carrera in charge of Guatemala. Some of his first acts included the restoration of the *fuero eclesiastico*, the reestablishment of religious orders, both male and female, and the repatriation of clerics who had been exiled by the liberal government. Carrera later invited the Jesuits to return. The Church played such a large role in the government that the Constitution of 1851 even granted the Church two seats in the congress. The rapprochement with the papacy also continued, and in 1852 Guatemala signed a concordat with the papacy. The concordat granted the right of patronage to the government in return for a declaration that the official religion of the country was the Catholic faith. The government would collect the tithe and also pay an annual stipend to the Church for its support. In essence, all of the reforms of the liberals were swept away. The conservatives remained in power in Guatemala until the 1870s.

While the Central American republics might seem to be indistinguishable in popular imagination, they have very different populations and have had unique histories. Costa Rica, as the most isolated country, had a different historical development following the dissolution of the federation. While a conservative regime took power in the immediate aftermath of the dissolution, the liberals quickly regained power, recalling Morazán from his exile in Peru. Yet his government came to a sorry end when the conservatives reasserted themselves and executed him. For the next forty years the conservatives held sway in Costa Rica, signing a concordat with the papacy in 1852, the same date as the Guatemalan agreement.

The remaining new republics of Central America, Honduras, El Salvador, and Nicaragua, had very similar experiences to Guatemala following the breakup of the federation. In these countries the local conservative elite gained authority and promptly moved to restore the Church privileges, welcome back religious orders, and declare the Church to be in charge of education, marriage, and other key aspects of social governance. El Salvador finally received its status as an independent diocese in 1841 while Costa Rica had to wait until 1850. Nicaragua signed a concordat with the papacy in 1862; Honduras joined Costa Rica and Guatemala in signing one in 1852.

Unquestionably the key feature of the history of the Catholic Church in the middle decades of the nineteenth century in Latin America was the working out of the manner in which the patronage would be inherited by the national governments. Linked to this negotiation, the deep-seated differences between the liberals and conservatives were largely rooted in their perception of the role of the Church in the modern state. Consequently, the role of the Catholic Church was unequivocally the central question that defined Latin American politics in the period. Independence for Latin America brought with it the need to confront how the independent country would relate to the Church, and this theme continued well beyond the middle decades of the nineteenth century.

The United States also began to take an active role in Latin America, particularly in Mexico and Central America. Through the Monroe Doctrine, the United States forcefully announced that it would not tolerate other countries' attempts to intervene in the region. Yet for most of the early and middle part of the nineteenth century, the United States was too weak or involved in its own internal affairs to effectively enforce the doctrine. In addition, the United States was itself expansionist and sought to occupy its sector of North America from the Atlantic to the Pacific. Mexico stood in the way, and so war was declared to gain that territory. And too, the United States had economic interests in its neighbors and realized that the internal affairs of those neighbors had repercussions on its own economic goals. This in turn caused further interventions, especially in Central America.

The native peoples of the Americas suffered greatly in the middle decades of the nineteenth century. While well-meaning governments passed legislation, which they thought would improve economic and social conditions, all too frequently they had the opposite effect, driving native peoples off of their land and forcing them onto the estates of large landowners and into the cities and towns. Moreover, changes in the nature of Church-and-state relations also meant that fewer priests were ordained, and consequently many parishes began to do without a priest for the first time since the seventeenth century. Changes in the legal status of confraternities and sodalities meant that the wealth that native peoples had invested in their own social organizations was frequently lost to the central government, which wished to reduce the power and influence of the Church. Taken as a whole, then, the period was one of turmoil and the realignment of political factions. But at the end of the period it was the natives and peasants who suffered the most as a result.

8

The Established Order and the
Threat of Popular Religion

The end of the nineteenth century and the dawn of the twentieth in Chile saw the slow change from one age to another, as in so many other places in Latin America. In many Latin American countries, power was consolidated among a handful of individual families, but the nature of their influence changed as the twentieth century began. The case of Chile highlights this phenomenon. During the *fin de siècle* in Chile, the Errázuriz family stood at the pinnacle of power and authority. The family was also famous for its wine production, and today the winery is one of the most famous in Chile.

In 1871 Federico Errázuriz Zañartu, was elected as president of the nation, heading up a conservative government. Errázuriz was the nephew of the archbishop of Chile, Rafael Valentín Valdivieso, who had held this position from 1848 to 1878. Errázuriz died before his uncle, passing away in 1876 at the end of his term of office. Two more members of the extended family also came to occupy the Chilean presidency. In 1896, following a civil war, Federico Errázuriz Echaurren was elected on the Liberal Party platform during a period in which the liberals and conservatives had a minimum of political cooperation. He suffered from fragile health and was unable to complete his presidential mandate, dying in 1901. Germán Riesco Errázuriz, a nephew of Errázuriz Zañartu, served as president in 1901. President Errázuriz's cousin, Fr. Crescente Errázuriz, became the archbishop in 1918, serving the archdiocese until his death in 1931.

Archbishop Fr. Cresente Errázuriz played an exceptionally important role in the development of Church-state relations in Chile in the early twentieth century. Early in Fr. Crescente's career, after his ordination to the priesthood, he worked as a writer and editor for two Catholic magazines. He also taught canon law on the faculty of Theology at the University of Chile. He eventually retired to the Recollect Dominican convent and entered the Dominican

Order. In the convent he became a librarian and set about writing the ecclesiastical history of the country, which was published in 1873. His fame as a historian grew, and he received several honors and accolades, rising to the presidency of the Chilean Academy of History in 1914.

Errázuriz's name was presented to the Holy See in 1917 when the government nominated him to become archbishop upon the death of his predecessor. This was a shrewd move on the part of the Chilean president. Appointed in 1920 at the age of 81, no one imagined that Fr. Crescente would serve for very long, but he lived for another eleven years and demonstrated his political acumen throughout that period. Although coming from a conservative tradition, he believed that the Church needed to rise above politics, thus paving the way for some of the dramatic events of the twentieth century. He was, in essence, a late-nineteenth-century figure who bridged the two eras.

His nephew, Rafael Valentín Errázuriz, was a powerful politician who served many terms in both the lower house and the senate, eventually becoming the minister of Foreign Relations, minister of the Interior, and lastly ambassador to the Holy See in Rome (1907–21) exactly during the period of his uncle's service as archbishop.

The Errázuriz family dominated much of the political spectrum in *fin de siècle* Chile. They were supporters of the Conservative Party in the nineteenth century, and eventually came to be standard-bearers for the liberals in the early twentieth. The family was a microcosm of the political life of the nation. Yet most importantly, it highlights the fact that in Latin America in the late nineteenth century only a very few influential families tended to control the entire political life of any given country. While the regimes espoused the principles of republican democracy, in effect the electorate was extremely limited, and the vast majority of people lived outside of the political life of the country.

The late nineteenth century saw a period of relative calm in Church-state relations. The conflicts between liberals and conservatives that marked the middle of the century had largely subsided. Most nations had achieved a balance between the two factions, sometimes favoring the liberals, other times favoring the conservatives. In some countries, however, the Church on the local level confronted stark conditions. The number of priests had declined significantly. The religious enthusiasm of the populace began to erode with the spread of what were perceived as "modern ideas," and the Latin American Church began to become more integrated into the larger world. Taken as a whole, however, it was a period in which religious devotion and personal piety took precedence over the role of the institutional church in large scale national issues.

Republican Brazil

The country that underwent the greatest turmoil in the late nineteenth century was Brazil. In 1889 the military helped to overthrow the emperor and establish a republican form of government. The role of the Church and clergy under the monarchy had manifested many of the themes seen elsewhere. As noted earlier, in Brazil the emperor successfully maintained some control over the Church in his realms although many of the local bishops began to acquire a greater allegiance to the international Church, and to the pope, than to the emperor. Yet, because most ecclesiastical posts fell under the patronage, lower clergy retained a far greater allegiance to the monarchy, which in reality controlled their livelihoods. By the end of the empire, when the emperor began to wield his power in a manner that was considered high-handed by the populace, imperial authority began to wane and the bishops gained credibility. At the same time that the monarch became increasingly regalist in his attitude toward the Church, the bishops became increasingly aligned with the papacy. The issues came to the fore when the emperor began to act unilaterally against the Church in general and individual clerics in particular. The controversy that this unleashed, as we read in chapter 7, came to be known as the "Religious Question." Opposition to the emperor by the bishops and other members of the upper clergy could have potentially aligned them with a republican form of government. Republicanism, however, was also associated with liberalism, a political philosophy that they opposed vehemently.

The republican movement in Brazil in the period prior to the fall of the monarchy was deeply imbued with liberal thinking. Not only did the leadership call for a separation of Church and state, but they also attacked the Church directly, railed against religious orders, and even denounced the dogma of the Immaculate Conception. The republicans, especially in the province of Rio de Janeiro, supported a full liberal agenda including civil marriage, civil registry of births and deaths, freedom of religion, secular education, and secularization of cemeteries. Freemasonry became a contentious political issue when various clerics were punished by their ecclesiastical superiors for membership in and participation in Masonic Lodges. Even when clerical leaders opposed to the emperor proposed alliance with the republicans, the latter declined, finding support of liberal principles more important than the abolition of the empire. Each side of the political divide had its own core political issues from which they would not vary, even to forge alliances.

When Dom Pedro II left for Europe to seek treatment for diabetes, he left his daughter in Brazil, the Infanta Isabel, along with her husband the Comte d'Eu, both devout Catholics. Since the Comte d'Eu was French, a wave of criticism among the republicans arose that the country might fall into the hands of foreigners. That the Infanta had issued pardons to some bishops for crimes under her father's regime caused criticism that the couple would undermine the local autonomy of the Brazilian Church (developed by her father) from the papacy and establish closer ties to Rome. Supporters of the monarchy and those who rallied to the Church, of course, opposed the liberal tendencies of republicanism. While earlier republican movements had drawn upon the lower clergy for some considerable support, by the end of the empire, neither the lower clergy nor many of the lay faithful supported a republic. Quite simply the clergy and laity feared that a republican government would be even worse for their cause than the monarchy had been, and they were far from supportive of the monarchy. Consequently, by the time of the fall of the monarchy, lines had been drawn in Brazil similar to those in the Spanish-speaking republics years and decades earlier. The true conservatives were forced to choose between the lesser of two evils, and threw their support to the emperor and his family.

Yet the conflict between Church and state in the latter years of the empire was not the only problem that confronted the monarchy. Among other causes, the liberals also fought for several decades to abolish slavery in Brazil, as it was the last country in Latin America to abolish the slave trade. It moved very slowly toward abolition, first with the passage of the "Law of Free Birth" whereby all children born of slaves after its promulgation would become free. This provided for the eventual elimination of slavery but not its abolition. Abolition came in 1888, on the eve of the revolt that ousted the monarch.

In the late 1860s Brazil became involved in a disastrous war against Paraguay. As a result of an alliance with a political faction in Uruguay, both Argentina and Brazil were drawn into conflict with Paraguay. Much to everyone's surprise Paraguay, convinced that its very existence was in jeopardy, successfully resisted and the war ground on for five more years. The war annihilated one-third of the male population of Paraguay but also had serious repercussions in Brazil. There, the emperor continued to press for a full victory, even when the war stagnated. This cost him much political credibility because he had traditionally been seen as a moderate seeking compromise. Liberals increasingly faulted the government for a host of sins, including unpreparedness and an inability to successfully conclude the war.

To complicate matters, in pursuing the war the Brazilians recruited slaves to fight, offering them freedom in return. This offended many of the conservative landowners, who constituted some of the emperor's strongest defenders. The military soon tired of the political bickering and came to resent political interference in what they felt was their own responsibility.

All of these issues came to a head after the promulgation of the abolition of slavery. Shortly thereafter the Brazilian military staged a coup, ousted the emperor, and proclaimed a republic. The republic began as a military state but quickly passed to the hands of politicians. Within two years a new constitution was written. The political environment of the early republic tended more toward liberal thought than conservative, although a few prominent conservatives did participate in the government. Quite simply, the liberals were republican and opposed the monarchy on a whole host of grounds. Yet some conservatives were able to disassociate their tendency to support the monarchy to recognize the strengths of a republican government. One important move was to disestablish the Church and begin to implement some liberal goals, such as civil marriage, and civil registry. Titles of nobility were outlawed; suffrage was expanded through the abolition of property requirements; and the republic became a federation of states.

One important theme within Brazilian liberal thinking was the influence of positivism. Founded by the French philosopher Auguste Comte, positivism attempted to subject all of human activity to the rigors of the scientific method. Comte, considered the father of the discipline of sociology, also believed that order and progress were intimately linked. Without order there could be no progress and with progress would come order. These ideals were embraced by a small group of influential Brazilian republicans. The positivist motto of "Order and Progress" became emblazoned on the Brazilian national flag. Positivism reached the level of religious devotion in Brazil, when a positivist church was established there in the waning days of the empire.

A deep political dichotomy developed in Brazil between the coast and the interior. The overwhelming majority of the population lived relatively near the coast, with notable exceptions being the regions of São Paulo and Minas Gerais. The religious life of the interior had traditionally relied heavily on missionaries, frequently members of religious orders. This pattern suffered its first disruption in 1759 when the Jesuits were expelled. Some religious orders, such as the Franciscans and Capuchins, attempted to fill the gap created by the expulsion but lacked the manpower to fully restore missions. Throughout the nineteenth century the hinterland remained poorly served by clergy. With the abolition of the monarchy and the system of Royal Patronage that supported parish priests, the interior again suffered a loss of priests. As a result, popular religious movements began to take root in the sparsely populated interior in the absence of a well-developed central Church.

The Church also suffered from a changing climate brought on by the new republic and by mandates coming from the Vatican. The disestablishment of the Church forced it to rely on its own resources, having been cut off from public financial support. There were so few priests in the interior that years might pass between their visits in any specific village. The clerics themselves had gone through many decades of a rather lax discipline. Many maintained families, had sporadic contact with their superiors, and adopted less than orthodox theologies. The lack of discipline and limited supervision of parish priests had become nearly normative. The Vatican was eager to impose greater control over the clergy and looked to local bishops to clean up morals to assure that priests were better educated. Yet the Church was confronted by financial crises and too few trained priests to serve the vast populations along the coast, let alone minister to the interior.

The period after the fall of the monarchy was one of considerable social turmoil and a mass movement of people: slaves fleeing the plantations, temporary workers moving to cities, and the arrival of new immigrants from Europe. In the interior, therefore, several non-orthodox religious movements began to appear. This tradition of popular religion developed due largely to the hinterland's isolation and infrequent contact with clergy.[1] Even in the coastal communities popular religion was powerful, with strong African components.

Canudos and Joaseiro

Perhaps the most famous popular religious uprisings in the interior was led by Antônio Conselheiro in the village of Canudos. Conselheiro, a mystical figure, gained a large following in 1893. He and his followers built a new settlement at Canudos, where he preached a mildly apocalyptic vision. While firmly rooted in Christianity, his message had additional influences from popular piety and local religion. What attracted the attention of the government was Conselheiro's strident opposition to the republic, opposition to civil marriage and civil registry, and support for monarchy, although he criticized the excesses of the monarchy during the ecclesiastical crises of the previous two decades. Canudos essentially seceded from the nation, relying on its own agricultural production, residents working in local estates, and donations from supporters throughout Brazil. As the republicans began to feel more threatened by monarchist plots in the wake of some assassination attempts against the new elected president and other leaders, they saw Canudos as the embodiment of the opposition and as a real threat. The army was sent to destroy the community. Although the villagers put up a valiant fight, in the end they were defeated. Villagers who had surrendered as part of an offer of clemency were murdered. Conselheiro was killed and then beheaded.

The rebellion at Canudos helped to bring many of the cultural and political divisions of Brazil to the fore. On the surface it contrasted the condition of the disestablished Catholic Church in the new republic with an apocalyptic popular religion, which had formed the heart and soul of the community. It also brought to public attention the vast cultural division between the interior and the coast. The political leaders of the time were largely of European descent, while Conselheiro's followers were from all races and mixtures. The positivist philosophy that guided many of the republic's leaders called for order and progress, but they were forced to use bloody force to bring down what was in essence a peaceful community. Finally, the weakness of the military became apparent because the army attempted four times to conquer the settlement before it actually succeeded. Deep fissures in the state emerged as a result of the reaction to Canudos.[2]

Roughly contemporary with Conselheiro and his utopia at Canudos was the development of the village of Joaseiro by Father Cícero Romão Batista. Father Cícero, a Catholic priest, was assigned to the village of Joaseiro in 1872. Throughout the waning years of the empire, Father Cícero comported himself in a manner expected of a clergyman, worked with his bishop, and supported the good works of various religious associations. Legend has it that in 1889 a miracle occurred. Blood appeared in the consecrated host as he administered it to a lay person. The miracle was taken up and proclaimed by various neighboring clergy, including the rector of the nearby diocesan seminary. Now, hundreds of pilgrims began to descend on Joaseiro to share in the miracle, but the place never became as self-supporting and closed a community as did Canudos. The ecclesiastical hierarchy did not accept the miracle, and in 1892 the bishop suspended Father Cícero from holy orders. A rift formed between the local secular clerics and the diocesan administration that was slow to heal. The local priests supported Father Cícero and opposed the actions of the bishop. Eventually, as Father Cícero became more estranged from the ecclesiastical hierarchy, he turned to local political leaders for support. He pledged his political neutrality in return for the leaders to vouch for his devotion to the Church and his orthodoxy. As a result of this bargain Joaseiro began to flourish, since it was tacitly removed from the political turmoil of the time. While political leaders were murdered, Joaseiro remained quiet. Then in 1908 Father Cícero entered into politics. He seemed to believe that he might use political influence to persuade the Vatican to choose Joaseiro as the capital town of a newly planned diocese for the region of Ceará. The ecclesiastical authorities, however, vehemently opposed this. Cícero did successfully gain recognition from the state government of the status of Joaseiro as a *vila,* gaining ascendency over other towns in the region, and from this point on Father Cícero became enmeshed in politics.

Joaseiro serves as a contrast to Canudos. In the wake of Church-state conflict under the empire, the republic disassociated itself from the Church. The populace had grown to support the Church more than the monarchy. In rural areas the clergy were too limited to effectively serve the people, so laypersons took on ecclesiastical functions and lay preachers arose, as did individuals who sought to emulate the dedication of members of religious orders while remaining laypersons. All this change created multiple spiritual responses. Conselhiero in Canudos sought to withdraw completely from the turmoil and focus instead on spirituality. Father Cicero's reaction was far more nuanced. Although he witnessed the original miracle, others began drawing attention to it. He was suspended from holy orders not because he publicized the miracle but because of opposition to the miracle by the bishop. Father Cicero became identified with the miracle initially only through association. He became involved in politics in part to regain his clerical status. One of the attendant miracles of Joaseiro was that in spite of political change all around it, the town was able to grow and prosper. The experiences of Conselhiero at Canudos and Father Cicero at Joaseiro mark two very different responses to the politics of the time.[3]

Mexico

In Mexico the Liberal Party had regained power following the expulsion of the French. In the years that followed the liberals began to systematically implement the wide range of policies they had already embodied in the Mexican Constitution of 1857. This included the nationalization of Church property, supplanting the Church sacraments with civil registry, suppression of noble titles, and the elimination of the vestiges of entailed estates. For the Church the worst was already over in many ways. The conflict and acrimony generated in the 1850s did not return to the same degree in the late 1860s and 1870s, largely because the supporters of the Church were so thoroughly defeated. The victorious Benito Juárez created a government office to administer the properties confiscated from the Church and to investigate properties rumored to belong to the Church.

Upon Juárez's death political factions began to emerge, both within the ruling liberals and among the shattered conservatives. There were those among the liberals who opposed Juárez in his later years, not because of his policies but because he had served four terms as president. Many liberals believed that term limits were necessary to keep a democracy from moving toward autocracy. In Juárez's defense, two of his terms of office were interrupted by war and so he could not effectively govern as president. His successor, Sebastián Lerdo de Tejada, pursued a rigorous campaign against the Church and clergy, proclaiming religious vows to be illegal, prohibiting any ecclesiastical institution from acquiring land or even taking out mortgages and loans with land as collateral. Yet among the liberals there was a faction that supported a more moderate approach with regard to the Church, at the same time that these same liberals held a more militant policy with regard to central tenets, such as opposition to reelection. Porfirio Díaz, a hero of the liberal cause as a result of his role in the defense of the city of Puebla during the French intervention, emerged as the leader of the moderate "no reelection" camp and won the presidency in 1876, following an abortive coup.

In terms of his relationship with the Church, Díaz took a more conciliatory stand than had his liberal predecessors and probably turned a blind eye when local officials chose to ignore many laws. His first term of office lasted until 1880. Other than a lax enforcement of the reform laws aimed at the Church, he made no major changes in policy. As the candidate of the no reelection faction, in 1880 he stepped down, and his designated successor, Manuel González, was elected. While some observers argued that González was a puppet for Díaz, most scholarship indicates that he was his own man. His term was one marked by a slow return to graft and corruption, something Díaz had largely either eliminated or kept contained. Díaz had also managed to stimulate the economy and improve conditions generally. In 1884, when Díaz again announced his candidacy for the presidency, it was a foregone conclusion that he would win.

After his electoral success of 1884, Díaz abandoned his no reelection philosophy and remained in power until 1911. An important component of his political program was a rapprochement with the Church. While maintaining a formal separation of Church and state, Díaz undermined the more onerous of the liberal policies. While nominally calling for enforcement, he took no actions to require local officials to crack down on offenders. Under Díaz the Church was able to recover much of the property and other wealth that it had lost after 1857. One estimate held that Church property actually doubled under Díaz and that as much as 10 percent of the capital available was again in the hands of the Church and clerics. The number of Catholic schools doubled under Díaz, and new churches and chapels were allowed once again to be built. The Church grew so much under Díaz that five new archdioceses and eight new dioceses appeared. Although Díaz publically rejected opening diplomatic ties with the Vatican and never claimed any of the old patronage rights, behind the scenes he was making suggestions to the Vatican about episcopal appointments.

The Díaz regime, like the Brazilian elite at the time of the fall of the monarchy, believed in the positivist philosophy of order and progress. Díaz came to rule with a stern hand, creating the order necessary for economic development and was successful in improving the Mexican economy. He invited American and British companies to assist Mexico in exploiting its natural resources, especially in the mining industry. Other external concessionaires helped to develop a fledgling railway system, operate the ports of the nation, and establish plantations and other agricultural industries. Díaz surrounded himself with intellectuals and advisors who embraced positivism and were known as the *científicos*. They saw the Church as an important ally in the development of the nation. The Church could help maintain social stability and order. The *científicos* also adopted what was called "Social Darwinism." Under this mistaken ideology, many of the elite, usually of European heritage, believed that they were in fact superior to the native and mixed race peoples. The success of the elite was believed to be proof positive that in the survival of the fittest, they were manifestly more fit. Biologically speaking, the members of the elite were clearly superior, and there was little the natives could do to change the situation, being that it was an inherent difference. The elite, then, had two options to follow regarding the natives and peasants: they could either limit the influence of the peasants on the society, or they could seek to somehow improve their conditions. Under the leadership of Díaz and the *científicos*, Mexico was transformed into a peaceful and, ostensibly, prosperous country. Its industrial output increased, it paid off its foreign debt, and it collected slightly more in taxes than it spent. However, in spite of the generally rosy aggregate view, things were terribly wrong.

While overall wealth increased in Mexico, it was at the cost of the lowest members of society. The rich got very much richer and the poor remained destitute. Some Mexicans increasingly felt like foreigners in their own country, as more and more industries and land were acquired by foreign interests. The Mexican elite had lifestyles that were very different from their compatriots. The former were heavily influenced by French and European fashions and tastes, while many of the latter lived in abject poverty and worked as tenant farmers on lands owned by others. While the Reform had confiscated much land owned by the Church, only to have Díaz return it later, it had also targeted any lands held communally or corporately. Therefore, much of the land owned by native communities was confiscated by the government since it was communally held. This land was then sold at auction, creating many large estates owned by wealthy Mexican and foreigners, and employing the local natives as either day laborers or tenant farmers.

Many of the *científicos* were not Roman Catholics, yet they tended to look upon the Church more as an ally than an enemy. The result was that the Church was then enlisted as a partner in the regime. For opponents of the regime, especially those of a more radical persuasion, the rapprochement between Church and state only reinforced the Marxists' dictum that religion was the "opium of the people." They felt that the state callously used the Church to maintain social stability and passivity.

While Antônio Conselheiro was founding Canudos and Padre Cicero was in Joaseiro (1889–97), a young woman named María Teresa Urrea began a millenarian movement in the Mexican state of Sonora. María Teresa grew up in the village of Cabora, the illegitimate daughter of a local notable and a native woman but raised in her father's home. In 1890, she suffered from a violent seizure, which left her in a coma for months. When she woke up from the coma she recounted talking with the Virgin Mary and told of other visions. Stories began to emerge that she had healing powers. Newspaper reporters dispatched to investigate published conflicting opinions about her. The local ecclesiastical leaders denounced her, and the civil authorities sought to determine if there were signs of insurrection in her preaching and actions. Thousands of pilgrims from throughout northern Mexico began to arrive daily at the village to hear her preach and receive her blessing. Followers then took the story of "La Santa de Cabora" or "Santa Teresa de Cabora" to their home villages.

Teresa's message seems to have focused on three ills: money, doctors, and priests. She argued that the Catholic Church was controlled by the Antichrist and that her followers did not need to follow its tenets nor embrace its sacraments. She indicated that reform was at hand. She similarly had no good words for the medical professions and claimed that people could heal themselves through traditional remedies, prayer, and devotion. She saw money and the state that supported it as being evil.

One of the villages where followers of Santa Teresa gained a political advantage was Tomochic, some 130 miles from Cabora. It was a mestizo town where most residents were a mixture of Spanish and native. There Cruz Chávez latched onto her message as a pathway to both salvation and political autonomy. Chávez had been among a group of young men seeking divine intervention to solve modern problems. Chávez became aware of Teresa through word of mouth from her village and from messages from her which were printed and distributed throughout the area. Her printed messages claimed to protect the holders from harm and that if they worshipped the Virgin and the Holy Cross, respected their superiors, gave alms, and avoided evil they would prosper. Teresa preached about the unequal distribution of land, where some individuals owned hundreds of thousands of acres, while others had nothing. She heavily criticized the political and ecclesiastical hierarchy, although she sent a mixed message since she also called on followers to respect authority.

Problems came to Tomochic when a local priest arrived and scolded the locals for their veneration of Teresa, claiming that she was no saint but a charlatan. Cruz Chávez emerged as the leader of the pro-Teresa faction in the village; he followed the priest out of town heaping insults on him. Rumors of a more widespread revolt began to trickle out of Tomochic and worried the local civil authorities. They dispatched a small force of soldiers to investigate. Their accounts told of Chávez acting like a priest, chanting and praying in the church. Later men came forward and he blessed their rifles while an assistant placed copper tacks into the stocks in the shape of the letter T. While all of this is equivocal as to the real intent of the followers of Teresa in Tomochic, the government interpreted it as signs of preparations for rebellion. In 1892, the army attacked the village. While accounts told of fierce fighting, not all the believers perished. They later rallied and began a march to Cabora, and both army and militia units harassed them on the way. Upon arrival in Cabora they discovered that Teresa had left, perhaps to avoid becoming involved in a political fight. She had, in fact, fled to the United States. The Tomochitecos entered her chapel, laid down their arms, and returned in small groups to Tomochic, swearing to die with their families. The fierce opposition that they had received at the hands of the army undoubtedly convinced them that they were marked men.

Once back in Tomochic, the believers continued to support Teresa but exercised their own judgment about which parts of her message they would embrace. It was not a closed town, people came and went, but in general those who opposed the believers fled to nearby towns and cities, and urged the government to take action to reestablish control in Tomochic. Although Teresa did not endorse the movement in Tomochic, she was in communication with it, as letters were later discovered between her and Cruz Chávez. The civil government entered negotiations with the believers in Tomochic, but little was accomplished. Many remaining villagers then fled, fearing a confrontation. The local army and militia were ordered to attack, but the results were muted since they did not want to fire on their neighbors. Eventually a force from the federal army was brought in to attack the village, and fighting began in earnest. After a week the villagers raised a white flag, and the women and children filed out; the flag was somehow lowered and hostilities ensued. At last the army staged an all-out assault on the village and killed everyone there.

The rebellion in Tomochic adopted the message of Santa Teresa de Cabora, but it was not directly her work. While the government branded the believers as ignorant Indians, they were in fact mestizos. The government also claimed that they were fanatics, but even this is open to debate. In their first siege on the village, when the believers left and went to Cabora, while surely devout, they did not act like fanatics. In the second and fatal siege, however, either the military engaged in excess in slaying everyone in the village, or the believers literally fought to the death, having sent away the women and children. While the overt message focused on religion, other messages from Tomochic were political. The followers refused to accept the political status quo in which government was the preserve of a few powerful men, large tracts of land were controlled by a few wealthy families, and a distant and isolated ecclesiastical hierarchy had indeed lost touch with the spiritual needs of their flock.[4]

Tomochic and Canudos were very different. Teresa did not lead in Tomochic, rather political leadership was embraced by Cruz Chávez. In Canudos, Conselheiro was both prophet and leader. Canudos was a refuge; Tomochic and Cabora were merely the towns where Teresa and Chávez lived, although Tomochic eventually became an armed camp. Conselheiro railed against the new republican government of Brazil and its restrictions on the Church, civil registry, and secularization. In Tomochic, Chávez preached nothing overtly against the state, although the impact of the message created concerns in the government. Many of the voices calling for the assault on Tomochic were villagers themselves who had fled and disagreed with Chavez, whereas it was purely the government that opposed Canudos. But at their core, both movements represented the power of a local religious cult, which took on political and social messages and became a threat to the existing power structures.

These movements are also indicative of the rise of popular religion that occurred in late-nineteenth- and early-twentieth-century Latin America, particularly in rural regions with high concentrations of native peoples. In the colonial period the Church was able to increase the number of priests who served in rural areas. Evangelization in many areas was far from complete, allowing for the development of hybrid religions, which incorporated both Christian and native belief systems. The unsettled ecclesiastical situation of the late colonial period, caused by the Bourbon Reforms and secularization of the parishes, and complicated by the turmoil of the movements for independence, created great instability in the rural areas. The conflicts between the liberals and conservatives particularly over the nature of the Church in the new republics, further destabilized the situation. Finally, the success of the liberals in most areas and the closure of seminaries meant that fewer priests were available to serve rural areas. As a result popular religious expressions emerged to fill the void.

Central America

Nearby Guatemala and other Central American countries experienced their own unique histories the last decades of the nineteenth and early years of the twentieth century. Many of the Central American nations embraced the basic tenets of liberalism, but while not openly hostile to the Church, they did little to support it either. In Guatemala in the nineteenth century some 70 percent of the population was considered to be members of indigenous groups. The remaining 30 percent was categorized as *ladino* (mestizo), persons of mixed native and European heritage. Following their success in 1871, the liberals embarked on several decades of essentially anticlericalism.

The case of Guatemala is especially curious because not only did the liberal government severely restrict the activities of the Catholic Church, it openly invited Protestant missionaries. Among other anticlerical acts, the government expelled the Jesuits and confiscated their properties, extinguished all-male religious orders, expelling foreigners, and took their properties. The government also created civil registry and civil marriage, and abolished the ecclesiastical courts. On the other hand, the liberals were convinced that part of the economic success of the United States and other developed countries was their embrace of Protestant ethics. The ladinos of the government, like their colleagues in Mexico, believed in what Max Weber would come to call the "Protestant ethic" at the same time they embraced notions of Social Darwinism. This latter ideology placed the native peoples on a level beneath their more well-educated compatriots. The government leaders believed that only time and much effort would raise the natives to the level of intellectual achievement of the ladinos. The government declared freedom of worship and then invited foreign missionaries, particularly to the regions of greatest native population. Political instability in Guatemala discouraged most missionaries, and it was not until a decade later that the first Presbyterian missionary arrived, taking up residence not in a native village, but in Guatemala City. The Protestants began to arrive in greater numbers in the last ten years of the nineteenth and first decade of the twentieth century.

The impact of these policies on the part of the government had a dramatic impact. By 1908, for a population of some 2 million people in Guatemala, only 120 diocesan priests and 12 priests who were members of religious orders served in all of that country's 101 parishes, while another 83 members of religious orders lived in the country. At about the same time there were only 16 students in the archdiocesan seminary.[5] In spite of these dismal statistics, the Protestants did not have much success in the first few decades of their missionary efforts. The missionaries chose to work mostly using Spanish, since the government had a policy of trying to eradicate the native languages by forcing them to speak Spanish. This, however, required them to use interpreters when out on mission. The missionaries also chose to convert through good works, to emulate Christian ethics, focusing their efforts on schools and hospitals. Yet none of these strategies brought about massive conversions from Catholicism. Openly anti-Catholic preaching of the missionaries and their desire to turn the natives into modern Westerners also met with icy resistance. The natives were comfortable in their own brand of Catholicism and did not wish to abandon their culture for the Western shoes and uncomfortable clothes of the missionaries.[6]

While the native population did not convert to Protestantism, neither did the Catholic Church exercise much control. As native communities saw less and less of the visiting priests, they maintained the spiritual life of the community through collective institutions that had existed for centuries. Even in the colonial period, the native communities had come to participate in their own churches. Natives assisted the local parish priest in a wide range of activities, serving as catechists, musicians and cantors, sacristans, and as officers in local sodalities. The sodalities came to occupy a very important place in local religion. Most religious celebrations revolved around the devotional calendar associated with the sodality. Members of the community passed through a system of leadership opportunities in both the civil (village) and religious hierarchies. This pattern of service came to be known as the *cargo* system, as the Spanish word *cargo* means a position of trust and authority (see chap. 4). A young man might begin with a minor civil post in the village government, then a minor post in the sodality, taking on offices of increasing responsibility in each hierarchy as he matured. The offices also carried with them the responsibility to organize *fiestas*, which would entail the periodic redistribution of wealth; as the officer became wealthier, he would need to put on more lavish celebrations. Moreover, the very tone of the celebration had much more to do with traditional native spirituality than Christianity. The relative absence of priests only ensured that native traditions could continue without major restriction.

The other republics of Central America differed in one degree or another from each other and from Guatemala insofar as their ecclesiastical histories developed in the late nineteenth and early twentieth centuries. El Salvador, however, mimicked Guatemala. The liberals were equally anticlerical and just as supportive of Protestant missionaries. In Honduras and Nicaragua, the conservatives were able to hold onto power longer, providing for an alternation of parties and a generally higher level of support for the Church; however, in Honduras the liberal regime after 1880 did begin to act in an anticlerical fashion, while this occurred fourteen years later in Nicaragua. Costa Rica differed from the others in that it never had a protracted period of anticlerical governments. In fact, Church-state relations remained cordial throughout the period.

South American Republics and Concordats

Several South American republics eventually succeeded in negotiating concordats with the Vatican. In Venezuela the concordat was never ratified locally, and with the strict anticlerical stance of the dictator Guzmán Blanco it became a dead letter. In Peru, while not an actual concordat, the pope did outline a formal relationship with the state in an 1874 bull granting to the state certain privileges. The bull was formally accepted by the government in 1880. In the next few decades there was a slow movement to implement the liberal causes of civil marriage for non-Catholics, civil cemeteries, and even freedom of worship. In Colombia, following fierce confrontations between various factions, in 1888 the pope issued a concordat, which was promptly ratified and served the country fairly well for the next half century. On the surface these three republics seem to be quite similar, but in fact they had three very different experiences.

In Venezuela, education remained firmly under the grip of the civil government, but it also allowed the existence of a few church-supported schools. By the 1920s one of the critical issues facing the Church in Venezuela was the severe shortage of priests, especially for rural and isolated areas. In addition, the Church had very little money. With the loss of support from the royal government and no tradition of regular giving from the laity, the Church had only its investments and property to support its activities, and these fell under civil scrutiny and much was lost. The state did provide a small subsidy from time to time, but it was not sufficient to support the existing activities of the Church. In short, the period at the end of the nineteenth century and the beginning of the twentieth found the Church in Venezuela in full decline.

In Peru, the Church did not suffer as much at the hands of the liberal governments as in Mexico or Venezuela; rather, a compromise developed. A radical constitution developed in 1869 did not last, and thereafter the liberals were content to slowly implement their program. Over the next few decades civil cemeteries were established, civil marriage for non-Catholics was allowed, followed by freedom of worship, and eventually universal civil marriage. Intellectuals and political leaders of Peru became enamored of positivism as a means of explaining the country's inability to modernize. Variously the native population and the dogmatism of the Church were cited as barriers to modernity. At the same time, Protestants appeared in Peru ready to evangelize. A large part of the ruling elite had become ambivalent to the Church, although their wives and daughters tended to be more fervent in their support. Eventually, by the early part of the twentieth century, grassroots organizations began to defend what they perceived as the traditional values of the Church. Some of the presidents during that period won their elections thanks to overt support from the Church. Those years also saw the founding of the Catholic University in 1917, Catholic printing presses, and the arrival of new religious orders and congregations. In 1919 President Augusto Leguía took office, to govern for eleven years. He actively sought to improve Church-state relations. The Church tried to reciprocate, but the success of the rapprochement was not clear. As in Venezuela, two important problems were the increasing shortage of priests and the decline in Church revenues.

In Colombia, the Church enjoyed many of the privileges denied it in Peru or Venezuela. The concordat of 1888 clearly granted various rights to both parties, and it also served as a framework to work out disputes, protected the Church from confiscations and other depredations, and granted to the civil government a modicum of control. The document recognized the state's ability to create civil cemeteries, for example, without infringing on Church-supported ones. The Church could still maintain civil registries, subject to submission to the government. Conversely, the government promised financial support to the Church, partially in recognition of confiscations that had occurred earlier, and the two parties would renegotiate the subsidy every ten years. In 1902 the government also offered to provide financial support to missionaries. It agreed that the missionaries could take on the responsibility of providing elementary education in the mission districts. The concordat succeeded because both the political factions of the liberals and conservatives saw the value of compromise. Most important, the Church in Colombia benefitted from government support and its protected status. The Colombian case provides a stark comparison to Venezuela and Peru: Venezuela marks an extreme case where the Church never regained its luster from the battles of the nineteenth century; in Peru a rapprochement was developed, but it was an uneasy truce; but in Colombia the Church and state were able to find common ground and work positively together.

One of the phenomena of the Southern Cone in the nineteenth century was the presence of British merchants. In Argentina, Chile, Brazil, and Peru there were large numbers of British commercial representatives. Early on, the British government made freedom of religion for these citizens a part of their foreign policy concerns. Anglican churches were founded to minister to these populations. By the late nineteenth century the population of Protestants in the Southern Cone had grown considerably beyond the Anglicans to include many other mainline denominations. Many of these churches had active programs to send missionaries to Latin America—both to evangelize native populations who had never embraced Christianity as well as to offer an alternative to Catholics.

In Argentina, the adoption of the Constitution of 1853 established a period of general stability in Church-state relations. That constitution was clearly modeled on that of the United States but had special provisions with relation to the Catholic Church. While the constitution did not declare the Catholic Church to be the official religion of Argentina, it did indicate that the state would support the Church. In doing this, the country left the door open to allow the state to exercise control over the Church. If the state supported the Church financially, there was the expectation that some aspect of the patronage would continue. The president was required to be a Catholic, but the government retained the right to approve papal communications before their publication and other issues related to the Church. The government sought a concordat with Rome but did not achieve one. There were several conflicts between the Argentine state and the Church, but none was truly serious. The government routinely nominated candidates for episcopal office, and they were subsequently approved by the Vatican. The government suggested the creation of new diocese, and the Vatican complied. And so, while a concordat never occurred, both parties acted as if one were in place.

In Chile, the late nineteenth century saw the emergence of debates regarding the Church and the rise of Protestantism. There had been a small but influential group of British and American merchants resident in Chile from the time of independence. Liberal governments pursued freedom of religion and thus protected some of these interests. The conservatives wished to maintain the Catholic Church as the official state church and to require everyone to follow the marriage laws of the Church. By the last third of the nineteenth century, Chilean politics had split into four factions. In addition to the traditional liberal and conservative parties, the National and Radical parties emerged. The National Party represented secular conservatives, those who supported most of the conservative agenda but who also supported freedom of religion and other social parts of the liberal agenda. The Radicals consisted of the most liberal politicians for whom the issue of freedom of religion and the diminution of the power of the Church was paramount.

The structure of the Chilean government seemed to mimic that in the United States, with a bicameral legislature and an elected president, who served for a maximum of two five-year terms (a single term after 1871). Yet in the latter part of the nineteenth century it became a de facto parliamentary system. Because of political fragmentation, presidents could not get their legislative initiatives passed without alliances among the parties. They began to apportion seats in their cabinets to the various factions and parties in an attempt to create a ruling majority. For the last three decades of the nineteenth century, the issue over which these factions and parties argued most was that of the role of the Church and the state.

The arguments in Chile differed little from those heard in the rest of Latin America. The central issue was the degree to which the Catholic Church would be the official state religion, whether the central government would control or support the Church, whether the state would adopt civil registry and civil marriage, and whether there would be secular education, and the role of the Church in providing it. Eventually, in 1883 the package of laws that would make up the "Theological Reform Laws" (*leyes reformas teológicas*) came into being. The first of these addressed the issue of burial. The law nationalized the ecclesiastical cemeteries and declared them to be new civil cemeteries. When the Church authorities protested, the government closed all ecclesiastical cemeteries and prohibited burials within the churches themselves, which caused many subsequent problems. Soon thereafter a law creating civil marriage emerged. It allowed for the civil registry of marriages and established a required civil ceremony for all marriages, even those which had first been performed by a priest. It also transferred all lawsuits regarding marriages to the civil jurisdiction, even allowing for legal separation, but not true divorce. Next, civil registry of all life events was enacted, adding to the civil registry of marriages the registry of births and deaths. While all of these laws moved Chile toward a state that would allow for freedom of religion, the constitution still mandated the Catholic Church as the official state religion. Even though the government was unable to amend the constitution, lacking sufficient political clout, freedom of religion existed in fact.

The religious question played an important part in the Chilean civil war of 1891. To the casual observer the war was a most curious one: the president was pitted against the legislature, the army against the navy. At its root was the quasi-parliamentary structure wherein a president needed legislative confirmation of his cabinet ministers. Between 1888 and 1891 the president, José Manuel Balmaceda, increasingly came to loggerheads with congress over the approval process. Of course, the factions were also split over the religious issues of the day. Although congress had passed the Theological Reform Laws, any subsequent congress could overturn them. At the same time the country was also suffering through a period of labor unrest. What had been isolated industries, mining, the ports, and agriculture, were now all being stopped by widespread strikes. Neither Balmaceda nor the congress would relent, and the government soon was without funds, since no appropriations bills had been passed nor taxes collected. Balmaceda called upon the army to pacify the country and to occupy the customs houses, one sure source of revenue. In turn, the navy supported the congress and occupied the ports. The congress also organized its own army, largely among striking nitrate miners, and eventually carried the day. Balmaceda committed suicide. What emerged was a true parliamentary form of government, with a fairly weak executive and powerful legislature. The power of the Church had been weakened, but it remained an institution central to Chilean identity. The state still provided it with an annual subsidy and from time to time intervened in ecclesiastical appointments. At the end of the nineteenth century the question was not whether there would be a separation of Church and state, but rather when it would be finally accomplished.

The latter half of the nineteenth century saw some general trends throughout Latin America. The conflict between liberals and conservatives worked out in slightly different ways in different countries. In some the conflict was moderate, with both sides recognizing the Church as an institution that provided continuity and stability in the face of rapid change. In others the Church was seen as an obstacle to modernization. In these cases, middle ground rapidly eroded. There simply was no place for liberals who believed in the value of the Church, or conservatives who questioned the more absolutist claims of the clerical supporters. Part of the beginnings of the Protestant churches in Latin America came from those liberals who were religious and increasingly saw the Catholic Church as intransigent or dogmatic. This became especially true as the Church increasingly opposed any type of liberal reform, most clearly embodied in the 1864 Syllabus of Errors, a curious document that listed eighty statements, which the pope found to be worthy of condemning. Pius IX unequivocally condemned such liberal thoughts such as freedom of religion and the separation of Church and state. Nine years later Pius published the encyclical *Etsi multa*, which was directed specifically to Switzerland and Germany, but the text also roundly criticized the liberal movements, particularly in Latin America.

For its part, the Church underwent a slow and steady change in this period, mostly directed from Rome. The Latin American Church had been largely isolated, certainly in the colonial period but even in the early decades of the nineteenth century. Improvements in communications and continual pressure on the part of the papacy had the effect of creating a more integrated ecclesiastical hierarchy. Freed from the rule of patronage, the pope could begin to appoint bishops and archbishops in accordance with a plan or system, mostly of creating more direct control over the Latin American Church. Even in those countries where the national government claimed or attempted to exercise the right of appointment to ecclesiastical office, the papacy had a large degree of freedom to negotiate and to slowly move toward greater control. One important event occurred in 1859 with the creation of the Colegio Pio Latino Americano, a school of superior studies in Rome for young men from Latin America and approved by Pius IX. The first director of studies was the Chilean priest José Ignacio Victor Ezayguirre. Although the founder was a secular priest, eventually Jesuits came to dominate the life of the college. This college created a core of highly skilled and well-trained priests. Rather than holding on to purely nationalist or local perspectives, these priests were trained in a truly *catholic* sense, to see the scope of the Church throughout the world, and the place of Latin America within that larger plan. They became more closely tied to Rome and the Vatican. In the first hundred years of existence the college educated more than 2,000 students. Half of these received doctorates, in theology, philosophy, and canon law. Some 1,500 became priests, while 183 eventually became bishops, and 7 rose to cardinalship, a truly impressive accomplishment.[7]

As the college was being developed, the pope also convened the First Vatican Council (1869–71), the first ecumenical council since Trent in the sixteenth century. No Latin American bishops were able to participate in the two-decade-long deliberations of Trent, but some forty bishops from the region did participate in Vatican I. The experience helped to heighten the sense of solidarity among the Latin American prelates. It further strengthened their ties to Rome and helped to create a sense of common destiny among them. The Latin American bishops voted solidly in the majority on major issues, including the recognition of papal infallibility when speaking *ex cathedra* on matters of faith and morals. The vote for papal infallibility can also be seen as a vote of support by the bishops in the pope's conflict with liberalism, coming as it did closely in the wake of the Syllabus of Errors. The net result of the canons of Vatican I was to make the Catholic Church even less willing to cooperate with liberals. It did however signal the creation of a new Catholic Church, united under the papacy in a way never before realized. Differences of national churches were lessened as dogma and practice for the whole Church entered a modern age of heightened communication, which allowed for greater uniformity throughout the Church.

In the wake of the experience of Vatican I, the bishops and archbishops of Latin America began to meet more or less regularly in Latin American Plenary Councils, starting in 1899. The impetus was the celebration of the fourth centenary of the Columbus's discovery of the Americas. Bishops from all the Spanish-speaking countries, Brazil, and Haiti were invited to the Colegio Pio Latino Americano in Rome. Fifty-three prelates attended (thirteen archbishops and forty bishops) from eighteen countries. The program was developed not by Latin Americans but by a working group in Rome consisting of Italians, Germans, and Spaniards, one of whom had missionary experience in Latin America. The sources for the deliberations of the group were the canons of Trent, Vatican I, and recent papal encyclicals and briefs. Curiously enough the rich tradition of provincial councils and synods in the Americas, held since 1555, were absent in the final decrees. The work of the Plenary Council was to truly bring the Latin American Church fully under the sway of Rome and make a clean break with its history under the Royal Patronage. In effect it applied the canons of Vatican I and the recent papal decrees for application to the Americas, in a manner similar to what the three Provincial Councils of Lima and Mexico had done for the canons and decrees of the Council of Trent (see chaps. 4 and 5). Although the assembled prelates resolved to meet every three years thereafter, it was more than a half-century before the next Plenary Council (1955).

While the Church hierarchy became more closely integrated into the Catholic Church and more closely aligned under the papacy, the local churches struggled with local political conditions and with the faithful who adhered to their own regional forms of religious practice. In fact, entering the twentieth century the Church in its local manifestations was less unified and less orthodox, and could only provide a large tent under which a broad range of practices coexisted.

Turmoil and change characterized Latin America at the end of the nineteenth century. In the rural areas, native peoples and other members of the lower classes found themselves at a significant economic disadvantage due to restrictions and reforms imposed by the elites. The countries became, in fact, two different worlds. In general the elites lived in cities where the benefits of modernization improved living conditions. The lower classes, predominately native peoples, remained in rural villages, cut off from the benefits of modernization. Moreover, well-meaning reforms of the nineteenth century frequently worked to further erode the fragile economic condition of the natives. To make matters worse, the elites then assumed that the disparity between their condition and that of the natives and peasants was due to inherent biological differences, through a misinterpretation of Darwinian biology. There was also a widespread emergence of popular religion as native peoples took control of their own lives and spirituality. Yet since these movements were not orthodox and since some of them threatened the stability of the state, they were either violently put down or otherwise isolated.

All of this would set the stage of the dramatic changes that occurred in the early twentieth century in Latin America. Some countries would be engulfed in civil war, others would see political change sweep away the old regimes, and in still others the military would take control of the power of the state to impose order. In all of these scenarios, the Church would sit at the eye of the storm.

9

Revolution and Reform

Mustachioed revolutionaries with bandoliers crossed over their chests, firing rifles into the air, riding horses at breakneck speed are a common image of the Mexican Revolution. These men, and the women who fought along with them, were glorified in popular culture, especially in the *corridos*, popular songs written to detail their exploits in overthrowing the dictatorship of Porfirio Díaz in 1910. The Mexican Revolution was a popular uprising against the political system that had dominated Mexico for several decades in the late nineteenth and early twentieth centuries. Yet it was not solely a political movement. Like many other revolutions it encompassed a broader spectrum of changes than merely political ones. In many ways the key issue of the revolution was access to land. Thousands of peasants in Mexico lived on the land but did not own it. They either worked on the estates of others or scraped out a meager existence on marginal plots rented from others. At the same time the wealthy controlled, but did not use, rich soils and fertile estates.

This dichotomy in Mexico was all the more poignant because access to land had been a central issue of the liberal reforms that had led to a series of civil wars in the nineteenth century. In those conflicts, the Church was a major protagonist because the liberals sought to confiscate the lands owned and controlled by the Church. Although the liberals were successful, and implemented programs to take over Church lands, the liberal program had unintended consequences. When the Church lands were confiscated, they were put up for sale, rather than distributed to the landless. As a result the program tended to concentrate even more wealth in the hands of a few. Additionally, while the law prohibited the ownership of land by a civil corporation (the legal definition of the Church), native villages and many other institutions were also civil corporations. Since native peoples owned land in common in many areas, those villages frequently lost their land through the zealous enforcement of the law. During his long years in office (1876–80 and 1884–1911) Díaz brokered a rapprochement with the Church, and in some instances the Church was able to reacquire its property. Regardless of whether the Church regained its land or not, it did become closely identified with the regime. Because the regime also violently silenced its opponents and was perceived as callously exploiting the peasants, dissent grew within the nation. The popular imagination of the Diaz regime pictured the bishops and clergy of the Church decked out in their bejeweled vestments, officiating before gold encrusted altars, raising chalices of silver and gems, while the great majority of the faithful were dressed in rags and faced a lifetime of starvation. The contrast provided fodder for the opponents of the Church.

The twentieth century in Latin America witnessed the rise of revolutions that would overthrow the traditional order of things. In some countries the revolutions were fought on battlefields. In others they were political revolutions, truly substantive changes but without the level of bloodshed of civil wars. In other regions change came about more through benign, or malignant, neglect, than through any clear plan. What is true is that the Church in Latin America would be dramatically transformed in the first half of the twentieth century.

Díaz and the Revolution

The single event that has captured the imagination was the Mexican Revolution. Mexico had already gone through several wrenching civil wars in the nineteenth century. These were followed by a long, relatively calm period of stability under General Porfirio Díaz. The Díaz regime fell to a violent and popular opposition in the wake of the election of 1910. The opposition to Díaz was widespread from moderate republicans to anarchists and others inspired by more radical European political philosophies. The Catholic Church ultimately became a participant in the conflict in support of the Diaz regime.

Various opponents to that regime found different issues upon which to base their opposition. The liberals could not tolerate the administrations' perpetuation of power through sham elections. Many of the liberals were strong federalists. The Díaz regime, though ostensibly liberal and federalist, had successfully concentrated all power in the hands of the chief executive and had made central intervention into the affairs of the states a way of life. Other opponents, particularly some of the more populist groups on the political Left, saw the Díaz regime as a continuation of the domination of a wealthy few over the general population. As a result of the confiscation of land held in common in some native villages, a large group of landless peasants was created. Others, taking their lead from European political theories, such as anarcho-syndicalism, socialism, and communism, saw conditions in Mexico as ripe for revolution and the possibility of creating a new political entity along the lines of their political philosophies. For several of these groups, the close relationship of the Church with the Díaz regime was but another reason for opposition. The peasants had seen the lands of the Church confiscated, just as their own lands had been, but eventually the Church regained control of some of its lands while the peasants did not. For the socialists, anarchists, and communists, there was little love lost with an institution to which they ascribed many of the ills of society. For the liberal democrats, however, while they might oppose the Church on a philosophical basis, they were largely faithful believers and felt that the contributions of the Church far outweighed its shortcomings.

The first phase of the revolution was brief. In November 1910 federal troops attacked a group of political opponents in Puebla, launching the military phase. Revolutionaries arose in many parts of the nation, all with various grievances with the Díaz regime. It quickly became clear that Díaz could not continue, and by May 1911 he had resigned and left Mexico. The leader of the opposition, Francisco Madero, then called for free and fair elections and a return to the rule of law as outlined in the national Constitution of 1857, the nominal ruling document under the Díaz regime. Madero was elected in a landslide but quickly demonstrated that his opposition to Díaz was political. He had opposed the dictator for *being* a dictator and for violating the rule of law, not particularly because of the specific practices of the regime. Madero slowly discovered that the revolution meant far different things to discrete constituencies, and the only cause uniting them was a common hatred of Díaz. He attempted to govern, but the rate of change was far too slow for many of his erstwhile supporters. At the same time, there were powerful elements that still supported Díaz. Within Madero's first year, revolts began to break out, both among the nominal revolutionaries and among the Díaz supporters.

Eventually in February 1913, a military coup overthrew Madero. After a week of bloody fighting in the capital, Madero and his vice president surrendered to the opposition and subsequently were assassinated. General Victoriano Huerta emerged as the leader of the opposition and de facto president. Once again, all of the revolutionary groups could unite in opposition to Huerta. The old divisions continued, with peasants, industrial workers, cattlemen from the north, anarchists, and others all finding common cause in opposing him. The Church hierarchy, however, supported Diaz and the remnants of the Diaz regime once the dictator was deposed. Those same Church leaders also supported the coup of General Huerta, believing that stability was essential for the future of the country.

The revolution dragged on for four more years. Various rebel groups gained control of the capital, Mexico City, only to withdraw within weeks or months. A coalition of rebel leaders eventually came to support Venustiano Carranza, a landowner from the north. He consolidated his power to become the first leader of the Revolution and called for a constitutional convention in Querétaro in 1917. The document that emerged is still the basic law of the country. Unlike the U.S. Constitution that outlines basic principles upon which the rest of the legal system might be established, the Mexican constitution speaks to many highly specific issues. As with all such instruments, it was a consensus document, and reflects the widely varying interests of the groups that eventually came to support Carranza.

The Mexican Constitution of 1917 marked a true turning point in Church and state relations in Mexico. A significant number of the delegates to the constitutional convention were strongly anticlerical. Led by Francisco Múgica, the more radical delegates succeeded in passing a series of items that severely restricted the Church. In addition to the goals of the nineteenth-century liberals, such as making marriage a civil ceremony and the civil registration of births and deaths, the left-wing delegates succeeded in striping clerical organizations of legal recognition, banning public and outdoor worship services, and expropriating all Church property by the state. Moreover the constitution clearly announced that the state would control the Church in nearly every way, from limiting the number of clergy in a given district to prohibiting the presence of foreign-born clerics to requiring clerics to register their presence with local authorities. The conflict between the extreme left-wing and the more traditional liberals focused on the issue of education. While both agreed that there should be free, obligatory primary education, the leftists declared that education could only be secular and that there could be no role for the Church in it. Other articles of the constitution proved to be equally innovative, governing issues such as landownership, labor rights, and social issues. But it was the sections dealing with the Church that laid the ground work for continuing violence in Mexico.[1]

While the Constitution of 1917 charted an entirely new course for the nation, in order for the changes to actually take effect, congress needed to pass implementing legislation. The process of implementing the constitution took many years, since not all members of congress were as supportive of the changes mandated by the document as were the writers of the constitution. It was not until after 1920, under President Alvaro Obregón, that congress passed and the administration began to implement and enforce the more onerous anticlerical articles of the constitution. Under his administration more than a thousand rural schools were constructed. Hundreds of teachers went into training, and expenditures on public primary education soared. Many people, however, opposed the public education program since they believed that it interfered in what they considered was one of the proper functions of the Church. Obregón did not totally oppose Church participation in the educational enterprise but rather saw it as a last resort, should the public program fail. He also openly encouraged Protestant missionaries to enter the republic and to assist in education, a move that piqued the ire of Catholic supporters.

The situation became critical in the administration of Plutarco Elias Calles, Obregón's successor. After 1924, Calles began a program of strict implementation and enforcement of the anticlerical provisions of the Constitution of 1917, which went far beyond what Obregón had begun. His efforts were paralleled in the various states as they too began to pass increasingly anticlerical laws, based on the federal precedent. In 1926, the archbishop of Mexico, José Mora y del Río, came out not only in opposition to these newly enacted laws, but to declare that Catholics should not support the constitution. Calles responded by vigorously enforcing the laws that had been mandated by that document, deporting foreign priests, closing church schools, and taking over monasteries and convents. Responding to these acts, the archbishop declared a clerical strike (a general local interdict) ordering that all churches be closed and that no masses be said or services performed anywhere in the Mexican Republic.

The confrontation between Calles and the archbishop became even more acute. While troops sought to enforce the law, local guerilla groups supporting the Church emerged. Particularly in the rich agricultural regions of central Mexico, the guerillas took up the battle cry of "Viva Cristo Rey" (Long Live Christ the King). This gave the movement the name of the *Cristero* Revolt. The conflict became an open civil war between forces loyal to the government and the constitution on one side, and the supporters of the archbishop and Church hierarchy on the other. As violence spread to many regions of the nation, the country also entered a presidential campaign period. In an odd turn of events, Alvaro Obregón was elected to a second, nonsuccessive term as president. The constitution prohibited the immediate succession of a president into a second term but was silent on the question of a nonsuccessive term. But before Obregón was inaugurated he was killed by an assassin. The assassin was linked to the antigovernment Cristero rebels.

With the death of Obregón, Calles became the de facto power governing Mexico. Because of the provisions of the constitution, he could not succeed himself. He orchestrated the congress to appoint an interim president until new elections could be held. Even with the elections, Calles remained the *Jefe Máximo* (Supreme Chief), having a direct influence on the nomination of the official candidates for president. Within the year, secret negotiations between the government and the Cristero leaders, assisted by the U. S. ambassador and prominent U. S. Catholic leaders, resulted in a compromise to end the revolt. The government held fast to most of the principles of the constitution but allowed religious instruction to take place in churches, permitted some of the exiled priests and bishops to return, and declared that it did not intend to destroy the Church. With this, the impasse was resolved. The government would not press many of the most egregious restrictions of the constitution while the Church would recognize the legality of the government and constitution. What ensued in Mexico was a tense peace between Church and state, neither side choosing to openly oppose the other.[2]

La Violencia *in Colombia*

The early decades of the twentieth century saw dramatic changes, although perhaps not on the scale of Mexico, in other Latin American countries as well. Colombia provides another example in which the Church became a participant in a period of widespread unrest and bloodshed. Church-state relations in Colombia had been a model for many other countries in the nineteenth century. While there had been conflicts between the liberals and the conservatives, the country was eventually able to negotiate a concordat with the papacy, which outlined mutual rights and responsibilities. At the same time, as a result of the concordat and the ability of the Conservative Party to maintain power, the Church became identified with that party, for better or worse.

The roots of the terrible violence that wracked the country in the 1940s and 1950s are generally traced back to the first major presidential win by the liberals in 1930. In that election the Conservative Party split between two mutually attractive candidates, allowing the liberals to gain power. In the year following the election there were incidents of violence against conservatives as a result of years of pent-up frustration on the part of some more-radical liberals. The liberals established freedom of religion, removed priests from politics and the Church from education, and it recognized religions other than the Roman Catholic Church. This, in turn, prompted some moderate liberals to find common cause with the conservatives. Slowly subsequent presidential regimes moved away from the radical liberal platform. The moderate regimes reinstated parochial education and successfully negotiated a new concordat in 1942. This pact required that candidates for bishop be approved by the state and be of Colombian nationality. While the agreement granted the state slightly greater control over the Church, including the Church's role in education, for many observers there was hardly a difference in practice between this and the former agreement.

The year 1946 saw a mirror image of the 1930 election: this time the Liberal Party was split between the moderate liberals and an even more reform-minded faction. With the ensuing conservative win, there were reprisals against liberals for the incidents sixteen years earlier. Unfortunately, the elected regime of conservative Mariano Ospina Pérez was unable to control the violence, and the country slowly drifted toward anarchy. He was succeeded in 1950 by Laureano Gómez, also a conservative, in an uncontested election. Gómez governed on and off until he was overthrown in 1953 by a military coup. Under the military, the violence began to abate, but economic problems dogged the regime, leaving Colombia greatly impoverished until 1957 when a coalition of liberals and conservatives developed a power-sharing arrangement.

In the period between 1946 and 1957, Colombia passed through a period of such extraordinary brutality that it became known simply as *la violencia*— the violence. Some argue that the problems with militias, drug smugglers, and violence in the late twentieth century can be traced back to this period. The most cogent explanations for the drastic situation point to the creation of two political parties, each of which offered patrimonial favors to its supporters. In fact, there were no other overriding national institutions that were able to offer the same degree of support, and the result was a dichotomous state. The Catholic Church played an important although perhaps unintentional role in the process. With the success of the conservatives in the late nineteenth and early twentieth centuries, the close alliance of the Church with that party, and with the central government through the concordat, the Church became widely perceived as yet another organ of the Conservative Party. Consequently, violence against the conservatives in 1930 also spilled over into violence against the Church, along with anticlericalism among certain sectors of the Liberal Party.

When the conservatives came back into power, the Church celebrated the success. Many clerics, from parish priests to bishops, openly rejoiced in the electoral victory. While the Church was not extremely partisan, it did clearly indicate its political preferences and became the target, yet again, of disgruntled liberals. During the height of the conflict there is evidence that some groups closely associated with the Church perpetrated attacks against liberal targets. In the whole of the society the violence had an escalating effect: atrocities meted out by one faction were matched by another faction, guerilla bands developed in the countryside to punish political opponents, and armed gangs in the cities engaged in reprisals, kidnappings, murder, rape, and countless brutalities on both sides. Kidnap for ransom, expropriation of properties and crops, and extortions, all helped to provide financial backing for the bloodshed.

The Church also contributed to the violence. Many sermons and the teachings of the Colombian Church in general blurred the line between party and state. Given that the political environment had become dichotomous, any opposition to the Conservative Party was interpreted as opposition to the Church, which tacitly supported it. What began as righteous indignation at insults real and imagined in the 1930 and 1946 elections escalated into virulent harangues and bloody repercussions on both parts. Pro-Catholic bands also attacked Protestant churches, pastors, and missionaries. Hundreds of schools, churches, and other properties of the Protestant missionaries were burned or destroyed in the violence. The conservative regime of Laureano Gómez had negotiated an agreement with the Vatican in 1951 to regulate missionary activity, designating parts of the country as missionary districts, and one particular clause in the agreement prohibited the practice of any Christian faith other than the Catholic Church.

Gómez was unable to contain the violence that had engulfed the nation. Now in ill health, he attempted to govern through a surrogate but was overthrown in a military coup by General Rojas Pinilla in 1953, supported by conservatives and moderate liberals. Rojas Pinilla continued the strong pro-Church policies of Gómez, even calling Protestants "revolutionary bandits" and comparing them to communists. Although he was able to bring about a diminution of conflict, it was short-lived. By the third year of Rojas Pinilla's presidency, bloodshed increased as did the repression. This continuing conflict, combined with an increasingly disastrous economy, led to his overthrow in 1957. The liberals and conservatives joined in opposing Rojas Pinilla by creating a bipartisan civilian alliance, which allowed healing to begin. By 1960 attacks and other acts of repression against Protestants started to abate.

In the wake of the regimes of Gómez and Rojas Pinilla, the Catholic Church set out to pursue a path that was clearly different from that of the Conservative Party and from military regimes. Church leaders in 1960 embraced Protestant leaders as colleagues in fighting Communism. The Church also began to look at larger social issues such as agrarian reform, the economic conditions of the country and its effect on the poorest citizens, and other social and economic issues. Many of these new concerns ran contrary to the policies of the conservatives.[3]

Mexico and Colombia provide two examples of the Church becoming involved in violent acts as part of a large national conflict. They also come from two rather different eras in the twentieth century. The Mexican example occurred from the time of the First World War, and the interwar period, while the Colombia example occurred after the Second World War. They thus represent two very different worlds. Not only are there great historical differences between the two countries, the world was a very different place in 1926 than in 1946. In other Latin American countries, but particularly in the Southern Cone of South America, the first few decades of the twentieth century brought sometimes dramatic change, but the Church, per se, was more frequently a bystander, not an active participant and not particularly affected by the outcome.

In many Latin American countries, as has been seen in Mexico and Brazil, the ideas of Auguste Comte and positivism had an important impact. By and large these ideas were embraced by the more conservative elements of the political society who saw in positivism an explanation for and justification of the stratified social system so common in the region. On the other hand, the old liberal movements increasingly began to embrace the more radical notions of Marx and Engels as socialism, anarchism, and communism began to take hold. While neither of these two philosophical poles could easily be reconciled with the teachings of the Church at that time, many bishops and other high-ranking churchmen expressed more sympathy for the positivist view, emphasizing the stability of the social structure and, by extension, the ecclesiastical hierarchy. This stance also led both Church leaders and the conservative elements to embrace the newly emerging ideology of fascism. Fascism called for a strong central authority, a paternalistic corporate model, and in Hispanic countries a return to the dogmas of the Church. A Pan-Hispanic vision of fascism also sought to strengthen the ties between the former colonies and the mother country. The paternalism of the system was manifested in workers unions organized by management, and controlled by management, so that industrial workers could be managed in a manner not dissimilar from the old patron-client system of the landed estates.[4]

Many of the lower clerics and other Catholic thinkers began to view the world more from the bottom up, and saw the Gospel as preaching a more egalitarian system. They began to focus on issues of social justice. For these idealists, the corporatist state envisioned by the conservatives was no progress at all but an attempt to re-create some of the less enlightened practices of the colonial period. Rather, they saw the modern nation as progressing more toward equality.

As the Second World War developed and wore on, and the Axis powers eventually defeated, the admirers of fascism in Latin America backed away from their earlier embrace of its teachings. Some of them recognized that if the Church did not take an active role in the improvement of the conditions of the poor, then other less amenable ideologies might carry the day. Many began to embrace a modified vision of social justice, one in which the Church, not secular institutions such as labor unions or political parties, took the leadership.

One of the major issues confronting the Church throughout Latin America in the late decades of the nineteenth century and the opening decades of the twentieth was the need for Catholic priests. Seminaries had been developed throughout Latin America and Brazil in the colonial period. The rupture with the mother country caused no great diminution of clergy. The character of the active clergy tended to become much more local, with fewer foreigners. Several religious orders still sent priests to Latin America, but the secular clergy came to be nearly completely local. Nevertheless, due to the protracted political rivalries between the liberals and conservatives, it became increasingly difficult to train new priests. Liberals closed seminaries, along with convents and monasteries. Many countries went for years at a time with no bishops being appointed, consecrated, or installed due to issues over the succession of the patronage. By the end of the nineteenth century, these trends resulted in sometimes severe limitations in the number of priests to administer the sacraments to the faithful. The shortage was compounded by xenophobic nationalism on the part of both the liberals and conservatives. The nationalists opposed the presence of priests from other countries, so that in many places foreign priests were expelled or others simply were prevented from entering the country. The end result of these policies was that the Church was severely understaffed by the early decades of the twentieth century. The shortage of priests had only a moderate effect in the rapidly growing cities of Latin America. While the density of priests declined, the presence of the Church remained. The newly emerging mass media reported on the religious life of the city, and the faithful still had access to churches and the mass. Yet the relationship was different because fewer priests could attend to only so many of the faithful. The countryside presented a different challenge. Many rural villages only occasionally saw a priest as those areas were largely cut off from the Church because of isolation and the absence of clergy. Thus, the faithful in the rural areas took more responsibility for their own faith and religious lives, as seen in the examples from Brazil and Mexico.

Argentina and Chile

Both Argentina and Chile had had a Protestant presence from the time of independence. Both countries developed somewhat strong ties to England by the middle of the nineteenth century. With this link came the increasing presence of British merchants and entrepreneurs, many of whom brought their Anglican religion with them. They were never a large population, but they were indeed a presence that had to be dealt with directly or indirectly. Early efforts at freedom of religion were usually for the benefit of the British. As the oligarchies developed their power in the late nineteenth century, they tolerated a degree of religious freedom. Slowly other Protestant groups began to enter the countries, sometimes as a result of the increased presence of merchants and businessmen from the United States. One important feature of the British and American immigration was that eventually these businessmen and merchants were incorporated into the ruling elite of the two countries through marriage. In the late nineteenth and early twentieth centuries, both countries also saw additional immigration. In Argentina this population came from Italy and other Mediterranean countries, with a few German and Swiss immigrants. Chile also saw some Italian and South European immigrants but also from Germany and northern Europe. These immigrants further muddied the ecclesiastical waters, bringing both Protestant faiths and communions different from, but recognized by, the Catholic Church, such as the Eastern Rite Catholics. By the early decades of the twentieth century, then, the presence of Protestants in Chile and Argentina had a fairly long historical tradition.

Brazil in the late nineteenth century also actively encouraged immigration from Europe and the United States. Some of the best-known programs occurred during the monarchy when Confederate supporters from the United States were welcomed by the Brazilians at the end of the U.S. Civil War. Later on, both under the monarchy and the republic, immigration programs targeted Germans, Swiss, Italians, and Eastern Europeans to settle the rich agricultural lands of the south, which created a very complex religious landscape. There were, for example, old Catholics, especially among the coastal elites; Protestants increasingly played a role in many regions of the country; and in the hinterland various types of popular religious beliefs flavored the Catholic ceremonies and rituals. Brazil also had a large population descended from Africans imported under the slave regime, so in areas with dense African populations, popular religions derived from African tribal religions were widespread.

The middle decades of the twentieth century saw military rule or dictators in nearly every country of the Southern Cone. The countries reached their point of dictatorship or military control through extremely diverse methods. In Chile the parliamentary system lasted two decades into the twentieth century, balancing out the political goals of the major factions. Unlike other Latin American republics, Chilean labor unions came to have a voice in politics in those early years. Chile had three main economic engines: mining, agriculture, and manufacturing. Two of these, mining and manufacturing, had been unionized relatively early, by Latin American standards. As a result organized labor could provide a national voice for workers. The rise of the labor unions also came at a time that Chile rapidly urbanized. From 1875 to 1902 the percentage of Chileans living in cities rose from 27 percent to 43 percent.[5] This meant that the third sector of Chilean labor, the rural laborers, increasingly fled the poor conditions of the rural areas for the lure of the cities. There they took on low-wage industrial labor, frequently outside of the unions. The mining industry came to dominate the Chilean economy, resting on the extraction of nitrates and copper. But nonmining industry represented a significant second place, with agricultural production in full decline. At this time, the urban elites found common cause with the rural elites. The newly rich urban elites saw acquisition of rural land as symbolic of their social arrival; the rural elites saw an opportunity to diversify their power and acquired interests in manufacturing and other urban activities.

In Chile the parliamentary system allowed for the creation of numerous smaller political parties, which ran the gamut of political opinion. The system tended to favor those political parties which sought the least change, since the mounting of a coalition to achieve change could be exceptionally difficult. Yet the system ultimately resulted in a powerful coalition of popular parties and middle-class supporters who desired more significant change. This movement came to fruition with the election in 1921 of Arturo Alessandri, a senator from the northern region of Tarapacá, as president. He carried with him a coalition of democrats and radicals from the parties seeking systematic change of the old patronal system, reduction in the power and influence of the Church, and an improvement in the working conditions for Chileans of all economic status. The Church hierarchy initially opposed Alessandri's efforts to separate Church and state, but eventually they too became convinced that the separation would be beneficial to the Church. Yet other reform efforts were stymied in the congress because of the factionalism that characterized the parliamentary system. Finally the military intervened, at the behest of a broad spectrum of political parties.

The military essentially ushered a mild reform package through congress, and also oversaw the writing of a new constitution in 1925 that did away with the parliament. The Church remained both a target and an important political force. Recognizing that the autonomy of the Church would be better served by separation, and possibly fearful of more radical attacks on it, Church leaders, specifically Crescente Errázuriz (see chap. 8), did not oppose the separation clause that had been incorporated into the constitution. This tacit cooperation provided an important precedent in Chile in that the Church might cooperate with the state, while the two entities pursued their own unique agendas. Not only did the 1925 Constitution separate Church and state, it provided for freedom of religion, and allowed all denominations to hold their own property in a tax exempt status. In the wake of the constitution, the conservatives continued to press for further support for the Church. At the same time, a new party arose, the Christian Democrats. The adherents of this party represented more liberal politicians who still supported the civil and social goals of the Church, while not actively supporting a reinstitution of its status as an official cult.

In Argentina there was an opening up of the electoral process following the passage the Saenz Peña Law in 1912, which established the universal, obligatory, and secret ballot for all male citizens. This allowed a new party, the Radical Civic Union, to gain power.[6] The Radical Party, as it was known, had been created many years earlier by a small group of liberals as an opposition to the ruling oligarchy. The liberal movement had been split, with some joining the conservatives in government. The others opposed the government and demanded secret, universal, and obligatory suffrage, leading to the formation of the new party. The Radical Party had called on its followers to simply abstain from voting in what it considered fraudulent elections. Finally in 1916, the party gained power with the election of Hipólito Yrigoyen. As a successor to the Liberal Party, the Radical Party shared many of the same anticlerical attitudes.

In Argentina at the end of the nineteenth century, the country was ruled by an oligarchy made up of elements from the old liberal and conservative movements (see chap. 7). In this political environment the Church recognized that if it took an active role in politics it would reinvigorate a latent anticlericalism among the political leaders, especially the old liberals. Argentina had adopted the U.S. constitutional model of the separation of Church and state in their own Constitution of 1853, and so by the early decades of the twentieth century the Argentine Church had begun to focus most directly on those areas outside of the political realm over which it could justly exercise control. While focusing on evangelism among the new immigrants to the country, the Church also saw itself as a national guardian, particularly of the morals and faith of the people. As was common elsewhere, the Church feared the growth of the more radical leftist ideologies of anarchism and socialism, and in many respects it made common cause with the oligarchy in opposing these perceived common enemies.

When the constitution recognized freedom of religion and the ideal of the separation of Church and state, it also claimed the right of patronage, especially in the appointment of bishops and archbishops. Moreover, public funds were used to foster religion. Both the federal and provincial governments provided funds to the Church, particularly for the support of the diocesan seminaries, although by the second decade of the twentieth century some of these payments became irregular.

The governments of the Radicals in Argentina lasted through the terms of Yrigoyen, his successor, Marcelo T. de Alvear, and another Yrigoyen presidency. Halfway through Yrigoyen's second term, he was deposed by a military coup in 1930. By this time the Radicals had split into two factions: one supported Yrigoyen, the other opposed him on the grounds that reelection was contrary to the political philosophy of the movement. More than anything else, it was likely the worldwide Depression that was pivotal in the failure of the second Yrigoyen administration. Nevertheless, support for him had begun to wane on many different issues.

The military government, in turn, allowed for the eventual rise of Colonel Juan Perón, who would be a feature of Argentine politics for two decades. The military ruled until 1938 and was followed by the governments of two Radicals, Roberto Ortiz and Ramón Castillo. The period is remembered in Argentina as an especially difficult time. Both military and civilian rulers were unable to control the rapid growth of labor unions and a massive flow of people from the countryside into the cities, particularly Buenos Aires. During this period the British gained significant concessions from the government regarding exports of Argentine beef and wheat. Both military and civilian governments were conservative and authoritarian. And when the Second World War began, the presidents attempted to maintain Argentine neutrality, while many in leadership felt sympathy for the Axis.

Peru and the Rise of APRA

In Peru, the early part of the twentieth century also saw political instability, the rise of a dictator, and the creation of a truly new political movement. The political system of Peru had provided a relatively peaceful succession of presidents for several decades of the late nineteenth and early twentieth centuries. In 1908 Augusto Leguía was elected president as the representative of the Civilista Party, a largely conservative one, deeply influenced by positivism with its dual goals of order and progress. The party also opposed the personalism that had characterized politics prior to the latter part of the nineteenth century. It supported the Church and the military as institutions to provide national cohesion, but not as alternatives to the civil political order. Leguia had previously served as minister of finance and prime minister in other Civilista governments and had lived in the United States as an employee and executive of the New York Life Insurance Company. Leguía's first term was largely uneventful and followed the pattern established by his predecessors. He focused on economic development, thanks to his professional training, and set about concluding boundary disputes with Brazil and Bolivia.

Leguía was succeeded by a liberal president, Guillermo Billinghurst. The liberals in this era represented mostly the middle class and sought to provide for a greater range of government services than the Civilistas. This platform won support from most political sectors in Peru, much to the chagrin of the Civilistas. After Billinghurst cut the military budget and proposed a series of economic reforms, including an eight-hour workday, a military coup overthrew him in 1914. In 1915 the Civilista José Pardo was reelected to the presidency, having already served from 1904 to 1908. Following his election, one important piece of legislation, the Toleration Act, was passed in 1915. This allowed Protestant missionaries to serve in Peru, while keeping the Catholic Church as nominally the official religion. In the end, however, Pardo, fared little better than Billinghurst and was in turn removed in a coup in 1919 for supposedly having attempted to rig the election of his anointed successor. The military installed Leguía, who had broken with the Civilistas and run in opposition to Pardo, as the new president.

Leguía would go on to rule Peru until his own deposition in 1930. In keeping with patterns seen elsewhere, one of Leguía's early actions was to convene a constitutional convention and write a new integral document for the country more in keeping with his own political goals. Leguía, who had a very cordial relationship with the Church saw the it as an important ally for maintaining stability in the country consonant with the essentially conservative nature of his policies. As in many other countries, Peru saw the rise of more militant opposition groups, including socialists and anarchists. Leguía and the Church leaders believed that the Church could offer a real alternative to the masses through its message of solidarity in the face of division. They also stressed the equality of all under God, while recognizing what they felt were the necessary social strata. Leguía found a close ally in the archbishop of Lima, Emilio Lissón y Chaves. Lissón y Chaves was a historian who saw the roots of the country in a common, shared experience, which focused on the unifying role of the Catholic Church. The alliance of Church and state under Leguía further fostered a sense of paternalism and played into the sentiments of both positivism and fascism, both of which explicitly proposed that the Church and the state knew what was best for the masses. If reform were to come, it would be at the behest of the upper classes. In the area of native affairs, Leguía claimed to be the strongest supporter of native rights but in the end, most analysts conclude that what laws were passed manifested a paternalism of the state rather than a true empowerment of the natives. Even after Leguía was overthrown, the Catholic Church, the Catholic University, and many Catholic thinkers in Peru would be heavily imbued with ideologies shared with the fascists because of the old vestiges of positivism and Social Darwinism. This trend faded with the defeat of Germany and Italy in the mid-1940s.

As Leguía consolidated his power, an important new political movement developed in Peru. The ideologue behind the new movement was Victor Raúl Haya de la Torre. During the Leguía administration Haya de la Torre began to embrace what were then revolutionary thoughts about social equality. He noted that throughout Peruvian history, the native peoples had been marginalized, deprived of political expression, and oppressed by the ruling classes. He founded a populist movement to give a voice to the underclasses. His vision was indeed unique for the times because it was not limited to his own country, Peru, but was to be for the entire continent. For this reason his party was founded not in Peru but in Mexico, with the assistance of the then Mexican secretary of education José Vasconcelos. They called the party the Popular American Revolutionary Alliance (*Alianza Popular Revolution-*

aria Americana, APRA). While much of the rhetoric of the early movement seems quite revolutionary, when distilled down it was actually more populist and democratic. Early on, Haya de la Torre was also specifically indigenist, supporting the native peoples. His vision soon became much broader. He especially opposed the participation of the military in politics and the paternalist character of the recent administrations in Peru. A close ally of Haya de la Torre in the early years before 1924 was José Carlos Mariátegui, a journalist and political thinker. He and Haya were close friends and worked together in the early phases of the creation of APRA, but they parted ways when Mariátegui concluded that socialism was the only solution for Peru's problems. The division between the two also highlighted that Haya focused on populist ideology, of both the working and the middle classes, while Mariátegui focused on the natives and lower-class workers. The APRA had no direct policy regarding the Church. Because of its populist base, it routinely criticized the Church hierarchy but was far more tolerant of local manifestations of religiosity. The APRA thus became a constant feature of Peruvian politics for the remainder of the twentieth century.[7]

Brazil and Getúlio Vargas

Brazil in the early twentieth century also saw the erosion of the power of the oligarchy. Ever since the revolution of 1889, which marked the end of the empire and the creation of the republic, the government of Brazil had been in the hands of a small cadre of local elites. The search for power among these elites pitted geographical regions against one another more than did ideological differences. The Church had suffered a significant decline during the "Old Republic." The Constitution of 1891 relegated the Church to an inferior position, withheld government funding, and denied it any role in government, formally bringing about a separation of Church and state. These actions led to a closer relationship between the Brazilian Church and Rome. It also placed the Church in a more tenuous financial position and led to a decline in the number of clerics in general. The result of these trends, as occurred elsewhere in Latin America, was an increase in the number of foreign-born priests and an influx of money for the Church from abroad.

The oligarchy began to lose power as the Brazilian economy began to confront the changing economic conditions of the twentieth century. Because landed elites dominated the oligarchy, their economic policies paid far more attention to agricultural issues than to industrialization and the concerns of the urban middle and lower classes, which condemned Brazil to a boom-and-bust economic cycle. As coffee, or sugar, or cotton prices rose, the national economy was stable; when prices for these goods fell, the nation was plunged into economic crisis. With the Depression of 1930, the Brazilian economy quickly foundered. Unrest among the middle classes, joined with concerns by the military, led to a bloodless coup against the newly elected president, Julio Prestes. Regional interests had also chaffed against the centralizing influences of the oligarchical government. In reaction to this, the military selected Getúlio Vargas as provisional president. Vargas came from the southern agricultural state of Rio Grande do Sul and had been elected to congress from there. He eventually became treasury minister in the central government, only to resign to run for governor in Rio Grande do Sul. As governor he loudly opposed the central government and the oligarchy, protested election fraud, and called for free and open elections with secret ballots. As a leading regional opponent of the oligarchy he provided the military with a perfect choice for president.

Once in office, Vargas had an uncanny ability to remain in power, governing Brazil for the next fifteen years. Vargas supported the industrialization of Brazil as a counterweight to the agricultural focus of the oligarchy, recognized the political potential of the working and middle classes, and formulated a populist platform to appeal to them. The coffee elite of the state of São Paulo vehemently opposed Vargas and attempted to overthrow him, but the military rallied to his defense. With his power consolidated, Vargas began to create a new state. He was deeply influenced by the rise of fascism and the allure of the corporatist state and relied heavily on the support of urban masses and a few special-interest groups in Brazilian society. Important among these special interests were the *tenentes* (literally "lieutenants") led by Carlos Luis Prestes (not related to presidential candidate Julio Prestes). The *tenentes* were low-level officers in the Brazilian army who had been trained by European and U.S. military advisors to form a more professional officer corps. Frustrated by their inability to break into the higher ranks of the army, they revolted against the oligarchical rule. Heavily influenced by Marxism, they sought the overthrow of the state. Early in his regime, Vargas was able to convince them to embrace his government. He was equally successful at co-opting other dissident groups in the country. It was his dealings with the Church that proved critical to the success of his efforts. Initially, Vargas had shown no support for recognizing the Catholic Church, although many Church leaders saw the 1930 revolt as just such an opportunity. When it became clear to Vargas that he could not be successful without the support of the Church, and to the faithful loyal to the Church, he indicated that while he did not reestablish the Church, he did recognize the "God of the people."[8] In so doing he tacitly recognized that the vast majority of the populace was Catholic and while his regime might have differences with the Church hierarchy, it could not discount the importance of the Church. In turn, this move provided the Church with the opportunity to begin grassroots political organizing in order to influence the government.

In 1934, Vargas oversaw the writing of a new constitution. Although he maintained his populist roots—with the Constitution and his policies thereafter—Vargas moved to the right. The 1934 Constitution was a stop on the way to his eventually assuming powers of dictator, authoring a coup, and writing yet another constitution in 1937. The main features of the old 1934 document had been the empowerment of the judiciary to take a more active role both in judicial affairs and in supervising the electoral process. The 1937 Constitution inaugurated Vargas's political vision of the *Estado Novo*, "The New State." This second constitution essentially placed all power in the hands of Vargas: the states lost the power to elect their own governors, and the president appointed an "intervenor" to govern the state. In effect, the constitution gave Vargas the authority to reshape the country as he wished. The end result was a state that had many similarities to Italy under Mussolini and Spain under Franco. While Catholic political organizations worked to elect representatives to the constitutional congress of 1934, Vargas and his closest advisors wrote the new 1937 document. During the *Estado Novo*, which ran until Vargas's overthrow in a coup in 1945, close ties developed between the dictator and the Church, especially as a result of their mutual opposition to Marxism and Communism.[9]

Catholic Action

Given the political environment in many of the South American countries, it is possible to observe some common themes in the history of the Catholic Church in the early twentieth century. In the late nineteenth century Catholic laypeople began to form local associations, which took various forms. Many were quite clearly outgrowths of the older tradition of religious sodalities but with more modern concerns and orientations. Others had more political or social goals. In Peru, for example, in several cities there emerged Catholic Unions and Catholic Circles. Some of these were created to combat the spread of what the members perceived as evils, including the Freemasons, Marxists, and other groups condemned by the Church. But these new Church associations were also proactive. Recognizing the need for protection of working-class members, they suggested the creation of Catholic-based trade unions. They called upon employers to improve working conditions for their workers and advocated the creation of night schools and Sunday schools for the education of the workers, as well as endorsing other progressive ideas. The membership, while generally from the upper and middle classes, did not exclude the natives and lower classes. At the same time, the families that generally supported the Church tended to come from the older landed families. These associations had at their core middle and upper class elements who, under the guise of Christian charity, sought to improve conditions for all social ranks. The organization of these Catholic associations was reminiscent of the older sodalities that had served to organize social groups in the colonial period and throughout the nineteenth century. The emergence of these popular lay organizations suggested a broadening of the core support for the Church after a long period of decline, with the creation of new organizations to address new issues. It also allows one to understand how support for the Church passed from the oligarchy in the late nineteenth century to the middle and lower classes by the middle of the twentieth century.

The cornerstone of the "modern" social concern of the Church was the papal encyclical *De rerum novarum* in 1891 (see chap. 9), promulgated by Pope Leo XIII. In this open letter Leo addressed the condition of labor in the world. The encyclical sought to refute socialist and other visions of labor, while supporting the rights of workers in a capitalist economic system. It recognized that the state had the right to regulate the justice of employer and employee relations, while it staked out for the Church the mediation of the moral elements. Importantly, it recognized the need for labor unions to protect the rights of workers and called upon the faithful to focus on social and economic issues, which hitherto had been thought of as solely in the realm of politics.

In the late nineteen-teens, movements began focusing on Catholic youth. In the case of Peru, a priest of the Congregation of the Sacred Heart, Jorge Dintilhac, founded a "Catholic Youth Action" at the order's college in Lima. The group then spread to the newly founded Catholic University of Peru. It served as a starting point for the careers of many of Peru's leading intellectuals and was eventually superseded by the Young People's Social Action, which also spawned many political and intellectual leaders of Peru. Many other similar groups, looking to improve society and to avoid the twin poles of capitalism and communism, emerged by 1930. Eventually most of these groups coalesced into the large movement in the Church known as Catholic Action.

Although there were many influences in the creation of Catholic Action, it was Pope Pius XI who served as the catalyst for change. Seeing the situation of the Church as it confronted both political and social movements that threatened it, Pius called for the creation of Catholic Action groups in all countries and dioceses. These were to combine laypeople and Church officials in a grassroots movement to support the Church and its social and political agenda. In Peru, and elsewhere, Catholic Action embraced the separation of Church and state, because the close relationship between the two was seen as potentially destructive to the Church. The movement sought to reinvigorate Catholics and make them far more militant, such as were the *Cristeros* in Mexico, although stopping just short of endorsing violence. Pius XI specifically mentioned the efforts of the Mexican Catholic Action in supporting the Church in the aftermath of the revolution.

Catholic Action fostered the development of a sensitivity regarding social issues, especially following various papal encyclicals that highlighted the social responsibility of the Church. Catholic Action groups throughout Latin America had several features in common. Each was directed by the laity but with a moral or spiritual advisor appointed by the local bishop. Often the group was even created at the behest of the local bishop. The groups were usually segregated by age and gender. So it would not be uncommon to find a men's group, women's group, and boys' and girls' movements, for example. The leadership was often selected by the ecclesiastical authorities and trained in the best ways to pursue political goals. In many countries there emerged highly specialized associations, such as Catholic Sports Leagues or Unions of Catholic Students. These more highly specialized groups tended to be more successful than the broad generic associations.

In Brazil, from the early twentieth century, the Catholic Church had to develop as an entity independent of the state, given the separation that occurred in the 1891 Constitution. While difficult, this shift allowed the Church to reflect local conditions, to a certain degree, while it also became more closely aligned with Rome. With the fall of the Old Republic and the rise of Vargas, the Church had an opportunity to position itself in the face of the new reality. The archbishop coadjutor of Rio de Janeiro, dom Sebastião Leme, encouraged the creation of popular organizations to advocate for causes close to the Church in the political realm. Leme felt that the time was ripe for the Church to reengage in political discourse. During the early phase of the Vargas regime, Leme organized popular demonstrations to articulate the Church's agenda. Leme did not favor the populist politics of the left, but rather a more authoritarian model, albeit with a well-organized and properly engaged laity. In this he manifested clearly to Vargas that the Catholic faithful were a key constituency to be considered. Part of Leme's agenda was the creation of the Catholic Electoral League in 1932, which fostered and supported the goal of persuading voters to support candidates who in turn supported the policies of the Church. The organization was fully endorsed by the Church, but ostensibly it was a lay organization. It was nonpartisan, evaluating candidates purely on the basis of their support for specific issues. Shortly thereafter, Leme supervised the creation of the Brazilian Catholic Action. Modeled after the Italian Catholic Action, it resembled other Catholic Action organizations throughout Latin America in seeking to both organize the faithful and articulate the social doctrine of the Church.

In Brazil, as in other countries of Latin America, the Church hierarchy opposed the creation of a Catholic political party, in effect meaning that Catholic Action would be a grassroots organization that could influence the regular political parties. Archbishop Leme tacitly encouraged support for the Brazilian Integralist Party (Vargas's political party), which saw large numbers of Catholic activists, priests, and bishops working for it, even holding public office under the party banner. The Integralist movement sought to find a "third way" between socialism and classical liberalism. Many of the supporters tended to be fascist in their orientation. The Brazilian Integralists appealed directly to the middle class and supported generally conservative ideologies, opposing revolution, seeking unity through nationalism, and especially seeing Catholicism as a central and unifying aspect of the nation. The alliance between the Church and the Integralists was of short duration, nor did the alliance have the outcome that they had hoped. When Vargas became the dictator and promulgated his *Estado Novo* he also outlawed political parties. Vargas, while benefitting from the support the Church had provided, was willing to ignore the Church as well. As a result only Catholic Action and the Catholic Electoral league remained. Both appealed to a rather small cadre of middle-class voters and intellectuals who supported the Church hierarchy and opposed both classical liberalism and socialism.[10]

In Chile, Catholic Action also played an important role in the 1930s. Early movements, such as the National Association of Catholic Students, targeted Catholic students who desired to deepen their faith while also dealing with the newly emerging social issues confronting the nation. These movements began in the 1920s and tended to proliferate. By the early 1930s they were all incorporated into the Chilean Catholic Action. Like other Catholic Actions it was an alliance of the Church hierarchy and the laity. While many members were loyal supporters of the Conservative Party, many others were not, such as members of the liberal movement who did not support the anticlerical-ism of classical liberalism. There were, however, two powerful camps within Catholic Action. There were many old-time conservatives, traditional Catho-lics who wished the Church to occupy a more prominent role in the political life of the republic, who saw the need for a personal spirituality and morality in the face of modern threats. Yet increasingly the younger members were inspired by the social message of the Church, calling for social change and the improvement of working conditions. Eventually the social Catholics came to outnumber the traditional ones, thus coloring the agenda of Catho-lic Action.

The papacy and the local Church hierarchy opposed the creation of Cath-olic political parties. However, a group of young people in Chile, active in Catholic Action, formed an association within the Conservative Party, called the National Phalanx (*Flanage Nacional*). Among these young men was Edu-ardo Frei, who would later go on to become president of Chile. In 1938 the Phalanx withdrew from the Conservative Party and presented its own roster of candidates. While opposing the ideologies of the Left, and the anticlerical position of the liberals, it also began a program to address issues of social justice. Some twenty years later this party, after having incorporated several other parties embracing the notion of Catholic social justice, became the Christian Democratic Party of Chile.

Conclusion

The early decades of the twentieth century in Latin America saw the Catholic Church at a crossroads. It began with popular movements in many coun-tries in which supporters manifested a popular piety and religious beliefs not entirely in line with Catholic teachings. The state frequently put down these movements with violence, as they challenged the established social and political order. In Mexico and Colombia the Church became involved in some of the bloodiest conflicts in the region. In other countries the Church continued to play an active political role, contesting with national govern-ments over the exact nature of Church-state relations.

While these high-level contests played out, among the faithful and a few members of the clergy there emerged the vision of the Church as a voice for social and economic justice, following a path described by Pope Leo XIII and reaffirmed by Pius XI. This movement was first embodied in the various Catholic Action associations. These lay associations in actual practice func-tioned in many ways like the older sodalities insofar as they were able to give the faithful a small group experience focusing on Catholic teachings. Sodalities at their peak had involved nearly all levels of society, but as they declined in importance in the nineteenth century, they were more commonly associated with native peoples and the lower classes. On the other hand, the new Catholic Action societies focused on the middle and upper classes. Yet as Catholic Action developed and engaged in the political discourse of the time, the Church itself began to change. The membership began to envision a society that was somewhat different from what the hierarchy had in mind, which was to expand the spiritual experience of the faithful and deepen their social awareness—but not necessarily bring about dramatic changes in society. As people became involved in the movement, they began to imagine a different social vision for the Church. The history of the Catholic Church in Latin America in the latter half of the twentieth century represents the playing out of the role of the Church as a voice for social and economic justice in a rapidly changing world.

10

The Mid-Twentieth-Century Church

Ernesto Cardenal (b. 1925) was a poet, priest, and revolutionary from Nicaragua. He came from a middle-class household, descended from nineteenth-century immigrants to the region. Early on he manifested a talent and passion for literature in general and poetry in particular. He attended the National Autonomous University in Mexico (1944–48) and Columbia University in New York (1948–49). Upon his return to Nicaragua he became involved in political movements, which opposed the government of Anastasio Somoza García (1936–56). Much of his poetry focused on political themes, including one that glorified the life and death of Augusto César Sandino, an early opponent of the Somoza regime.

In 1957 Cardenal was forced to flee Nicaragua following the repression that beset Nicaragua after Somoza's assassination in 1956. He chose to go to Gethsemani, a Trappist monastery in Kentucky, where he spent two years as a novice and studied under the famous spiritual author Thomas Merton. Illness forced Cardenal to leave the monastery in 1959. He went to Cuernavaca, Mexico, where he continued his theological formation in a Benedictine abbey and thereafter to La Ceja Seminary in Colombia. He was eventually ordained to the priesthood in Madrid in 1965, establishing a religious community on the island of Solentiname in Lake Nicaragua, in Nicaragua. Although committed to his vows as a priest, he was equally committed to his vocation as a writer and to his political opposition to the Somoza family regime. Because of his support for the anti-Somoza movement, when the Sandinista Liberation Front took over the Nicaraguan government after the ouster of Anastasio Somoza Debayle in 1979, Cardenal became a member of the inner circle of advisors to Daniel Ortega, the revolutionary leader who became the country's leader. Cardenal was appointed as minister of culture. His participation in the Sandinista government caused him to be publicly criticized by Pope John Paul II in 1983, since canon law dictated that serving in a government office was incompatible with being a priest. By 1988, the ministry of culture was abolished, although Cardenal remained a loyal Sandinista until 1994, when he publically broke with President Ortega. Cardenal continued to work for social justice and was an active poet and advocate for literacy.

The life of Ernesto Cardenal demonstrates the manner in which many priests and faithful Catholics became involved in movements that championed human rights and social justice in Latin American in the middle decades of the twentieth century. These individuals began with a faith that called them to serve the humanity of their fellow men and women, and to oppose regimes that they believed did not foster social justice and the equality of all persons.

Fluctuations in the Number of Clergy

The period between 1930 and the 1950s saw many Latin American countries under the rule of dictators, military and otherwise. In the face of the persistence of authoritarian regimes, those who have studied Latin America have wondered if there were something in the Latin American past that made those countries more susceptible to dictatorship or military rule. The period is very important in the history of the Church because the first major shifts in its political and social orientation began in this period. At the time of the Great Depression (1928–40), which had serious effects also in Latin America, the Catholic Church worldwide began to change its social and economic policies dramatically, at the same time that the societies in which it served were also undergoing significant change.

One of the major changes in the Church was an increase in the number of clergy in some Latin America countries. The ranks of the clergy had declined significantly in the late nineteenth and early twentieth centuries, but by about 1930 the number of priests began to grow again due to several important trends. As the dichotomy between liberals and conservatives gave way to new political parties, the ruling elites in nearly all countries accepted an apolitical role for the Church. This meant that liberals and their political heirs no longer opposed the Church as they had for nearly a century. By the 1930s, Marxism and socialism began to influence political opposition to ruling elites. For these new left-wing opponents, the Church was at best a marginal institution. While they viewed it as a tool of the dominant classes, they focused their ire not on the Church but on the politicians who allowed the Church to continue to monopolize many areas of potential social development, such as education and charitable works for the poor.

As restrictions on the Church lessened in the middle decades of the twentieth century, more young men from middle- and lower-class families began to see careers in the Church as viable options, and ones that also carried a modicum of social mobility. For the first time in decades, there was an increase in native-born priests, and the Church was allowed to open seminaries again. In many Latin American countries, religious orders began to reemerge after decades of relative absence. Many of these orders were missionary in approach, seeking to continue the missionary efforts of the sixteenth-century friars. With new religious orders came new priests and brothers to increase the numbers of clergy. In particular, many of these orders focused their efforts on rural parishes, where the shortage of priests had become acute. Additional priests also came from many foreign countries, in particular the United States and Spain.

Before the Second World War, Spain was caught up in a bloody civil war. After the victory of the forces of General Francisco Franco in 1939, the Church in Spain came to occupy an important place as an institution capable of uniting a badly divided country. One result was that the number of priests being produced was in excess of the number needed to serve the Spanish Church, so many Spanish priests chose to become missionaries to Latin America. These men tended to be more conservative and viewed the Church as an agent for social stability. The Church for them was the manifestation of the Gospel of Christ as handed down through teachings, traditions, and interpretations of the ecclesiastical hierarchy, a traditional view of the Church as an institution, which was embraced by many in Latin America as well. At the same time a number of priests from other countries, including the United States, Italy, and France, also served as missionaries in Latin America, and some of them carried with them a new vision for the Church. Rather than being a hierarchy, which enhanced social stability, for them the Church was the corporate body of all the faithful. The institution of the Church existed merely to serve the needs of the faithful. This new conception of the Church would need several decades before it became widely accepted as an alternative vision. The working out of this new vision formed an important part of the development of the Latin American Church in the 1950s.

As the ranks of the Catholic clergy began to grow again in the mid-twentieth century, Protestant missionaries also began to make significant inroads in many parts of Latin America. Because of the absence of Catholic clergy, hostility to the institutional Church by liberal governments, and a desire on the part of some politicians to emulate what they believed to be the success of the United States and Britain, Protestant missionaries also found a relatively accessible mission field. Many of these missions were based around the provision of medical care, schools, and other primary services that had been neglected in Latin America over much of the early twentieth century. The neglect grew partially from insufficient funds in government coffers and some lingering attitudes, which reasoned that the poor did not deserve the same services as the middle and upper classes.

Finally, the rise of socialist, communist, and other left-leaning ideologies had a dramatic effect on Latin American politics. As early as the Mexican Revolution (1910–17), there had been fears that a socialist state would arise in the Americas. While the Mexican post-revolutionary state espoused many leftist ideologies, it became more of an institutionalized revolution, committed to slow change and acting as a power broker among major political factions in the country. Yet, the more enthusiastic leftists sought deep and abiding change in Latin America. In spite of the alliance between the United States and the Soviet Union during the Second World War, the United States definitively rejected socialism. As a result, it worked actively with Latin American governments to discourage leftist political movements. In some instances the United States actively intervened when it felt its interests were threatened. In Nicaragua, the United States had sent in Marines in 1912 to reinforce the government in the face of liberal opposition, since it was still interested in Nicaragua as a possible site for an interoceanic canal. The Marines remained until 1925, with other U.S. troops staying on until 1932. In neighboring Guatemala in 1954, the United States, working covertly through the Central Intelligence Agency, helped to overthrow the popularly elected government of Jacobo Arbenz, which was seen as being too leftist for American sentiments.

The Catholic Church also opposed Marxism, socialism, and other leftist ideologies. Following in the logic of the Syllabus of Errors (1864), the Church felt that these movements sought to replace the Church with their own ideology. Clearly many of these movements were also strongly egalitarian and saw the ecclesiastical hierarchy as being antithetical to their beliefs. The Church now began to call upon the faithful to address social ills in a manner consistent with the teachings of the Church, and which was sanctioned and supervised by the Church hierarchy in order to counter the leftist movements. What emerged were various groups dedicated to Catholic Action. These became particularly important in Latin America in the 1930s and 1940s. Catholic Action was a movement, which originated with and was directed by the laity (see chap. 9). There were four main characteristics of Catholic Action: (1) the thrust of the movement was to put apostolic principles into action: to feed the hungry, clothe the naked, house the homeless; (2)

it was sanctioned and approved by the local ecclesiastical hierarchy, in most instances the local bishop; (3) the actual associations were divided along gender and frequently age lines; and (4) for those movements that had an international thrust, papal recognition was expected.

In Latin America, Catholic Action represented a new vision of the nature of the Church. Since the Council of Trent, the Church had been envisioned as the hierarchy that ran the gamut from each of the faithful to the clergy and bishops then all the way to the pope. It was an institution defined by its structure, not by its action. Ministry under the older concept of the Church was vested in the hierarchy and spread out to the laity. The rise of Catholic Action changed the way people envisioned the nature of the Church and changed their ecclesiology. People began to think of the Church as the assembly of all the faithful acting in the world in the name of Jesus. The call to ministry was not vested solely in the priesthood and hierarchy, but rather extended to all believers. Catholic Action did not generally create political parties, although there were exceptions. Instead, Catholic Action empowered the laity to act on their own, with the blessing of the Church, to solve the problems of the world, consistent with the Gospel and teachings of the Church.

The period from about 1950 until 1975 in Latin America would prove decisive in the evolution of the Church. Following the Second World War, Latin America began to confront issues related to dictatorship and the role of the military in politics. Most of the countries also entered the world economy at a level not seen before. These two themes had a tremendous impact on the role and function of the Church. Some of the major countries had strongmen using dictatorial powers to govern. Argentina, for example, had a military government that eventually became the dictatorship of Juan Perón. In Brazil, Getúlio Vargas ruled as dictator, and the military eventually took over after a few elected governments. In others countries, the military routinely entered the political fray, including in Chile, Peru, Ecuador, Colombia, and Venezuela as well as in Brazil and Argentina. In Central America political instability and economic dependence, particularly on the United States, created an atmosphere where power became vested in the hands of a very few, usually allied to the military. The Church and the faithful had to negotiate a difficult political and cultural landscape.

Church and Juan Perón

The relationship of the Church to dictators and military governments in the twentieth century was a complex one. In the case of Porfirio Díaz of Mexico (see chaps 8 and 9), although he had begun his political career as a liberal and thus antagonistic to the Church, he eventually embraced the Church and used it as an agency of social control. The Church of the early and mid-twentieth century grappled with issues of authority and hierarchy. Confronted with ideologies that sought to empower the individual within the state, some elements of the Church felt that it was necessary to stress the authority and tradition of hierarchy as an important value of the Church. This approach gave the Church a unique identity but did not necessarily attract more supporters.

In Argentina, in the middle decades of the twentieth century, the politics of the nation revolved around the person of Juan Perón. Perón, a military officer, was carried into power by a military coup when he served as part of a governing junta. By allying himself with labor unions, the disenfranchised masses, and to a certain degree with the Catholic hierarchy, Perón was able to consolidate power to emerge as the sole ruler. The military had an unclear relationship with the Church. After the coup, the junta members began to ally themselves with the more conservative elements in the Church and sought to revert to an earlier period of Church and state conservative solidarity. Unfortunately, by the middle of the twentieth century, the Church no longer commanded the same mass support that it had in earlier epochs, so the junta moved to a more populist message. Perón emerged as the leader since he was able to garner support from several of the most powerful labor unions in the country. At the same time, many elements in the Church remained strong allies of Perón for many years.

Following the coup and Perón's consolidation of power, he made overtures to the Church, supporting compulsory religious instruction in public schools, for example. Nonetheless, in the election of 1945, in which Perón hoped to become a legitimate democratically elected president, the Church declined to publically support any particular party or candidate. Still, Perón's opponents espoused clearly anticlerical policies such as the abolition of religious instruction in the public schools as well as the legalization of divorce and consequently Perón achieved victory with the tacit approval of the Church. Perón, in turn, more publically endorsed ecclesiastical initiatives and praised the papal encyclicals of *De rerum novarum* (1891) and the other keystones of modern Catholic Action. These actions caused Perón opponents to also turn their wrath on the Church.

Catholic Action in Argentina had become relatively powerful in the 1930s and '40s. As in other parts of Latin America, it represented a more conservative perspective, frequently xenophobic and nationalistic, although it avoided outright political activity. Its strenuous opposition to the tolerance of Protestants, Jews, and other non-Catholics became closely intertwined with xenophobia, seeing *all* non-Catholics as outsiders. In spite of its policy to remain outside of politics, Catholic Action became part of the more vocal support for Perón. In Perón many conservative Catholics saw an opportunity to improve the status of the Church within society at large, making it a central institution of the nation. Yet the alliance of Perón and Catholic Action was relatively short-lived.

By the middle years of his rule, and certainly by 1955, Perón increasingly came into conflict with the leaders of the Catholic Church. Between 1950 and 1955 Perón allied his policies with labor unions more than with the Church. He opposed Catholic influences in the labor movement, fearing an alliance of those two institutions, and he also harbored fears that some institution might gain sufficient power to oppose him. Since the Church was not wholly supportive of his regime, he kept a wary eye on it. While the hierarchy had largely supported Perón, there were clerical opponents to him even in the early days of his government. The role of his wife, Eva Duarte de Perón, and her philanthropic foundation also caused tensions with the Church. Founded in 1948, the foundation quickly became a quasi-governmental agency distributing charity throughout the nation and the world. The foundation came to largely supplant the charitable works of the Church, which it also sought to control, directly or indirectly.

By 1954 Perón initiated a clear break with the Church. He condemned elements in the Church, which he felt were trying to undermine the integrity of the nation and declared them enemies of the government. Shortly thereafter several priests were arrested for their political activity, especially in labor unions. Catholic newspapers closed up shop, and Perón halted the support of religious instruction in the public schools. Soon congress legalized divorce, eliminated all aid to Catholic schools, and closed some Church-supported schools. The government continued to imprison clerics who spoke in opposition to it. These actions offended not only conservative supporters of the Church and opponents of Perón, but large swaths of the political spectrum as well.[1]

The Catholic hierarchy emerged in clear opposition to the regime and expressed a determination to defend itself from the Peronista attack; Catholic Action also came out strongly against the Perón government. Eventually the papacy excommunicated all governmental authorities who had participated in the arrest and eventual deportation of two prelates who had been arrested for opposing government policies. Perón, unable to head off a diplomatic confrontation with the papacy, could not get the excommunication lifted. By September 1955 the regime lost its popular support, and a military coup overthrew the government, restoring the political and legal framework to a relatively pre-Perón state. Unfortunately for the Church, it emerged from the Perón era with a damaged reputation for having supported the regime early on, only to have to defend its own integrity in the face of governmental threats. Subsequent military and civilian governments established cordial relations with the Church, and subsequently negotiated with the Vatican over the creation of dioceses and the appointment of bishops and archbishops.

While the institutional Church continued to play an important political role in many Latin American countries, by the middle of the twentieth century it was fading rapidly. The Church increasingly was not a monolithic institution with a unified set of goals in the political realm. The rise of Catholic Action had created an active laity, willing to support the hierarchy but with their own ideas about the political process. Moreover, the movement for social justice, begun with *De rerum novarum* and continued through other popes, began to have a real impact on the laity. While the Church hierarchy might be allied with conservative political forces, a new group of laypersons and clergy emerged for whom issues of social equity were part and parcel of the Gospel message. For them the traditional support given to the Church hierarchy and its emphasis on structure rather than change did not coincide with what they found in the social teachings of the Gospel. Some intellectuals did indeed embrace Marxism as a reasonable response to the alliances of the institutional Church with dictators and conservatives. And by the 1950s, the Church was in turmoil from within, with the hierarchy tending to be conservative, opposing what it saw as atheism in Marxist thought. At the same time a few priests and laypersons openly embraced Marxism and Communism as fully consistent with the Gospel.

The Origins of Liberation Theology

The Catholic Church now confronted several different perceived threats. First of all was the unstable political realm in which the Church chose to ally itself with various political factions, suffering losses of prestige when those groups lost political power. The latter part of the middle decades of the twentieth century also saw a second decline in the number of clergy available to minister to the faithful. In many countries the number of young men seeking careers in the Church began to decline around the time of the Second World War, after having enjoyed an increase in the 1920s and 1930s even into the

1940s. Some political regimes suppressed seminaries and hindered clerical formation. In some countries economic and social conditions also tended to discourage young men from the clergy, instead seeking economic opportunities that were emerging in the middle decades of the century. With more open economies, young men from middle- and lower-class families did not have to rely on becoming priests for upward social mobility. Those from the poorest families, however, still saw the Church as a viable option for social mobility, and many young men from the wealthiest families also entered the priesthood as part of the social attitudes of their class. At more or less the same time, the Church hierarchy saw the rise both of Protestant missionaries and of Marxist reformers as a direct threat.

The Catholic Church became involved in the Cold War, maintaining its longtime skeptical stance regarding any Marxist movement. Yet due to the trends initiated with the encyclical *De rerum novarum* and reiterated in *Quadragesimo anno* (1931) Catholic efforts for the furtherance of social and economic justice continued to have life. Because of the confrontations of the nineteenth century, in much of Latin America the Church had taken on a less politically active role by the middle of the twentieth century, focusing more on tradition and less on social or economic change. Nevertheless, within the Church there were elements that continued to strive for social and economic justice and to play a political role. As seen in Argentina, such endeavors could have an unfortunate outcome if the regime supported by the Church proved to be something other than expected.

As we read earlier, Catholic Action in Latin America was formed in the 1930s mostly to support the Church hierarchy and to invigorate the faithful. In most of Latin America these groups remained fairly conservative, often extremely conservative tending toward xenophobia. In Brazil, however, a slightly different pattern emerged. The Brazilian Catholic Action (*Ação Católica Brasileira*) appeared in 1935. Within a relatively short time it became the leading Catholic lay organization in the country. The Church hierarchy created Catholic Action, appointed its leaders, and directed its interests. Under the leadership of dom Sebastião Leme, archbishop of Olinda and later cardinal, Catholic Action became a strong force lobbying the political parties, not a substitute for a political party (see chap. 9). Leme was convinced that while direct political action was useful, a political party would not further the causes espoused by the Church hierarchy. As Getúlio Vargas rose to power and eventually became a dictator in 1937, Leme's decision to have Catholic Action act as a lobby rather than a political party, and to offer only limited support to Vargas on specific well-chosen issues, kept the movement from suffering embarrassment as the dictator took control and changed his various policies. Only in their mutual opposition to Communism did Catholic Action and Vargas support one another in any significant way. This was important because Vargas tacitly supported the newly created Catholic Workers Circles (*Círculos Operários*) as a bulwark against communist organizations in the labor sector. With Vargas's eventual fall in 1945, these labor groups also lost significant power, but in the meantime an important trend had begun, namely of a Church-based organization promoting the conditions of the workplace. The Catholic Action organization that survived Vargas was a more progressive entity than many of its peers in Latin America.

Vargas made a brief constitutional comeback in 1950, but the political environment had changed by the early 1950s. For the Church in Brazil this period saw the coming together of several important trends, evident throughout Latin America. Perhaps one of the most crucial was the continued decline in the number of clerics. Conflicts between liberals and conservatives and the uncertain role of the Church in the late nineteenth century were definite factors in the decline. The number of priests had begun to rise early in the twentieth century, but by the middle decades of the twentieth century only young men from wealthy rural families, where the clerical estate still held high social import and whose families could afford to pay for their education entered the clergy, along with a very few poor candidates who were given scholarships to study in the seminaries. For decades the Brazilian Church was unable to recruit enough local men into the priesthood and increasingly relied on priests from other countries, frequently Europe and to a degree the United States.

In the absence of sufficient clergy, some of the duties of the parish priest that did not require ordination could be passed to the laity. And now, with the second decline in the number of priests, there was a concomitant rise in lay leaders. The duties of these lay leaders included leading prayer meetings, such as the praying of the rosary. They ran catechism sessions for young people preparing for their first communion and confirmation. They could also supervise minor liturgies of prayer as long as they avoided the sacramental services of the Eucharist and Confession. There also emerged a pattern of holding some of these services in private homes rather than in the Churches. Several areas in Latin America adopted a program of Christian base communities (*comunidades de base*) to provide for support for individuals through small groups within a parish.[2] Consisting of small assemblies of several families, these small communities provided both support for their members as well as participation in the liturgical and social life of the parish. A technique that would play an important role by the late 1950s in training lay leaders was the *Cursillo de Cristiandad* (a short course in Christianity, known simply as *cursillo*). The *cursillo* is a three-day experience, led by clergy and the laity, which provides an intensive introduction to Christianity aimed at believers by providing a deeper and more significant emotional and religious experience. It provides a deeper relationship with God and prepares them to be lay apostles in the world. The movement began in Spain around 1949 and quickly spread through Spanish-speaking congregations elsewhere. All of these responses would work to create a new perspective on the part of the laity as to the function of the Church and priesthood.

The last major trend to emerge in the period following the Second World War was the increase in the number of Protestant missionaries in Brazil in particular and in Latin America in general. While the mainline Protestant denominations invested resources in the conversion efforts, some of the fastest growth has occurred since World War Two—not among the mainline churches but in the Pentecostal and Evangelical churches. All Protestant churches offer a truly new religious experience to a greater or lesser degree. Rather than a ritual dependent on an ordained priest, much of the celebration is communal and egalitarian. Protestant denominations tend to have firm beliefs about a "priesthood of all believers," without need for mediation to the divine. The clergy are married and participate fully in the life of the community, and the Protestant churches allow individuals to sidestep traditional social hierarchies. The Catholic Church was seen as reinforcing social hierarchies, and thus by joining a Protestant sect the individual could opt out of the traditional Church-mediated social hierarchy. The idea that the Church mediated the social hierarchy was reinforced by the fact that a large percentage of priests came from the rural upper class. In the Pentecostal and Evangelical churches in particular, the lowest classes had an equal opportunity with upper-class individuals for leadership. Pentecostal Christianity also includes an emotional and charismatic element not unlike the syncretic cults already prevalent in Brazil, such as *Candomblé* and *Macumba*.

In many ways communism offered the same types of rewards as did the Protestant missionaries. It was a new social and economic system that would remove the individual from the traditional structures. It offered a new network within which to operate and a promise of improved conditions. Communism also offered an ideology to replace the traditional Catholic doctrine, but it did not, in general, offer the same emotional response that a Catholic liturgy or Pentecostal celebration did.

For the Catholic Church, Eucharistic congresses provided a mechanism for emphasizing the important liturgical differences between Catholicism and Protestantism, and communism for that matter. Eucharistic congresses are assemblies—regional, national or international—that celebrate the centrality of the Eucharist in the public worship of the Church. One of the significant differences at the personal level between Catholicism and its competitors is liturgical. While the Pentecostal movement might have opportunities for high emotion, music, and celebration, as did certain other Protestant sects, the Catholic Church offered unity, vestments, emotion, drama, and music in its liturgy. The celebration of the Eucharist was one means of heightening the unique nature of the Catholic faith. Eucharistic congresses began in France as a sociopolitical response to secularist trends in the French state, but were adopted throughout the Catholic world in the early twentieth century as a means of galvanizing public enthusiasm for the Church, in the very public celebration of its central sacrament. Two important international Eucharistic congresses were held in Latin America: first in 1934 in Buenos Aires, and then in 1955 in Rio de Janeiro. In both of these instances thousands came to participate in activities organized around the celebration of the Eucharist. Several countries had their own national Eucharistic congresses as well, with Brazil celebrating some seven of them between 1922 and 1955.

While all of these trends were developing, the Brazilian hierarchy also was changing. One of the themes of the colonial period and early Republican periods had been the centralization of political authority. Brazil is a large nation and, like the United States, has struggled with the opposing trends of centralization and regionalization. The Church, especially under the leadership of powerful figures like Cardinal Leme, had enjoyed more centralization than many national institutions. With Leme's death in 1942 there began a slow but seeming inexorable decentralization as power began to flow to regional bishops. Moreover, the bishops also differed greatly from one to the other over their vision for the large Brazilian Church, let alone the condition of the Church in their particular diocese.

In Brazil in the 1950s the Church sought to actively take control of its own future. One of the first actions was the creation of a National Conference of Bishops, the *Conferência Nacional de Bispos Brasileiros* (CNBB), in 1952. The impetus behind this development was a proposal made by dom Helder Câmara. Câmara had been the chaplain to the Catholic Action in Brazil, and then became an auxiliary bishop of Rio de Janeiro at roughly the same time that Pope Pius XII appointed Armando Lombardi as papal nuncio to Brazil. In 1950 Câmara met with the nuncio and proposed the creation of a national conference to improve communication among the bishops, and to regain some of the focus of the national Church as a substitute for the centralizing power of Archbishop Cardinal Leme. Câmara later made his proposal in Rome, and in 1952 the conference received papal approval. Câmara emerged as the de facto leader of the new conference, with the title of general secretary. This was, for all intents and purposes, the first national conference of bishops created in Latin America. Nuncio Lombardi had as his mission to support the conference and to help play a role in the renovation of the Brazilian Church. The actions of Helder Câmara and Nuncio Lombardi had the effect of bypassing dom Jaime Cardinal de Barros Câmara (no relation to dom Helder), the cardinal archbishop of Rio de Janeiro, a very conservative cleric and the putative head of the Brazilian Church, though the creation of the bishops conference clearly had the blessing of the papacy.

Not all of the Brazilian bishops or clergy supported the conference. Many conservatives felt that the Church needed to maintain its traditional structure and opposed the influence of a national conference. While the CNBB spoke ostensibly for the whole of the Catholic bishops, its policies were those promoted by Câmara, the nuncio, and their allies in the conference. In the context of the times, these policies were largely progressive. While the conference supported the anticommunist rhetoric coming out of the United States and endorsed by the Brazilian government, it also supported economic development efforts fostered by the United States.

In the period between 1950 and 1964—the peak years of cooperation between Câmara and Nuncio Lombardi—the Brazilian hierarchy grew rapidly, adding eleven archbishoprics and forty-eight bishoprics, plus other minor jurisdictions. Of the bishops appointed in this period none came from the ranks of the conservatives. At the same time large numbers of North American and European priests came to serve as missionaries in Brazil, comprising nearly half of the priests in the country by 1964.[3] These actions all created a truly Brazilian Church, which looked significantly different from many other national Churches. They also developed the groundwork for dramatic developments in the 1960s and 1970s as Latin America began to react to the Cuban Revolution and other significant upheavals.

The course sought by Câmara and by other leaders in Brazil was development. While the world of the 1950s and 1960s did not lack for models, between the poles of capitalist Europe and the United States on the one hand, and the communist bloc on the other, the path frequently defined by progressive Church leaders in Latin America was a path of development, consistent with the traditions and culture of the region. This was seen as a program in which the Church fostered labor movements, popular housing, and financial institutions for the poor. These movements also placed a good deal of responsibility in the hands of the persons receiving the benefits. The key was that these institutions were closely allied to the Church and the local clergy.

In Chile this tendency took on a distinctive tone when some young leaders used the Christian Democratic Party as a vehicle to push for greater development for the country. In this period these political efforts were both progressive and strongly anticommunist. The party appealed to members of the middle class who saw a progressive agenda as a hope for better economic conditions, as well as offering young men and women a new and attractive political movement. The party attempted to find a middle ground in world politics, allied to Christian Democrats in Europe, and supportive of some U.S. initiatives, like the Alliance for Progress, but not averse to state participation in the economy for the purpose of development. The Alliance for Progress was a program, initiated by President Kennedy, to foster the rapid economic and social development of Latin America within the framework of democracy and to keep communism at bay. The key for many political activists within the Christian Democrats was to plot an autonomous economic policy and to create a political and social system that would be more open than the one inherited from the colonial period and nineteenth century, and not completely reliant on the United States.

While many national Churches were coming to grips with the reality of the Cold War, fending off perceived threats from communists and Protestants, and concerned about changing political alliances in their own countries, there were several supranational trends at work as well. One of these focused on the coordination of the activities of the regions' bishops, while the other sought to provide superior education for priests.

In 1955 the bishops of the region organized the Latin American Bishops' Conference (CELAM). Some of the prime movers of this group were Bishop Manuel Larraín of Talca, Chile, and Archbishop Helder Câmara of Brazil. Both believed that to be effective pastors, Latin American bishops needed a venue in which to share ideas and initiatives. Each was a progressive in his own right. Larraín worked hard to assure that all social groups were included in the mission of the Church. He feared that the popular classes would feel disenfranchised from the Church, long seen as a bastion of elites in many Latin American countries, and that this was a greater threat than communism to the Church. CELAM became instrumental in developing regionwide policies and practices to combat communism, addressing issues of underdevelopment, and spreading the Gospel in the face of growing Protestant missions. CELAM also fit into a new vision being developed in the Vatican of transnational agencies created to coordinate ecclesiastical programs. In fact, CELAM and other regional associations became prototypes for institutions to be encouraged by the reforms of Vatican II (1962–65).

The Second Vatican Council

The 1950s saw several key developments. One was the creation of national bishop's conferences, such as the one in Brazil, which brought bishops together to allow for more coordinated efforts in evangelization, renewal, fighting communism, and seeking economic and social development for their nations and regions. The character of the local priesthood changed as large numbers of European and North American priests arrived to serve as missionaries and parish priests. They brought with them modern ideas concerning social change and social and political structures. Because of the relative scarcity of priests, many communities developed methods of continuing the work of the Church in the absence of clerics, such as Christian base communities. The confrontation with communism and Protestants forced the Catholic Church to look to messages that would best counter these forces. Frequently this was to emphasize the liturgical focus of the Church and to emphasize more social and economic issues rather than purely structural, institutional questions. In the end, many bishops, such as Larraín and Câmara believed that the Church needed to address issues of social and economic underdevelopment in order to best counter the inroads of communism and Protestantism. CELAM provided a mechanism for the sharing of ideas on these issues among all the bishops of the region.

The 1960s and 1970s provided a few watershed events in the development of the Catholic Church in Latin America. The period began with two extremely important occurrences: the success of the Cuban Revolution under Fidel Castro, and the call for the Second Vatican Council, both in 1959. The Cuban Revolution had a powerful impact on the Latin American Church. Cuba, by objective measures, was not the place many theorists would have anticipated a communist revolution. It took the Church by surprise. Many local bishops and national bishops associations recognized the threat posed by Cuba in their efforts to fight communism, and they redoubled their efforts to support development programs in their own countries to keep revolutionary fervor at bay. Like the Alliance for Progress, the Church adopted a policy of favoring economic development at the grassroots. This tended to shift attention away from a traditional alliance with elites, upon whom the

Church had relied for centuries in Latin America, to a new concern for the poor.

The impact of Vatican II on the Latin American Church was profound. The Council was announced by Pope John XXIII in 1959, the purpose of which was to modernize the Church to better prepare it to deal with the changing world. In particular, issues of liturgy, inter-Christian relations, the nature of revelation, and organizational structure, especially as it related to the powers of bishops, were key elements. But perhaps the greatest impact of the council was that it presented a different definition of what constituted the Church. Prior to the council, at least in Latin America, the Church was institutional and structural.

Vatican II met in four sessions lasting from 1962 to 1965. Its deliberation resulted in a flurry of documents, which would govern and guide the Church in the future. One of the early decisions of the council was to redefine the Church as the "pilgrim people of God." This implied that the Church is the body of all the faithful, engaged in a journey of revelation moving toward the full and complete revelation of the kingdom of God. The Church changed into an organic network of all the faithful, committed to bringing about the works of the Gospel. Moreover, greater emphasis was placed on the importance of the laity in doing the work of the Church in the world. Both the ordained clergy and the laity were seen as important parts of the body of the Church, each with special gifts for ministry.

The council reiterated that the Bible was the central authoritative document for the Church. The pope and ecumenical councils also were recognized as inerrant in directing the moral and spiritual life of the Church. Bishops were authoritative within their own dioceses, mediated by the primacy of the pope. The council restored the permanent diaconate, with or without celibacy, which meant that men seeking ministries within the Church could be ordained permanent deacons, whether or not they were married. And finally, the council also undertook a complete reform of the liturgy.

For most practicing Catholics the major changes in the liturgy—the words and manner in which the sacraments of the Church are celebrated, mandated by the Vatican Council—constituted a dramatic shift. Breaking with centuries of tradition, the Council not only approved the use of the vernacular in Church ceremonies and services, but it severely restricted the use of the old Latin Mass. It called for a reexamination of the liturgical calendar and especially the obligatory veneration of some saints who were no longer considered to have been historical figures, such as Saint Christopher. Another change allowed national Churches to develop their own liturgies for the sacraments, based on the formulas and traditions from Latin. It encouraged local innovation. In Latin America this change stimulated efforts to look back to popular religion as it had developed locally and to attempt to incorporate those elements into the celebrations.

In defining the Church as an institution in the world, the Council stressed the dignity of the individual human, the importance of the Church's influence on culture, the equality of all humans, and the importance of continued teaching on social issues. It reaffirmed the importance of Catholic Action, as well as calling on the laity to further social and economic opportunity. Papal encyclicals also emphasized the right of all persons to a decent standard of living, to education, and to participate in politics. While recognizing older, more traditional measures to address social and economic issues, Vatican II also called upon the faithful to transform the world in accordance with Catholic norms of equity and mutuality. It tacitly recognized that lessons could be learned from the social sciences and applied to the work of the Church. This allowed theologians, and others, to begin to incorporate many ideas and methodologies from disciplines such as politics and sociology to create a more encompassing theology. Poverty need no longer be tolerated by hoping for a greater reward in heaven, but rather the faithful should transform the world to prepare for the kingdom; they should move to abolish poverty as a precondition for the coming of the kingdom.

The various decrees of the council outlined the importance of the office of bishop, and for the first time it established a compulsory retirement age for bishops. The council walked a fine line between declaring the Catholic faith as the one true pathway to salvation and the need to enter into dialogue with other faiths and creeds, especially to seek the unity of all branches of the Christian faith. Much of the debate focused on the life of the priest. The council lifted up the vocation of priest as a high calling, along with practical issues such as the need for more priests and a more equitable distribution of priests throughout the populations of the world. It stressed the need for a well-educated priesthood and called for the creation of more seminaries. Along with the priesthood, the religious life was extolled and found necessary even within modern society. The contemplative life offered a stark contrast to the hectic and busy life of most people. Missionary efforts also warranted a formal decree. The council called for the spreading of the Gospel to all cultures, and approved efforts to make it understood and relevant in different cultural settings. The council also promulgated decrees regarding the laity. The laity was seen as exercising an important calling within the Church, on a par with the calling of the early apostles. Catholic Action, in particular, was singled out as an important mission for the laity. Taken as a whole, the Second Vatican Council considered nearly every aspect of the Church and attempted to bring canon law and ecclesiastical practice into the twentieth century.

The middle decades of the twentieth century saw the Church move in directions that only a few decades earlier would have been unimaginable. In the 1930s much energy was still expended on resolving issues regarding the relationship between the Church and the state. By the 1960s these issues, while not forgotten, had become less important. Energy was now focused on bringing the Church to the people. The emphasis shifted from the Church as a hierarchy, defending the magisterium (the teaching authority of the hierarchy), to the Church being the living body of the faithful, working out God's plan of redemption for the world in concrete efforts to change social and economic standards throughout the region. The decades to follow would witness nothing short of the complete renovation of the Church into a new and strikingly different institution, but not without great tension and debate.

While the numbers of priests experienced a modest growth early in the century, by the 1950s fewer and fewer young men entered the priesthood. This caused individual communities to have to come to grips with the very nature of the Church. The Vatican Council addressed this issue by opening up much of the ministry of the Church to lay people, except in those areas where canon law dictated the need for a priest, such as in the celebration of the Eucharist, absolution of sins, marriage, and other sacraments. In isolated communities where large populations of native people still lived, there was far less change. Having been largely ignored since independence, they continued to practice popular forms of Christianity. In addition large slums around major cities developed where the vast majority of the population was not in regular contact with the Church. Now, however, Catholic missionaries from abroad, Protestant missionaries, and, in some instances, revolutionaries began to see these populations as prime targets for their efforts.

The Decline of Liberation Theology

Leonardo Boff was born Genezio Darci Boff to a large family in Concordia, in the Brazilian state of Santa Catarina. In 1949, at the age of ten, he entered the Franciscan elementary school for young men interested in joining the order. Upon entering the Franciscan novitiate he took the name of Leonardo and was ordained to the priesthood in 1964 in Brazil. He traveled to Europe where in 1970 he received the doctorate in theology from the Ludwig-Maximilian University in Munich. Boff's research considered the sacramental nature of the Church in the light of the canons and decrees of the Second Vatican Council. In 1972 he returned to Brazil where he embarked on a teaching career while also actively publishing and serving several scholarly journals.

Many of Boff's works were co-authored by his brother, Clodovis Boff, a member of the Order of the Servants of Mary. In 1985 Leonardo broke into the international scene when his book, *Church: Charism, and Power* was translated into English. In this book, Boff criticized the institutional structure of the Church from what seemed to be a Marxist orientation. He argued that similar to the way in which industrialists held a monopoly on the means of production, so the Church taught that it held a monopoly on God's grace. This position brought Boff to the attention of the Congregation of the Doctrine of the Faith, headed by then Joseph Cardinal Ratzinger (later Pope Benedict XVI), which reprimanded Boff and officially demanded that he refrain from preaching, teaching, or publishing for one year. Following his year of silence, Boff resumed his writing, embracing such controversial themes as the ordination of women and the acceptance of married priests. In the face of his refusal to comply with its directives, the Congregation issued a formal refutation of his works, and the following year he was removed from one of his editorial positions with a leading Catholic Brazilian publisher.

Boff also continued his work on the institutional nature of the Church. In keeping with his interpretation of the decrees of Vatican II, he wrote that

Christian communities were an equal vehicle for salvation, not necessarily subject to the Church. In 1992, Boff renounced his vows as a Franciscan and of the priesthood. He subsequently married. Following his break with the Catholic Church, he remained active in his own local Christian community, and has continued to write on theological and ecclesiological themes while exploring issues of climate change and ecology. He has taught ethics, philosophy of religion, and ecology at the State University of Rio de Janeiro. Boff, along with other priests and theologians in Latin America, has attempted to use new methodologies to better understand the relationship of the Church to the modern economic realities especially as found in the less developed parts of the world. His research brought him into conflict with the teaching of the Church, yet it was an important component in what was a transformational dialogue within the Church.

The Catholic Church in Latin America in the last four decades of the twentieth century underwent a dramatic transformation, brought about by many different impulses but focused mostly on the working out of the Second Vatican Council and the actions of the Latin American bishops, meeting in regional councils, which sought to bring the reforms of Vatican II to the region. At the same time Latin America underwent two political transformations. While popularly elected governments typified the region in the 1950s, these were replaced in the mid-1960s and '70s with military governments, only to recover civilian governments by the last fifteen years of the century. This turmoil and change brought to light a way of being a Church and doing God's will, and which came to be known as liberation theology.

In the twentieth century, the United States had continued its interventionist approach, developed in the nineteenth century. The Monroe Doctrine was frequently invoked following the 1960 revolution in Cuba. Other than the failed invasion at the Bay of Pigs, the United States did not overtly attack Cuba. It did send troops on numerous occasions into Central America and to various islands of the Caribbean, sometimes for political reasons, sometimes for more financial reasons. Many theorists in the United States envisioned the world as a chess game in which the United States and the Soviet Union played for dominance. As a result, any regime that manifested tendencies that could be interpreted as supportive of the Soviet Union would quickly encounter opposition from the United States. This U. S. involvement in Latin America ran the gamut from covert operations to destabilize regimes, such as a 1952 CIA plot to overthrow the government in Guatemala, to funding secondary agents to carry out guerrilla warfare against regimes, as occurred in Nicaragua during the administration of Ronald Reagan.

While not all Latin American governments were democratically elected in the period immediately following the Second World War, by the late 1950s and early '60s perhaps a greater number were elected in this way than had ever been before. Many of the governments were mildly progressive. They eagerly sought to cooperate with the United States in creating new economic opportunities in their countries to counteract the spread of communism, a threat made manifest by the Cuban Revolution. Communism and other leftist ideologies were certainly prevalent throughout the continent among intellectuals, residents of shanty towns, and poor landless peasants in the rural regions. In several countries the political leaders had begun modest programs of social and economic development, in some instances with the cooperation of the local bishops and clergy. The two best examples of these efforts are found in Brazil and Chile.

Brazil and the Generals

Brazil in the 1950s and early 1960s was politically fragile. It had lived through the *Estado Novo* of Getúlio Vargas, who was eventually overthrown by a military coup, only to return as an elected president. When Vargas was no longer able to govern effectively, confronted with mounting political opposition and threats of a military coup, he committed suicide. In the regular elections already scheduled for 1955, Jucelino Kubitschek was elected president on a platform of economic development in a three-way race. Although a Christian Democratic Party existed in Brazil, having been founded after the first Vargas regime, it had neither close ties to the Church hierarchy nor an extensive following. Kubitschek ran as the head of a generally pro-Vargas coalition, but he lacked a clear mandate, headed a minority government, and was not thoroughly trusted by the military. He ruled by offering something to everyone, which resulted in a growing deficit and the beginnings of inflation in the economy. It was Kubitschek who began the risky venture of creating Brasilia, a new national capital in the interior.

Kubitschek was succeeded by Jânio Quadros, a political outsider and not really a member of any party, who created a coalition of supporters. Although endorsed by one of the leading parties, he renounced that endorsement in order to manifest his independence. While charismatic, Quadros was simply unable to govern. Given the complexity of the problems confronting Brazil, Quadros had no effective program or response, and so resigned less than a year into his presidency. He was succeeded by his vice president, João Goulart. Both Quadros and Goulart had friendly relations with the communist and socialist parties. When Che Guevara visited the country in 1961, Quadros awarded him Brazil's highest medal given to a foreigner. Goulart, though an experienced politician, was unable to resolve Brazil's most pressing problems: a continuing need for economic development and a growing problem of inflation. As well, the political middle was rapidly shrinking as the Far Left and the Far Right each sought to increase their support in the economic crisis. Finally, the military staged a coup, convinced that Goulart was unable to govern effectively and that he was leading the country even farther leftward.

During the Kubitschek and Goulart era, the Church had been active in promoting its own social and economic programs in Brazil. The experience of the Church, having allied with Vargas only to be betrayed and eventually losing credibility, deeply colored the bishops' approach to the political situation. Within the Church, a significant segment of the laity and clergy were energized by the prospects of social and economic development. Some independent Catholic labor unions and peasant groups in the interior and northeast were created. The Catholic University Youth were deeply inspired by the Cuban Revolution and began to become more political, moving significantly toward the Left. Some Catholics founded political parties, which were independent of the Church but drew heavily from a Catholic perspective on development and social change. Most of these movements lacked any clear endorsement of the Church hierarchy, although individual bishops participated in their activities with some clergy and laity playing a dominant role. With the coup of 1964, all political parties were abolished. A period of repression, which grew by the end of the decade, followed this action.

The dictatorship of the generals falls into three periods.[1] In the first period (1964–67), both the Church and the military proceeded cautiously, finding common cause where possible, although groups within each manifested deep mistrust of the factions of the other. In general, Brazilians welcomed the military coup, fearing a greater radicalization under Goulart, or at worst political chaos. The military expressed its willingness to work with the Church on issues of economic development and social justice. The Church, for its part, saw the coup as saving the country from the threat of communism. At the same time, more conservative bishops took over the Council of Bishops. Helder Câmara was transferred from auxiliary archbishop of Rio de Janeiro to archbishop of the distant Olinda and Recife archdiocese. He ceased to serve as secretary general of the council. In Olinda and Recife he organized the sixteen local bishops into a regional conference that stood in partial opposition to the more conciliatory stance of the National Council of Bishops regarding the government. For his work in speaking out for the poor and the oppressed, Câmara was nominated four times for the Nobel Peace Prize.

In the middle period (1970–78), the military exercised violent repression against all potential opponents, including the Church. Starting as early as 1967 the military government began to clamp down on opposition. As opposition groups sprouted up, the military sought to eliminate them, using legal and extralegal means as necessary. The police were watchful of the political activities of members of the clergy, and numerous clashes ensued as priests and bishops were targeted by the security forces of the military government, arrested, and in some cases deported. Finally in 1968, the government promulgated Institutional Act 5, which eliminated habeas corpus and most other civil liberties. The military government created a secret police to monitor the opposition, guerrilla groups sprang up throughout the country, and violence became widespread. The generals specifically targeted the Church in their efforts to eliminate opposition. Extreme repression followed. Some conservative groups within the Church supported the military repression, denouncing what they saw as a leftist attempt to subvert both the Church and the government. Eventually even the moderately conservative National Council of Bishops spoke out against the repression after more priests were arrested, detained, and even murdered for their political opposition to the military government.

During the repression, the Church became one of the few organized voices of opposition to the military government, most other institutions having been silenced by the generals. As the repression mounted and the National Council of Bishops sought a moderate path, changes were afoot within the episcopacy. First, in 1968 dom Aloísio Lorscheider became the secretary general of the council. Lorscheider, a Franciscan, then bishop of Santo Angelo in Rio Grande do Sul, had attended the Second Vatican Council. He was one of the more liberal bishops, outspoken in his work to alleviate the crushing poverty in his country. His rise manifested a new approach on the part of the episcopacy in the face of military repression. In 1970 the pope appointed Cardinal Rossi, the moderate, conservative head of the Council, as head of the Congregation for the Evangelization of the Peoples in Rome. He was replaced on the council by dom Paulo Evaristo Arns, also a Franciscan and auxiliary bishop of São Paulo, who was named a cardinal in 1973. Arns was, in turn, succeeded by Lorscheider, who became archbishop of Fortaleza in the northeast in 1973 and a cardinal in 1976. Under Lorscheider, the National Council of Bishops turned into one of the most vocal opponents to the military regime and its repression. The support that these bishops received from the papacy, in their elevation to the College of Cardinals, also understood that the Roman Church was indeed serious about confronting not only poverty but also repression.

The National Council of Bishops then published a series of open letters to the public opposing the military repression and the savage attacks mounted by paramilitary groups allied with the government. In the first of these, the bishops equated the military government with repressive communist states. Other pastoral letters outlined the obligations of a Christian in the political order, which repeated many of the earlier arguments, noting that the nation consisted of *all* the people and the state was merely a servant of the nation, not the other way around. The bishops also supported the protection of the rights of the poorest members of the Brazilian nation, such as the natives of the Amazon Basin. In response, attacks by right-wing terrorists and paramilitary groups escalated against Church targets.

In the final period (1978–85), the military realized that it had to return the country to democratic principles, and it sought to improve relations with the Church, as one national institution that could actually help in the transition. This period began with the selection of General Ernesto Geisel to run the government. One of his first acts was to rescind the hated Institutional Act 5, restoring civil liberties. He then lifted restrictions on the media, followed by the approval of the return of dozens of exiles, and, not least, an amnesty for all exiles. The Church, sensing a new openness, embraced these actions and began to cooperate with leading members of the parliament on democratization. In response to this, too, the National Council of Bishops issued a series of pamphlets on democracy and participation in elections. In 1979, General João Batista Figueiredo was elected president in a modestly free election. He manifested the rapprochement with the Church by visiting the office of the National Council of Bishops shortly after his election, before formally taking office.

During the years of the military dictatorship, the Church had begun to be transformed in a very fundamental way. In an effort to counter the effects of a serious shortage of priests, local parishes saw the development of Christian base communities (CEB) These groups are small, usually consisting of twelve to fifteen families. They are sub-units of a local parish in which the members take on part of the responsibility for maintaining the Christian life of the group, teaching catechism, studying the Bible, being missionaries within their own larger community, and providing support mechanisms for their fellow CEB members. The earliest examples date from the early 1960s, particularly in Brazil. The activities of the CEB conform closely with many of the new ideas that were just then coming out of the Vatican II meeting. Importantly, they seem to have sprung up from below, rather than being imposed from above and provided a great cohesiveness for their members. Moreover, the CEB made the larger Church and its ministries more approachable, since the Church was and is merely a larger scale of the small, personal, and family-oriented community.

There are three main implications of the CEBs. The most important is their role as a system of mutual support. In an increasingly industrialized society with a breakdown of the traditional extended family support systems for the poor, the CEBs provide a network of individuals who work to support one another, providing day care, financial assistance, and many other basic human needs. They serve to educate their members not merely about the doctrines of the Church but also about their responsibilities as members of a larger community, often with a significant political tone. And they are important missionary institutions. The CEB is expected to grow through the inclusion of new families who have not yet been incorporated into the Church. In these ways, the CEB provided a direct answer both to threats from communism and from Protestants.

In Brazil, the rapid growth of the CEBs corresponded to the period in which the military government cracked down on political parties, labor unions, and many other public institutions. Some have posited that the base communities grew as one of the few places where people could freely express their thoughts. As the more public institutions of the Church suffered under attack from paramilitary groups and right-wing death squads, the base communities continued to survive more or less out of sight. As such they provided an important venue in which to carry on the political debate necessary for a free society. Needless to say, the CEBs became political entities in this atmosphere, most frequently embracing leftist ideologies. While politicized, they did not, however, become political. They usually retained their focus on being the Church to their members. Base communities also provided a voice for women, who in earlier periods had been largely marginalized in the life of the Church, and therefore women came to take up many leadership roles in their small communities. The strength of the CEBs also provided for a smoother transition to democracy as the military loosened their control over the government.

Chile: From Democracy to Dictatorship

The experience of Chile was quite different, although that country too saw a military dictatorship in the 1970s. By the 1930s the Catholic Church in Chile had opted to remain on the sidelines politically. In the past, the alliance with the conservatives had not served the institution well. Although the hierarchy continued to be supportive of the anticommunist and anti-liberal stance of the conservatives, there were those who sought a different political path. In the 1940s a group of young politicians emerged ready to create a Christian party of the center. As we have seen, Catholic Action had a modest success in Chile in the early decades of the twentieth century. In 1937 and 1938, a group of young men formed by that movement broke from the Conservative Party to establish a new political group, which they called the National Phalanx (*Falange Nacional*). While they supported many of the traditional policies of the conservatives, generally opposing the anticlerical stance of the liberals yet definitively anticommunist, they broke with tradition in also pursuing a program of social justice. The Phalanx never gained widespread support, but it had sufficient numbers of followers to remain politically viable. In the period after the Second World War other political groups emerged pursuing similar programs, some more, others less conservative than the Phalanx. Finally in 1957 the Phalanx merged with another more conservative group to create the Chilean Christian Democratic Party. It was strongly anticommunist but supported a wide range of enlightened social policies, as part of an economic strategy to encourage economic development. Eduardo Frei, one of the original founders of the Phalanx, emerged as the leader of the new group.

While the Phalanx had grown out of Catholic Action, the party did not always have a cordial relationship with the Church hierarchy. In the late 1930s and '40s, Catholic Action supported the citizen's freedom to join whichever party he or she desired, with the caveat that the party respect Catholic values. Catholic Action also was a strong voice in favor of the freedom to create labor unions, that workers live in decent housing, and that they collect just wages, all of which was based on papal encyclicals. Yet as the postwar period developed and the threat of communism became more imminent, the episcopacy began to align itself more clearly with the more conservative political parties. The Phalanx, while also anticommunist, had no interest in allying with more conservative parties and thus pursued a more moderate voice, especially in social and economic issues. Although Catholic Action was directly tied to the episcopacy, the Phalanx was not. That group steered a more pragmatic course, sometimes allying with leftist parties in order to accomplish common goals, something the bishops found unsettling. A rupture between the Phalanx and many of the bishops occurred in 1948 when the government passed the "Law in Defense of Democracy," which outlawed the Communist

Party. Most of the bishops warmly supported the law; the Phalanx opposed it on constitutional grounds.

In Chile, in the absence of a powerful liberal government in the last half of the nineteenth century, there had been few restrictions on the number of men entering the priesthood, unlike the situation in most other countries. Yet in the opening decades of the twentieth century, the country had been plagued by fewer and fewer young men entering the priesthood. In the late 1940s and early '50s, Chile received hundreds of foreign priests to alleviate a severe shortage. At the same time, Catholic Action continued to surge in popularity. Catholic Action also began numerous outreach efforts to bring the urban masses into the Church. Many bishops who supported social and economic reform were now being appointed to various dioceses; by the end of the decade of the 1950s more progressive bishops held a clear plurality, if not majority. The Christian Democratic Party benefitted from this increased interest on the part of the Catholic faithful. The traditional parties had begun to fracture over internal issues. The once-powerful Radical Party fell into a decline when it was unable to bring about the reforms it had previously championed. Many former supporters of reform then moved into the Christian Democratic Party.

In the 1960s the Christian Democratic Party emerged as one of the most powerful in Chile, along with the Marxist *Frente de Acción Popular* (Popular Action Front) and the conservatives. In response to the Cuban Revolution and the initiatives coming from Vatican II, the bishops of Chile began significant outreach efforts, added new parishes especially among new migrants from the rural areas into the cities, and developed evangelization materials to attract the newcomers. In support of land reform, two bishops even donated land in their dioceses for a pilot program. Like Brazil, they organized a national bishops' conference, led by Archbishop Raul Silva Henríquez, of Santiago. Silva had been the head of Carítas, the leading relief agency for the Chilean Church, prior to his appointment and was seen as a strong supporter of social and economic reform. The spirit initiated by Vatican II also prompted the bishops to become more supportive of social justice issues, calling for reform and actively supporting various initiatives on their own. The hierarchy became increasingly allied with the Christian Democrats as the older, more conservative bishops were replaced with more progressive ones. As a result the Christian Democratic Party gained more influence in political circles and consequently also gained more partners for its own programs. When Eduardo Frei was elected president in 1964, a significant number of his appointees came from Catholic Action and from the many programs established by the bishops throughout the country.

The close ties between the Frei government and the Church were not completely beneficial. Many Catholics on the left felt that the reform agenda of the government was too slow. At the same time, many on the right who supported Frei as the lesser of two evils (his opponent was the Marxist Salvador Allende) strongly opposed attempts at land reform, which the bishops had supported. A decline in the worldwide price of copper put severe economic constraints on the government, and it was hampered in its effort to fund its reform agenda. All of these things convinced the bishops that blanket support for the government would ultimately compromise them and that they needed to cherry-pick those issues to support or oppose. In formal communications the Council of Bishops called for the creation of a more just society, noting the need for programs to provide more housing, employment, and education, but leaving to the faithful the exact policies whereby to accomplish these goals. As the election of 1970 approached, the bishops urged priests and laypersons working for the Church to avoid political activity, stressing the neutrality of the Church. In the election the Christian Democratic candidate came in third behind Salvador Allende, the Marxist leader of the Popular Unity Party, and the liberals.

With the election of the first openly Marxist president, the Catholic hierarchy charted a course wherein the bishops would serve as moral guides for the nation, attempting to moderate the voices on either side of the political spectrum. This was no small task since there were many voices within the Church urging the bishops to openly support Allende's programs and policies. Archbishop Silva supported the general direction of the new president's reforms, and he even declared that socialism had much to be admired. The Allende government had widespread support among the poorest Catholics in the cities' slums and popular neighborhoods. Still, the political spectrum continued to fragment, and the Church itself was not immune to the fragmentation, with more radical Catholics supporting the government and more traditional Catholics in vehement opposition to it. As the regime began to face trouble, both from the weakening internal economy and from sanctions imposed by the United States, the hierarchy did not actually take sides but the Christian Democrats aligned with the conservative parties in blocking government policies. In spite of the political turmoil, in the midterm elections of 1973, Allende's Popular Unity coalition gained seats in Congress.

As the political situation deteriorated, Archbishop Silva, now Cardinal Silva, sought to mediate by calling together Allende and leaders of the other political parties, particularly the Christian Democrats. These talks proved futile. The hierarchy worked diligently to avoid civil war and to calm the political waters, but all efforts failed. In 1973 the military, under the leadership of General Augusto Pinochet, staged a coup d'état during which Allende died. In the aftermath the Council of Bishops attempted to remain neutral, tacitly recognizing the regime but lamenting the loss of life in the struggle. Cardinal Silva sought to work with the military regime to smooth the eventual transition back to democracy, but was viewed by the military as too closely allied with the Christian Democrats. The military also mistrusted the cardinal for his efforts to negotiate with Allende and the Christian Democrats prior to the coup. Moreover, Silva had been among the first voices calling for a restoration of democracy, political freedom, and an independent judiciary, and he had also criticized the army for removing the leadership of the Catholic University and replacing them with friends of the military. Nonetheless, Silva would remain an important voice for the Catholic Church throughout the thirteen years of the military government.

Within the first year after the coup, it became clear that the Pinochet regime was not a brief military interlude in a generally democratic country; the generals intended to govern as long as possible. The Catholic Church then became one of the many voices calling for a return to democracy, finding partners in sometimes strange places. While the threat of Protestantism had been significant in Brazil, in Chile nearly a quarter of the population was already Protestant. The mainline Protestant churches allied themselves with the Catholic Church to form first the Cooperative Committee for Peace in Chile, and later the Vicariate of Solidarity. The first organization was disbanded due to government pressure when activists were involved in an armed confrontation with police. While the committee was an alliance of Lutherans and Jews, the Vicariate was organized as an office within the Archdiocese of Santiago, under the direct control of Cardinal Silva. At the same time that the Catholic Church and many Protestant denominations opposed the actions of the military government, many of the Pentecostal and some Evangelical Christian churches embraced it.

The Catholic opposition to the Pinochet regime was vested in the Vicariate of Solidarity. It differed from other similar institutions in that it was an office under the personal supervision and control of Cardinal Silva, not of the Conference of Bishops. In fact, several of the bishops opposed any such activity and were far more supportive of the regime. It also was not ecumenical as its predecessor, the Committee for Peace, had been. The Vicariate became one of the leading voices in protection of human rights in Chile. In the face of a well-organized state security office, the DINA (Directorate for National Intelligence), the Vicariate offered its assistance in the defense of human and civil rights. Thousands of Chileans were arrested by the DINA on charges of subversion; hundreds were murdered by agents of the state. The Vicariate served to keep the world informed of these actions and to provide direct aid to those who had been arrested and tortured regardless of their religious affiliation. It acted as a means to channel support from outside of Chile to those in need in the country, working with Amnesty International, Lutheran World Relief, and other human rights agencies. Needless to say, Pinochet viewed the Vicariate as a major threat to his regime and he became openly confrontational.

In 1983 Cardinal Silva retired as archbishop of Santiago, replaced by the more conservative Juan Francisco Fresno, who soon was elevated to the rank of cardinal. Fresno was far more willing to seek reconciliation with the regime, although he assured the Vicariate of his continued support. The country experienced several sharp encounters between the regime and the Church, although Fresno remained steady in his belief that reconciliation was possible and that the Church had a moral duty to spur dialogue, not cause a confrontation. He convened a meeting of the major political parties of the center representing some 80 percent of the political spectrum. These representatives agreed upon an accord for the transition to democracy, which Fresno presented to Pinochet. The general would not accept the blueprint, but later many would see in this accord the seeds of the restoration of democracy in Chile.

Important in the transition back to democracy was the visit of Pope John Paul II in 1987. Even though the pope remained scrupulously detached from politics, his visit was seen as a legitimization of the regime. Pinochet exploited the opportunity to have his photo taken with John Paul. The pope, however, had many interviews, including those who opposed the regime. In the end, the lack of violence during the trip helped pave the way to reconciliation, a word mentioned more than once by the pope.

In the events leading to the end of the regime, a plebiscite, and then full elections, the Church hierarchy took a back seat. In communications with the government, and in letters to the faithful, the bishops stressed the importance of a free election. While the bishops called for the election of someone who could lead the country to democracy, tacitly excluding Pinochet, they did not endorse any particular candidate. In the end the citizens voted to abolish the military regime and then elected Patricio Aylwin of the reorganized Christian Democratic Party as president.

During the military regime, the Church continued to support many programs that had been instituted in earlier periods. One curious side effect of the dictatorship was an increase in clerical vocations. During the Frei and Allende years, fewer men had opted to join the priesthood in Chile, but under Pinochet that number increased. The Chilean bishops also supported many of the programs already seen in Brazil, such as Christian base communities and community organizations for support of various groups, workers, students, mothers, and the like. The success of the Church came from its grassroots work. Although the communists and socialists had significant power in Chile as did the Protestants, the Catholic Church, because of its ministries to all income levels and manifest concern for social and economic reform, was able to emerge as a voice for the improvement of the country. It had one period where it became too closely allied with the Christian Democratic Party, but generally it sought to move the nation through pastoral concern and moral teaching rather than overt political action.[2]

The Church in an Age of Transitions

While we have focused on Brazil and Chile, many other countries in Latin America found themselves in similar situations in the 1970s and 1980s. In Argentina the military ruled for seven years, waging what has been called the "dirty war" against individuals suspected of leftist leanings. In Bolivia, the country went through a revolution in 1952, sought democracy, but endured various military regimes in the 1970s and 1980s. Peru had a unique leftist military government in the late 1960s and early 1970s, replaced by a civilian government that was then confronted by the Shining Pathway terrorists, only to have a civilian dictator in the person of Alberto Fujimori. While variations occurred, the Church followed a similar path in most countries: Catholic Action developed a group of priests and laypersons committed to social and economic reform and development; concurrently the Church strove to be an agency which was not in alliance with a particular regime or political party but dedicated to ensuring the human and civil rights of all.

During the 1960s and 1970s three basic positions developed within the Catholic Church in Latin America. The position that broke most clearly from the past was that of the priest, prelate, or layperson who openly embraced revolution as a key manifestation of Christianity. Among the numerous rebel groups in Latin America, one could find devoted and committed Catholic priests and laypersons, who firmly believed in the theological correctness of armed struggle. Many prelates and clerics remained within the conservative political fold and actively sought to roll back those changes that had already occurred in society, seeking to limit the activities of Protestants, vest all education in the Church, and empower the state to exercise more social control. Yet one of the themes of the development of the Catholic Church in Latin America has been a clear movement on the part of much of the priesthood and hierarchy toward a more moderate political orientation. Increasingly, bishops and priests, along with female religious, embraced policies aimed at creating social justice and economic development. These positions were fully consonant with the concerns manifested in the papal encyclicals of the late nineteenth century and embodied in the Second Vatican Council. Thus, the Church in this period manifested three factions: the Right, a highly conservative group seeking to limit social change; the center, made up of those who sought economic and social reform within the political realm; and the Left, those who advocated the violent overthrow of government to create a more radical social and economic change.

Camilo Torres of Colombia is a lasting example of the revolutionary priest. Coming from an upper-middle-class family in Bogotá, Torres studied sociology and was deeply influenced by French ideas of social Catholicism. In 1954, upon entering the priesthood, he traveled to Louvain, in Belgium, to pursue advanced study in sociology. On his return to Colombia in 1959, he served as a university chaplain and as a lecturer in sociology. Yet increasingly he became impatient with the slow process of molding popular opinion and the persuasion of the elites. In a confrontation with the cardinal archbishop, Luis Concha Córdoba, in 1962, Torres resigned from the university and began to work on the problem of land reform. His work and further study convinced him that the type of change necessary to address the social and economic ills of Colombia would not come about through normal political processes. First he embraced the notion of a peaceful revolution, but later acknowledged that significant change would come only through armed struggle. He wrote that Christians should ally themselves with Marxists to bring about this change, that the love of the Christians would counter the hate of the Marxists. He then founded a political movement, the United Front, in 1965. This led him into even more conflict with the Church hierarchy, at the end of which he accepted a voluntary renunciation of his vows and a return to the laity. Within a few months he had joined the National Liberation Army, a pro-Castro revolutionary group of guerrillas. A few weeks later, in February 1966, he was killed in a skirmish with an army patrol. Although he was only thirty-seven when he died, he would become the symbol of the radical Catholic response to issues of social and economic development. Nor was he unique within recent Latin American history. Many others shared his beliefs, to a greater or lesser degree. This type of radical interpretation of the political and economic reality of the region provided an important influence on liberation theology.

On the opposite political extreme, several countries, including Brazil and Chile, saw the development of an articulate conservative response to the issues of modernization. In many countries these were embodied in organizations known as Societies for the Defense of Tradition, Family, and Property (TFP). The conservative branch of the Catholic Church holds that the Church is a hierarchical institution, not merely an assemblage of people. This tradition argues that instead of seeing society strengthened through economic and social development, societies should embrace traditional structures such as the family and the Church. The conservatives strongly support the tenets of capitalism whereby each individual is an economic actor free to succeed or fail through his or her own efforts. They tend to reject most of the liturgical reforms of Vatican II, preferring the Latin mass. They are strongly committed to social stability and powerful central governments. For example, in much of Latin America, members of the ultraconservative Opus Dei have formed the core of the response to modernity. Opus Dei, founded by Josemaría Escrivá de Balaguer, a Spanish priest, seeks to have everyday people seek holiness in their everyday activities.

The political middle has been the area of greatest change. In general, many priests, religious orders, and the hierarchy in Latin America have moved to more centrist or even left-of-center policies. Part of this shift came as a result of the infusion of European and North American priests into the region. They also supported the creation of modern seminaries for the education of local priests. In addition, many of the brightest local priests continued their theological studies in the United States and Europe where they also encountered more progressive policies and ideologies. Catholic Action, responding to papal encyclicals, began to emphasize the importance of social justice, human rights, and economic development. Under the direction of John XXIII, Paul VI, and John Paul I, there was a clear preference for bishops of a more moderate to progressive outlook. This period corresponded with the sessions of Vatican II and the implementation of its canons and decrees, along with the efforts to manage social and economic reform in the face of threats from communism and other movements in the Far Left. Even though the Church has generally attempted to remain outside of politics, it has taken on a role of teaching the importance of human rights, social justice, and economic development.

CELAM and Medellín

Just as councils and conferences of bishops developed in individual countries in the 1950s and 1960s, so the bishops of Latin America began to interact more with one another across national boundaries. As we read in chapter 10, in 1955 the bishops of the region organized the Latin American Bishops' Conference (CELAM). Following the initial meeting, CELAM played an important role in the Second Vatican Council. Latin American bishops made up nearly 25 percent of all the bishops who participated, compared to about 30 percent from Europe. The group held two other conferences of tremendous importance to the development of the Church in the region: the first of these was in Medellin, Colombia, in 1968; the other in Puebla, Mexico, in 1979.

The Medellin conference of the Latin American bishops had as its goal the full implementation of the reforms of Vatican II in Latin America. The agenda and support materials were developed by the secretary general, Manuel Larraín, bishop of Talca in Chile. Larraín was close to the Brazilian bishop dom Helder Câmara and to the cardinal archbishop of Santiago de Chile, Raúl Silva Henríquez. Larraín had taken a decisive step for social justice a few years earlier when he divested his diocese of several hundred acres of land for an experiment in land reform. Unfortunately, Larraín died in an automobile accident en route to the conference.

The conference had an auspicious beginning, inaugurated by Pope Paul VI in the first-ever papal visit to Latin America. In his remarks Paul called upon the bishops to repudiate violence as a means for social change. Yet he urged the prelates to bring Christ to the poor and hungry of the region. While not diminishing the importance of the institutional and hierarchical Church, Paul called on the assembled bishops to be agents of change and reform. Based upon papal encyclicals and on developments in the field in the decades leading up to the conference, the pope exhorted the bishops to promote justice, understand social problems, and channel the energy of the clergy and laity to resolve them. He posed three particular areas of interest for their deliberations. First he highlighted that bishops and priests are called upon to serve as examples of a balanced spiritual life to the world. Next he discussed pastoral orientations, specifically that central to the pastoral role is the exercise of charity. Last, he pointed the bishops toward social issues. Looking back at the origins of the Church, he asked the bishops to embrace poverty, to renounce violence, and to seek peace.

The Medellín conference occurred with a backdrop of turmoil around the world. In the United States protests against the Vietnam War had become widespread, and police had beaten hundreds of demonstrators in Chicago at the Democratic National Convention. In France factory workers and students had violently protested working conditions and other issues. In Mexico the government had brutally put down demonstrations on the eve of the Olympic Games to be held there. Within the Catholic Church there were increasing debates about the role of the hierarchy in the post–Vatican II era. Consequently, with rebellion in the air, the bishops who conferred in Medellín found themselves surrounded by a powerful movement for change.

The bishops approached the issues in a manner generally outlined by the pope in his opening homily. They first looked at the current situation in which many different philosophies were making inroads in Latin America and that the region was beset periodically by military governments and dictatorships, investigated the theology relevant to that situation, and then made recommendations for a pastoral response to that situation. The Medellín resolutions were to mark a new period in the development of the Catholic Church in Latin America. Much of the concern of the bishops had to do with social justice and economic development, leading then to develop a path between liberal capitalism and Marxism. In their conclusions they wrote:

> The system of liberal capitalism and the temptations of the Marxist system on our continent seem to exhaust the possibilities of transformation of economic structures. Both systems affront the dignity of the human person. One has as its foundation the primacy of capital, its power and its discriminatory utilization as a function of wealth; the other, although ideologically it might seem to support humanism, looks mostly to collective mankind and in practice becomes a totalitarian concentration of power in the State. We must protest that Latin America is seen as caught between these two options and must remain dependent on one or the other centers of power directing its economy.[3]

The bishops called for a transformation of society based upon Gospel principles. Yet within their vision there was a basic tension. On the one hand, the bishops generally accepted the idea that Latin America needed further economic development in order to resolve many of the thorny problems it confronted, especially poverty. They saw the Church as providing guidance and moral authority to countries facing economic development and concomitant social transformation. Yet among the ranks of the bishops there were those who believed that development alone would not resolve the problems of the region. This group looked to transform both the society and the economy to provide greater justice and access for all. For these bishops the Church, seen as the people of God, would provide both the moral and concrete example for a more liberated political, social, and economic system. In the end, both of these positions were incorporated into the final resolutions. Yet they reflect two very different conceptions of the Church and its role in the world.

One word in particular—"liberation"—began to appear in the documents generated by the bishops at Medellín. In their discussion of their foundation in Christian doctrine, the bishops wrote: "Thus, for our true liberation, all of us as humans need a profound conversion such that the Kingdom of Justice, of love and peace, comes to all of us. . . . In The History of Salvation the divine labor is an action of integral liberation and of the promotion of mankind in all its dimensions which has love as it sole motive."[4] The bishops characterized liberation as a process of breaking away from the history and context of the past into a new endeavor for the future. A large part of this process was also education and the creation of awareness in individuals of their status and reality.

The message that many observers took away from Medellín was that the meeting was a watershed in the development of the orientation of the Church in Latin America. With the changes brought about by the Second Vatican Council and the response in many countries to changing political and economic conditions, the Church was in a process of change. This change would move the Church from being an institutional entity, based upon a hierarchical structure linking the faithful at the bottom of the pyramid to the pope at the top, to a new reality in which the Church was the body of all the faithful working through the inspiration of the Holy Spirit. With this change in orientation and vision, the roles and functions of each part of the Church were linked closely to their specific powers and callings, and it had the effect of empowering the laity to take on many functions previously seen as falling within the clerical domain, especially evangelization, education, and other ministries. The shift from a developmental model to one of liberation also triggered a new way of studying God's relationship to mankind. In particular, the bishops called for an awakening of the consciousness of all Christians.[5] They called for consciousness-raising among the popular classes so that they could recognize the nature of their political and economic situation, and respond to it in a fully Christian manner.

Liberation Theology

Responding to the historical reality of the 1960s, a new theological method came into being, that of "liberation theology." This theology incorporated the canons of Vatican II as well as the development of the Church at the lowest levels in Latin America, as it responded to social and economic change, repression by military government, and the perceived threats from Protestant churches and communism. The documents of the Medellín conference became a kind of Magna Carta, a defining charter of areas to study and assumptions about God's relationship with man, especially in the Latin American context. What developed was a method of doing theology that takes into account the interrelated nature of theory and praxis, along with the social, economic, and political environments, looking particularly at the inequities inherent in them.

The lynchpin of liberation theology became the poor. The phrase that came to be central to many of the discussions of this method was the "preferential option for the poor." This position held that throughout the Hebrew Bible and the New Testament, God has manifested his concern for the physical and spiritual welfare of the poor. Rather than consoling the poor that their suffering on earth will result in glory in heaven, liberation theology seeks to use the Gospel message as a means of freedom for the poor. In many ways this is as much a way of acting out the Gospel than a tool for the study of man's relationship to God.

Liberation theology takes as its starting point an analysis of the current reality, looking particularly at discrepancies of power, wealth, and social status within countries and among countries. The dependency that comes from these discrepancies of power is identified as the cause of the inequality. In order to move beyond dependency, the goal must be liberation and not simply development. Liberation theology is indeed critical of development theory, noting that development merely reinforces the ties of dependency and inequality. In this new theology the structure of the Church and its mission is also a subject for investigation. Looking at the evangelization, the colonial period, and the nineteenth century, the Church itself developed and fostered a condition in which native peoples and others were kept in a dependent position. Liberation theology calls, then, for a more egalitarian ecclesial structure in which the laity play an important part in the work of the Church. Symbols and practices, which in the past reinforced the dependency, need to be recovered and recast to assist in the process of liberation.

The area of greatest contention regarding liberation theology had to do with the nature of violence. The bishops at Medellín had distinguished two types of violence. One was the oppression by unjust and unequal social and political structures, which the bishops characterized as "institutionalized violence." The bishops declared this sinful because it prevented people from pursuing a truly Christian life. Running counter to this was "defensive violence" whereby persons could protect their individual rights and oppose the sinful social and political structures brought about by prolonged and clear tyranny. That this type of theology condoned violence and even seemed to embrace it in certain political and social situations proved to be very disturbing.

Liberation theology grew out of many of the themes explored by the bishops at Medellín. It also responded to the wave of military governments that swept through Latin America in the late 1960s and '70s. While Peru and Brazil became important zones wherein the theology was explored and expounded, Central America also became a proving ground. Central America in this period came to occupy much of the attention of the world and of the United States in particular due to confrontations between leftists and conservatives.

The Church in Central America

Central America offered a unique location for the working out of many aspects of liberation theology: the region had never enjoyed the economic development present in places like Argentina, Chile, or even Mexico. The five small Central American nations, each with a unique character and history, lacked both the population and resources of the larger nations of Latin America. Several of the countries had significant indigenous populations, such as Guatemala and Honduras; others essentially lacked native population, such as Costa Rica. What economic development did occur tended to be in a boom-and-bust cycle, where typically an agricultural monoculture would dominate, as with cacao or bananas, until a worldwide decline in prices. The countries tended to be dominated by a few wealthy families and so political activity was limited to a ruling elite.

In the ecclesiastical realm in Central America, conflicts between the liberals and conservatives in the nineteenth century, and ensuing liberal regimes into the early twentieth century, hampered the development of clergy (see chaps. 7 and 8). Some Central American countries suffered from severe shortages of priests. As in other places, this created a fertile field in which Protestant missionaries could operate, and it offered an opportunity for indigenous religions to return. It also created a situation in which the laity increasingly took over many of the duties of the local parish priest, outside of those reserved by canon law to the clergy. The rise of active Catholic missionaries also brought important new institutions such as Christian base communities to the region. This provided native peoples with a new structure within which to both practice their spirituality and to provide one another with mutual support and assistance. Here, individuals trained in theology and doctrine acted as catechists teaching others about the faith, and they organized their own liturgies and prayer groups. In many ways the base community came to fill part of the void created when sodalities and confraternities declined in the late nineteenth century. These practices were not unique to the Catholic Church but were adopted by Protestant missionaries as well, often allowing the base community to identify individuals who might seek ordination as pastors and assume leadership in the faith communities.

Although the Catholic Church was quite distinct in Nicaragua, El Salvador, and Guatemala, several features appeared in all three states in the period from the 1960s until the 1990s. All three countries had different historical traditions, and by the latter third of the twentieth century, all of them went through significant political turmoil. In each country the Church evolved from being allied with the conservative oligarchy to playing a role in the social development of the country to being a target of right-wing terrorists to playing an important role as mediator.

Of the three countries, Guatemala has the longest history of turmoil involving the Church. The political conflict between liberals and conservatives in the nineteenth and early twentieth centuries had left the Church significantly weakened. Following the Second World War foreign missionaries, both Protestant and Catholic, came to the country. Moderate politicians also took power nationally and began modest reforms, including land reform. Guatemala had for several decades seen large tracts of land under the control of a few powerful families and outside corporations, such as the United Fruit Company. In 1951 a former military man, Jacobo Arbenz, was elected president. The next year, Arbenz nationalized several thousand acres of land held by United Fruit as part of a land reform program. This caused serious concerns in the United States. Although Arbenz was far from being a communist, his enemies succeeded in painting him as a radical reformer. In the end, the CIA organized a coup against Arbenz and assisted in the creation of a military government.

Repression and political violence soon became central features of the Guatemalan political process. The target of the violence tended to be the native communities, which represented the vast majority of Guatemalan citizens. In the relative absence of any real left-leaning political parties, moderates were seen by the military and the oligarchy as a threat. In the rural areas, though, some revolutionaries had attempted to organize. This led the military government and right-wing death squads to repeatedly attack rural areas where they believed revolutionary movements were active. The situation came to a crisis under the presidency of General Efraín Ríos Montt. Ríos Montt had run as a presidential candidate from the Christian Democratic Party but lost the election, due to what he perceived to be government fraud. By the time he assumed power as a military dictator, he had also undergone a personal transformation: in the wake of his electoral defeat he became an evangelical Protestant. Upon assuming the leadership of the government, Ríos Montt surrounded himself with other Protestants from the military. Earlier military governments had seen all religious organizations as a threat since they provided a countervailing authority to the military; under Ríos Montt, evangelical Protestants were recruited to support the military while direct action was taken against Catholics and many mainline Protestant groups. This policy was targeted specifically at the rural zones of the country where the population was overwhelmingly Maya. The military was dominated by persons of European ancestry and *ladinos* (mestizos), groups who viewed the native population with suspicion. More than one hundred thousand Indians were murdered or disappeared during this period. The rural areas were patrolled by paramilitary units frequently consisting of *ladinos* and natives who were forced to participate. Hundreds of villages were simply destroyed and as many as half a million persons were uprooted in the process.

Toward the later years of Ríos Montt's government, the Catholic Church in Guatemala underwent a transformation with the death of the long-serving Archbishop Mario Casariego. Casariego was an old-fashioned archbishop, closely allied to the military and oligarchy. Upon his death, the Guatemalan Church became a vocal opponent of the bloodshed had gripped the country and began to seek to serve as an intermediary between the military, the natives, and the various revolutionary groups. The Church became the focus of human rights advocacy in the country as well as a strong proponent for land reform. Revolutionary movements lost impetus with the decline in communism in Europe. As the military slowly backed away from its violent oppression, and as the political defeat of the Sandinistas in nearby Nicaragua along with the eventual overthrow of Ríos Montt, the Church was able to pursue a dialogue among the various factions.

The peace negotiations lasted eight years (1987–96). The Church played an active role until the final phases, when it withdrew in favor of United Nations supervision. The Church also played an active role in the reconstruction of the Guatemalan countryside, supervising aid shipments, education, and social development projects. Unlike in the other Central American countries, the Guatemalan Church remained largely in the background, although it was still a target of repression and a focus of development. It had entered into the period of turmoil in an extremely weak position, but in spite of the turmoil the Guatemalan Church in the local communities remained strong, due to missionary activity and the creation of specialized ministries to serve the indigenous communities. At this time, local native religions have risen to a position of importance, and Protestant groups have had great success in evangelization.

In El Salvador, the Church was stronger by the middle decades of the twentieth century than it had been earlier in the century, but it was certainly weaker than in many other countries. Although the country was controlled by a small oligarchy, the Church had been strengthened by large numbers of foreign missionaries. Politically the country was governed by the party of the oligarchy and the military. A Christian Democratic Party, largely consisting of middle-class supporters, provided an opposition. The Communist Party had been established in the 1930s in an early attempt to overthrow the oligarchy that controlled the economy and the production of coffee, Salvador's main cash crop.

Political positions hardened in the late 1970s as the military and oligarchy consolidated power, deporting the leader of the Christian Democrats. Various leftist groups then formed an alliance and began an insurgency against the government, calling themselves the *Farabundo Martí National Liberation Front* (FMLN), named after the founder of the Salvadorian Communist Party. The civil war that ensued cost the nation tens of thousands of lives, displaced half a million citizens, and forced hundreds of thousands to emigrate, out of a population of approximately 5 million. Because of the Sandinista political victory in neighboring Nicaragua, the United States poured millions of dollars of military aid into El Salvador, training and supplying the army and paramilitary groups to carry out a war against the insurgents to prevent the spread of communism in the region.

The Catholic Church in El Salvador during their civil war had been deeply engaged in fostering the reforms mandated by the Second Vatican Council and Medellín. Christian base communities had sprung up in the countryside. Increasingly workers and peasant groups were organized with Church assistance to seek protection for their basic rights. More than a few peasants and workers were radicalized by their participation in various Church-supported movements. They, and more radical supporters of the Christian Democratic Party, went on to found a new revolutionary movement, the Revolutionary Army of the People (ERP, *Ejército Revolucionario del Pueblo*). These and other activities prompted strong opposition from many of the leading economic leaders of the country and were criticized by conservative politicians. In 1977, Oscar Romero was named archbishop of San Salvador. His appointment was seen by many as a move to placate the conservatives, since he was not known as a supporter of the reform movement. Nevertheless, as the government increasingly began to violate human rights and pursue a very repressive agenda, Romero transformed himself into an advocate for the poor and the voiceless. Although he initially supported the military coup of 1979, increasingly the military saw him as a threat. Romero denounced the excesses of the military and of paramilitary groups. In 1980 he was assassinated while saying Mass. It is generally believed that Romero was killed by supporter of a right-wing political movement. In the following months and years Jesuit priests and several female religious were also murdered by policemen and right-wing squads. The revolutionaries also conducted their own acts of terror, and the country slipped into a bloody civil war of reprisals.

Arturo Rivera Damas succeeded Romero as archbishop. Rivera sought to be a voice for reconciliation and peace between the warring factions, but there were many missteps in the process. The two extremes, the FMLN and the right wing ARENA (Republican Socialist Alliance, *Alianza Repúblicana Socialista*) Party, had deep mistrust of one another. ARENA was directly implicated in the death of Archbishop Romero; the FMLN was avowedly Marxist and had conducted its own terrorist attacks. Rivera finally succeeded, after many attempts, to bring the parties together, facilitated in great measure by the end of the Cold War and the end of the Reagan administration in the United States. In essence the external parties funding the factions ceased their active involvement. The Church, although implicated in the rise of some of the revolutionary movements, still commanded respect from the largest segment of the Salvadoran populace and was thus able to serve as an objective mediator between the factions.

In Nicaragua, the role of the Church in the political life of the country was far more complicated. From 1933, when the U.S. Marines finally left the country after a long occupation, one family dominated Nicaraguan politics: the Somozas. First under Anastacio Somoza García, then Luis Somoza Debayle and Anastacio Somoza Debayle, his sons, the family ruled the country more or less like a private property. Their status was generally legitimized through their leadership of the National Guard, although others might actually occupy the office of presidency. When the United States Marines pulled out in 1933, the National Guard had been constituted as a unified defense and police force. The Church generally had a cordial relationship with the Somozas. For many years guerillas had carried out strikes against the government from rural outposts, and in 1961 the rebels organized themselves as the Sandinista National Liberation Front (FSLN, *Frente Sandinista de Liberación Nacional*). Although carrying out guerrilla attacks, the movement itself was dominated by the urban middle class.

In the 1960s and 1970s the Church in Nicaragua, as in many other places, saw an influx of priests and other missionaries from abroad. At one point over 60 percent of the priests in the country were foreigners. With these missionaries, and as part of the worldwide reforms of Vatican II and the Medellín conference, the Nicaraguan Church embraced change. Christian base communities sprouted; Catholic Action movements became worker or peasant movements; catechists were trained to spread the Gospel to rural and poor urban areas; and *cursillo* and other renewal movements touched the middle classes. In short, the Catholic Church in Nicaragua began to break out of its postcolonial dormancy and become active in many areas. This created a tension within the Church, since many of the more reformed-minded clergy were foreign born, but the local priests tended to be more conservative. Empowered by Medellín, the bishops began to move away from their blind support of the Somoza regime with the selection of Miguel Obando y Bravo as archbishop of Managua.

In 1972, Nicaragua was struck by a devastating earthquake. The ineffective response of the Somoza dictatorship to the natural disaster began to erode support among the middle classes, seeing that much of the relief was being siphoned off by corrupt government officials. A few years later a leading opposition voice and editor of the Managua daily, *La Prensa*, Joaquín Chamorro, was assassinated by government operatives in response to his articles against the government.

The Sandinista movement emerged as the largest single political party in this period of instability. Unlike many other revolutionary and quasi-revolutionary movements, many leaders of the Sandinistas came from the clergy or were otherwise closely allied with the Catholic Church. The attacks of the Sandinistas from their rural outposts proved to be ineffective, so they began a new program. They approached the middle and lower classes in the cities and towns, especially those who had become active in various Church programs, seeing in these individuals persons who were more aware of issues of social and economic inequality. In the wake of the earthquake, the Sandinistas began to draw more heavily from Church organizations. Two priests, Fernando Cardenal and Miguel D'Escoto, became part of the public image of the movement.

In order to call for free elections, the Sandinistas now began to pressure the Somoza government in the form of public protests in the cities and towns and continued guerrilla attacks in the rural areas as part of a general plan of destabilization. Finally, in 1979, Anastacio Somoza Debayle fled the country, and the Sandinistas entered Managua in triumph. This sequence of events led many observers to instantly compare the Nicaraguan revolution to the Cuban experience. Yet there were significant differences, especially as far as the involvement of the Church. Most importantly, in Cuba not only did the Church not participate in the revolution, the Castro regime quickly isolated the Church and concertedly worked to undermine its power and authority. In Nicaragua, the Sandinista movement embraced the Church, and included many priests and laypersons in positions of authority, it also sought to cooperate with the Church on a wide range of progressive programs. Importantly, the Carter administration in the United States recognized the Sandinistas.

Although the Sandinistas enjoyed a broad range of political support in Nicaragua, especially among the middle and lower classes, there was not unanimity. Archbishop Obando was frankly lukewarm toward the movement. While recognizing many of the positive elements of the Sandinistas, Obando was fearful of a communist takeover of Nicaragua through the Sandinistas. He focused therefore on Church unity and the ongoing programs of the Church, without allying himself too closely with the government. This position was embraced by many in the middle class. The segment of the population that was most conservative, the elites and many in the middle class, opted to oppose the Sandinistas actively. Yet they found in Obando an acceptable spokesperson, although they were also against many of the reforms going on in the Church. In the United States, the newly inaugurated Reagan administration saw the Sandinistas as a foothold of communism on the American continent and pledged to do everything possible to overthrow the regime.

Unlike Rivera Damas, who maintained a certain distance from both factions in the Salvadorian civil war, Obando soon became identified with the opposition to the Sandinistas and was unable, or unwilling, to serve as a mediator. Yet within the Church many priests and laypersons openly and strongly supported the Sandinistas. This broad support in the Church, nearly half of all priests, made the Sandinista experiment in Nicaragua far different from any other communist or Marxist government. But, due to both internal and external factors the situation rapidly deteriorated. Archbishop Obando formally protested to the Vatican that five priests had taken positions of authority in the Sandinista government. The Vatican allowed them to keep the offices, but forbade the clerics from serving as priests during their government tenure. Obando also met with former Somoza leaders to see about the creation of a center-right coalition to oppose the Sandinistas.

The United States resolved to begin providing arms and materiel to the opponents of the regime, who came to be known as the Contras. Although the Sandinistas held elections in 1984, with participation from a wide range of political factions, the Contras chose not to present candidates. The Reagan administration refused to recognize the elections, in which the Sandinistas increased their control of the government. When John Paul II visited Nicaragua in 1983, his advisors characterized the government as Marxist and anti-Christian. The pope believed that the Nicaraguan experience was similar to what he had known in Poland. Seeing the Sandinistas as nothing more than communists, the pope called upon the faithful to reject philosophies that did not align with Christian principles. This had a disheartening effect on many members of popular Church organizations aligned with the government who earnestly felt that they were helping to create a new Christian experiment.

In the later 1980s in Nicaragua positions hardened. The episcopacy, under the direction of Obando, continued to oppose the government, yet many of the faithful and a broad section of the clergy saw the administration as putting Christian principles into action. Even the Vatican began to question the aggressive opposition to the regime, especially the military actions supported by the Reagan administration. It was clear that the issue of support for the regime was dividing the Nicaraguan Church into two factions. North American and European bishops also expressed their concerns about support for the Contras. Through the nuncio in Managua, the Vatican began to explore the possibility of Obando serving as a mediator between the Contras and the government. When other Central American presidents called upon the parties to enter into discussions, the Sandinista government had the opportunity to begin dialogue without being perceived as being forced into talks. Also key was the end of the Cold War and the emergence of détente between the United States and the Soviet Union, which allowed for a calming effect in regional confrontations where surrogates of the two powers were in conflict. The waning of the Reagan administration enabled politicians in the United States to begin to focus their energy on new issues. Finally in 1990 elections were held in which nearly all parties participated. Although polls had the Sandinistas holding a clear advantage, the election favored the united opposition, known as the UNO (National Opposition Union, *Unión Nacional Opositora*). Daniel Ortega, head of the Sandinistas, admitted defeat and, by doing so, paved the way to a peaceful transfer of power. The Church has played an active role in the ensuing years, helping to incorporate the Contras back into society and to maintain many of the social and economic programs of development.

Taken as a whole, the Central American experience found the Church in an extremely delicate position. Many of the groups that grew out of Catholic Action, which were empowered by Vatican II, eventually produced more than a few progressives. The presence of a large percentage of foreign-born priests also brought new ideas and new reforms into the Central American countries. Yet the Church was deeply divided among those who supported the traditional oligarchies and institutional Church, and those who adopted the Vatican Council's vision of the Church as the pilgrim people of God. Added to these divisions, there was the larger geopolitical conflict between the United States and the Soviet Union. Progressive movements in Central America were usually branded as communist, thus polarizing the situation and inviting intervention from the United States. Where communists actually participated, such as in the case of Nicaragua, it was as part of a broad movement for social and economic justice, which had as it core many Christian principles. Still, this was all caught between the opposing ideologies of the United States and the Soviets. Where the institutional Church maintained neutrality in the political realm, it had a better chance to mediate the internal conflicts. Similarly once the external pressures were removed, the Church could then intervene internally to bring warring factions to the table.

While much has been written about Archbishop Oscar Romero of El Salvador, he was not the prototype of a Central American prelate. In fact, Obando was far more typical, if not perhaps progressive by comparison. The vast majority of prelates in Central America were not comfortable with many of the reforms that resulted from Vatican II and Medellín. But as we have seen, perhaps a majority, or at least a plurality, of the clergy did embrace the reform in some manner. The large numbers of European and North American priests and male and female religious serving in the region became a vanguard in the diffusion of the new ideas.

Puebla

By the 1980s some in the Church began to question the validity of liberation theology, and this change came as a result of two rather broad concerns. One stemmed from the Central American situation where critics saw liberation theology as creating more radical opposition to the established order. The radicalization of priests and the laity was a deep concern to many. The other came from the Vatican. Pope John Paul II, using his personal experience in communist Poland, had deep concerns about any theology that advocated political, social, and economic transformation. Many in the Vatican believed that liberation theology was merely a Marxist interpretation of traditional Gospel teachings, and perhaps even a perversion of the Gospel. Liberation theology placed great emphasis on the *doing* of theology, the praxis, rather than just the study of theology. This emphasis on action, in the eyes of its critics, led its practitioners into error. There is little doubt that many of the first proponents of liberation theology, while not Marxist, did understand the world from a perspective that placed greater moral value on ministry to the poor: class struggle was for them a reality.

In 1979 the bishops of Latin America met in Puebla, Mexico. This meeting was the successor to the one held in Medellín ten years earlier. Obviously, much had changed in both the life of the Church and in the political, social, and economic conditions in Latin America. On the larger scene, there was a slow but steady move from authoritarian regimes to more democratic ones. The region was beginning to enjoy the first stages of economic growth that would transform it over the next two decades. The bishops who attended the Puebla conference also had gained much insight into the evolving role of the Church in the region. At no time since Independence did the Church enjoy quite such a unified purpose. While there were still great divisions among the prelates, there was a consensus that the Church needed to continue to integrate social and economic development as true manifestations of the Gospel message. The means of doing so and the relationship of the Church to the state and the economic powers were still topics that would be hotly contested.

In general, the bishops gathered at Puebla endorsed the outline of action passed at Medellín. Several concepts, though, emerged from Puebla with redoubled emphasis. Perhaps one of the most important was the role of small groups within the parish to support, teach, and nurture the faithful. Whether they were fully organized ecclesial base communities or more informal support networks, the power of these small groups was evident to the bishops. There was an enthusiastic endorsement of these groups as basic building blocks for the Christian community. The bishops also embraced the notion that the defense of human rights was central to the Christian calling in the modern world. One of the hallmarks of the meeting was the importance of adapting the universal truths of the Christian message to the regional issues of the Americas. This orientation provided the prelates with a clearly unified perspective. While some national differences persisted, the Church throughout Latin America was again embracing a common agenda. Since the left wing of the Church had seen the elements of Medellín as insufficient to address the problems of the region, many of the subsequent solutions manifested more of that philosophical perspective than they did of the more conservative traditional perspective. Yet rather than envisioning the debate as having winners and losers, the bishops recognized that one of the most glaring problems facing the region was the abject poverty of so many people. It was this realization—as interpreted by the Gospel message of love for one's neighbors—that moved the Church, and not a particular ideology.

On the political front, while the Church had clearly opposed authoritarian regimes from either political persuasion and advocated for human rights and human dignity, the Church had learned to avoid actively participating in or being seen as supporting any political factions. This strategy too informed the bishops in Puebla, and they agreed that the Church had to be involved in the political process, if for no other reason than to keep the Gospel message in the political marketplace. The political role obviously was fraught with contradictions and nuance, so the consensus was to be vocal in political debates but not to be converted either to a political party or to the endorsement of a political party. This paradox was more difficult under authoritarian regimes, where the Church alone could provide a unified voice as an opposition. In that situation, there was general agreement that the Church must continue to defend the poor. This stance was seen as consistent with the pastoral calling of the bishops in particular and the Church in general. As well, the Church could also call for political pluralism. In the end, one of the great contributions of the Puebla meeting to the development of the Church in Latin America was the return to the notion of the pastoral responsibility both of the bishop and of the Church as a whole.

Distilled to its essence, the message of Puebla was, then, twofold. On the one hand the bishops emphasized the importance of communion and participation: that the Eucharist was the central unifying rite of the Church, bringing all together to the Lord's table. Furthermore, it called for participation of all the faithful within the broad ministries of the Church, thus validating the work of the ecclesial base communities. In compliment to this position the bishops articulated the now-famous "preferential option for the poor." This mandate called upon all to work to bring about social justice in the economic realm. The bishops went so far as to suggest that service to the poor was an important, though not the unique, measure of how well one followed the teachings of Christ.

While the importance of the participation of all within the life of the Church was consonant with the reforms of the Second Vatican Council, there was some concern that it could lead to a diminution of the authority of the hierarchy of the Church. More conservative bishops pointed out that the Church continued to be the repository of the teachings of Christ as interpreted over the centuries and as communicated through the magisterium of the Church. There was simply no place for the creation of a popular church to supplant the Catholic Church.

In the wake of the Puebla meeting, political events changed the face of Latin America. The Cold War began to wind down. This removed one potential point of conflict, as was seen in the case of Central America in general, and Nicaragua in particular. The military dictatorships that had characterized the region in the 1960s and 1970s began to cede power back to civilians. Brazil, Argentina, and Chile all gained popularly elected governments. In countries like Mexico where one party had ruled the country for most of the twentieth century, a system of political pluralism emerged. These developments dramatically changed the entire political atmosphere.[6]

The Vatican and Liberation Theology

By the late 1980s the Vatican had grown wary of some aspects of liberation theology. In 1984 Joseph Cardinal Ratzinger (elected Pope Benedict XVI in 2005), head of the Congregation of the Doctrine of the Faith, issued an "Instruction on Certain Aspects of the Theology of Liberation." The purpose of the document was to diminish the authority of many liberation theologians and to reinforce traditional Catholic teachings. The document had the unexpected consequence of reaffirming many of the conditions regarding which the liberation theologians had been preaching, such as the importance of human rights, the problem of unequal distribution of wealth, and the role of the Church in addressing the ills of society. Yet the Congregation reached far different conclusions based upon these conditions than did the liberation theologians. As part of this new offensive, the Vatican suspended the permission of several theologians, such as Leonardo Boff of Brazil, to teach theology in Catholic universities, and imposed other strictures. As seen earlier, while Boff complied with the initial restriction issued by the Vatican, he eventually left the Franciscan order and renounced holy orders. The incident, however, indicated that the Vatican was serious about exercising greater scrutiny over liberation theology. While Boff and others, such as Jon Sobrino and Gustavo Gutiérrez, continued to write, their works were closely analyzed by the Vatican to assure that they complied with Church teachings. As a result, in the last two decades of the twentieth century, while liberation theology has continued to be a powerful voice in Latin America and much of the underdeveloped world, it has become far more restrained, especially in the political aspects of its message.

In the early years of the twenty-first century, the message of liberation theology, while continuing to emphasize the "preferential option of the poor," has begun to look at social disequilibrium in a more complex and nuanced fashion. One particularly viable thread has been to support efforts for sustainable development. Yet in going in this direction, practitioners are slowly moving away from a method for doing theology to developing new methods for economic development. Thus, while liberation theology continues to be an important methodology, it has not supplanted other more traditional methods. Moreover, it continues to suffer from the perception of being rooted in Marxist thought and from its having been circumscribed by the Vatican. In the end, its power and its shortcoming is that it is at its very essence more of a set of theological practices rooted in the Gospel than a systematic method of theological thought.

During the papacy of John Paul II, the bishops appointed to the various dioceses around the world tended to reflect orthodox teachings, to have had seminary experience, and also to have served as pastors. These conditions are also seen in the bishops appointed in Latin America. The bishops have tended, therefore, to be strongly committed to a dual role for the episcopacy: teaching and pastoral care. On the basis of experience, Latin American bishops are sympathetic to the needs of the poorest in their society. Due to their responsibility as pastors to their entire flock and as caretakers for the ongoing authority of their office, however, they necessarily respond to more conservative and institutional demands. These conditions mean that while recognizing the power of liberation theology to address issues of social and economic justice, most bishops will stop short of fully embracing the application of that theology to all situations within their dioceses. Taken as a whole, the bishops appointed by John Paul II were notably more conservative than those named by popes since Pius XII in the 1950s.

In response to concerns regarding liberation theology, other movements have also sprung up to respond to some of the needs it addressed. An example of one of these is the *Sodalitium Christianae Vitae* (Society of Christian Life) movement, seen particularly in Peru. This movement focuses on the theology of reconciliation as the basis for the creation of a theology that is more attractive and potentially more orthodox than liberation theology. *Sodalitium Vitae* originated among those who were concerned with the politically liberal aspects of liberation theology that they felt were divorced from the true mission of the Church. It is rooted in reconciliation as an attempt to find common ground among the disparate units of society and the Church, particularly through nonviolent means.

Another response within the Catholic Church has been the charismatic movement, specifically Catholic Charismatic Renewal. This movement has gained widespread popular support in many Latin American countries. It benefits from two very important characteristics. First, it has a large popular appeal, using pop or rock bands to spread the Word, mass meetings with a very high emotional content, and it is extremely participatory. Furthermore, it is embraced, generally, by the Church hierarchy. The movement is based firmly in traditional theology, which teaches that the Church is guided by the inspiration of the Holy Spirit, the third person of the Trinity. While it shares some features with Pentecostal churches, especially the influence of the Holy Spirit upon the individual, the Catholic Charismatics place the Virgin Mary in a far more prominent position. The bishops, however, have exercised caution, since they fear that if individuals seek inspiration through the Holy Spirit without the agency of the clergy, nothing might inhibit them from private confession and absolution, marriage, or any number of other sacraments with the sole mediation of the Spirit. For these reasons, several bishops have banned the movement from their dioceses, seeing it as ultimately detrimental to the cohesion of the Church.

With the re-emergence of democracies around the region, there also came a greater tolerance for divergent political and religious thought. Protestant missionaries have become active as political conditions stabilized. In Brazil, in particular, there has been also a resurgence of other religious movements, particularly Afro-Brazilian religions, such as Candomblé. The Catholic Church has thus found itself competing with many more religious options than at any time in the history of the region. So at a time when the Catholic Church is as unified as it has ever been in its recent history, in terms of the community of thought of its leaders and their ecclesial vision for the future, it has also faced a world of increasing pluralism. Although unified, those in the Catholic Church have sentiments that range from anti-Vatican II and support of a Tridentine Church to the progressive liberationists and Catholic Socialists.

In part the Church has been responsible for the situation. The emphasis since Medellín on popular lay movements such as the, ecclesial base communities, had the effect of empowering individual to take greater responsibility for his or her own spiritual formation. For four hundred years, the Catholic Church had a near monopoly on religion in Latin America. In the last decades of the twentieth century and opening years of the twenty-first, the religious horizon has expanded greatly. This increased attention has led to greater experimentation in religion and developed a "religious marketplace" where adherents of other religions could actively seek to engage followers.

For the Catholic Church there are clear trends for the future. Having had great success, ecclesial base communities will continue to serve as a means for evangelization and for the support and education of the faithful. There will continue to be many faithful who see the Gospel as a call for social and economic justice; there will be segments that reject many of the reforms of Vatican II and look to an older tradition. Popular religion, rooted in Catholic practice, will also continue to be an important aspect of Catholic culture in Latin America. Small groups such as religious sodalities and Christian base communities will continue to provide support for their members in a broad range of ways. The hierarchy will continue, although there will be tension between the various varieties of Catholicism and the orthodoxy of the hierarchy. Most importantly, the institutional Church will reclaim and exercise the magisterium to a higher degree than in the recent past. This development, combined with appointments as bishop to individuals who reflect Vatican thinking, will create a stronger hierarchy and teaching mission of the Church closely linked to Rome.

At the local level, in the native villages, in the rural regions, in the slums, there will continue to be competition among churches. Catholics will continue to serve the poor. Protestants, specifically Evangelicals and Pentecostals, will continue to make significant inroads into the population, as their message allows individuals to create a personal faith outside of the bounds of a hierarchy, and because their worship services are exciting and vital. The resurgence of popular religions among native groups and persons of African descent will actually expand, being embraced by the middle class, as persons seek new and unique means to encounter the divine. All of these will, in turn, also create a new Catholic Church as it adapts to the new religious marketplace and adopts new measures to remain an attractive spiritual option.

Clearly there has been an increasing secularization of society in Latin American in recent decades. For a host of reasons, people have turned away from the traditional affiliation with the Catholic Church and have been attracted to other denominations and even other religions. Protestant churches are experiencing rapid growth in Latin America. The reasons are manifold. Part comes from the more secular society and the idea of the religious marketplace. The growth of ecclesial base communities might have contributed as well, given more power over religious issues to small groups not directly supervised by clergy. The disintegration of traditional society has also played an important role. Ties of ritual kinship, the decline of the patron-client system in rural areas, and the egalitarian nature of urban areas have also eroded ties to the Church. The fastest growing groups, Pentecostals and Evangelicals, offer emotionalism, popular music, and a wide range of other attractions in their worship. Their practical social doctrines often strengthen the traditional family, also attracting those who feel lost in a rapidly changing society.

Last, indigenous religions, be they local adaptations to Christian theology such as indigenous Pentecostal ministries or hybrid religions based on African or American roots, have grown in recent decades. Many of these religions respond to the emotional and mystic in a manner beyond that found in more traditional religion. They have deep roots in the popular conscience of the lower classes, where they merge with popular religion. In addition, and perhaps most importantly, they are not associated with any hierarchy either within or outside of the country and thus are seen as being more intimate and local in their orientation.

The last decades of the twentieth century and the first years of the twenty-first have seen dramatic changes both in Latin America and the Church. The region passed from an epoch of widespread repression and dictatorship to one of generally democratically elected governments and an opening up of the social, political, and economic systems. The Church has moved from being the voice of opposition to repression and dictatorship to being merely one player in an increasingly complex religious marketplace. The coming years and decades will be crucial for the Church. It is quite possible that Latin America will eventually manifest the same religious plurality that has occurred in Western Europe. In that model the Catholic Church, while still a significant institution, will become just one player in a very complex religious environment, in which increasingly large numbers of people simply ignore all forms of organized religion altogether.

Conclusion

As we have seen, the history of the Catholic Church in Latin America is as complex and multifaceted as the region is itself. The missionaries who arrived in the Americas were far from homogeneous, representing several religious orders and the secular, or diocesan, clergy. They came from many different regions of Spain and Portugal and throughout Europe. The areas in which they landed were home to a wide variety of native peoples, climates, topographies, flora, and fauna. Yet the evangelization efforts of the Europeans were unitary in that they sought to bring the Gospel to the natives of the New World and to have them embrace the Christian faith.

Looking at the question of what constitutes authority in the modern Latin American Church, Daniel H. Levine has posited that there are two conflicting ecclesiologies, i.e., models of the Church. One was clearly articulated in the Second Vatican Council: the Church as the pilgrim people of God. The other ecclesiology is the traditional view of the Church as an institution, governed by a hierarchy under divine authority.[7] The model expressed by Vatican II is a view of the Church from the ground up: namely that the Church consists of *all* of its members, brought together by the Holy Spirit. The institutional model is a vision from the top down, that the Church is the continuum of authority from God, through the pope and ecclesiastical hierarchy, down to and including all of the faithful. Needless to say, these two visions are quite different and have dramatic implications, depending on which vision is applied. The history of the Church in Latin American can be seen as the working out of these two visions. Taking this as a point of departure, let us look again at the various periods of the history of the Church in Latin America.[1]

During the early years of the Church in Latin America, the different evangelical styles of the Franciscans and the Dominicans manifested the dichotomy of perspectives regarding the nature of the Church. These two orders originated in Europe at the same time; Dominic and Francis were contemporaries, and each sought to reinvigorate the medieval Church. Francis followed the path of emulating Christ's humility and worldly poverty. He believed that people would be attracted to Christianity, or to a deeper version of Christianity, by seeing individuals who truly emulated Christ and his humility. Dominic emphasized the power of the Word of God, as found in Scripture, but more importantly as preached by the ministers of the Church. He believed that non-Christians could be attracted to the faith through the power of preaching, and that preaching could deepen the faith of believers.

In the New World, the Franciscans, emboldened by a millenarian theology predicting the imminent end of the world, believed that through the example of their own lives they could attract the natives to the faith. By caring for the poor, feeding the hungry, clothing the naked, and ministering to the needs of the individual, the friars believed that the natives would see the physical manifestation of the power of the Christian faith and be drawn into following it. The Franciscans could then talk about the power of God and his incarnation in Jesus, leading the natives to a profound personal belief. The Dominicans, on the other hand, believed in a more formal, fuller, and deeper teaching of the rudiments of the faith. The natives needed to not just embrace the new faith on an emotional level, but rather they needed to understand it on an intellectual level. The Dominicans believed in the importance of the intellectual acceptance of the teaching of the Christian faith, which would then be manifest in actions.

The two orders held deeply divided opinions concerning the administration of the sacrament of Baptism, the entry point whereby individuals became Christians. The Franciscans saw Baptism as the initiation of the Christian relationship, that all people were children of God. The Dominicans saw the sacrament as a gating mechanism which concluded the process of becoming Christian. This also colored their views of the Church. The Franciscans viewed the Church as the mystical body of Christ, a stance that can be seen as a precursor of the modern notion of the pilgrim people of God. The Dominicans, with their emphasis on teaching and preaching, embraced the idea of the institutional Church, consisting of laws and procedures.

The other religious orders and the diocesan clergy fell within these two poles of missionary praxis. Obviously the diocesan clergy fully embraced the model of the institutional Church, since that was the structure of their worldview. The Jesuits manifested both poles, as they preferred to attract the natives to the faith, but also placed great emphasis on indoctrination. Mercedarians, Carmelites, and Augustinians generally fell closer to the Dominican position, but many individual missionaries had a deep sympathy for the Franciscan technique. As time passed, however, even the Franciscans began to move away from their early embrace of attraction to the faith; they adopted a more Dominican orientation, eventually relying on military force to assist them in bringing natives to their missions, as they moved out of the core regions with large populations of sedentary native populations into regions with more nomadic peoples.

The dichotomy seen in the early phase of the evangelization waned with time. That is not to say, however, that there were not significant differences among the religious orders and diocesan clergy over the best manner of evangelization, but debate changed to new topics. The early distinction, however, was essential in the development of the Church, since the pure Franciscan vision of attraction through example lost out to a more structured catechistic approach whereby persons were taught and then incorporated. This meant that some people always remained at the margin of the Church.

In the middle years of the colonial period the dichotomy of vision regarding the nature of the Church had to do with the funding of missionary efforts and Church activities in general. Again, the Franciscans took one extreme. In keeping with the Rule of Saint Francis, the foundational document of the order, the Franciscans supported themselves and their enterprise through alms given by the faithful. This conformed to the vision of the Church as the body of all the faithful. Obviously one part of the body of the faithful would willingly support another. The Franciscans could approach their mission freed from worries about financial support, confident that the Holy Spirit would sustain them. They fully participated in a model in which all members of the body supported one another.

The Jesuits represented the other extreme in funding. The Jesuits established commercial enterprises, usually landed estates, to produce goods for the market. The order used the profits from these estates to support the wide-ranging activities of the order. Most other religious orders engaged in some commercial enterprises at one point or another in the colonial period, although none to the degree of the Jesuits. This vision conformed more to the notion of the Church as hierarchy in which ancillary enterprises could exist for purposes other than ministry in order to develop resources for the primary ministry. It was more of a modern business model, based on hierarchical organization.

The diocesan clergy received support from the tithe on agricultural production and from fees charged for the administration of the sacraments. The tithe went directly to support the hierarchy, which was seen as the physical embodiment of the Church. The participation of the Church in both the system of agricultural production and in the credit market had very serious implications in Latin American history. While it provided much needed revenue to the Church in the colonial period, by the time of independence people's understanding of the nature of the Church was colored by its financial successes. Even the crown saw the Church as a successful financial institution that could be used to further royal programs. This detracted from the vision of the Church as the body of all believers. The Church increasingly became a specialized type of economic system, not the sacramental bride of Christ.

Both the landed estates producing for the market economy and the credit market relied at their very core on real estate, since most loans were types of mortgages based on real estate. By the late eighteenth century, with changes in royal policy brought about by conditions in Europe, the Church faced the loss of its financial underpinnings. The Bourbon kings began the process of stripping the Church of capital and real estate. After the movements for independence, the new governments in Latin America inherited this same process, and consequently the vision of the Church as a hierarchy eventually had disastrous implications as the Church itself became embroiled in disputes over wealth and power in society. First, in the late colonial period the Crown attached all of its investments; in the early nineteenth century, national governments fought with the Church over the degree to which it needed to own property. The long-term effect of these conflicts was to weaken the Church and embroil it in political disputes not central to its mission of spiritual guidance and support for the faithful.

The nineteenth century in Latin America saw the great conflict between liberals and conservatives played out in nearly every country. The Church was a part of this debate because the liberal movement wanted to separate the state from the Church. For the liberals the Church was simply one of many civil institutions, like a club or civic association and as such should not have special privileges. Furthermore, the Church acted as a damper on the free flow of goods and property because, liberals reasoned, it controlled a significant amount of real estate, owned either outright or through mortgages. Thus, the liberals sought to divest the Church of its control over real estate. On a more crass level, one can also posit that the liberals, like most other governments of the time, coveted the wealth of the Church. Conservatives saw the Church as an essential institution for the maintenance of social order and the continuation of civilization. While they too coveted the wealth of the Church, they sought to use it in partnership with the state rather than by stripping it for the state.

This struggle manifested the two visions of the Church. For the liberals the Church was the hierarchy; a powerful social institution that owned land, made loans, and acted in a concerted way on the society and economy of the country. On the other hand, the conservatives envisioned the Church as the sum total of all the faithful, manifested in the religious orders, the secular clergy, and the various other constituent institutions. Although respecting the hierarchy, conservatives envisioned the Church as a unitary institution. Ironically, there was no consensus within the Church about the very nature of the Church. By this time some of the clergy had begun to accept the Church not as hierarchy but as the body of all believers. Members of religious orders also maintained skepticism about the unitary nature of the Church. The conflict with the state nearly destroyed the Church. The two political positions vied for power in the nineteenth century, with the liberal position eventually gaining ascendency.

The rise of the liberals in the late nineteenth century was extremely harmful to the Church. In many countries seminaries were closed and prohibitions made on men entering the clergy. In nearly all countries the Church had extreme financial difficulties as political factions squabbled about Church revenues. The number of priests declined, and many parishes found themselves, sometimes for decades, without clergy. This created yet another problem for the Church. In areas of large native populations, the local response to the lack of clergy resulted in a resurgence of popular religion, wherein the locals took control of their own celebrations and rituals. This also meant that when Protestant missionaries began to reach the region, there was a deep desire on the part of many local communities to have some sort of access of organized worship, even if it were not Catholic. Responses to the difficulties of the late nineteenth century had at their core two different visions for the Church. Most priests and bishops believed that the Church was the hierarchy. Without government support, without finances, the Church could not operate as it had before. Yet on the local level, for many of the faithful and for a small number of the clergy, the Church continued since they were committed to the continuation of their faith lives, with or without a local priest. For these, the Church was the fellowship of believers and the system of beliefs they embraced.

During the nineteenth century, the Church, through its bishops and clergy, realized that a return to the favored position of the seventeenth century was no longer feasible and sought to embrace the new political order. Increasingly the Church began to distance itself from the political fray and focus on issues of the faith. The Church also began to perceive the rise of socialism in all of its variants as being a very real threat to its continued existence. In order to counter the threat, the Church openly opposed socialism and other leftist ideologies as being antithetical to the faith. Church leadership also assumed that by addressing the root causes of dissatisfaction they might lessen the attractions of the new ideology. Thus, in the late nineteenth century the principles of social justice began to develop within the Church. Ministries emerged to address the greatest needs of the poor along with various types of Catholic Action associations. The Church in Latin America fell more directly under Vatican control than in the previous centuries. Yet its internal divisions became more prominent. One faction within the Church included clerics devoted to the traditional teachings and reliant upon the strong hierarchical structure to impose orthodoxy. This faction eschewed overt political action, arguing the Church needed to be focused on salvation in the hereafter. The other faction included clerics who sought to address the important social and economic problems of the region and who called for the faithful to live out their faith in the political realm. As the Church evolved, the hierarchy and many priests began to see that the Church was indeed the body of the faithful. While the hierarchy could create an environment for social change, the real action occurred at the grass roots. This marked an important turning point in the life of the Church in Latin America.

The dichotomy between Church as the faithful and Church as *institution* became manifest in the wake of the Second Vatican Council. On the one hand, many bishops and clergy favored the full range of reforms offered by the council, and were willing to push them to their logical extreme. On the other hand, many bishops and priests were highly critical of the reforms, seeking to maintain the traditional liturgies, ministries, and theologies of the Church. In the reforming camp a new way of doing theology emerged, which came to be known as liberation theology. Thus the last period of dichotomies in the history of the Church in Latin America had to do with the tension between the reforming spirit of Vatican II, as manifest in liberation theology, versus the more traditional orientation of the Church. On the surface the reforms of the Second Vatican Council should have guaranteed the success of the vision of Church as body of the faithful. Nevertheless, a more nuanced reality has come about, at least in Latin America.

When Pope Benedict XVI was still a cardinal, he demonstrated his concerns about the perceived excesses of liberation theology. The appointment record of his predecessor, Pope John Paul II, in filling episcopal vacancies in Latin America demonstrates the Vatican's unease regarding the more reform-oriented factions within the Church. The power and influence of those who sought to further the ideas of liberation theology waned in recent years because of the subtle and sometimes open opposition of the Vatican.

In most areas of Latin America, liberation theology has been intimately associated with the social justice movement. The movement for social justice within the Church has, however, made an important contribution. Furthermore, in Latin America institutions such as Christian base communities and social justice committees have changed the very nature of the Church in the lives of many people. Outreach efforts by local Church organizations and missionaries from abroad have also changed the face of the Church. While the faithful continue to embrace the Church, social justice continues to be an important goal. At the same time, most of the attention of the local bishops and councils of bishops has been on structural and institutional issues, and thus one can see that the vision of Church as hierarchy has not yet fallen by the wayside.

Another concern for the Catholic Church in Latin America is the explosive growth of Protestant groups, in particular Pentecostal and Evangelical Protestant churches, along with nativistic religions such as Candomblé in Brazil. As the numbers of clerics declined in the nineteenth and early twentieth centuries, the mission field was left open to Protestant groups, which offered a totally new way of looking at the individual's relationship to God and the society at large. While the Catholic Church has been closely identified with the dominant culture and socioeconomic structure, the new churches allow the believer to throw off the old ties and take on a new persona. This spread of Protestantism—and particularly Pentecostal and Evangelical movements—will continue to be a major challenge to the Catholic Church in the coming years. The rise of Protestantism offers yet another view into the nature of the Church. For the Protestant sects the focus is continually on the individual spiritual experience. The Church in this context is unequivocally the body of the faithful, for in most Catholic parishes and missions identification with the larger Church is an important component in the total religious experience.

The idea of two competing visions for the Church helps to illuminate the conflicts and transitions that have occurred throughout its history in Latin America. There are other methods that can also assist us in looking at change over long periods of time. One of these is known as the Hegelian dialectic. In the study of history as a discipline, the Hegelian dialectic has been a very useful tool. It became well known because of its adoption by Marxists, and thinkers of the Left in general, through their concept of "dialectical materialism." The dialectical approach in its simplest form assumes that a society exists in a specific state or condition, which generically is known as the status quo, the current situation. In Hegelian thought this status quo is called the thesis, based upon concepts from medieval debates. Within society, at any given moment, there will appear individuals who oppose the status quo, and espouse a model of the state in opposition to it. In Hegelian thought the stance in opposition to the status quo is "antithesis," since it stands against the status quo, or thesis. The medieval debate attempted to rationalize these two opposing ideas into a third position, combining certain aspects of both, resulting in a synthesis. In historiography, the status quo is the essential nature of the political, social, and economic system in any given period. Opposition arises to the status quo in the form of an opposing ideology. Rather than having a debate on the merits of each position, usually the status quo and the opposition are tested out, or rationalized, in a period of conflict, sometimes in civil wars and revolutions, sometimes in political conflict and tension. In the end, the historian using this technique analyzes the results in terms of it being a synthesis of the two opposing ideologies. Finally, the synthesis becomes the new thesis, or status quo, for the ensuing period.

Looking, then, at the history of the Church in Latin America, each epoch has its thesis, its dominant practice or worldview. In each period a countervailing position arose. As times and conditions changed, the two positions also changed, creating a new thesis or status quo. While the periods are not crisply demarcated, nor are the dominant, or antithetical, states cleanly defined, taken as a whole and viewed from a distance, the pattern emerges. The shortcoming of this approach is this: once one begins to focus in on a specific country or a specific time period, the clarity of scheme is lost. All of the nuances that are so important in the everyday reality of the Church, and of the faithful living their lives of faith, distract from the larger movements and themes.

Using this approach, to look at the Church in Latin America, the period of discovery and conquest can be characterized as the conflict between the native cultures of the Americas versus the European culture, including Christianity. The conquest and settlement of the New World was the rationalization of these two themes, with the resulting colonial period becoming the synthesis. The culture of colonial Latin America was largely European but with important components of native influence.

The colonial period developed according to pressures unique to Latin America. By the eighteenth century, the established system for the colonies was opposed by none other than the ruling houses of Spain and Portugal. The Bourbon monarchs of Spain and the Marquis of Pombal in Portugal imposed new rules and regulations on the colonies. The Church was actively involved in this conflict because the reforms sought to make significant changes in how the Church operated. Yet the rationalization of these two opposing ideologies (the old colonial period versus the new reforms) could not occur because of an external event—the French invasion of the Iberian Peninsula. The conflict and tensions caused by the opposition of these two themes continued into the early nineteenth century.

Independence was a relatively simple case of the dialectic, in which the modified colonial system was opposed by ideologies of nationalism. Independence was marked by warfare between supporters of the opposing ideologies, and the resultant synthesis consisted of the independent national state. Yet the ensuing synthesis was extremely complex because many of the supporters of independence actually wished to restore conditions to a situation prior to the reforms of the eighteenth century: the status quo ante, in Hegelian terms. As a result the early nineteenth century witnessed a complex interplay of ideas and ideologies from across two centuries. In order to characterize them in Hegelian terms, however, the conservatives represented the status quo (or even status quo ante), while the liberals were the antithesis. The late nineteenth century saw yet another rationalization as the liberals gained ascendency, creating a new synthesis. The Church played a central role in this process having been closely identified with the conservatives and thus punished by the liberals.

By the early twentieth century the old dichotomy of the liberals and conservatives broke down. The new status quo was a generally liberal state, with an opposing ideology that sought to open up the political system even more. In Chile and Argentine the Radicals were the opposition; in Brazil a similar movement was represented by Getúlio Vargas; in Mexico it was revolutionaries. The rationalization of these opposing ideologies occurred both through civil war and through the ballot box. The resulting synthesis, however, did not gain sufficient support among all sectors of the nations, and so in many countries over the next few decades the military would intervene to oppose change. The Church in Latin America, by this time, had begun to move away from an active role in politics and thus was able in many places to act as a mediator between the military and the opposition.

The most recent rationalization occurred as nations threw off their military governments and again embraced democracy. The model of liberal democracy has become the status quo for most of Latin America. Yet there are ideologies that have arisen to oppose this model, mostly in the form of left-leaning nationalist governments, such as those currently found in Venezuela, Bolivia, and Ecuador.

While the Church no longer takes an active a role in politics, one might also extend the Hegelian dialectic to the Church itself. One can see the rise of liberation theology as an ideology opposing the vision of the Church of the early twentieth century. The CELAM meetings of Latin American bishops were the manifestation of the working out of the status quo with the new ideology. The resultant synthesis, mediated by the pope and his criticisms of liberation theology have left us with a new synthesis in which concerns for social justice remain an important topic within the Church, with somewhat less emphasis on social and political change than advocated by some liberation theologians.

The Church in Latin America is central to understanding change in the region for the last five hundred years. In some instances it was the agent of change. In other situations it opposed change. But when one looks across the five-hundred-year history of the Church in Latin America, there is little doubt that it is the central institution in the history of the region. No other institution has survived or continued to play such an important role as has the Church. The Church remains.

The future of the Church in Latin America will build on the foundations laid in this long history. Change will continue. The issue of the Church as body of the faithful will still be debated by those who see the Church as hierarchy. Neither side will win a clear-cut victory simply because the Church is both, and it transcends both. That dichotomy fails to address the central issue: the Church is the earthly manifestation of God's divine purpose, the rest is interpretation. In the end, the history of the Church in Latin America is in reality all of this—the large interplay of great ideas and theologies, and the daily faith of the millions of people working out the story of salvation in their own lives and in their own time and place.

Glossary

abbot. The head of a monastery, popularly elected by the members of the religious order.

arancel. Schedule of fees to be paid by parishioners to the parish priest for the performance of specific rituals or sacraments such as Baptism and Marriage.

archbishop. The chief administrative officer of a region of the Church, who has some administrative supervision over neighboring bishops.

archdeacon. The second most important member of a cathedral chapter charged with assisting the bishop in his duties in the cathedral.

benefice. A guaranteed ecclesiastical income, frequently based on an investment.

bishop. The chief administrative officer of a region of the Church.

bull. A type of official papal document, sealed with a large lead ball impressed with the papal seal.

canon. One of ten members of a cathedral chapter ranking beneath the dignitaries but above the prebendaries.

capellanía. See **chantry.**

cargo system. A political system in native villages wherein adult males proceed through alternative offices in the religious and civil hierarchy.

cathedral. The principal church of a diocese that houses the bishop's throne, the cathedra

cathedral chapter. The body of clerics appointed to assist in the celebration of the liturgy in the cathedral, and to also take on specific functions within the diocese.

CEB. Christian base communities.

chantry. An endowment under which a priest is contracted to perform a specific number of masses for the benefit of the patron.

cofradía. See **sodality.**

concordat. A treaty between the Vatican and a country outlining mutual rights and privileges regarding the operation of the Church within the country.

confraternity. See **sodality.**

congregación. A program in colonial Latin America whereby widely dispersed small native villages were brought together into a single, larger community.

convent. A religious house for friars, especially Franciscans.

Creole. A person of pure European ancestry, born in the New World.

curate. The person who serves as a parish priest, literally, a "cure of souls."

cursillo. A short course on Christian life.

dean. The chief officer of a cathedral chapter.

definitor. One of the three members who advises the provincial of a religious province.

dignitary. One of the five high ranking members of a cathedral chapter.

diocesan clergy. Clergy who are not members of religious orders, who are directly subject to the local bishop. Also known as secular clergy.

diocese. The territory governed by a bishop

encomendero. An individual who receives the right to collect tribute from a specific group of natives, in return for accomplishments in the conquest and settlement of the Americas.

encomienda. The jurisdiction of natives who must pay tribute to an *encomendero.*

encyclical. A type of papal communication generally sent to a specific group of bishops.

episcopal. Of or pertaining to a bishop.

erection. The papal bull that orders the creation of a new diocese and which stipulates how it will be governed.

exequatur. A declaration which allows a papal communication to be promulgated within a specific jurisdiction.

friar. A brother within a religious order, generally used for Franciscans and Dominicans.

fuero (eclesiástico). The privilege of a member of the clergy to have certain law suits heard in an ecclesiastical court, rather than in the royal or other courts.

Holy Office of the Inquisition. The court appointed to hear cases dealing with heresy, apostasy, and violations of the sacraments, originally within the powers of the local bishop, but later granted to the secular authority of the king.

ladino. Someone who is a new speaker of Spanish, usually refers to a mestizo

laissez-faire. The liberal idea of allowing economies to operate unfettered by regulations, from the French.

league. A measure of distance approximately 3.5 miles.

maestrescuelas. A dignitary on the cathedral chapter charged with supervision of schools in the diocese. See also **schoolmaster.**

magisterium. The teaching authority of the Catholic Church

medio-racionero. One of the minor prebendaries on a cathedral chapter.

mendicant. A member of a religious order, which is supported through alms, such as the Franciscans or Dominicans.

mestizo. A person of mixed European and Native American ancestry.

monastery. A religious house for members of certain religious orders, such as Benedictines.

monk. A member of a monastic order, such as the Benedictines.

mortmain. Literally "dead hand;" the status of certain lands held by the Church which could not be sold or otherwise alienated.

mulatto. A person of mixed European and African ancestry.

nuncio. A papal ambassador.

oposición. a competitive examination to choose the best prepared candidate for certain positions such as parish priest of canon.

ordinary. The power of the bishop which comes from the office

patronage. The right of an individual who endows a benefice or other ecclesiastical position to name the person who will enjoy the fruits of the office. It also refers to the right (Royal Patronage) claimed by the kings of Spain and Portugal to administer the Church in the American territories.

pious work. Any endowment created for a pious or ecclesiastical purpose. See also **chantry.**

prebendary. One of six lower members of a cathedral chapter. See also *racionero*.

prior. The head of a religious house, elected by the members of the order.

province. An ecclesiastical jurisdiction consisting either of many religious houses, in the case of the regular clergy, or of many dioceses and an archdiocese, in the case of the secular clergy.

provincial. The member of a religious order elected to supervise a province.

provisor. The chief administrative officer of a diocese under the bishop.

racionero. One six lower members of a cathedral chapter. See also **prebendary**.

Radical. A political party in Argentina and Chile, which sought to return to the roots of the nation.

recurso de fuerza. A legal procedure wherein a person whose rights had been violated in a legal proceeding could request that royal official intervene.

regular clergy. Members of religious orders.

religious. Of or pertaining to a religious order.

schoolmaster. A dignitary on the cathedral chapter charged with supervision of schools in the diocese. See also *maestrecuelas*.

secular clergy. Also known as diocesan clergy. Those clerics who are not members of religious orders and are directly subject to the authority of the local bishop.

secularization. The process whereby parishes administered by religious orders were transferred to the secular, or diocesan, clergy.

sodality. A religious guild or association established for purposes of devotion and mutual aid, often in veneration of a particular saint or object such as the Blessed Sacrament.

suffragan. The relationship of a bishop to the supervising archbishop.

tenente. A junior commissioned officer in Brazil.

tithe. A 10 percent tax on agricultural and pastoral production for the support of the Church.

treasurer. Dignitary on the cathedral chapter charged with supervising the cathedral finances, and by extension those of the diocese.

vicar. An ecclesiastical judge.

vicar-general. The superior ecclesiastical judge of a diocese and the chief administrative officer under the bishop.

Notes

NOTES TO CHAPTER 1

1. In Spanish the word meaning "to entrust" is *encomendar* from which these words are derived.

2. The term "ordinary" in ecclesiastical parlance means "One who has, of his own right and not by special deputation, immediate jurisdiction in ecclesiastical cases, as the archbishop in a province, or the bishop or bishop's deputy in a diocese." *Oxford English Dictionary,* s.v. "ordinary."

3. The cathedral is the principle church of the diocese. It houses the bishop's throne, or *cathedra,* a physical symbol of episcopal authority. The clerics assigned to the cathedral served a dual function: they supervised the religious services of the cathedral, and they had various administrative responsibilities in conjunction with the bishop.

4. Each of these groups is known by several names. The Aztecs should better be called the Mexica, the name of their particular tribe. They belonged to a larger cultural group called the Nahua, after the language they spoke. The Maya lived in powerful, independent city-states, and while modern archeologists consider them a single cultural entity, they most likely did not consider themselves as such. Inca refers to the title of the ruler of the group. The people themselves might best be referred to as the Quechua, after their language. Cognizant of these facts, however, for clarity I will refer to these native people by their common, if inaccurate, names.

5. For example, Spanish and English are actually quite close to one another. They are both members of the Indo-European language family. Nahuatl and Maya are not members of the same language family. They are totally distinct languages.

NOTES TO CHAPTER 2

1. A papal bull is any important papal communication carrying the authority of the pope. The term comes from the Latin *bulla* (related to the English word "ball"), which described the large, round, lead seal used to seal the document. Bulls are traditionally named after their opening words in Latin.

2. Samuel Eliot Morison, *Admiral of the Ocean Sea: A Life of Christopher Columbus* (New York: Little Brown, 1942), 397, 432, 484.

3. *Encomienda*, that which is entrusted , comes from the Spanish verb *encomendar*, which means to entrust. *Repartimiento*, a distribution, comes from the Spanish verb *repartir* meaning "to distribute." The term *encomienda* harkened back to the military-religious orders in the Reconquest when the large estates they held were called *encomiendas* and would be administered by an officer called a *comendador*.

4. A Spanish league was approximately 3–3.5 miles.

5. Anthony Pagden, *Spanish Imperialism and the Political Imagination* (New Haven, CT: Yale University Press, 1990), 18–22.

6. The passage originally came from Isa. 40:3, "A voice cries: 'Prepare in the desert a way for Yahweh'" (New Jerusalem Bible) and is used in all the Gospels to describe the ministry of John the Baptist. See Matt. 3:3, Mark 1:3, Luke 3:4, John 1:23.

7. Lewis Hanke, *The Spanish Struggle for Justice in the Conquest of America* (Philadelphia: University of Pennsylvania Press, 1949), 17–19.

8. Eccles. (Sirach) 34:18–19, "The sacrifice of an offering unjustly acquired is a mockery; the gifts of the impious are unacceptable. The Most High takes no pleasure in offerings from the godless, multiplying sacrifices will not gain pardon for sin" (NJB).

9. In Spanish he would be referred to simply as Casas, but in English we have adopted the practice of calling him Las Casas.

10. Hanke, *Spanish Struggle for Justice*, 60.

11. The tithe is a 10 percent tax imposed by the Church on certain goods.

12. A benefice is an ecclesiastical office, usual that of a parish priest, which enjoys a permanent income, usually from an endowment.

13. Shiels, *King and Church*, 82–91.

NOTES TO CHAPTER 3

1. Details of this period can be found in John Hemming, *The Conquest of the Incas* (New York: Harcourt, Brace, Jovanovich, 1970), chaps. 9–13. The biographies of the conquerors can be found in James Lockhart, *The Men of Cajamarca* (Austin: University of Texas Press, 1972), 12–16.

2. The Catholic clergy historically has consisted of two groups: the secular and regular clergy. Secular clerics are directly subject to the local bishop and as priests they serve as the common parish priest. The term "secular" comes from the fact that they live and work out in the world (Lat. *saeculum*). Regular clerics are members of organized religious orders. In addition to the normal vows of the clergy, they take special vows and follow a rule of life (Lat. *regula*).

3. John F. Schwaller, *Church and Clergy in Sixteenth-Century Mexico* (Albuquerque: University of New Mexico Press, 1987), 71–75.

4. Lockhart, *Men of Cajamarca*, 201–7, 465–66.

5. For a detailed discussion of this event and the historiography surrounding it, see Patricia Seed, "'Failing to Marvel': Atahualpa's Encounter with the Word," *Latin American Research Review* 26 (1991): 7–32.

6. Lockhart, *Men of Cajamarca*, 465–68.

7. See Díaz del Castillo, *Historia verdadera* 1:162–63.

8. "Paréceme, señor, que en estos pueblos no es tiempo para dejarles cruz en su poder, porque son desvergonzados y sin temor, y como son vasallos de Montezuma no la que-

men o hagan alguna cosa mala. Y esto que se les ha dicho basta, hasta que tengan más conocimientos de nuestra santa fe." Díaz del Castillo, *Historia verdadera* 1:184.

9. Hemming, *Conquest of the Incas*, 62–63.

10. Fr. Peter of Ghent was neither a priest nor a deacon. He was, however, a member of the Franciscan Order, having taken full vows. As a result he was a layman, but a member of the order, consequently called a lay brother.

11. Hernán Cortés, *Cartas y Documentos* (Mexico: Editorial Porrúa, 1963), 237–39.

12. W. Eugene Shiels, *King and Church: The Rise and Fall of the Patronato Real* (Chicago: Loyola University Press, 1961), 211–15.

13. Antonio Muro Orejón, "Las leyes nuevas, 1542–1543," *Anuario de Estudios Americanos* 2 (1945): 833.

14. James Lockhart, *The Nahuas After the Conquest: A Social and Cultural History of the Indians of Central Mexico, Sixteenth through the Eighteenth Cenuries* (Palo Alto, CA: Stanford University Press, 1992), 445.

15. Antonine Tibesar, *Franciscan Beginnings in Colonial Peru* (Washington, DC: Academy of American Franciscan History, 1953), 9–20 and throughout.

16. Rubén Vargas Ugarte, *Historia de la iglesia en el Peru*, vol. 1 (Lima: Imprenta Santa María, 1953), 109–10.

17. Eduardo Hoornaert, "The Catholic Church in Colonial Brazil," in *Cambridge History of Latin America*, vol. 1, 541–42.

NOTES TO CHAPTER 4

1. Eduardo Enrique Rios, *The Life of Fray Antonio Margil OFM*, translated by Benedict Leutenegger (Washington, DC: Academy of American Franciscan History, 1959).

2. The rule of the order refers to the set of rules established to govern a particular order. For example, the Franciscan Order is governed by the Rule of Saint Francis.

3. John F. Schwaller, *The Church and Clergy in Sixteenth-Century Mexico* (Albuquerque: University of New Mexico Press, 1987), 6–17.

4. John F. Schwaller, *The Origins of Church Wealth in Mexico: Ecclesiastical Revenues and Church Finances, 1523–1600* (Albuquerque: University of New Mexico Press, 1985), 9–28.

5. Ibid., 111–17.

6. The word *cargo* in Spanish means "office." In the *cargo* system individuals moved from one office to another as they matured and took on greater responsibilities in their communities.

7. Richard Greenleaf, *Zumárraga and the Mexican Inquisition, 1536–1543* (Washington, DC: Academy of American Franciscan History, 1961), 69–75.

8. Charles, E. P. Simmons, "Palafox and His Critics: Reappraising a Controversy," *Hispanic American Historical Review* 46 (Nov. 1966): 394–408.

9. Kathryn Burns, *Colonial Habits: Convents and the Spiritual Economy of Cuzco, Peru* (Durham, NC: Duke University Press, 1999), 15–16.

10. Asunción Lavrin and Loreto L. Rosalva, eds., *La escritura femenina en la espiritualidad barroca novohispana, siglos XVII y XVIII* (Puebla: Universidad de las Americas y Archivo General de la Nación, 2002), 5–9.

11. Ronald J. Morgan, *Spanish American Saints and the Rhetoric of Identity, 1600–1810* (Tucson, AZ: University of Arizona Press, 2002), 67–97.

NOTES TO CHAPTER 5

1. Charles R. Boxer, *The Golden Age of Brazil* (Berkeley: University of California Press, 1969), 179–80.

2. Michael P. Costeloe, *Church Wealth in Mexico: A Study of the "Juzgado de Capellanias" in the Archbishopric of Mexico, 1800–1856* (Cambridge: Cambridge University Press, 1967), 16–28.

3. Antonine Tibesar, "The Peruvian Church at the Time of Independence in the Light of Vatican II," *The Americas* 26 (Apr. 1970): 349–50.

4. Juan Carlos Garavaglia and Diane Melendez, "Economic Growth and Regional Differentiations: The River Plate Region at the End of the Eighteenth Century," *Hispanic American Historical Review* 65 (Feb. 1985): 70.

5. Five million pesos annually, if collected fully at 10 percent. Records indicate that 5 percent might be a more reasonable figure.

6. Costeloe, *Church Wealth*, 22–23.

7. Ibid., 2, 17, 22, 86–87.

8. Asunción Lavrin, "The Role of Nunneries in the Economy of New Spain in the Eighteenth Century," *Hispanic American Historical Review* 46 (Nov. 1966): 377–81.

9. Ibid., 380–81.

10. Burns, *Colonial Habits*, 161–62, 183–84.

11. Lavrín, "Role of Nunneries," 385–86.

12. Linda Greenow, *Credit and Socioeconomic Change in Colonial Mexico: Loans and Mortgages in Guadalajara, 1720–1820* (Boulder, CO: Westview Press, 1983), 71–75.

13. Luis Martin, *Daughters of the Conquistadores: Women in the Viceroyalty of Peru* (Albuquerque: University of New Mexico Press, 1983), 270.

14. Donald L. Gibbs, "The Economic Activities of Nuns, Friars, and their Conventos in Mid-Colonial Cuzco," *Americas* 45 (Jan. 1989): 359–61.

15. Nicholas P. Cushner, *Farm and Factory: The Jesuits and the Development of Agrarian Capitalism in Colonial Quito, 1600–1767* (Albany: State University of New York Press, 1982), 157–59.

16. Stuart B. Schwartz, "The Plantations of St. Benedict: The Benedictine Sugar Mills of Colonial Brazil," *Americas* 30 (July 1982): 1–22.

17. David A. Brading, "Tridentine Catholicism and Enlightened Despotism in Bourbon Mexico," *Journal of Latin American Studies* 15 (May 1985): 10; Francisco Morales, "Mexican Society and the Franciscan Order in a Period of Transition, 1749–1859," *Americas* 54 (Jan. 1998): 324.

18. Brian Hamnett, "The Appropriation of Mexican Church Wealth by the Spanish Bourbon Government: The 'Consolidación de vales reales,'" *Journal of Latin American Studies* 1 (Nov. 1969): 91–92.

NOTES TO CHAPTER 6

1. For the most complete study of Brazilian politics during the transition from colony to indepdendence, see Roderick E. Barman, *Brazil: The Forging of a Nation, 1798–1852* (Palo Alto, CA: Stanford University Press, 1988).

2. For an overview of Mexican Independence seen through the lens of Mexico City, see Timothy E. Anna, *The Fall of Royal Government in Mexico City* (Lincoln, NE: University of Nebraska Press, 1978).

3. For a general survey of independence in South America, see John Lynch, *The Spanish-American Revolutions, 1808–1826* (New York, Norton, 1973).

4. The single work that focuses on the role of the Church in Latin America the nineteenth century is J. Lloyd Mecham, *Church and State in Latin America: A History of Politico-Ecclesiastical Relations,* rev. ed. (Chapel Hill, NC: University of North Carolina Press, 1966).

5. The word *mazorca* means "ear of corn" and refers to the fact that members were as close to one another as kernels of an ear of corn. Opponents made a play on words, noting that the word was pronounced the same as "*más horca*" which means "more hanging."

6. The best biography of Rosas in English is John Lynch, *Argentine Dictator: Juan Manuel de Rosas, 1829–1852* (New York: Oxford University Press, 1981).

7. Entails were estates that had been legally bound together and could not be broken up or sold. They had to pass on to the next generation completely intact. This process was used by large landowners as a means of avoiding the Spanish inheritance system that called for the equal division of an estate among the heirs.

8. The politics of Chile in the Independence period is studied by Simon Collier, *Ideas and Politics of Chilean Independence, 1808–1833* (New York: Cambridge University Press, 1967).

9. To best understand the period, see Charles A. Hale, *Mexican Liberalism in the Age of Mora, 1821–1853* (New Haven, CT: Yale University Press, 1968).

NOTES TO CHAPTER 7

1. There are several editions of Echeverría's "The Slaughterhouse," known in Spanish as "*El matadero.*" One modern edition is Roberto González Echevarría, *The Oxford Book of Latin American Short Stories* (New York: Oxford University Press, 1997), 59–72.

2. Still the best biography of Santa Anna is Oakah L. Jones, *Santa Anna* (New York: Twayne, 1968).

3. Much has been written on Church-state relations in Mexico in the nineteenth century. The period before 1857 is the topic of Michael P. Costeloe, *Church and State in Independent Mexico: A Study of the Patronage Debate, 1821–1857* (London: Royal Historical Society, 1978).

4. The economic aspects of these policies is covered by Jan Bazant, *Alienation of Church Wealth in Mexico: Social and Economic Aspects of the Liberal Revolution, 1856–1875,* ed. and trans. Michael P. Costeloe (Cambridge: Cambridge University Press, 1970).

5. The best source for the history of the Peruvian Church in the national period is Jeffrey L. Klaiber, *The Catholic Church in Peru, 1821–1985: A Social History* (Washington, DC: Catholic University Press, 1992).

6. Helen Delpar, "Aspects of Liberal Factionalism in Colombia, 1875–1885," *Hispanic American Historical Review* 51 (1971): 250–74.

7. The 1974 agreement was declared unconstitutional some twenty years later. Colombia currently has a new concordat dating from 1992. The text of the 1887 agreement can be found in J. Lloyd Mecham, *Church and State in Latin America,* rev. ed. (Chapel Hill: University of North Carolina Press, 1966), 126–31.

8. Mary Watters, "The Present Status of the Church in Venezuela," *Hispanic American Historical Review* 13 (1933): 23–36.

9. George C. A. Boehrer, "The Church and the Overthrow of the Brazilian Monarchy," *Hispanic American Historical Review* 48 (1968): 380–91.

1. The interior was called the *sertão* in Portuguese, roughly equivalent to backlands.

2. Robert M. Levine, "Canudos in the National Context," *Americas* 48 (1991): 207–22.

3. The best study of the impact of Joaseiro is: Ralph Della Cava, *Miracle at Joaseiro* (New York: Columbia University Press, 1970); see also Ralph Della Cava, "Brazilian Messianism and National Institutions: A Reappraisal of Canudos and Joaseiro," *Hispanic American Historical Review* 48 (1968): 402–20.

4. The best study of Teresa de Cabora is Paul J. Vanderwood, *The Power of God Against the Guns of Government: Religious Upheaval in Mexico at the Turn of the Nineteenth Century* (Stanford, CA: Stanford University Press, 1998).

5. Ramírez Colom, José María. "Santiago de Guatemala," *Catholic Encyclopedia,* vol. 7 (New York: Robert Appleton Company, 1910).

6. Virginia Garrard-Burnett, "Liberalism, Protestantism, and Indigenous Resistance in Guatemala, 1870–1920," *Latin American Perspectives* 24 (Mar. 1997): 35–55.

7. José Oscar Beozzo, "The Church and the Liberal States (1880–1930)," in *The Church in Latin America, 1492–1992,* ed. Enrique Dussel, 131 (Maryknoll, NY: Orbis Books, 1992).

1. A good overview of the Church during the Revolution, see Robert E. Quirk, *The Mexican Revolution and the Catholic Church, 1910–1929* (Bloomington: Indiana University Press, 1973).

2. The best survey of the *Cristero Revolt* is Jean A. Meyer, *The Cristero Rebellion: The Mexican People Between Church and State, 1926–1929* (Cambridge: Cambridge University Press, 1976).

3. Norman A. Bailey, "*La Violencia* in Colombia," *Journal of Inter-American Studies* 9 (Oct. 1967): 561–75.

4. Frederick B. Pike, "Church and State in Peru and Chile Since 1840: A Study in Contrasts," *American Historical Review* 73 (Oct. 1967): 42–44.

5. Frederick B. Pike, "Aspects of Class Relations in Chile, 1850–1960," *Hispanic American Historical Review* 43 (Feb. 1963): 18.

6. The name of the party is misleading to modern readers. The term "radical" in the party name merely indicated that it would remain faithful to the roots of the larger movement, the Civic Union, in its demand for secret ballots. The older movement had been incorporated into the government without having won the suffrage it sought.

7. Richard Lee Clinton, "APRA: An Appraisal," *Journal of Interamerican Studies and World Affairs* 12 (Apr. 1970): 280–97.

8. Ralph della Cava, "Catholicism and Society in Twentieth Century Brazil," *Latin American Research Review* 11 (1976): 14.

9. Margaret Todaro Williams, "Integralism and the Brazilian Catholic Church," *Hispanic American Historical Review,* 54 (Aug. 1974): 431–52.

10. Della Cava, "Catholicism and Society," 7–50.

NOTES TO CHAPTER 10

1. David F. D'Amico, "Religious Liberty in Argentina During the First Perón Regime," *Church History* 46 (Dec. 1977): 490–503.
2. Also known as ecclesial base communities. CEB comes from the Spanish *communidades eclesiales de base* or Portuguese *comunidades eclesiais de base.*
3. Ralph Della Cava, "Catholicism and Society in Twentieth-Century Brazil," *Latin American Research Review* 11 (1976): 37–38.

NOTES TO CHAPTER 11

1. Jeffery Kaliber, *The Church, Dictatorships, and Democracy in Latin America* (Maryknoll, NY: Orbis Books, 1998), 23–30.
2. Michael Fleet and Brian H. Smith, *The Catholic Church and Democracy in Chile and Peru* (Notre Dame, IN: University of Notre Dame Press, 1997), 43–75; 111–37.
3. Medellin Documents, 15 (1. Justicia, III. PROYECCIONES DE PASTORAL SOCIAL, (c) Empresas y economía, 10, Párrafo 2), translation mine. "El sistema liberal capitalista y la tentación del sistema marxista parecieran agotar en nuestro continente las posibilidades de transformar las estructuras económicas. Ambos sistemas atentan contra la dignidad de la persona humana; pues uno tiene como presupuesto la primacía del capital, su poder y su discriminatoria utilización en función del lucro; el otro, aunque ideológicamente sostenga un humanismo, mira más bien al hombre colectivo, y en la práctica se traduce en una concentración totalitaria del poder del Estado. Debemos denunciar que Latinoamérica se ve encerrada entre estas dos opciones y permanece dependiente de uno u otro de los centros de poder que canalizan su economía."
4. Medellin Documents, 13 (1. Justicia, II. FUNDAMENTACIÓN DOCTRINAL, Para. 3 and 4). "Por eso, para nuestra verdadera liberación, todos los hombres necesitamos una profunda conversión, a fin de que llegue a nosotros el 'Reino de Justicia, de amor y de paz.'" "En la Historia de la Salvación la obra divina es una acción de Liberación integral y de promoción del hombre en toda su dimensión, que tiene como único móvil el amor."
5. This position is based upon the works of the Brazilian educator and philosopher Paulo Freire. He used the term *conscientização,* usually translated as "awakening of consciousness" or "consciousness-raising."
6. Alexander Wilde, "Ten Years of Change in the Church: Puebla and the Future," *Journal of Interamerican Studies and World Affairs* 21 (Aug. 1979): 299–312.

NOTES TO CONCLUSION

1. Daniel H. Levine, "Authority in Church and Society: Latin American Models," *Comparative Studies in Society and History* 20 (Oct. 1978): 522.

Bibliography

The bibliography of works on the Church in Latin America is extensive. The works listed here are those written in English, which can provide insight into specific topics and point of departure for further reading.

Anna, Timothy E. *The Fall of Royal Government in Mexico City.* Lincoln, NE: University of Nebraska Press, 1978.

Archer, Christon I. "'Viva Nuestra Señora de Guadalupe!' Recent Interpretations of Mexico's Independence Period." *Mexican Studies/Estudios Mexicanos* 7 (Winter 1991): 143–65.

Archibald, Robert. *The Economic Aspects of the California Missions.* Washington, DC: Academy of American Franciscan History, 1978.

Aufderheide, Patricia. "True Confessions: The Inquisition and Social Attitudes in Brazil at the Turn of the Seventeenth Century." *Luso-Brazilian Review* 10 (Winter 1973): 208–40.

Bailey, Norman A. "*La Violencia* in Colombia." *Journal of Inter-American Studies* 9 (Oct. 1967): 561–75.

Bamat, Thomas. "The Catholic Church and Latin American Politics." *Latin American Research Review* 18 (1983): 219–26.

Barman, Roderick E. *Brazil: The Forging of a Nation, 1798–1852.* Stanford, CA: Stanford University Press, 1988.

Bastide, Roger. *The African Religions of Brazil: Toward a Sociology of the Interpenetration of Civilization.* Translated by Helen Sabba. Baltimore, MD: Johns Hopkins University Press, 1978.

Baudot, Georges. *Utopia and History in Mexico: The First Chronicles of Mexican Civilization, 1520–1569.* Translated by Bernard R. Ortiz de Montellano and Thelma Ortiz de Montellano. Niwot, CO: University Press of Colorado, 1995.

Bauer, Arnold J. "The Church and the Spanish American Agrarian Structure." *The Americas* 28 (July 1971): 78–98.

———. "The Church in the Economy of Spanish America: *Censos* and *Depósitos* in the Eighteenth and Nineteenth Centuries." *Hispanic American Historical Review* 63 (Nov. 1983): 707–33.

Bazant, Jan. *Alienation of Church Wealth in Mexico: Social and Economic Aspects of the Liberal Revolution, 1856–1875.* Edited and translated by Michael P. Costeloe. Cambridge: Cambridge University Press, 1970.

Beirne, Charles J. "Latin American Bishops if the First Vatican Council, 1869–1870." *The Americas* 25 (Jan. 1969): 265–80.

Berryman, Phillip. *Liberation Theology: Essential Facts About the Revolutionary Movement in Latin American and Beyond*. Philadelphia: Temple University Press, 1987.

———. *The Religious Roots of Rebellion: Christians in Central American Revolutions*. Maryknoll, NY: Orbis Books, 1984.

———. *Stubborn Hope: Religion, Politics, and Revolution in Central America*. Maryknoll, NY: Orbis Books, 1994.

Block, David. "Links to the Frontier: Jesuit Supply of Its Moxos Missions, 1683–1767." *The Americas* 37 (Oct. 1980): 161–78.

Boehrer, George C. A. "The Church and the Overthrow of the Brazilian Monarchy." *Hispanic American Historical Review* 48 (1968): 380–401.

Boff, Clodovis. *Theology and Praxis*. Maryknoll, NY: Orbis Books, 1987.

Boff, Leonardo, and Clodovis Boff. *Salvation and Liberation*. Maryknoll, NY: Orbis Books, 1984.

Bonpane, Blase. "The Church and Revolutionary Struggle in Central America." *Latin American Perspectives* 7 (Late Spring/Summer, 1980): 178–89.

Borah, Woodrow W. "The Collection of Tithes in the Bishopric of Oaxaca During the Sixteenth Century." *Hispanic American Historical Review* 21 (Aug. 1941): 386–409.

———. "Tithe Collection in the Bishopric of Oaxaca, 1601–1867." *Hispanic American Historical Review* 29 (Nov. 1949): 498–517.

Boxer, Charles R. *The Church Militant and Iberian Expansion, 1440–1770*. Baltimore, MD: Johns Hopkins University Press, 1978.

———. *The Golden Age of Brazil, 1695–1750: Growing Pains of a Colonial Society*. Berkeley: University of California Press, 1969.

Boyer, Richard. *Lives of the Bigamists: Marriage, Family, and Community in Colonial Mexico*. Albuquerque: University of New Mexico Press, 2001.

Brading, David A. *Church and State in Bourbon Mexico: The Diocese of Michoacan, 1740–1810*. Cambridge: Cambridge University Press, 1994.

——— "Tridentine Catholicism and Enlightened Despotism in Bourbon Mexico." *Journal of Latin American Studies* 15 (May 1983): 1–22.

Bricker, Victoria. *The Indian Christ, the Indian King: The Historical Substrate of Maya Myth and Ritual*. Austin: University of Texas Press, 1981.

Brown, Kendall W. "Jesuit Wealth and Economic Activity within the Peruvian Economy: The Case of Colonial Southern Peru." *Americas* 44 (July 1987): 23–43.

Bruneau, Thomas C. *The Catholic Church in Brazil: The Politics of Religion*. Austin: University of Texas Press, 1982.

——— "Church and Politics in Brazil: The Genesis of Change." *Journal of Latin American Studies* 17 (Nov. 1985): 271–93.

——— *The Political Transformation of the Brazilian Church*. New York: Cambridge University Press, 1974.

——— "Power and Influence: Analysis of the Church in Latin America and the Case of Brazil." *Latin American Research Review* 8 (Summer, 1973): 25–51.

Burdick, John. *The Church at the Grassroots in Latin America: Perspectives on Thirty Years of Activism*. Westport, CT: Praeger, 2000.

Burkhart, Louise M. *The Slippery Earth: Nahua-Christian Moral Dialogue in Sixteenth-Century Mexico*. Tucson: University of Arizona Press, 1989.

Burns, E. Bradford. "The Rise of Azeredo Coutinho in the Enlightenment of Brazil." *Hispanic American Historical Review* 44 (1964): 145–60.

Burns, Kathryn. *Colonial Habits: Convents and the Spiritual Economy of Cuzco, Peru*. Durham, NC: Duke University Press, 1999.

Butler, Matthew. "Keeping the Faith in Revolutionary Mexico: Clerical and Lay Resistance to Religious Persecution, East Michoacán, 1926–1929." *The Americas* 59 (July 2002): 9–32.

Cabal, Hugo Latorre. *The Revolution of the Latin American Church*. Norman: University of Oklahoma Press, 1978.

Cahill, David, "*Curas* and Social Conflict in the *Doctrinas* of Cuzco, 1780–1814." *Journal of Latin American Studies* 16 (Nov. 1985): 241–76.

Calcott, Wilfred Hardy. *Church and State in Mexico, 1822–1857*. Durham, NC: Duke University Press, 1926.

Camp, Roderic A. *Crossing Swords: Politics and Religion in Mexico*. New York: Oxford University Press, 1997.

Campbell, Leon G. "Church and State in Colonial Peru: The Bishop of Cuzco and the Tupac Amarau Rebellion of 1780." *Journal of Church and State* 22 (Spring 1980): 251–70.

Cardozo, Manoel. "The Holy See and the Question of the Bishop-Elect of Rio, 1833–1839." *Americas* 10 (July 1953): 3–74.

Carrasco, David. *The Religions of Mesoamerica*. New York: Waveland Press, 1990.

Cervantes, Fernando. *The Devil in the New World: The Impact of Diabolism in New Spain*. New Haven, CT: Yale University Press, 1994.

Chance, John K., and William B. Taylor. "Cofradías and Cargos: An Historical Perspective on the Mesoamerican Civil-Religious Hierarchy." *American Ethnologist* 12 (February 1985): 1–26.

Chesnut, R. Andrew. "A Preferential Option for the Spirit: The Catholic Charismatic Renewal in Latin America's New Religious Economy." *Latin American Politics and Society* 45 (Spring 2003): 55–85.

Cleary, Edward, ed. *Born of the Poor: The Latin American Church since Medellin*. Notre Dame, IN: University of Notre Dame Press, 1990.

———. "The Brazilian Catholic Church and Church-State Relations: Nation Building." *Journal of Church and State* 39 no. 2 (1997): 253–72.

———. *Crisis and Change: The Church in Latin America Today*. Maryknoll, NY: Orbis Books, 1985.

Cleary, Edward, and Hannah Stewart-Gambino, eds. *Conflict and Competition: The Latin American Church in a Changing Environment*. Boulder, CO: Lynne Rienner, 1992.

Clendinnen, Inga. "Disciplining the Indians: Franciscan Ideology and Missionary Violence in Sixteenth-Century Yucatan." *Past and Present* 94 (1982): 27–48.

———. "Ways to the Sacred: Reconstructing 'Religion' in Sixteenth-Century Mexico." *History and Anthropology* 5 (1990): 105–41.

Cline, S. L. "The Spiritual Conquest Re-examined: Baptism and Church Marriage in Early Sixteenth-Century Mexico." *Hispanic American Historical Review* 73 (Aug. 1993): 453–80.

Clinton, Richard Lee. "APRA: An Appraisal." *Journal of Interamerican Studies and World Affairs* 12 (Apr. 1970): 280–97.

Coleman, William. *Latin American Catholicism: A Self-Evaluation*. Maryknoll, NY: Orbis Books, 1958.

Cole, Jeffery, ed. *The Church and Society in Latin America*. New Orleans: Tulane University, Center for Latin American Studies, 1984.

Collier, Simon. *Ideas and Politics of Chilean Independence, 1808–1833.* New York, Cambridge University Press, 1967.

Cook, Guillermo, ed. *New Face of the Church in Latin America.* Maryknoll, NY: Orbis Books, 1994.

Cooney, Jerry, "The Destruction of the Religious Orders in Paraguay, 1810–1824." *The Americas* 36 (Oct. 1979): 177–98.

Costeloe, Michael P. "The Administration, Collection, and Distribution of Tithes in the Archbishopric of Mexico, 1800–1860." *The Americas* 23 (June 1966): 3–27.

———. *Church and State in Independent Mexico: A Study of the Patronage Debate, 1821–1857.* London, Royal Historical Society, 1978.

———. *Church Wealth in Mexico, 1800–1856.* Cambridge: Cambridge University Press, 1967.

Crahan, Margaret. "Civil-Ecclesiastical Relations in Hapsburg Peru." *Journal of Church and State* 20 (Winter 1978): 93–111.

Crosby, Harry W. *Antigua California: Mission and Colony on the Peninsular Frontier, 1697–1768.* Albuquerque: University of New Mexico Press, 1994.

Cushner, Nicholas P. *Farm and Factory: The Jesuits and the Development of Agrarian Capitalism in Colonial Quito, 1600–1767.* Albany: State University of New York Press, 1982.

———. *Jesuit Ranches and the Agrarian Development of Colonial Argentina, 1650–1767.* Albany: State University of New York Press, 1983.

———. *Lords of the Land: Sugar, Wine, and Jesuit Estates of Coastal Peru, 1600–1767.* Albany: State University of New York Press, 1980.

———. *Why Have You Come Here? The Jesuits and the First Evangelization of Native America.* Oxford: Oxford University Press, 2006.

D'Amico, David F. "Religious Liberty in Argentina During the First Perón Regime." *Church History* 46 (December 1977): 490–503.

Dean, Carolyn. *Inka Bodies and the Body of Christ: Corpus Christi in Colonial Cuzco, Peru.* Durham, NC: Duke University Press, 1999.

Della Cava, Ralph. "Brazilian Messianism and National Institutions: A Reappraisal of Canudos and Joaseiro." *Hispanic American Historical Review* 48 (1968): 402–20.

———. "Catholicism and Society in Twentieth Century Brazil." *Latin American Research Review* 11 (1976): 7–50.

Delpar, Helen. "Aspects of Liberal Factionalism in Colombia, 1875–1885." *Hispanic American Historical Review* 51 (1971): 250–74.

Diacon, Todd A. *Millenarian Vision, Capitalist Reality: Brazil's Contestado Rebellion.* Durham, NC: Duke University Press, 1991.

Díaz Balsera, Viviana. *The Pyramid Under the Cross: Franciscan Discourses of Evangelization and the Nahua Christian Subject in Sixteenth-Century Mexico.* Tucson: University of Arizona Press, 2005.

Dodson, Michael. "Liberation Theology and Christian Radicalism in Contemporary Latin America." *Journal of Latin American Studies* 11 (May 1978): 203–22.

Drekonja, Gerhard. "Religion and Social Change in Latin America." *Latin American Research Review* 6 (Spring 1971): 53–72.

Dulles, Avery. "John Paul and the New Evangelization." *America* 166, no. 3 (1 Feb. 1992): 52–59.

Durston, Alan. *Pastoral Quechua: The History of Christian Translation in Colonial Peru, 1550–1650.* Notre Dame, IN: University of Notre Dame Press, 2007.

Dussel, Enrique, ed. *The Church in Latin America, 1492–1992*. Maryknoll, NY: Orbis Books, 1992.

Eagleson, John, and Philip Sharper, eds. *Puebla and Beyond: Documentation and Commentary*. Maryknoll, NY: Orbis Books, 1979.

Early, John D. *The Maya and Catholicism: An Encounter of Worldviews*. Gainesville: University Press of Florida, 2006.

Edgerton, Samuel. *Theaters of Conversion: Religious Architecture and Indian Artisans in Colonial Mexico*. Albuquerque: University of New Mexico Press, 2001.

Farriss, N. M. *Crown and Clergy in Colonial Mexico, 1759–1821: The Crisis of Ecclesiastical Privilege*. London: The Athlone Press, 1968.

Fitzgibbon, Russell H. "Components of Political Change in Latin America." *Journal of Interamerican Studies and World Affairs* 12 (Apr. 1970): 187–204.

Fleet, Michael. "The Church and Revolutionary Struggle in Central America." *Social Text* 7 (Spring/Summer, 1983): 106–14.

Fleet, Michael, and Brian H. Smith. *The Catholic Church and Democracy in Chile and Peru*. Notre Dame, IN: University of Notre Dame Press, 1997.

Foroohar, Manzar. "Liberation Theology: The Response of Latin American Catholics to Socioeconomic Problems." *Latin American Perspectives* 13 (Summer 1986): 37–58.

García-Rivera, Alex. *St. Martín de Porres: The "Little Stories" and the Semiotics of Culture*. Maryknoll, NY: Orbis Books, 1995.

Garneau, James F. "The First Inter-American Episcopal Conference, Nov. 2–4, 1959: Canada and the United States Called to the Rescue of Latin America." *American Catholic Historical Review* 87 (2001): 662–87.

Garrard-Burnett, Virginia. "Liberalism, Protestantism, and Indigenous Resistance in Guatemala, 1870–1920." *Latin American Perspectives* 24 (Mar. 1997): 35–55.

———. *On Earth as It Is in Heaven: Religion in Modern Latin America*. Wilmington, DE: Scholarly Resources, 2000.

———. "Protestantism in Rural Guatemala, 1872–1954." *Latin American Research Review* 24 (1989): 127–42.

Gaudino, Pedro. "La preparación del Concilio Plenario Latinoamericano, según la documentación Vaticana." *Teología* 72 (1998): 105–32.

Gill, Anthony J. *Rendering Unto Caesar: The Catholic Church and the State in Latin America*. Chicago: University of Chicago Press, 1998.

Gómez Treto, Raúl. *The Church and Socialism in Cuba*. Maryknoll, NY: Orbis Books, 1988.

González, Ondina E., and Justo L. González. *Christianity in Latin America: A History*. Cambridge: Cambridge University Press, 2008.

Greenleaf, Richard E. "The Inquisition and the Indians of New Spain: A Study in Jurisdictional Confusion." *The Americas* 22 (Oct. 1965): 138–66.

———. *The Mexican Inquisition of the Sixteenth Century*. Albuquerque: University of New Mexico Press, 1969.

———, ed. *The Roman Catholic Church in Colonial Latin America*. New York: Alfred A. Knopf, 1971.

———. *Zumárraga and the Mexican Inquisition, 1536–1543*. Washington, DC: Academy of American Franciscan History, 1961.

Greer, Allen, and Jodi Bilinkoff, eds. *Colonial Saints: Rediscovering the Holy in the Americas*. New York: Routledge, 2003.

Griffiths, Nicholas. *The Cross and the Serpent: Religious Repression and Resurgence in Colonial Peru.* Norman, OK: University of Oklahoma Press, 1996.

Gutiérrez, Gustavo. *A Theology of Liberation.* Maryknoll, NY: Orbis Books, 1976.

Guzmán C., Germán. "La rebeldía clerical en América Latina." *Revista Mexicana de Sociología* 32 (Mar./Apr. 1970): 357–94.

Hale,Charles A. *Mexican Liberalism in the Age of Mora, 1821–1853.* New Haven, CT: Yale University Press, 1968.

Hamnett, Brian R. "The Appropriation of Mexican Church Wealth by the Spanish Bourbon Government, The 'Consolidación de Vales Reales,' 1805–1809." *Journal of Latin American Studies* 1 (Nov. 1969): 85–113.

——. "Process and Pattern: A Re-Examination of the Ibero-American Independence Movements, 1808–1826." *Journal of Latin American Studies* 29 (May 1997): 279–328.

Hanke, Lewis. *The Spanish Struggle for Justice in the Conquest of America.* Philadelphia: University of Pennsylvania Press, 1949.

Haskett, Robert. "'Not a Pastor, but a Wolf': Indigenous-Clergy Relations in Early Cuernavaca and Taxco." *The Americas* 50 (Jan. 1994): 293–336.

Hennelley, Alfred, ed. *Santo Domingo and Beyond: Documents and Commentaries from the Fourth General Conference of Latin American Bishops.* Maryknoll, NY: Orbis Books, 1993.

Hewitt, W. E. *Base Christian Communities and Social Change in Brazil.* Lincoln: University of Nebraska Press, 1991.

——. "Catholicism, Social Justice, and the Brazilian Corporative State Since 1930." *Journal of Church and State* 32 (Autumn 1990): 831–51.

——. "Origins and Prospects of the Option for the Poor in Brazilian Catholicism." *Journal for the Scientific Study of Religion* 28 (June 1989): 120–36.

Hyland, Sabine. *The Jesuit and the Incas: The Extraordinary Life of Padre Blas Valera, SJ.* Ann Arbor: University of Michigan Press, 1994.

Ireland, Rowan. *Kingdoms Come: Religion and Politics in Brazil.* Pittsburgh: University of Pittsburgh Press, 1991.

Ivereigh, Austen. *Catholicism and Politics in Argentina, 1810–1960.* New York: St. Martin's Press, 1995.

Jackson, Robert H., and Edward Castillo. *Indians, Franciscans, and Spanish Colonization: The Impact of the Mission System on California Indians.* Albuquerque: University of New Mexico Press, 1995.

Jones, Oakah L. *Santa Anna.* New York, Twayne, 1968.

Kadt, Emanuel de. "Paternalism and Populism: Catholicism in Latin America." *Journal of Contemporary History* 2 (Oct. 1967): 89–106.

Keleman, Pal. *Baroque and Rococo in Latin America.* 2 vols. 2nd ed. New York: Dover, 1967.

Kellogg, Susan, and Mattew Restall, eds. *Dead Giveaways: Indigenous Testaments of Colonial Mesoamerica and the Andes.* Salt Lake City: University of Utah Press, 1998.

Kennedy, John J. *Catholicism, Nationalism, and Democracy in Argentina.* Notre Dame, IN: University of Notre Dame Press, 1958.

Keogh, Dermot, ed. *Church and Politics in Latin America.* New York: St. Martin's Press, 1990.

Kirk, John M. *Between God and the Party: Religion and Politics in Revolutionary Cuba.* Tampa: University of South Florida Press, 1989.

——. *Politics and the Catholic Church in Nicaragua.* Gainesville: University of Florida Press, 1992.

Klaiber, Jeffrey L. *The Catholic Church in Peru, 1821–1985: A Social History.* Washington, DC: Catholic University Press, 1992.

———. "The Catholic Lay Movement in Peru, 1867–1959." *The Americas* 40 (1983): 149–70.

———. *The Church, Dictatorships, and Democracy in Latin America.* Maryknoll, NY: Orbis Books, 1998.

———. "Prophets and Populists: Liberation Theology, 1968–1988." *The Americas* 46 (July 1989): 1–15.

———. "Religion and Revolution in Peru, 1920–1945." *The Americas* 31 (Jan. 1975): 289–312.

Knowlton, Robert J. *Church Property and the Mexican Reform, 1856–1910.* Evanston: North Illinois University Press, 1976.

———. "Expropriation of Church Property in Nineteenth-Century Mexico and Colombia: A Comparison." *The Americas* 25 (1969): 387–401.

Konrad, Herman W. *A Jesuit Hacienda in Colonial Mexico: Santa Lucia, 1576–1767.* Stanford, CA: Stanford University Press, 1980.

Kress, Lee Bruce. "Argentine Liberalism and the Church under Julio Roca, 1880–1886." *The Americas* 30 (Jan. 1974): 319–40.

Kubler, George. *Mexican Architecture of the Sixteenth Century.* 2 vols. New Haven, CT: Yale University Press, 1948.

Lafaye, Jacques. *Quetzalcoatl and Guadalupe: The Formation of the Mexican National Consciousness, 1531–1813.* Translated by Benjamin Keen. Chicago: University of Chicago Press, 1976.

Langer, Erick D. "Mission Land Tenure on the Southeastern Bolivian Frontier, 1845–1949." *The Americas* 50 (Jan. 1994): 399–418.

Langer, Erick, and Robert H. Jackson, eds. *The New Latin American Mission History.* Lincoln: University of Nebraska Press, 1995.

Landsberger, Henry A., ed. *The Church and Social Change in Latin America.* Notre Dame, IN: University of Notre Dame, 1970.

Lanning, John Tate. "The Church and the Enlightenment in the Universities." *Americas* 15 (Apr. 1959): 331–50.

Lara, Jaime. *Christian Texts for Aztecs: Art and Liturgy in Colonial Mexico.* Notre Dame, IN: University of Notre Dame Press, 2007.

———. *City, Temple, Stage: Eschatological Architecture and Liturgical Theatrics in New Spain.* Notre Dame, IN: University of Notre Dame Press, 2004.

Larkin, Brian R. "Liturgy, Devotion, and Religious Reform in Eighteenth-Century Mexico City." *The Americas* 60 (Apr. 2004): 493–518.

Lavrin, Asunción. "The Execution of the Law of *Consolidación* in New Spain: Economic Aims and Results." *Hispanic American Historical Review* 53 (Feb. 1973): 27–49.

———. "The Role of the Nunneries in the Economy of New Spain in the Eighteenth Century." *Hispanic American Historical Review* 46 (1966): 371–93.

———, ed. *Sexuality and Marriage in Colonial Latin America.* Lincoln: University of Nebraska Press, 1989.

Lavrin, Asunción, and Edith Couturier. "Dowries and Wills: A View of Women's Socioeconomic Role in Colonial Guadalajara and Puebla," *Hispanic American Historical Review* 59 (May 1979): 280–304.

Lee, James H. "Church and State in Mexican Higher Education, 1821–1861." *Journal of Church and State* 20 (1978): 57–72.

———. "Clerical Education in Nineteenth-Century Mexico: The Conciliar Seminaries of Mexico City and Guadalajara, 1821–1910." *The Americas* 36 (1980): 465–77.

Lernoux, Penny. *Cry of the People: The Struggle for Human Rights in Latin America—The Catholic Church in Conflict with U. S. Policy.* 2nd ed. New York: Penguin, 1982.

———. "The Latin American Church." *Latin American Research Review* 15 (1980): 201–11.

———. "Latin America's Insurgent Church." *Nation* 222, no. 20 (May 22 1976): 618–25.

Levine, Daniel H. "Authority in Church and Society: Latin American Models." *Comparative Studies in Society and History* 20 (Oct. 1978): 517–44.

———. "Church Elites in Venezuela and Colombia: Context, Background, and Beliefs," *Latin American Research Review* 14 (1979): 51–79.

———. *Popular Voices in Latin American Catholicism.* Princeton: Princeton University Press, 1992.

———. *Religion and Political Conflict in Latin America.* Chapel Hill: University of North Carolina Press, 1986.

———. *Religion and Politics in Latin America: The Catholic Church in Venezuela and Colombia.* Princeton: Princeton University Press, 1981.

———. "Religion and Politics, Politics and Religion: An Introduction." *Journal of Interamerican Studies and World Affairs* 21 (Feb. 1979): 5–29.

Levine, Robert M. "Canudos in the National Context." *The Americas* 48 (1991): 207–22.

———. *Vale of Tears: Revisiting the Canudos Massacre in Northeastern Brazil, 1893–1897.* Berkeley: University of California Press, 1992.

Liebscher, Arthur R. "Institutionalization and Evangelization in the Argentine Church: Córdoba under Zenón Bustos, 1905–1919." *The Americas* 45 (Jan. 1989): 363–81.

Livi-Bacci, Massimo, and Ernesto J. Maeder. "The Missions of Paraguay: The Demography of an Experiment." *Journal of Interdisciplinary History* 35 (Autumn 2004): 185–224.

Lockhart, James. *The Nahuas After the Conquest.* Stanford, CA: Stanford University Press, 1992.

Loy, Jane Meyer. "Primary Education during the Colombian Federation: The School Reform of 1870." *Hispanic American Historical Review* 51 (May 1971): 275–94.

Lynch, John. *Argentine Dictator: Juan Manuel de Rosas, 1829–1852.* New York: Oxford University Press, 1981.

———. *The Spanish-American Revolutions, 1808–1826.* New York, Norton, 1973.

MacCormack, Sabine. *Religion in the Andes: Vision and Imagination in Early Colonial Peru.* Princeton: Princeton University Press, 1991.

Mainwaring, Scott. *The Catholic Church and Politics in Brazil, 1916–1985.* Stanford, CA: Stanford University Press, 1986.

Mainwaring, Scott, and Alexander Wilde, eds. *The Progressive Church in Latin America.* Notre Dame, IN: University of Notre Dame Press, 1989.

Manchester, Alan K., "The Paradoxical Pedro, First Emperor of Brazil." *Hispanic American Historical Review* 12 (1932): 176–97.

Martin, David. *Tongues of Fire: The Explosion of Protestantism in Latin America.* Oxford: B. Blackwell, 1990.

Martin, Edward J. "Liberation Theology, Sustainable Development, and Postmodern Public Administration." *Latin American Perspectives* 30 (July 2003): 69–91.

Martín, Luis. *Daughters of the Conquistadores: Women of the Viceroyalty of Peru.* Albuquerque: University of New Mexico Press, 1983.

Martin, Percy A. "Causes of the Collapse of the Brazilian Empire." *Hispanic American Historical Review* 4 (1921): 4–40.

McAndrew, John. *The Open-Air Churches of Sixteenth-Century Mexico: Atrios, Posas, Open Chapels, and Other Studies.* Cambridge, MA: Harvard University Press, 1965.

McCloskey, Michael B. *The Formative Years of the Missionary College of Santa Cruz of Querétaro, 1683–1733.* Washington, DC: Academy of American Franciscan History, 1955.

McGovern, Arthur F. *Liberation Theology and its Critics: Toward an Assessment.* Maryknoll, NY: Orbis Books, 1989.

Meacham, Carl E. "Changing of the Guard: New Relations between Church and States in Chile." *Journal of Church and State* 29 (1987): 411–33.

Mecham, J. Lloyd. *The Church and State in Latin America: A History of Politico-Ecclesiastical Relations.* Rev. ed. Chapel Hill: University of North Carolina Press, 1966.

———. "The Papacy and Spanish-American Independence." *Hispanic American Historical Review* 9 (May 1929): 154–75.

Méndez, Jesús. "Church-State Relations in Argentina in the Twentieth Century: A Case Study of the Thirty-Second International Eucharistic Congress." *Journal of Church and State* 27 (1985): 223–43.

Metcalf, Alida C. "The Entradas of Bahia of the Sixteenth Century." *The Americas* 61 (Jan. 2005): 373–400.

Meyer, Jean A. *The Cristero Rebellion: The Mexican People Between Church and State, 1926–1929.* Cambridge: Cambridge University Press, 1976.

Mills, Kenneth. *Idolatry and its Enemies: Colonial Andean Religion and Extirpation, 1640–1750.* Princeton, NJ: Princeton University Press, 1997.

Morales, Francisco. *Ethnic and Social Background of the Franciscan Friars in Seventeenth Century Mexico.* Washington, DC: Academy of American Franciscan History, 1973.

———, ed. *Franciscan Presence in the Americas: Essays on the Activities of the Franciscan Friars in the Americas, 1492–1900.* Potomac, MD: Academy of American Franciscan History, 1983.

Morgan, Ronald J. *Spanish American Saints and the Rhetoric of Identity, 1600–1810.* Tucson: University of Arizona Press, 2002.

Mörner, Magnus, ed. *The Expulsion of the Jesuits from Latin America.* New York: Alfred A. Knopf, 1965.

———. "The Expulsion of the Jesuits from Spain and Spanish America in 1767 in Light of Eighteenth-Century Regalism." *The Americas* 23 (Oct. 1966): 156–64.

———. *The Political and Economic Activities of the Jesuits in the La Plata Region: The Hapsburg Era.* Stockholm: Victor Pettersons Bokindustri Aktiebolag, 1953.

Mulvey, Patricia A. "Slave Confraternities in Brazil: Their Role in Colonial Society." *The Americas* 39 (July 1982): 39–68.

Mutchler, David. *The Church as a Political Factor in Latin America, with Particular Reference to Colombia and Chile.* New York: Praeger, 1971.

Nesvig, Martin Austin, ed. *Local Religion in Colonial Mexico.* Albuquerque: University of New Mexico Press, 2006.

Norris, Jim. *After "The Year Eighty": The Demise of Franciscan Power in Spanish New Mexico.* Albuquerque and Berkeley, CA: University of New Mexico Press and the Academy of American Franciscan History, 2000.

Padden, Robert C. "The *Ordenanza del Patronazgo* of 1574: An Interpretive Essay." *The Americas* 12 (Apr. 1956): 333–54.

Pagden, A. R. *Spanish Imperialism and the Political Imagination.* New Haven, CT: Yale University Press, 1990.

Pang, Eul-Soo. "The Changing Roles of Priests in the Politics of Northeast Brazil, 1889–1964." *The Americas* 30 (Jan. 1974): 341–72.

Pardo, Osvaldo F. *The Origins of Mexican Catholicism: Nahua Rituals and Christina Sacraments in Sixteenth-Century Mexico.* Ann Arbor: University of Michigan Press, 2004.

Pattridge, Balke D. "The Catholic Church and the Closed Corporate Community during the Guatemalan Revolution, 1944–54." *The Americas* 52 (July 1995): 25–42.

Peña, Milagros. "The *Sodalitum Vitae* Movement in Peru: A Rewriting of Liberation Theology." *Sociological Analysis* 53 (Summer 1992): 159–73.

Phelan, John Leddy. *The Millenial Kingdom of the Franciscans in the New World.* 2nd rev. ed. Berkeley: University of California Press, 1970.

Pike, Frederick B. "Aspects of Class in Chile, 1850–1960." *Hispanic American Historical Review* 43 (Feb. 1963): 14–33.

———. "Church and State in Peru and Chile since 1840: A Study in Contrasts." *American Historical Review* 73 (Oct. 1967): 30–50.

———, ed. *The Conflict Between Church and State in Latin America.* New York: Alfred A. Knopf, 1964.

Pizzigoni, Caterina. *Testaments of Toluca.* Stanford, CA: Stanford University Press, 2007.

Poblete, Renato. "From Medellin to Puebla: Notes for Reflection." *Journal of Interamerican Studies and World Affairs* 21 (Feb. 1979): 31–44.

Poole, Stafford. "Church Law on the Ordination of Indians and *Castas* in New Spain." *Hispanic American Historical Review* 61 (Nov. 1981): 637–50.

———. *Our Lady of Guadalupe: The Origins and Sources of a Mexican National Symbol, 1531–1797.* Tucson: University of Arizona Press, 1995.

———. *Pedro Moya de Conteras: Catholic Reform and Royal Power in New Spain, 1571–1591.* Berkeley: University of California Press, 1987.

Pottenger, John R. *The Political Theory of Liberation Theology: Toward a Reconvergence of Social Values and Social Science.* Albany: State of New York University Press, 1989.

Powers, Karen Viera. "The Battle for Bodies and Souls in the Colonial North Andes: Intraecclesiastical Struggles and the Politics of Migration." *Hispanic American Historical Review* 75 (Feb. 1995): 31–56.

Quirk, Robert E. *The Mexican Revolution and the Catholic Church, 1910–1929.* Bloomington: Indiana University Press, 1973.

Raine, Philip. "The Catholic Church in Brazil." *Journal of Interamerican Studies and World Affairs* 13 (Apr. 1971): 279–95.

Ramirez, Susan E., ed. *Indian-Religious Relations in Colonial Spanish America.* Syracuse, NY: Maxell School of Citizenship and Public Affairs, Syracuse University, 1989.

Rausch, Jane M. "Frontiers in Crisis: The Breakdown of the Missions in Far Northern Mexico and New Granada, 1821–1849." *Comparative Studies in Society and History* 29 (1987): 340–59.

Reed, Nelson. *The Caste War of the Yucatan.* Stanford, CA: Stanford University Press, 1964.

Reff, Daniel T. *Plagues, Priests, and Demons: Sacred Narratives and the Rise of Christianity in the Old World and the New.* Cambridge: Cambridge University Press, 2005.

Remmer, Karen L. "The Timing, Pace and Sequence of Political Change in Chile, 1891–1925." *Hispanic American Historical Review* 57 (May 1977): 205–30.

Ricard, Robert. *The Spiritual Conquest of Mexico: An Essay on the Apostolate and the Evangelizing Methods of the Mendicant Orders in New Spain: 1523–1572.* Translated by Lesley Byrd Simpson. Berkeley: University of California Press, 1966.

Riley, Carolyn L. *The Kachina and the Cross: Indians and Spaniards in the Early Southwest.* Salt Lake City: University of Utah Press, 1999.

Riley, James D. "The Wealth of the Jesuits in Mexico, 1670–1767." *The Americas* 33 (Oct. 1976): 226–66.

Ríos, Eduardo Enrique. *Life of Fray Antonio Margil, OFM.* Washington, DC: Academy of American Franciscan History, 1959.

Rivera, Luis N. *A Violent Evangelism: The Political and Religious Conquest of the Americas.* Louisville, KY: Westminster/John Knox Press, 1992.

Rozeman, Stephan L. "The Evolution of the Political Role of the Peruvian Military." *Journal of Interamerican Studies and World Affairs* 12 (Oct. 1970): 539–64.

Saeger, James S. "Another View of the Mission as a Frontier Institution: The Guaycuruan Reductions of Santa Fe, 1743–1810." *Hispanic American Historical Review* 65 (Aug. 1985): 493–517.

Salles-Reese, Verónica. *From Viracocha to the Virgin of Copacabana: Representation of the Sacred at Lake Titicaca.* Austin: University of Texas Press, 1997.

Sanders, Thomas G. "The Church in Latin America." *Foreign Affairs* 48 (Jan. 1970): 285–99.

Sandos, James A. *Converting California: Indians and Franciscans in the Missions.* New Haven, CT: Yale University Press, 2004.

Sanks, T. Howland, and Brian H. Smith, "Liberation Ecclesiology: Praxis, Theory, Praxis." *Theological Studies* 38 (Mar. 1977): 3–38.

Schmitt, Karl. "Church and State in Mexico: A Corporatist Relationship." *The Americas* 40 (Jan. 1984): 349–76.

Schoultz, Lars. "Reform and Reaction in the Colombian Catholic Church," *The Americas* 30 (Oct. 1973): 229–50.

Schroeder, Susan, and Stafford Poole, eds. *Religion in New Spain.* Albuquerque: University of New Mexico Press, 2007.

Schwaller, John F. *The Church and Clergy in Sixteenth-Century Mexico.* Albuquerque: University of New Mexico Press, 1987.

———, ed. *The Church in Colonial Latin America.* Wilmington, DE: Scholarly Resources, 2000.

———. "The *Ordenanza del Patronazgo* in New Spain, 1574–1600." *The Americas* 42 (Jan. 1986): 253–74.

———. *The Origins of Church Wealth in Mexico: Ecclesiastical Revenues and Church Finances, 1523–1600.* Albuquerque: University of New Mexico Press, 1985.

Schwaller, Robert F. "The Episcopal Succession in Spanish America, 1800–1859." *The Americas* 24 (Jan. 1968): 207–71.

Schwartz, Stuart B. "The Plantations of St. Benedict: The Benedictine Sugar Mills of Colonial Brazil." *The Americas* 29 (July 1982): 1–22.

Seed, Patricia. "'Failing to Marvel:' Atahualpa's Encounter with the Word." *Latin American Research Review* 26 (1991): 7–22.

————. *To Love, Honor, and Obey in Colonial Mexico: Conflicts over Marriage Choice, 1574–1821.* Stanford, CA: Stanford University Press, 1988.

Segundo, Juan Luis. *The Theology of Liberation.* Maryknoll, NY: Orbis Books, 1976.

Serbin, Kenneth P. "Church-State Reciprocity in Contemporary Brazil: The Convening of the International Eucharistic Congress of 1955 in Rio de Janeiro." *Hispanic American Historical Review* 76 (Nov. 1996): 721–51.

————. "Latin America's Catholics: Postliberationism?" *Christianity and Crisis* 52 (Dec. 14, 1992): 403–7.

————. *Needs of the Heart: A Social and Cultural History of Brazil's Clergy and Seminaries.* Notre Dame, IN: University of Notre Dame Press, 2006.

————. *Secret Dialogues: Church-State Relations, Torture, and Social Justice in Authoritarian Brazil.* Pittsburgh: University of Pittsburgh Press, 2000.

Shiels, W. Eugene. *King and Church: The Rise and Fall of the Patronato Real.* Chicago: Loyola University Press, 1961.

Simmons, Charles, E. P. "Palafox and His Critics: Reappraising a Controversy." *Hispanic American Historical Review* 46 (Nov. 1966): 394–408.

Smith, Brian H. *The Church and Politics in Chile: Challenges to Modern Catholicism.* Princeton, NJ: Princeton University Press, 1982.

————. "Religion and Social Change: Classical Theories and New Formulations in the Context of Recent Developments in Latin America." *Latin American Research Review* 10 (Summer 1975): 3–34.

Smith, Christian. *The Emergence of Liberation Theology: Radical Religion and Social Movement Theory.* Chicago: University of Chicago Press, 1991.

Spalding, Karen. *Huarochirí: An Andean Society Under Inca and Spanish Rule.* Palo Alto, CA: Stanford University Press, 1984.

Stein, Stanley J. "The Historiography of Brazil, 1808–1889." *Hispanic American Historical Review* 40 (May 1960): 234–78.

Stenger, Francis M. "Church and State in Peru." *Hispanic American Historical Review* 7 (1927): 410–37.

Stern, Steve J. *Peru's Indian Peoples and the Challenge of Spanish Conquest: Huamanga to 1640.* Madison: University of Wisconsin Press, 1982.

Stewart-Gambino, Heather. *The Church and Politics in the Chilean Countryside.* Boulder, CO: Westview Press, 1992.

Sullivan-González, Douglass. *Piety, Power, and Politics: Religion and Nation Formation in Guatemala, 1821–1871.* Pittsburgh: University of Pittsburgh Press, 1998.

Swatos, William H., ed. *Religion and Democracy in Latin America.* New Brunswick, NJ: Transaction Publishers, 1995.

Taylor, William B. *Magistrates of the Sacred: Priests and Parishioners in Eighteenth-Century Mexico.* Stanford, CA: Stanford University Press, 1996.

————. "The Virgin of Guadalupe in New Spain: An Inquiry into the Social History of Marian Devotion." *American Ethnologist* 14 (Feb. 1987): 9–33.

Tibesar, Antonine. "The *Alternativa*: A Study in Spanish-Creole Relations in Seventeenth Century Peru." *The Americas* 9 (Jan. 1955): 229–83.

————. *Franciscan Beginnings in Colonial Peru.* Washington, DC: Academy of American Franciscan History, 1953.

———. "The Peruvian Church at the Time of Independence in the Light of Vatican II." *The Americas* 26 (Apr. 1970).

———. "The Shortage of Priests in Latin America: A Historical Evaluation of Werner Promper's *Priesternot in Lateinamerika*." *The Americas* 22 (Apr. 1966): 413–20.

Tombs, David. *Latin American Liberation Theology*. Boston: Brill Academic Publishers, 2002.

Torres, Sergio, and John Eagleson, eds. *Theology in the Americas*. Maryknoll, NY: Orbis Books, 1976.

Vallier, Ivan. *Catholicism, Social Control, and Modernization in Latin America*. Englewood Cliffs, NJ: Prentice Hall, 1970.

Van der Vat, Odulfo. "The First Franciscans of Brazil." *The Americas* 5 (July 1948): 18–30.

Van Oss, Adriaan C. *Catholic Colonialism: A Parish History of Guatemala, 1524–1821*. Cambridge: Cambridge University Press, 1986.

Vanderwood, Paul J. "Millenarianism, Miracles, and Materialism." *Mexican Studies/Estudios Mexicanos* 15 (Summer 1999): 395–412.

———. *The Power of God Against the Guns of Government: Religious Upheaval in Mexico at the Turn of the Nineteenth Century*. Stanford, CA: Stanford University Press, 1998.

Vásquez, Manuel A. *The Brazilian Popular Church and the Crisis of Modernity*. Cambridge: Cambridge University Press, 1999.

———. "Toward a New Agenda for the Study of Religion in the Americas." *Journal of Interamerican Studies and World Affairs* 41 (Winter 1999): 1–20.

Vásquez, Manuel A., and Philip J. Williams. "The Power of Religious Identities in the Americas." *Latin American Perspectives* 32 (Jan. 2005): 5–26.

Wadsworth, James E. "In the Name of the Inquisition: The Portuguese Inquisition and Delegated Authority in Colonial Pernambuco, Brazil." *The Americas* 61 (July 2004): 19–54.

Warren, Fintan B. *Vasco de Quiroga and His Pueblo-Hospitals of Santa Fe*. Washington, DC: Academy of American Franciscan History, 1963.

Watters, Mary. "The Present Status of the Church in Venezuela." *Hispanic American Historical Review* 13 (1933): 23–45.

Weigel, George. "Catholicism and Democracy in the Age of John Paul II." *Logos* 4 (Summer 2001): 36–64.

———. *God's Choice: Pope Benedict XVI and the Future of the Catholic Church*. New York: HarperCollins, 2005.

Wethey, Harold E. *Colonial Architecture and Sculpture in Peru*. Cambridge, MA: Harvard University Press, 1949.

Wilde, Alexander. "Ten Years of Change in the Church: Puebla and the Future." *Journal of Interamerican Studies and World Affairs* 21 (Aug. 1979): 299–312.

Willeke, Venâncio. "Three Centuries of Missionary Work in Northern Brazil Franciscan Province of St. Anthony, 1657–1957." *The Americas* 15 (Oct. 1958): 129–38.

Williams, Margaret Todaro. "Church and State in Vargas' Brazil: The Politics of Cooperation." *Journal of Church and State* 18 (1976): 443–62.

———. "Integralism and the Brazilian Catholic Church." *Hispanic American Historical Review* 54 (Aug. 1974): 431–52.

———. "The Politicization of the Brazilian Catholic Church: The Catholic Electoral League." *Journal of Interamerican Studies and World Affairs* 16 (Aug. 1974): 301–25.

Williams, Philip. *The Catholic Church and Politics in Nicaragua and Costa Rica*. Pittsburgh: University of Pittsburgh Press, 1989.

Wright, Almon R. "Argentina and the Papacy, 1810–1827." *Hispanic American Historical Review* 18 (1938): 15–42.

Index

Callao, 125, 127
Calles, Plutarco Elías, 193–194
Callistus II, pope, 35
Câmara, Helder, 224–227, 233–235, 246
Canary Islands, 34
Candomblé, 223, 263, 272
Cano, Melchior, 41
canon, 78–79, 87
canon law, 41, 60, 77, 83, 87
canónigo. See canon
Cantabrian Mountains, 14
Cantigas de Santa María, 16
Canudos, 171–173, 176, 178
capac apu, 30
Capac Apu Sapa Inca, 30
Capac Raymi, 28
Cape Bojador, 34
Cape of Good Hope, 35
Cape of Storms, 35
Cape Verde, 34, 40, 49
capellanía. See chantry
capitalism, 208
Capitulaciones de Santa Fe, 37
Capuchin Order, 170
Caracas Company, 126
Cardenal, Ernesto, 213–214
Cardenal, Fernando, 256
cargo system, 85, 180–181
Caribbean, 1–2, 42, 52
Carítas, Chile, 239
Carmelite Order, 62, 69, 73, 267, discalced, 92
Carolina, diocese, 76–77
Carranza, Venustiano, 192
Carrera, Rafael, 164
Cartagena, diocese, 77
Carvalho e Mello, Sebastião José de, 10, 110–112, 273
Casariego, 252
Casas, Bartolomé de las. *See* Las Casas, Bartolomé de
caste system, 20
Caste War, 141
Castile, 16–18
Castillo, Ramón, 202
Castro, Fidel, 227

catechisms, 63
cathedra, 78
cathedral, 72, 78
cathedral chapter, 20–21, 78–80, 87; property, 103
Catherine of Siena, saint, 92
Catholic Action, 11, 207–212, 216 –217, 245; Argentina, 218–220; Brazil, 224; Chile, 238–240; and Liberation Theology, 221–222; and the military, 243; Nicaragua, 255; Vatican II, 229
Catholic Charismatic renewal, 263
Catholic Circle, 207
Catholic Electoral League, 210
Catholic Kings, 18, 20–21, 36–37
Catholic Union, 207
Catholic University of Chile, 241
Catholic University of Peru, 182, 204, 208
Catholic University Youth, Brazil, 234
Catholic Workers Circles, 222
Catholic Youth Action, 208
Ceará, diocese, 173
ceiba, 24
Ceja seminary, 213
CELAM, 226–227, 246–250, 258–261, 275
cemeteries: Chile, 184, Venezuela 158
Cempoala, 57
Central America, 22, 53, 66, 74, 250–258; nineteenth century, 162–165, 179–181; United States, 145
Central Intelligence Agency, 216, 232, 251
centralism, Argentine, 143, Mexico, 140
ceque, 29
Ceuta, 33
Chac, 23–24
Chamorro, Joaquín, 255
chanter. See precentor
chantry, 82–83, 92–93, 97–106; in Brazil, 111
Chantry and Pious Works Court, 83, 97–106, 113–114
chantry, beneficiary, 83
chapter, religious order, 75
charism, 73
charismatic movement, 263
Charles II, king of Spain, 106

Nombre de Jesús Province, 65
Nuestra Señora de Gracia Province, 67
Nuestra Señora de Guadalupe, colegio, 74
Nuestra Señora del Rosario, chapel, 92
nun, 15, 89–94
Núñez, Rafael, 155
nunnery, 94–95

oath taking, 86
Oaxaca, 64; convents, 103; diocese, 77
Obando y Bravo, Miguel, 255–258
obedience, vow of, 75
Obregón, Alvaro, 193–194
offerings, 80
O'Higgins, Ambrosio, 127
O'Higgins, Bernardo, 127, 137
Old Republic, 205, 209
Olias, Juan de, 65
oligarchy, Brazil, 205
Olinda, archdiocese, 221, 234; bishop, 161–162
Olmedo, Bartolomé de, 52, 55–56, 58
Olympic Games, Mexico, 247
Omecihuatl, Lady of Duality, 26
Ometecuhtli, Lord of Duality, 26
Ometochtzin, Carlos, 86
Omnimoda, 60–61
Omnium Sanctorum, college, 94
only way, 73
oposición, 87
Opus Dei, 245
oracle, 31
oracle, Peruvian, 58
Ordenanza del Patronazgo, 87, 107
Order and Progress, 170
ordinary, 77
ordination, 60–61, 64
organ music, 72
Orinoco River, 37, 127
Ortega, Daniel, 213–214, 258
Ortiz, Roberto, 202
Ospina Pérez, Mariano, 195
Otomi Indians, 62

Pachacamac, 31, 58
Pachamama, goddess of Earth, 28

Pachuca, 64
Padroado Real. *See* Royal Patronage
Páez, José Antonio, 157
Palafox y Mendoza, Juan de, 89, 110
Panama, 67
Pané Ramón, 37
Pánuco, 62
papacy, 8, 9, 11, 18–20, 35, 39–42, 45–47, 50, 60–62, 75, 107, 111, 272; Argentina, 151, 183–184, 218, 220; Brazil, 129, 158–162, 169, 171, 235–236; Colombia, 154–156, 195–196; Costa Rica, 164; Guatemala, 164; Honduras, 164; Independence, 131, 145; Latin America, 150–151; Liberation theology, 261–263; Mexico, 175; modernism, 186; Nicaragua, 164, 257; Peru 152–153; Venezuela, 157
papal nuncio, 111
Pará, 69
Paraguay War, 169–170
Paraguay, 31; Indpendence, 126, 134; missions, 97
Pardo, José, 203
parish priest, 7, 9; appointment, 87, 108
parliamentary system, Chile, 184
parochial dues. *See* fees
pase regio, 107
Pastry War, 144
Patagonia, 22
paternalism, 197, 204
patron client system, 197
patron, of pious work, 83
patronage, 20–21; Argentina, 135–136, 202; Bolivia, 136–137; Central America, 163; Chile, 138; Colombia, 155–157; Independence, 131–132; nineteenth century, 165; Peru, 152–153; Venezuela, 157–158
Patronato Real. *See* Royal Patronage
Paul III, pope, 46, 88
Paul VI, pope, 245–246
Pedro I, king of Brazil, 120–121, 128, 158–159
Pedro II, king of Brazil, 159–162, 169
penance: and the Inquisition, 86; sacrament, 63, 222
penitential theology, 87

penitentiary canon, 87
Pentecostal Protestants, 12, 223–224, 264–265, 272
permanent diaconate, 228
Pernambuco, 49
Perón, Eva Duarte de, 219
Perón, Juan, 202, 217–220
Peron populism, 218
personal journals, of nuns, 91
Peru, 27, 55, 66, 71; Catholic Action, 207; conquest, 54–57; early twentieth century, 203–205; ecclesiastical income, 99; evangelization, 65–67; extirpation, 86; Independence, 128; Jesuit estates, 105–106; late nineteenth century, 182–183; military, 217, 243; nineteenth century, 152–153; religious estates, 83; religious provinces, 66–67; viceregal government, 121
Phillip, duke of Anjou, king of Spain, 106
piety in worship, 72
Pilgrim people of God, 228, 258, 266
pilgrimage, 13
Pinochet, Augusto, 241–242
pious works, 82–84
Pius IX, pope, 153, 186
Pius XI, pope, 209, 211
Pius XII, pope, 224, 262
Pizarro, Francisco, 54–59, 65
Pizarro, Hernando, 58
Plenary Councils, Latin American, 187
political thought, and the Inquisition, 86
Pombaline Reforms, 110–113, 118, 120
Popular Action Front, 239
Popular American Revolutionary Alliance. See APRA
popular religion, 264–265, Independence, 129–130
Popular Unity Party, Chile, 240
Portales, Diego, 138, 151
Porto Santo, 34
Portugal, 3, 4, 5, 8, 9; age of discovery, 33–37, 40, 46–50; Reconquest, 13–22; ruling family, 120
Portuguese (language), 1
positivism, 170, 175, 197, 204

potato, 29
poverty, vow, 81
praxis versus theology, 259
Preaching Order, 17
prebendary, 78–79
precentor, 78
preferential option for the poor, 249, 260, 262
Presbyterian mission, Guatemala, 180
Prestes, Carlos Luis, 206
Prestes, Julio, 206
priest, 15
priesthood of all believers, 223
priesthood, Vatican II, 229
Prieto, Joaquin, 138
prior, 75
Propagation of the Faith, Congregation (*Propaganda Fide*), 74
property, Church in Mexico, 146–147
property rights, Venezuela, 158
prostitute, 90
Protestant ethic, 179
Protestant Reformation, 50, 88
Protestants, 199–200, 215, 219, 223, 226, 249, 264, 272; Argentina, 151; Brazil, 159–160; Central America, 251–253; Chile, 137, 152, 184, 241, 243; Colombia, 196; Guatemala, 179–181; late nineteenth century, 186; Latin America, 244; Peru, 182, 203
province, 75
provincial, 74
provincial councils, 187
provincial prior, 75
provisor, 78
Puebla, 246, 258–261
Puebla de los Angeles, diocese, 89
Puerto Rico, 1, 38, 42, 47, 76; Spanish loyalists, 126
purity of blood. See *limpieza de sangre*
Pyrenees, 14

Quadragesimo anno, encyclical, 221
Quanta Cura, encyclical, 161
Quechua, 27, 30, 59
Querétaro, 117; convents, 101; missionary college, 73

Quetzalcoatl, Plumed Serpent / Twin, 26
quipu, 30
Quito, 54, 66–67; Jesuit college and estates, 105–106

Racionero. See prebendary
Radical Civic Union, 201–202
Radical Parties, 274
Radical Party, Chile, 184, 239
Ratzinger, Joseph. *See* Benedict XVI, pope
Reagan administration and El Salvador, 254; Nicaragua, 256–257
Reagan, Ronald, 232
real estate, 97–106; Bolivia, 136; Mexico, 174–175; religious orders, 81–84
Recife, archdiocese, 234
reconciliation, sacrament. *See* penance
Reconquest (Reconquista), 13–22, 33, 37
recurso de fuerza, 109
Reform in Mexico and Díaz, 176
regula, 21
regular clergy, 55, 81, 88–89; Brazil missions, 97; family, 92; organization, 72–76; powers of, 60–61; prohibitions on, 96
regular clergy and wars of independence, 132–133
regular priest, 21
"Religion and Privileges," 148
religious order, 21, 46–47, 55, 60, 88–89, 94, 267; Brazil, 111; family, 92; finances, 98–106; limitations, 108–110; organization, 72–76; pious works, 83–84
Religious Question: Brazil, 161–162, 168; Chile, 151
rents, ecclesiastical, 98–106
republican, 190, 123–124; Brazil, 168
Requerimento, 42
Requirement, 42
Restorer of the Laws, 143
revolution, 11
Revolutionary Army of the People (ERP), 254
Ricke, Jodoco, 66
Riesco Errázuriz, Germán, 166

Rio de Janeiro: archdiocese, 209, 224–225, 234; bishop, 96, 161–162; imperial capital, 120; International Eucharistic congress, 224; royal judiciary, 111; State University, 232
Rio de la Plata, viceroyalty, 126, 134
Rio Grande do Sul, state, 206
Ríos Montt, Efraín, 252
Rivadavia, Bernardino, 134–136
Rivera Damas, Arturo, 254, 256
Rodeñas, Pedro, 66
Rodríguez de Francia, Dr. José, 126
Rodríguez, Juan, 66
Rojas Pinilla, Gustavo, 196
Roman Empire, 14
Rome, 39
Romero, Oscar, 254, 258
Rosas, Juan Manuel de, 135, 143, 151
Rose of Lima, saint, 92
Rossi, cardinal, 235
Royal Patronage, 35, 39–40, 46–48, 50–51, 77, 87–89, 107–110; Argentina, 135–136; Brazil, 128, 158–160, 170–171; Independence, 131–132
royalist, 123–124
Rule of Saint Francis, 268

sacrament of penance, 27
sacraments, administration of, 88–89
Saenz Peña Law, 201
Sahara, 33–34
Saint Clare, order of, 90, 92
Saint Dominic, 17
Saint James the Greater (Santiago), 13, 16
Saint John the Baptist, 28
saints, 91
Salamanca, university of, 93
Salvador da Bahia, 49, 68, 93, 120; diocese, 77
San Agustín de Chile Province, 67
San Agustín del Perú Province, 67
San Francisco de Zacatecas Province, 65
San José de Yucatan Province, 65
San Juan Bautista del Perú Province, 65–66
San Juan de Ulua, 60
San Juan, diocese, 76

San Marcos, university, 94
San Martín, José de, 127
San Miguel de Quito Province, 67
San Miguel Piura, 66–67
San Nicolás de Tolentino Province, 65
San Pedro y San Pablo Province
San Pedro, confraternity of, 84, 129
Sandinista National Liberation Front,
     213–214, 252–253, 255–258
Sandino, Augusto César, 213
Santa Anna. *See* López de Santa Anna,
     Antonio
Santa Catalina, convent, 91, 93, 103
Santa Catarina, State in Brazil, 231
Santa Clara de Jesús, convent, 101
Santa Clara do Desterro, convent, 93
Santa de Cabora, 176
Santa Lucia, hacienda, 106
Santa Maria, 33
Santa Maria de Gracia, convent, 102
Santa Mónica, convent, 102
Santa Paula, cemetery, 144
Santa Teresa de Cabora, 176
Santiago, archdiocese, 239
Santiago Campostela, 13, 16
Santiago de Jalisco Province, 65
Santiago, military religious order, 16
Santísima Trinidad, Antonio de la, 65
Santísimo Sacramento, confraternity, 84
Santo Angelo, diocese, 235
Santo Domingo de Guzmán, 17
Santo Domingo, 43, 126, 154; diocese, 76;
     university, 94
Santo Evangelio Province, 65
Santo Tomás de Aquino, university, 94
São Francisco River, 69
São Paulo, 49, 68–69, 170; diocese, 235;
     state, 206
São Vicente, 49
schedule of fees, 80; abolished in Mexico, 147
school master, 78
schools, 63
secular clergy, 46, 76–80, 88, 267–268; Bra-
     zil, 96, 111, 161; family, 92; Independence,
     132–133; Mexico, 62; Peru, 66; powers
     of, 60–61

secular priest, 21, 55
secularization, 88, 108, 115
separation of church and state, 131
Servants of Mary, order, 231
Seven Books (*Siete Partidas*), 16
Seville, archdiocese, 76
shaman, 32
Shining Pathway, 243
Sierra Leone, 34
Siete Partidas, 16, 20
Silva Henríquez, Raul, 246
Slaughterhouse, 143
slavery, abolition: Brazil, 169–170; Mexico,
     140
slavery, Jesuit estates, 106
slaves, 4, 5, 6
Sobrino, Jon, 262
Social Darwinsim, 175, 179, 204
socialism, 191, 197, 202, 204, 208, 210, 214,
     216, 270–271; Brazil, 233–234
Society of Christian Life, 262–263
Society of Jesus. *See* Jesuit Order
sociology and positivism, 170
Sodalitium Christianae Vitae, 262–263
sodality, 84–85, 114, 207–208; Brazil,
     161–162; Guatemala, 180–181; Indepen-
     dence, 129–130,
soldier, 38
Solentiname, 213
Somoza Debayle, Anastacio, 213–214,
     254–256
Somoza Debayle, Luis, 254
Somoza Garcia, Anastacio, 213, 254
Songs to the Virgin Mary, 16
Sosa, Juan de, 57, 66
Sousa, Tomé de, 49, 68
South America, 36
Soviet Union, 232, 257–258
Spain, 3, 4, 5, 8, 9, 33–48, 144; civil war, 215;
     claims to the New World, 40–42; cur-
     sillo, 223; invasion of Mexico, 148–149;
     Reconquest, 13–22; Royal Patronage, 50
Spanish (language), 1
Spanish Succession, war, 106–107
spiritual conquest, 9–10, 59
square-rigging, 34

About the Author

JOHN FREDERICK SCHWALLER is president of the State University of New York at Potsdam. He is the author or editor of seven books, including *The Church in Colonial Hispanic America: A Reader* and *The Church and Clergy in Sixteenth-Century Mexico.*